THE G8 SYSTEM AND THE G20

Global Finance Series

Edited by
John Kirton, Munk Centre for International Studies, Trinity College, Canada,
Michele Fratianni, Indiana University, USA and Paolo Savona, LUISS University,
Italy

The intensifying globalisation of the twenty-first century has brought a myriad of new managerial and political challenges for governing international finance. The return of synchronous global slowdown, mounting developed country debt, and new economy volatility have overturned established economic certainties. Proliferating financial crises, transnational terrorism, currency consolidation, and increasing demands that international finance should better serve public goods such as social and environmental security have all arisen to compound the problem.

The new public and private international institutions that are emerging to govern global finance have only just begun to comprehend and respond to this new world. Embracing international financial flows and foreign direct investment, in both the private and public sector dimensions, this series focuses on the challenges and opportunities faced by firms, national governments, and international institutions, and their roles in creating a new system of global finance.

Also in the series

Corporate, Public and Global Governance
The G8 Contribution
Edited by Michele Fratianni, Paolo Savona and John J. Kirton
ISBN 978-0-7546-4046-2

Elements of the Euro Area
Integrating Financial Markets
Edited by Jesper Berg, Mauro Grande and Francesco Paolo Mongelli
ISBN 978-0-7546-4320-3

New Perspectives on Global Governance
Why America Needs the G8
Edited by Michele Fratianni, John J. Kirton, Alan M. Rugman and Paolo Savona
ISBN 978-0-7546-4477-4

Governing Global Banking
The Basel Committee and the Politics of Financial Globalisation
Duncan Wood
ISBN 978-0-7546-1906-2

The G8 System and the G20

Evolution, Role and Documentation

PETER I. HAJNAL
University of Toronto, Canada

ASHGATE

HF
1359
.H34
2007

Published by
Ashgate Publishing Limited
Gower House
Croft Road
Aldershot
Hampshire GU11 3HR
England

Ashgate Publishing Company
Suite 420
101 Cherry Street
Burlington, VT 05401-4405
USA

Ashgate website: http://www.ashgate.com

British Library Cataloguing in Publication Data
Hajnal, Peter I., 1936-
 The G8 system and the G20 : evolution, role and
 documentation. - (Global finance series)
 1. Group of Eight (Organization) 2. Group of Twenty
 3. Economic policy - International cooperation 4. Summit
 meetings
 I. Title
 337.1

Library of Congress Cataloging-in-Publication Data
Hajnal, Peter I., 1936-
 The G8 system and the G20 : evolution, role and documentation / by Peter I. Hajnal.
  p. cm. -- (Global finance)
 Includes bibliographical references and index.
 ISBN: 978-0-7546-4550-4
 1. Group of Eight (Organization)--Handbooks, manuals, etc. 2. International economic
relations. 3. Economic policy. 4. Summit meetings. 5. Group of Eight
(Organization)--Bibliography. 6. Group of Twenty. I. Title. II. Title: G eight
system and the G twenty.
 HF1359.H34 2007
 337.1--dc22

2006100188

ISBN: 978-0-7546-4550-4

Printed and bound in Great Britain by TJ International Ltd, Padstow, Cornwall.

Contents

List of Tables

Foreword

Sir Nicholas Bayne

I am happy to write this foreword to Peter Hajnal's new book, as I did to its predecessor, *The G7/G8 System*. Back in 1999, when the first book appeared, the reforms which had converted G7 into G8 were very recent and no one could foresee how the transition would work out. But already the G7 and G8 had developed an extensive apparatus that operated at below summit level. Peter Hajnal then provided the first available guide or manual to the entire G7 and G8 system and it has held the field ever since.

Since that time the G8 has endured: all the member countries have hosted a summit, including Russia in 2006; and the tenth G8 summit will be held at Heiligendamm in Germany in June 2007. But over this period the G8 has changed in many ways, both at the summit and at lower levels: there are new subjects, new actors and new processes at work. So Peter Hajnal's new book, *The G8 System and the G20*, is timely and welcome. It updates and enriches the subjects covered in the earlier volume. Thus it explains the expanding agenda of both economic and political subjects and of issues that combine economics and politics, like the revival of Africa, and which were rarely attempted by the G7. It describes the full absorption of Russia into the G8 and the growing practice of outreach to non-G8 countries which now play a much greater role in the international system. It sets out with admirable clarity all the details of the G8 system, which has continued to diversify despite – or even because of – the simpler, heads-only, format prevailing at the summit itself. All these explanations are underpinned by a lucid presentation and analysis of the documentation whereby G8 debates and decisions are recorded.

In this breadth of coverage Peter Hajnal's book is already without parallel. But the new volume offers additional content, not to be found elsewhere. For the first time, he has looked into the government archives now becoming accessible and provided an authoritative account of how the summits began, based on confidential documents of the time. In this he has opened a door through which other scholars can follow. Secondly, he has recorded the striking growth of non-government interest and involvement in the G8 process since his earlier volume. The reader is thus the beneficiary of Peter Hajnal's close study and detailed knowledge of civil society attitudes. Thirdly, he has complemented his account of the G8 system with a parallel analysis of the G20 finance ministers' grouping, founded by the G8 in the late 1990s but now operating with complete autonomy. Finally, he has analysed thoroughly and wisely the growing debate on how the G8 might be improved and reformed, both in its composition and its approach to issues. This treatment unites G8 and G20, in that one proposal is that the G20 should meet at leaders' level – L20 – to complement or replace the existing G8 summit.

The many changes in the G8 and the evolution of the G20 are admirably captured in this book. But one thing does not change. The G8 is still run entirely by its members and it has no common apparatus that works on behalf of all. That means that it has no information department, to explain publicly its objectives and achievements. As the G8 chair rotates, each annual host puts out explanatory material, which may contain thoughtful analyses of the summit and its history. The best example of this is the bilingual *The G7/G8 from Rambouillet to Genoa* written by two Italian diplomats and issued before the summit of 2001. But such reflective treatment is rare: most of what is issued publicly by G8 hosts is ephemeral and affected, to some degree, by national bias. Thus Peter Hajnal's book, like other publications issued by the University of Toronto's G8 Research Group, fills a real gap, in that it provides an accurate, balanced and authoritative account of what the G8 does and what it aims to do.

Peter Hajnal is well equipped to undertake this task. He is by profession a librarian/archivist. He thus puts a high premium on tracking down original sources and on meticulous accuracy in recording both broad trends and essential details. As a member of the G8 Research Group, he has followed the evolution of the G8 system over many years, with particular expertise in the interaction between its state and non-state aspects. Therefore his knowledge is exhaustive and his judgements are soundly based. He has produced a book that goes far beyond its distinguished predecessor and will be essential for all those interested in summitry, the G8 and the G20: for those already expert in the subject as such, who want to keep up to date; for those following particular subjects, who want to learn how the G8 treats them; and for those coming to summitry for the first time, who want a guide through the labyrinthine system.

Preface

Much has changed since the predecessor of this book was published in 1999 with the title *The G7/G8 System: Evolution, Role and Documentation*. The G8 has evolved further as an institution, incorporating Russia as truly a full member, presiding over the G8 – and hosting its first regular summit – in 2006. It has attained a greater sense of continuity, if not permanence, since the 2002 Kananaskis summit set the calendar for the leaders' annual meetings until 2010 rather than simply signalling the following year's summit. Although official membership has not grown since Russia's joining, recognition has been increasing of the necessity to include major developing and other systemically important countries (particularly China, India, Brazil, South Africa and Mexico) in deliberations of the summits. Parallel with this development, it has become gradually clearer to all stakeholders that international organizations, from the United Nations (UN) to the World Trade Organization (WTO) and the African Union and others, as well as civil society and the business sector, had to be involved in tackling global problems.

The G8 agenda has broadened, too, reflecting changing global realities – and so has the larger G8 system, incorporating more and more G8 ministerial fora, task forces and expert groups, some going beyond G8 members. The emergence and development of the G20 finance ministers' forum has been a particularly notable development, and a major step toward greater representativeness and legitimacy.

Initiatives to reform the G7 and G8 have proliferated. Proposals have ranged from membership changes, restructuring, rationalizing the G7 and G8 agenda and processes, and, more radically, abolishing the G8 or replacing it with a new, either expanded or more restricted, forum. The L20 initiative that would turn the finance ministers' G20 into a leaders' level Group of 20 is especially significant.

The documentation of the G7 and G8 has undergone major quantitative and qualitative changes in recent years, making it imperative to re-think its typology and situating the various kinds of public documents in an appropriate context. Beyond public documentation, the importance of other sources of information has become clear by the opening of the archives of several governments of the original G7 countries. Research in these archives has uncovered a wealth of source material providing new insight into the negotiations, national priorities and background studies that preceded the launching of the leaders' summits; the quasi-secret history of the G5 finance ministers' forum both before and after the birth of the G7; and much formerly secret or confidential information about the early years of the G7. These information sources enhance our understanding of the processes and other complexities of the G7 and G8 system and the G20. All these developments have made this new book both possible and necessary.

In view of the increasing influence of the G7 and G8 system and the G20, and growing awareness of it worldwide, it is hoped that the book will be a worthwhile addition to the scholarly literature and will serve as a useful work of reference and analysis for academics and students in the fields of political science, economics, information studies and other disciplines. It also aims to be helpful to government officials, financial institutions, research libraries, the news media, and to members of the interested public.

Peter I. Hajnal
Toronto, October 2006

Acknowledgements

Many people, not all of whom can be named here, have helped in various ways in developing the ideas for, and researching and preparing, this book. First of all, I would like to express my deep gratitude to two summit veterans and scholars: Sir Nicholas Bayne and Dr. Sylvia Ostry, for their mentorship, insight, encouragement and numerous productive ideas. My special thanks go to my colleague Professor John Kirton, director of the G8 Research Group who, for many years, has supported my participation and inspired my work with the Group, and to Madeline Koch, managing director of the Group for her intellectual, logistical and technological help and for her cheerful and unflappable presence. I am grateful to a number of other academic colleagues for their insight, support and many-faceted assistance: Thomas Axworthy, C. Fred Bergsten, Andrew Cooper, Wendy Dobson, John English, Gerald Helleiner, Ella Kokotsis, Marina Larionova, Victoria Panova, Amandine Scherrer, Gina Stephens, Junichi Takase, Heidi Ullrich, George von Furstenberg, and Chen Xiaojin.

I express my special thanks to the Centre for International Governance Innovation (CIGI) for a research support grant that made it possible to conduct research in governmental archives in the UK and the US, attend conferences relevant to this project, and engage a research assistant. I also thank the Gerald R. Ford Foundation for a travel grant to assist with expenses for research in the Gerald R. Ford Library. I am grateful to the Munk Centre for International Studies for continuing support and the director of the Centre for International Studies within the Munk Centre, Professor Louis Pauly, for his help and encouragement.

A number of civil society friends and colleagues gave me a fresh, much-needed perspective on the G7 and G8: Nigel Martin (Forum international de Montréal), Kumi Naidoo (CIVICUS), James Orbinski (Médecins Sans Frontières), Ella Pamfilova (Civil G8), Peter Ritchie (Chatham House and the Green Globe Network), Muthoni Wanyeki (FEMNET), and several activists of ActionAid, Amnesty International, Greenpeace, Oxfam, and various other NGOs including some in Russia. Former and present officials of Canada, Japan, the UK and the US, and of international organizations, generously shared with me their experience and advice.

I had the good fortune to benefit from the expertise of highly competent and helpful archivists in several official archives: the Gerald R. Ford Library, Ann Arbor, Michigan, especially Geir Gundersen and Helmi Raaska; The National Archives, London, in particular Stephen Twigge and Tim Padfield; the Jimmy Carter Library and Museum, Atlanta, Georgia, especially Keith J. Shuler; and Library and Archives Canada, Ottawa, particularly Christian Rioux.

I express my grateful appreciation to my research assistant Gillian Clinton for her highly professional, tenacious work, flexibility in the face of many unexpected twists and turns in the preparation of the manuscript, for her editorial assistance, keen eye for accuracy and many good ideas. I thank Sara Newman as well for her assistance. I am grateful to Vanessa Corlazzoli, Diana Juricevic, Stanislav Orlov, Denisse Rudich, Janel Smith, Laura Sunderland and other members of the G8 Research Group who have helped in various phases of research.

Kirstin Howgate, Margaret Younger, Donna Hamer, Carolyn Court, Sarah Cooke and other colleagues at Ashgate Publishing deserve my thanks for their help and co-operation in preparing and publishing this work. And last but certainly not least, I thank my wife Edna for her patience during the long process of researching, writing, re-writing and nursing the manuscript through publication, and for her good common sense and editorial assistance. I also wish to thank the anonymous reviewers of the manuscript for their helpful suggestions.

My gratitude is due to all of them for their help in making this book better. Any omissions or inaccuracies are entirely mine.

Abbreviations and Acronyms

ACUNS	Academic Council on the United Nations System
AI	Amnesty International
APF	Africa Partnership Forum
APR	Personal Representative for Africa
ASEAN	Association of Southeast Asian Nations
ATTAC	Association pour une Taxation des transactions financiers pour l'aide aux citoyens/Association for the Taxation of Financial Transactions and the Aid of the Citizen
AU	African Union
BIS	Bank for International Settlements
BMENA	Broader Middle East and North Africa
C20	Committee of 20
CAFOD	Catholic Fund for Overseas Development
CFGS	Centre for Global Studies (University of Victoria, British Columbia)
Chatham House	Royal Institute of International Affairs
CIGI	Centre for International Governance Innovation (Waterloo, Ontario)
CIS	Commonwealth of Independent States (Azerbaijan, Armenia, Belarus, Georgia, Kazakhstan, Kyrgyzstan, Moldova, Russia, Tajikistan, Turkmenistan, Uzbekistan and Ukraine)
CLAAAC	Collective of Anti-authoritarian and Anti-capitalist Struggles
The Compact	UK's Agreement with the Voluntary and Community Sector
CSCE	Conference on Security and Co-operation in Europe
CSO	Civil society organization
CRID	Centre de Recherche et d'Information pour le Développement
DATA	Debt AIDS Trade Africa
Dissent	A network of resistance against the G8
DOT Force	Digital Opportunities Task Force
EBRD	European Bank for Reconstruction and Development
EC	European Community
ECB	European Central Bank
ECOSOC	Economic and Social Council (UN)
EEC	European Economic Community
EU	European Union

FAO	Food and Agriculture Organization (UN)
FATF	Financial Action Task Force on Money Laundering
FEMNET	African Women's Development and Communication Network
FIM	Forum international de Montréal/Montreal International Forum
FIP	Five Interested Parties (Australia, Brazil, the EU, India and the US)
FOE	Friends of the Earth International
FSF	Financial Stability Forum
G05	Global Democracy 2005 (FIM conference)
G5	Group of Five (finance ministers – France, Germany, the UK, the US and Japan)
G6B	Group of 6 Billion (counter-summit before Kananaskis 2002)
G7/G8	Group of Seven/Group of Eight industrialized countries (Canada, France, Germany, Italy, Japan, United Kingdom, United States plus Russia)
G15	Group of Fifteen [actually 17] (Algeria, Argentina, Brazil, Chile, Egypt, India, Indonesia, Jamaica, Kenya, Nigeria, Malaysia, Mexico, Peru, Senegal, Sri Lanka, Venezuela and Zimbabwe)
G20	Group of Twenty Finance Ministers and Central Bank Governors
G22	Group of 22, also known as Willard Group
G33	Group of 33
GAB	General Arrangements to Borrow
GATT	General Agreement on Tariffs and Trade
GCAP	Global Call to Action against Poverty
GDP	Gross Domestic Product
Global Fund	Global Fund on HIV/AIDS, Malaria and Tuberculosis
GMO	Genetically modified organisms
GNP	Gross National Product
GPWG	Global Partnership Working Group (against Weapons and Materials of Mass Destruction)
GSF	Genoa Social Forum
GW8	Global Warming 8
HIPC	Heavily Indebted Poor Countries
HIV/AIDS	Human Immunodeficiency Virus/Acquired Immune Deficiency Syndrome
IAEA	International Atomic Energy Agency
ICC	International Chamber of Commerce
ICFTU	International Confederation of Free Trade Unions
ICT	Information and communication technology
IDA	International Development Association
IEA	International Energy Agency
IFAD	International Fund for Agricultural Development
IFI	International financial institution
IGO	International governmental organization

ILO	International Labour Organisation
IMF	International Monetary Fund
IO	International organization
IOSCO	International Organization of Securities Commissions
IPR	Intellectual property rights
L20	Leaders' 20 Summit (proposed)
LAC	Library and Archives Canada
Lyon Group	Senior Experts' Group on Transnational Organized Crime
MGIMO	Moscow State Institute on International Relations
MPH	Make Poverty History
MSF	Médecins Sans Frontières
NARA	National Archives and Records Administration (US)
NATO	North Atlantic Treaty Organization
NBC	Nuclear, biological and chemical
NEPAD	The New Partnership for African Development
NGO	Non-governmental organization
OAU	Organization of African Unity
OECD	Organisation for Economic Co-operation and Development
OI	Oxfam International
OPEC	Organization of Petroleum Exporting Countries
OSCE	Organization for Security and Co-operation in Europe
P8	Political 8 (G7 + Russia)
PRSP	Poverty Reduction Strategy Paper
The Quad	Trade Ministers Quadrilateral (the US, Canada, Japan and the EU)
SGP	Strengthening the Global Partnership Project: Protecting Against the Spread of Nuclear, Biological and Chemical Weapons
SIG	Support Implementation Group
SME	Small and medium-sized enterprise
START	Strategic Arms Reduction Treaty
TNA	The National Archives (UK)
TOES	The Other Economic Summit
UK	United Kingdom
UN	United Nations
UNCED	United Nations Conference on Environment and Development (also known as the Earth Summit)
UNCTAD	United Nations Conference on Trade and Development
UNDP	United Nations Development Programme

UNEP	United Nations Environment Programme
UNICEF	United Nations Children's Fund
UNIDO	United Nations Industrial Development Organization
US	United States
USSR	Union of Soviet Socialist Republics
WDM	World Development Movement
WEF	World Economic Forum
WHO	World Health Organization
WIPO	World Intellectual Property Organization
WLAN	Wireless Local Area Networks
WMD	Weapons of mass destruction
WTO	World Trade Organization

Chapter 1

Introduction

The Group of Seven/Group of Eight (G7/G8) – launched in 1975 originally as G6, turning into the G7 in 1976 and the G8 in 1998 – has become one of the central components of global governance. It plays an expanding role, bringing together seven major industrial democracies (France, the United States, the United Kingdom, Germany, Japan, Italy and Canada) and – since 1998 – Russia, as well as the European Union. Unlike more structured international organizations that are based on intergovernmental agreements and permanent secretariats, the G7 and G8 have remained relatively informal and less encumbered by bureaucracy. This has enabled the leaders of member countries to develop good personal relationships and to understand one another's respective domestic political and economic circumstances and constraints. It has also provided them with a unique means to achieve policy co-ordination and to co-operate on policy initiatives in an ever-greater number and variety of issue areas. During its more than thirty years of existence, the G7/G8 has achieved respectable results on many economic, political, security and other global issues, although its performance has not been consistently high. It continues to draw criticism because of its lack of representativeness and (real or perceived) lack of legitimacy and efficiency. Increasingly, it has also inspired reform proposals ranging from abolishing the G8 altogether, through restricting or expanding its agenda, and increasing, reducing or changing its membership. Non-state actors (civil society and business) are increasingly active in promoting such ideas, influencing the agenda of G8 meetings, and lobbying for more fundamental reforms.

Over the years, an elaborate system has evolved around the annual summits that are still the foundation of the G8. Related meetings take place several times each year to discuss and make decisions on summit-related issues. The leaders' summits remain at the core of the G7 and G8 system, but the leaders' work is complemented by an expanding network of ministers, sherpas (the leaders' personal representatives), African Personal Representatives, and (ad hoc or continuing) working groups and task forces. Some of these, initially launched by the leaders, have taken on a life of their own either with an agenda that diverges from the main concerns of the summits, with different composition, and others that no longer have direct ties with the G7 and G8. The book discusses these 'G8+' entities (for example, the Financial Action Task Force and the Digital Opportunities Task Force or DOT Force). Particularly interesting is the now several years-old G20 finance ministers' forum which is the model for recent proposals of a leaders'-level group of 20 that would either supplement or replace the G8 and concentrate on a carefully focused agenda. Such an L20 is seen by its proponents as making the institution more representative and democratic by including important countries that are not at present members of the more restrictive G8 club.

The complex system of institutions related to or originated by the G7 and G8 has generated a great deal of varied and often significant information (usually embodied in documents) in the course of its work. Its own documentation is the principal primary source of information about the broader G7 and G8 (including the G20) and its activities, but because of the absence of a central G8 secretariat to pull together, disseminate and analyze the document output, there is a great need for making this source material known and available, and to assess it carefully and systematically. As well, there now exists an impressive corpus of analytical and descriptive work, along with personal recollections of major participants and, increasingly, material that is becoming accessible in the archives of member countries, at least for the earlier years of the G7. The documents in these archives throw much additional light on the financial/economic origins of the G7 and provide lessons for the future of the G8-G20.

Objectives of this Work

This book has four main objectives.

- To discuss the origins, characteristics, role and agenda of the G7 and G8 system, including a systematic survey of its components, and to introduce the major debates and questions about the G7 and G8 in the scholarly literature;
- To review changes that have occurred in recent years in G8 membership, agenda, *modus operandi*, and outreach to non-G8 countries, international organizations and non-state actors (business and civil society);
- To examine proposals to reform the G7/G8 and the G20; and
- To provide a detailed study of the complex, elusive and changing patterns of documentation of the broader G7 and G8 system and the G20, including electronic information, and to describe archives and other sources of information on the G7 and G8.

What is the G7/G8?

The Group of Seven/Group of Eight (G7/G8) is an unorthodox international institution. Traditional international governmental organizations (IGOs) are based on a founding charter or an international treaty or agreement among the founding governments; and they have a secretariat charged with the implementation of policies and other decisions of the governing body of the organization. The G7/G8 is a less structured international arrangement; it was not established by formal international agreement, and it has no secretariat. The UK government, prior to hosting the 1998 Birmingham summit, characterized the G8 as 'an informal organisation, with no rules or permanent Secretariat staff' (UK 1998). The G7/G8's informal *modus operandi* and the fact that it is relatively unencumbered by bureaucracy have enabled the leaders of its member countries to get to know one another on a strong personal basis and to understand one another's domestic political and economic constraints and priorities. It has also given them a forum and venue for policy co-ordination, joint initiatives and interaction with other actors, state and non-state.

Occasional proposals to establish a form of permanent, continuing machinery have met with stiff resistance from at least some members. Nonetheless, the G7/G8 has become an important and influential actor on the international scene and has evolved into a broader G7 and G8 system. The best-known part of that system is the series of annual meetings of heads of state or government. These annual summit meetings are covered in great detail, albeit unevenly, by the news media and increasingly by scholarly and other specialized writing, but the resulting documentation is not widely understood. This book explores the context, typology and evolution of that documentation; beyond that, it discusses the nature of G7 and G8 information not reflected in public documents.

'G7', and later 'G8' or 'G7 and G8' or 'G7/G8' – depending on the context – have become the predominant terms when referring to the institution and the system around it.[1] Earlier the annual meeting was called the economic summit, the summit of industrialized countries, the Western economic summit, and the seven-power summit.[2] None of these names was ever completely accurate. For many years, the summit has not been merely economic; political questions and a whole gamut of global issues have taken on increasing importance on the agenda. Prior to 1998, it had not always been strictly a summit of the seven; the first summit had six participants, only the second had seven, and subsequent meetings had seven countries plus the European Union (EU; formerly European Community (EC)). Beginning with the 1994 Naples summit (following post-summit meetings with the USSR in 1991 and then Russia in 1992 and 1993), Russia became directly associated with the political aspects of the summit which, for this purpose, came to be termed the P8 ('Political 8'). In 1997, Russia's association with the G7 deepened, forming the 'Summit of the Eight' and leaving only financial and certain other economic issues to the core G7. In Birmingham in 1998 the G7 became officially the G8, with Russia as a full member, although the G7 configuration continued not only to survive but to thrive alongside the G8 for a number of years, especially for financial and other economic matters (the G7 finance ministers' forum still exists). Because of the participation of the EU, the 'G8' is not precisely the G8, either. The term 'Western' is accurate in a geopolitical rather than a geographic sense; Japan is a founding member and Russia is an Asian as well as European state. Finally, some major industrialized and democratic countries remain outside.

There are several scholars who affirm the unique character and growing importance of the G7/G8. John J. Kirton wrote in 1995: 'the G7 system of institutions is the late twentieth century global equivalent of the Concert of Europe that helped produce peace among the great powers, and prosperity more widely, from 1818 to 1914'. He argued that 'the G7 Summit system has become the effective centre of global governance, replacing the order earlier provided by the 1919-1945 [League of Nations and] United Nations and [from] 1947 Atlantic family of institutions, and recurrently creating consensus and inducing compliance among its members and other

---

1   The term 'G7 and G8' is generally used throughout this book, except when the subject is only the G7 or only the G8. 'G7/G8' is only used exceptionally.

2   In German the summit continued to be called *Wirtschaftsgipfel* or *Weltwirtschaftsgipfel* (economic summit or world economic summit) for most of the existence of the G7 and G8.

states and international institutions' (Kirton 1995: 64-65).[3] Cesare Merlini (1994), on the other hand, in 1994 expressed the view that the G7 'is not an international institution in the real sense of the term .... [It is] a quasi institutional structure ... semi-personal and at the same time semi-institutional.' In the same year, Philippe Moreau Defarges (1994), stating a French view, wrote: 'the G-7 summit cannot and must not be a Western council'; Michael R. Hodges (1994) gave the British view that the G7 'is a forum rather than an institution'. In a speech he gave just before the Birmingham summit, the late Dr. Hodges remarked that 'an institution has a cafeteria and a pension plan' and the G8 has neither. If he were writing today, he would likely add that an institution also has a website (the G8 as such has no website, although the G8 countries, particularly the host country, do).

Andrea de Guttry (1994: 68), viewing the dynamic development of the institutionalization of the summit, notes 'the total absence of a fixed summit structure or any kind of administrative/bureaucratic support' at the summit's beginnings, and the gradual process whereby, over the years, 'the structure of the summit has slowly, almost unconsciously, become more complicated'. Nicholas Bayne and Robert D. Putnam (1995: 1-2) contrast the 'stand-alone' G7 summit with other kinds of summits which had become common and which depend on a parent international organization for their existence, such as the United Nations (UN) 'Earth Summit' in 1992, or the periodic summit meetings of the EU, the Commonwealth and the Francophonie. G. R. Berridge (1995: 83-84) lists G7 summits among the category of 'serial summits', in contrast with *ad hoc* (usually one-time only) summits and with a third type, high-level exchanges of views. Bayne (1995: 494) observes that '[t]he G7 Summit is at the same time an institution and an anti-institution. This ... may be the secret of its survival.' For practical reasons, this book refers to the G7/G8 as an institution or forum.

Its leaders declare from time to time that the G8 is not a *directoire*, an executive board. Yet, it is often perceived by the media and the public as just that. Writing just before the 2005 Gleneagles summit, one observer noted that the eight leaders 'are now the *de facto* world executive committee' and a permanent political mechanism, moving in to fill the vacuum left by a 'moribund and scandal-ridden United Nations', an EU that is unable to agree on a constitution or a budget, and a WTO that is still struggling to establish a viable trade framework for the world. The observer, George Kerevan (2005: 26), marshals three reasons for the G8's success: democratic legitimacy (given that the leaders are dependent on their electorate), the clear capacity to act, and the newly acquired popular mandate 'via Sir Bob Geldof'. The only two gaps, according to Kerevan, are the absence of China and of the security dimension.

Drawing on a number of analyses, Kirton (2005c: Appendix 15-1, 15-2; 255-56) distinguishes nine models of the G7/G8 and its performance:

- The 'American leadership' model, as developed by Putnam and Bayne (1984; 1987), stipulating the ability and willingness of the US to assume leadership, with the support of at least a second G7 leader.
- The 'concert equality' model, assuming that the member states have equal capabilities (but that collectively they can predominate), equal vulnerability

---

3   See also Kirton (1999).

to external shocks, common principles of democracy, sufficient domestic control and political capital, and restricted participation in the G7 (Wallace 1984; Kirton 1989a).

- 'False new consensus': declining G7 performance in the 1990s, due to the false new consensus that economic globalization makes governments impotent (Bergsten and Henning 1996).
- 'Democratic institutionalism': increased level of performance due to effective multilateral organizations controlled by the G7; institutionalization of the G7 at ministerial and official levels; strong bureaucracies in G8 governments; commitment of the leaders to international co-operation; and popular support for the leaders (Ikenberry 1993).
- 'Neoliberal hegemonic consensus': G8 performance that is increasingly effective, yet contested by globalization, financial market dominance and other factors (Gill 1999).
- 'Collective management': increasingly effective G7/G8 performance, due to new global problems, the inadequacy of other global institutions, constraints imposed by globalization on independent action by major powers, and the institutionalization of the 'leaders only' format and focused agenda of the G8 (Bayne 2000; 2005b).
- 'Ginger Group' (caucusing group): increasingly effective performance of the G8, due to the globalization of financial markets, and the G8's being a small private club with a common world view (Hodges 1999; Baker 2000).
- 'Group hegemony': constantly high performance due to the G8's concentration of power, group identity, economic liberalism, system of interaction and other factors (Bailin 2001; 2005).
- 'Meta-institution': increasingly high performance, due to the concerted power of G8 members and the failure of the established international organizations (Pentillä 2003).

Other models can be added to this list. One of the most persuasive is the 'network of networks' concept of Anne Marie Slaughter (2004: 16, 19, 54). She argues that financial regulators, for example, prefer to think of the new financial architecture as a combination of networks: the G7, G8, the Basel Committee, IOSCO (International Organization of Securities Commissions) and others. Finance ministers hold regular meetings under the auspices of the G7, the G20 and the IMF Board of Governors. Many of the groups spawned by the G7 and G8 have grown in membership beyond the G7 and G8, thus networking within larger groups. All this shows the G7 and G8 as networking with various other specialized groups in a broader international context.

Chapter Summaries

Chapters 2 through 6 may, in a sense, be considered to be the core of this book. Chapter 2 traces the events, circumstances and various national positions leading to the eventual launch of the leaders' meetings that have become annual summits; sketches the main economic developments that drove the need for such summits;

and discusses the history of the meetings of G5 finance ministers – a series of get-togethers that predated the summits. It concludes that the five major democracies – France, West Germany, the UK, the US and Japan (later joined by Italy) recognized their common vulnerability to economic shocks and other major international developments, and saw the need to find solutions to these problems in a co-ordinated fashion, in a way that existing international institutions could not. Therefore, they instituted the periodic meetings of their finance ministers. These meetings laid the groundwork for later summits and eventually an expanded system of ministerial and other fora.

Chapter 3 surveys the summit meetings over 32 years, discusses the deliberative, direction-giving, decision-making, global governance-related and domestic political management role of the G7 and G8, and illustrates the perspectives and personal reflections of leaders and other present and former officials of the G7 and G8. It shows how summits have evolved from the first, one-time, meeting to an elaborate annual event whose informality and flexibility have permitted the relatively like-minded leaders of major democratic, market-economy countries to exchange views freely and in confidence. It argues that such candid and private interaction would be unlikely in larger, more cumbersome, and economically and politically more diverse formal organizations with large bureaucracies.

Chapter 4 reviews the evolution of membership from the initial G6 of 1975 through the years of the G7 and (from 1998) the G8; examines the contentious issue of Russia's membership; and outlines the case for and against other candidates for membership. It concludes that the difficult, incremental increase of membership raises questions about possible trajectories of the G8's further evolution into a larger group, a smaller core group, or a looser, issue-based forum.

Chapter 5 discusses the process of G7 and G8 agenda setting, traces the evolution of the agenda through summit history, and outlines the effects of important unexpected events around the time of the summits. It concludes that the changing agenda reflects both the global economic and political realities and a process of continuity. It also finds that in addition to the public agenda, the leaders tend to discuss various other issues privately, as they see fit, and that this is a function of the dynamics of the G7 and G8 as an informal, confidential forum.

Chapter 6 introduces and comments on the various components of the evolving and growing G7 and G8 system (other than the leaders' summits and the G20 which are the subject, respectively, of Chapters 3 and 11): the panoply of ministerial fora; the sherpas and personal representatives for Africa; and task forces, working groups and expert groups. A number of these ministerial and other fora have developed a more or less independent existence from the summits that had originally created them. This chapter also gives a summary of typologies of the components of the G7 and G8 system.

The next three chapters focus on the relationship of the G7 and G8 with other groups of actors. Chapter 7 outlines the nature and evolution of the relationship of the G7 and G8 with international organizations. It shows that the G7 and G8 have always recognized the essential role of international organizations, and have continually expanded their links with them, and that G7 and G8 issues are more and more routinely remitted to those organizations for action.

Chapter 8 discusses the nexus of the G7 and G8 with the private (business) sector. It concludes that the G7 and G8 and the private sector have long recognized each other as essential interlocutors. This mutual recognition is reflected by G7 and G8 statements and other documents, and by analysis originating from business organizations. Several recent summits have launched initiatives to promote corporate responsibility. Moreover, both parties have come to value multi-stakeholder approaches and have, on occasion, established working partnerships.

Chapter 9 examines the evolving relationship of nongovernmental organizations (NGOs) and other civil society organizations (CSOs) and coalitions with the G7 and G8 (these relations are largely informal in nature, unlike the long-established and well-structured NGO relations with formal international organizations such as the UN) and identifies various modes of this interaction. It concludes with a review of lessons learned and factors contributing to a more successful relationship. It shows that the four dimensions of civil society action – dialogue, demonstrations, parallel summits and partnerships – have played an important role in the evolving relations with the G8. The usefulness of productive dialogue, successful partnerships, forceful but peaceful demonstrations and creative parallel summits has been clearly shown.

Chapter 10 notes that critical comments began to be made almost as soon as the first summit met at Rambouillet and they have intensified and diversified around later summits. In addition to much journalistic writing about the events and the issues and personalities involved in the G7 and G8, and assessments of results by civil society and other stakeholders, a body of scholarly analysis has arisen. The chapter focuses on three sets of such scholarly evaluations, each with its own objectives and approach: Putnam and Bayne (1997), and Bayne (2005) assess summits on the basis of co-operative achievement of the leaders; von Furstenberg and Daniels, and later Kirton and Kokotsis evaluate compliance with measurable or verifiable commitments by the summits; and the Foreign Policy Centre in London uses the 'scorecard' approach to assess the record of summit host countries. The chapter concludes that examining and analyzing the leaders' co-operative achievements are an important method of assessing summit performance, along with some other approaches such as the tracking of compliance with summit commitments and the newer 'scorecard' method of evaluating summit host countries, even though the different premises of these methods of evaluation makes them difficult to compare, but together they yield evaluations over a period of thirty-two years and reveal successes and failures.

Chapter 11 describes the origins, mandate, membership, structure, ministerial and other meetings, and evolution of the agenda of the Group of Twenty (G20) finance ministers' and central bank governors' forum. It then reviews the G20's connections with international organizations, fora, and other actors; and discusses the documentation and publications of the G20. In conclusion the chapter shows that the G20 was created to address the need to deal adequately with key issues of the international monetary and financial system, to strengthen the international financial architecture, and to serve as a platform for discussing other pressing international economic questions, and that the group reflects a much broader global constituency and thus greater legitimacy than its parent, the G7, even though it still excludes representation of the poorest developing countries. As well, the G20 does not have sufficient capacity to deal with a host of global issues linked to economic and financial matters.

Chapter 12 reviews the numerous initiatives that emerged over a number of years to reform the G7 and G8. Reform proposals have ranged from membership changes, restructuring, rationalizing the G7 and G8 agenda and processes, and, more radically, abolishing the G8 or replacing it by a new – more restricted or expanded – forum. The chapter concludes that there is a widespread perception of the structural, procedural, democratic and other shortcomings of the G8 as it is now constituted, and of the need to reform or replace it. Many reform proposals have merit, and some have had high-level advocates. But the ultimate outcome will need the endorsement and agreement of the leaders of the present G8.

The next three chapters focus on sources of information from and about the G7 and G8 system. Chapter 13 takes account of the varied and often significant documents that the G7 and G8 summits have generated in the course of their history. Because this public documentation is the principal primary source of information about the G7 and G8, and because of the absence of a G8 secretariat to gather, disseminate and analyze the document output, there is a clear need for systematic assessment of this source material. Responding to that need, this chapter surveys the types, characteristics, subject matter, production and dissemination of the documents of the G7 and G8 summits; and assesses the evolution and importance of the documentation. In conclusion, the chapter argues that the documentation of the G7 and G8 system, in all its complexity, is an essential source of information not only about the G7 and G8 but also on a whole range of vital economic, political and other global issues. Interpretation of the documents is necessary in order to get beyond their jargon and their often repetitive character. It further underlines the importance of looking beyond the primary G7 and G8 documentation to complementary sources, notably archives, memoirs, and informed writings about the G7 and G8 and related issues. Archival resources will be of increasing significance in future years as more material becomes accessible.

Chapter 14 discusses the documentation of parts of the G7 and G8 system apart from documentation of the leaders' summits: ministerial fora, task forces, working groups and expert groups. It concludes that, while the pattern over the years of the G7 and G8 system's existence demonstrates increasing transparency and at times even eagerness to communicate with the media and the public, the exact details of actual deliberations tend to remain confidential.

Chapter 15 highlights several types of information sources about the G7 and G8 system and the G20, with illustrative examples: writings about the G7 and G8; research groups active in G8-related projects; archives; memoirs and other writings by former prominent summit participants; and websites. In conclusion, the chapter argues that all these information sources contribute to greater understanding of the complexities of the G7 and G8 system and the G20.

The final chapter (16) presents a number of conclusions about the G7 and G8 system, the evolution of its agenda, and efforts to reform it. It also draws conclusions about the G20, relations of the G7 and G8 with international organizations, civil society and the business sector, the documentation and other information emanating from the summits, the broader G7 and G8 system and the G20, and problems of evaluating summit results.

References

Note on internet addresses (URLs): Websites tend to appear, change or disappear, often without warning. Addresses cited in this source list were accurate and active at the time of writing (August 2006) unless otherwise noted.

Bailin, Alison (2001), 'From Traditional to Institutionalized Hegemony', *G8 Governance*, 6, www.g8.utoronto.ca/scholar/bailin/bailin2000.pdf.

Bailin, Alison (2005), *From Traditional to Group Hegemony: The G7, the Liberal Economic Order and the Core-Periphery Gap*, Ashgate, Aldershot, UK.

Baker, Andrew (2000), 'The G-7 as a Global "Ginger Group": Plurilateralism and Four-Dimensional Diplomacy', *Global Governance: A Review of Multilateralism and International Organizations*, 6:2, 165-89.

Bayne, Nicholas (1995), 'The G7 Summit and the Reform of Global Institutions', *Government and Opposition*, 30:4, 492-509.

Bayne, Nicholas (2000), *Hanging in There: The G7 and G8 Summit in Maturity and Renewal*, Ashgate, Aldershot, UK, The G8 and Global Governance Series.

Bayne, Nicholas (2005b), *Staying Together: The G8 Summit Confronts the 21st Century*, Ashgate, Aldershot, UK.

Bayne, Nicholas and Robert D. Putnam (1995), 'Introduction: The G-7 Summit Comes of Age', in *The Halifax G-7 Summit: Issues on the Table*, 1-13, Sylvia Ostry and Gilbert R. Wynham (eds), Centre for Foreign Policy Studies, Dalhousie University, Halifax.

Bergsten, C. Fred and C. Randall Henning (1996), *Global Economic Leadership and the Group of Seven*, Institute for International Economics, Washington, DC.

Berridge, G. R. (1995), *Diplomacy: Theory and Practice*, Prentice Hall/Harvester Wheatsheaf, London; New York.

Defarges, Philippe Moreau (1994), 'The French Viewpoint on the Future of the G-7', in *The Future of the G-7 Summits*, 177-85, (*The International Spectator* 29:2, April/June, Special Issue).

Gill, Stephen (1999), 'Structural Changes in Multilateralism: The G7 Nexus and the Global Crisis', in *Innovation in Multilateralism*, 113-65, M. Schechter (ed.), St. Martin's Press, New York.

Guttry, Andrea de (1994), 'The Institutional Configuration of the G-7 in the New International Scenario', in *The Future of the G-7 Summits*, 67-80, (*The International Spectator* 29:2; April/June, Special Issue).

Hodges, Michael R. (1994), 'More Efficiency, Less Dignity: British Perspectives on the Future Role and Working of the G-7', in *The Future of the G-7 Summits*, 141-159, (*The International Spectator* 29:2, April/June, Special Issue).

Hodges, Michael R. (1999), 'The G8 and the New Political Economy', in *The G8's Role in the New Millennium*, 69-73, Michael R. Hodges, John J. Kirton and Joseph P. Daniels (eds), Ashgate, Aldershot, UK.

Ikenberry, G. John (1993), 'Salvaging the G-7', *Foreign Affairs*, 72:2, 132-39.

Kerevan, George (2005), 'How UN Failure Cleared the Way for G8 Power', *The Scotsman*, 26, 7 July.

Kirton, John J. (1989a), 'Contemporary Concert Diplomacy: The Seven-Power Summit and the Management of International Order', Paper prepared for the annual meeting of the International Studies Association and the British International Studies Association, London, March 29-April 1. Unpublished in print. www.g7.utoronto.ca/scholar/kirton198901/index.html.

Kirton, John J. (1995), 'The Diplomacy of Concert: Canada, the G7 and the Halifax Summit', *Canadian Foreign Policy* 3:1, 63-80.

Kirton, John J. (1997), 'Economic Cooperation: Summitry, Institutions, and Structural Change', Paper prepared for a conference on 'Structural Change and Co-operation in the Global Economy', Center for International Business Education and Center for Global Change and Governance, Rutgers University, New Brunswick, N.J., 19-20 May, www.g7.utoronto.ca/scholar/kirton199702/index.html. Also in *Structural Change and Co-operation in the Global Economy* (1999), John Dunning and Gavin Boyd (eds), Edward Elgar, London.

Kirton, John J. (2005c), 'New Perspectives on the G8', in *New Perspectives on Global Governance: Why America Needs the* G8, 231-57, Michele Fratianni et al. (eds), Ashgate, Aldershot, UK.

Merlini, Cesare (1994), 'The G-7 and the Need for Reform', in *The Future of the G-7 Summits. The International Spectator*, 29:2, 5-25, April/June, Special Issue, www.library.utoronto.ca/g7/italiano/merlini_i1.html (Italian).

Penttilä, Risto E. J. (2003), *The Role of the G8 in International Peace and Security*, Adelphi Paper, 355. Oxford University Press for the International Institute of Strategic Studies, Oxford.

Putnam, Robert D. and Nicholas Bayne (1984), *Hanging Together: Cooperation and Conflict in the Seven-Power Summits*, Harvard University Press, Cambridge, MA.

Putnam, Robert D. and Nicholas Bayne (1987), *Hanging Together: Cooperation and Conflict in the Seven-Power Summits*, rev. ed., Harvard University Press, Cambridge, MA.

Slaughter, Anne-Marie (2004), *A New World Order*, Princeton University Press, Princeton; Oxford.

United Kingdom, Foreign and Commonwealth Office (1998), *G8 Structure: An Informal Club*. London.

Wallace, William (1984), 'Political Issues at the Summits: A New Concert of Powers?', in *Economic Summits and Western Decision-Making*, 137-52, Cesare Merlini (ed.), Croom Helm; St. Martin's Press in association with the European Institute of Public Administration, London; New York.

Chapter 2

Origins of the G7 Summit[1]

This chapter traces the events, circumstances and various national positions leading to the eventual launch of the leaders' meetings that have become annual summits. It sketches the main economic developments that drove the need for such summits; discusses the history of the mostly secret meetings of G5 finance ministers – a series of get-togethers that were the predecessors of the summits; and draws some conclusions.

The Library Group and the G5 Finance Ministers' Forum

Several shocks and major events in the early 1970s had a profound effect on the world economic system:

- the collapse of the Bretton Woods monetary system based on fixed exchange rates and on the United States dollar's convertibility into gold. The two Bretton Woods institutions, the International Monetary Fund (IMF) and the World Bank, tried to set up the necessary reforms, but were not successful in this effort;
- the first enlargement of the EC (European Community), with Britain, Denmark and Ireland joining the original six members;
- the first oil crisis, when the Organization of the Petroleum Exporting Countries (OPEC) placed an embargo on oil supplies following the October 1973 Yom Kippur War. Western countries disagreed about how to respond to the embargo and to the resulting sharp price increases; and
- the 1974 economic recession in Organisation for Economic Co-operation and Development (OECD) countries, in which inflation and unemployment rates rose sharply.

With these developments, 'the traditional organs of international co-operation were no longer able to reconcile the differences among the leading Western powers or to give them a sense of common purpose' (Putnam and Bayne 1987: 25-27).

It was in this context that Valéry Giscard d'Estaing and Helmut Schmidt, then finance ministers of France and West Germany, participated in the 18 December 1971 monetary meeting at the Smithsonian Institution in Washington, DC. The Smithsonian meeting discussed exchange rates following the devaluation of the US

---

1   I am especially grateful to Sir Nicholas Bayne for his insightful comments and suggestions, and for valuable background information.

dollar. Subsequently, US Treasury Secretary George Shultz suggested that the three of them, along with their British and Japanese counterparts, meet informally in the White House library. These ministers then decided to meet periodically, without any publicity, to review developments of the international monetary system. This confidentiality was motivated, at least in part, by their desire to avoid influencing the exchange market (Giscard d'Estaing 1988: 125).

The finance ministers of France, Germany, the UK and the US met on 25 March 1973 in the White House library, forming the 'Library Group'. The four ministers met again in July and from September 1973 were joined by Japan. This group met periodically for a number of years and came to be known as the Group of Five finance ministers (G5). The participants welcomed its compactness and informality, in contrast with the more formal proceedings in the Committee of 20 (C20) and other IMF meetings. The governors of the central banks of the Five sometimes joined the finance ministers at these meetings. (The C20 was established on 26 July 1972 and consisted of finance ministers or central bank governors from each constituency of the IMF Executive Board, and was succeeded in 1974 by the IMF Interim Committee, later International Monetary and Financial Committee (Kenan 2004: 20).) By the time Giscard, now President of France, called the Rambouillet summit for November 1975, the G5 had been going for two years and it continued to exist as a parallel entity, usually meeting in secret, for more than another decade. The 22 September 1985 Plaza Accord on 'managed floating' of exchange rates was its greatest achievement. But it did not survive the public emergence of the G7 finance ministers' forum, established by the 1986 Tokyo G7 summit, and has not met since February 1987.[2]

With the opening of archival records covering the early and mid-1970s in at least some original member countries of the G7, a good deal of information is becoming gradually available to the public. UK, US and Canadian official archives were searched for this book, yielding valuable documentation of the pre-history and early history of the G7. As the official archives of G7 countries gradually open their holdings, more information will come to light. (For a more detailed discussion of archives as sources of information, see Chapter 15.)

The following is a list of G5 finance ministers' meetings known to have occurred or been proposed:

- September 1973, Nairobi, Kenya, on the margins of the annual meetings of the Boards of Governors of the IMF and the World Bank;
- 24-26 November 1973, Tours, France;
- 15 January 1974, Rome, Italy. Exceptionally, Italy managed to convene and take part in this meeting. This was the first of the two meetings of the group that Italy attended;
- 11 June 1974, Washington, DC, US (on board the presidential yacht Sequoia);
- 7-8 September 1974, Paris, France: Following a last-minute invitation, Italy was present for part of the meeting only;

---

2   Funabashi (1989) is an excellent source of information on the Library Group, the G5, and the G5's relationship to the G7. Healey (1989) includes some interesting anecdotes about the early G5 meetings and the personalities involved. See esp. pp. 416-20.

- 28 September 1974, Washington, DC: finance/foreign ministers' joint meeting, followed by G5 finance ministers' and central bank governors' meeting on 29 September;
- 4-5 November 1974. Proposed by the US but not verified whether it actually took place;
- 13 January 1975, Washington, DC. Proposed by Schmidt but not verified whether it actually took place;
- 29 May 1975, Paris, France: dinner on the margins of the OECD ministerial meeting;
- 30 August 1975, Washington, DC (on board the presidential yacht Sequoia).[3]

After the summits began with Rambouillet in November 1975, the finance ministers continued to meet up to three times a year on their own cycle. In 1976-1979, meetings were often held in Versailles, France, as Raymond Barre combined the posts of French Prime Minister and finance minister, and found it hard to travel. Post-Rambouillet meetings included:

- 22-23 April 1977, Versailles;
- 4-5 December 1977, Versailles;
- 12-13 February 1978, Versailles;
- 16 September 1979, Paris;
- 10 April 1981, London;
- 11-12 December 1982, Frankfurt;
- 17 January 1985, Washington;
- 22 September 1985, Plaza Hotel, New York;
- 6 October 1985, Seoul;
- 18-19 January 1986, London;
- 26 September 1986, Washington;
- 21 February 1987, Louvre, Paris (a day before the historic Louvre meeting of the G7 finance ministers which was boycotted by Italy). This was the last G5 meeting.

A summary of the 24-26 November 1973 G5 finance ministers' meeting in Tours, France indicates that the following topics were discussed: reform of the international monetary system; oil; exchange rate and balance of payments prospects; export credit interest; and US controls on capital exports. A provisional date (16 January 1974) and place (Nice, France) for the next meeting were also discussed. ('Group of Five Meeting, Château d'Artigny, Montbazon, 24-26 November 1973'; The National Archives (UK) [hereafter referred to by its official acronym, TNA], T354/52.) In the event, Italy, which resented its exclusion from the group, contrived to host the January 1974 meeting, so it briefly became G6.

---

3   In its 31 August/1 September issue, *Le Monde* reported the fact and likely topics of the G5 meeting in Washington on 30 August. The article, 'Français et Américains vont s'opposer à nouveau sur le système de change et l'utilisation de l'or', was likely written on 30 August.

In preparation for the G5 finance ministers' meetings, the ministers' deputies held their own series of meetings. The ministers also used the deputies' meetings to try out possible ideas for further development. (Letter, Peter H. R. Marshall [Under-Secretary, Financial Relations Department] to J. G. Littler [Under-Secretary, General], HM Treasury, 13 December 1973; TNA, T354/52, pp. 43-45.)

At the 15 January 1974 Rome meeting (actually held in a house half-way between Rome and Viterbo), the G6 finance ministers had a fairly wide-ranging discussion. They talked about oil prices and balance of payments; exchange rate relationships; the recycling of Arab money surpluses; gold; world liquidity; and export credit. As the meeting took place in Italy, that country could not be excluded from participating. ('Group of Six Meeting, 15 January 1974', Memorandum, D. J. Mitchell; TNA, T354/52, pp. 55-60.) This was the last meeting for three of the group's founders. Schmidt became German Chancellor in April 1974; Giscard was elected President of France in May; and Schultz left the US government in the same month.

On 11 June 1974, the G5 finance ministers and central bank governors (France was represented by its central bank governor only) met on board the presidential yacht Sequoia near Washington, DC. The meeting discussed gold, and the economic situation in Italy. Afterwards, their agreement on gold was a topic at the informal dinner of G10 ministers the same evening. ('Meeting of Group of Five on Tuesday, 11 June 1974, on the Presidential Yacht "Sequoia", Washington, DC', Memorandum, D. J. Mitchell, 19 June 1974; TNA T354/167, pp. 2B-2C).

Notes of the G5/G6 meeting of the finance ministers on 7-8 September 1974 in Champs-sur-Marne, France reveal that in addition to finance ministers, the governors of the central banks also participated again. Italy had protested its exclusion, turned up uninvited and was admitted to part of the meeting. It was hoped, nonetheless, by at least some of the G5 'that it would be possible in future for the group to revert to five countries'. The meeting held three sessions, and its agenda included: Euro-dollars and the recycling of surplus money of the oil-producing countries; preparations for the upcoming meeting of the World Bank and IMF; inflation and national economic policies of the participating countries; guidance to the press about the meeting; and arrangements for future meetings of the group. On the last point, it was assumed that central bank governors would continue to be invited to the meetings and that the next meeting of the group would take place on 28 September 1974 in Washington. (TNA, FCO 59/1097, p. 27A ff.) Another summary of the same meeting appears in FCO telegram No. 1904, dated 13 September 1974, which states: 'The meeting was one of the series of occasional meetings arranged to enable finance ministers of leading countries to exchange views privately. It is essential that the secrecy of the discussions be respected.' (TNA, FCO 59/1097, p. 30A, 3 pages.)

Although unhappy over their frequent exclusion from these meetings, the Italians 'had lived with the situation in the past because they had been assured that the meetings would take place only occasionally. But now it looked as if they were being institutionalised. The Italian Government could not understand why they were excluded, because on … grounds [of] size of economy, population, involvement in international trade and finance – they were surely qualified.' ('G.5 and Italy'. Note, C. W. France, 25 September 1974. TNA, FCO 59/1098, p. 81, 2 pages.) In fact, there was no clear G5 support for 'institutionalizing' these meetings; the French, in particular, 'opposed further collective meetings of G5 officials'. (TNA, FCO 59/1099, p. 157, 4 pages.) In fact, the Italian bid to get into the group failed and it remained as G5.

In addition to the Italians, the Dutch and the Belgians also resented being left out of the G5 finance ministers' meetings, although their objections were more muted. This is clear from various sources; for example, telegram No. 1950, dated 20 September 1974. (FCO 59/1097, p. 55.)

It was at Champs-sur-Marne that the idea for a joint meeting of the G5 finance and foreign ministers on oil prices was voiced, to take place in Washington on 28 September 1974. This was reported to be US Secretary of State Henry Kissinger's initiative, supported by US Secretary of the Treasury William Simon. (I. P. Wilson's [Higher Executive Officer, Private Secretary, Treasury] note of a meeting in Sir D[erek] Mitchell's office at the UK Treasury on 12 September 1974; TNA, FCO 59/1097, p. 29, 2 pages.) An account of the 28 September meeting describes the gist of the discussions, including summaries of comments by participants. (British Embassy, Washington, Telegram No. 3158, 29 September 1974; TNA, T354/169, pp. 98-101.) At the meeting, Kissinger circulated 'illustrative proposals' for co-operation among the major industrial oil-consuming countries in the following areas: demand restraint (conservation); financial solidarity; and economic relations between oil producers and consumers. ('Oil and the World Economy', Note, Donald Maitland, 17 October 1974, TNA, FCO 59/1100, p. 202; 2 pages.) The following day, on 29 September 1974, the G5 finance ministers and central bank governors met, also in the State Department in Washington but without the foreign ministers. ('Record of a Meeting in the State Department, Washington, DC, on the Morning of Sunday, 29 September 1974'; TNA, T354/169, pp. 162ff.)

Schmidt proposed another G5 finance ministers' meeting for 13 January 1975 in Washington. Reportedly, Presidents Giscard and Gerald R. Ford endorsed the idea. (Memorandum, Derek Mitchell, 17 December 1974; TNA, T354/170, pp. 50-51.) It could not be verified whether that meeting took place. From then on, the heads of government took less interest in the G5, being absorbed with their plans for a summit. But the G5 finance ministers met again in 1975, in May and August – as known from press reports – and they continued to meet subsequently two or three times a year. The G5 remained distinct from the summit, though finance ministers, with foreign ministers, attended the summits from the outset, at US insistence. This practice continued until the 1997 Denver summit. At the 1998 Birmingham summit, the leaders finally agreed to meet without their ministers as Giscard and Schmidt originally intended, and they have done so ever since, with finance and foreign ministers getting together separately just before each summit (Bayne 2005b: 8). (See Chapter 12 for a discussion of the Birmingham summit reforms.)

Problems of publicity continued to haunt the participating governments. A note drafted in the UK Treasury Department just before the 14 January 1974 G5 finance ministers' meeting suggests that in case of a news leak of the forthcoming meeting there should be a simple confirmation of an informal meeting and the fact that no communiqué would be issued. There would also be a brief reference to the previous meeting of the group, and to the fact that the discussion was expected to cover the same topics as the last meeting ('Draft Form of Words for Use if the News of the G5

Meeting Breaks', 11 January 1974; TNA, T354/166, p. 12.) G5 ministers from EC countries realized that they ought to inform their EC colleagues of at least the gist of the meetings, to assuage disquiet over these discussions taking place in a restricted forum rather than officially in the EC. ('G5: Problems of Publicity', Memorandum, C. W. Fogarty [Deputy Secretary, International Monetary, Treasury] to Mr [D. J.] Mitchell [Second Permanent Secretary, Overseas Finance, Treasury], 9 January 1974; TNA, T354/166, p. 125/14; 2 pages.)

The Idea of the Summit

Presidents Giscard and Ford held a meeting in Martinique on 16-17 December 1974. There the two leaders 'decided to take the initiative in calling additional intergovernmental meetings'.[4] But the summit was the idea of Giscard and Schmidt, as shown clearly by various sources; for example, in Schmidt's memoir *Men and Powers*, Callaghan's memoir *Time and Chance*, Putnam and Bayne's *Hanging Together* (both the first and the revised editions), and Schmidt's July 1975 private memorandum (all of which are quoted elsewhere in this chapter). As well, *Le Monde* reported as early as 9 July 1975 that, in an interview with two American journalists of the Hearst newspaper chain, Giscard proposed the holding of an informal summit meeting in Autumn 1975 in Paris, with France, the US, the UK, Germany, Japan and Italy (and perhaps other major industrial countries) participating. The summit would deal with the monetary crisis (La Lutte … 1975: 24).

Giscard and Schmidt based their idea on their favourable experience in the Library Group and the G5 finance ministers' forum. And in a later letter to Ford, dated 24 October 1975, Giscard confirmed that the summit would be only of heads of state and government plus the foreign and finance ministers, in order to keep the meeting personal and restricted. (Letter, President Giscard to President Ford, 24 October 1975; Gerald R. Ford Library [hereafter referred to as Ford Library], Box 1, National Security Adviser, Presidential Correspondence with Foreign Leaders, 1974-1977; France – President Giscard d'Estaing (1).)

Kissinger's account varies from this. Aboard Air Force One flying the US delegation home from the Rambouillet summit, he stated:

> The idea of this summit came up first in a vague way at a meeting I had with Giscard in May. It was then put forward in a more formal way at Helsinki by Giscard to the President [Ford]. At that point we decided that we would send … George Shultz … to see Giscard, Schmidt, [Harold] Wilson, and [Shultz] reported to us afterwards that he thought there was a good basis for a summit and only after we had that report did we make the decision to go ahead. (White House Press Release, November 17, 1975: Press Conference of Henry A. Kissinger, Secretary of State, and William E. Simon, Secretary of the Treasury aboard Air Force One; Ford Library, Box 5, John W. 'Bill' Roberts Papers, 1973-1977, Presidential Subject File, Foreign Trips, November 14-17, 1975 – France – Press Releases.)

---

4   Quoted from the Martinique communiqué in Putnam and Bayne (1984: 15). On the Martinique meeting see also Garavoglia (1984: 8).

The Helsinki Quadripartite Luncheon

The quadripartite luncheon that launched the G6 (later G7, and still later G8) leaders' summits took place on 31 July 1975 from 1:25 to 3:25 PM at the residence of the British Ambassador in Helsinki, during the Conference on Security and Co-operation in Europe (CSCE) where 35 heads of state and government were present to sign the Final Act of the conference. The following participated in the luncheon: UK Prime Minister Harold Wilson and Foreign Secretary Callaghan; French President Giscard and Minister of Foreign Affairs Jean Sauvagnargues; Federal Republic of Germany Chancellor Schmidt, Foreign Minister Hans-Dietrich Genscher, and interpreter Gisela Anders; and US President Ford, Secretary of State Kissinger, and interpreter Harry Obst. Excerpts from conversations at this luncheon, found in an originally secret but now declassified record in the archives of the Ford Library in Ann Arbor, Michigan, USA, reveal that the agenda of the luncheon conversation consisted of the following: Finnish President Urho Kekkonen's dinner at the CSCE plenary; reaction to Soviet President Leonid Brezhnev's speech at the CSCE summit; the state of Brezhnev's health; and the Middle East. The excerpts cover only the first hour (1:25-2:25 PM) of the conversation at the lunch table. The rest of the conversation, for another hour, was held in the garden by the four leaders and their foreign ministers only, without interpreters or note-takers. (Memorandum of Conversation: Excerpts from Conversations at the Quadripartite Luncheon in Helsinki (US, UK, France, FRG), 31 July 1975; Ford Library, Box 14, National Security Adviser, Memoranda of Conversations.)[5] It was in the course of that hour in the garden, devoted to economic issues, that Giscard's call for the Rambouillet summit was discussed and accepted, but since no excerpt of conversation during the second hour has been unearthed, the researcher must rely on memoirs of participants and other insider accounts (see also Putnam and Bayne 1987: 25).

This fairly detailed account of the luncheon serves to illustrate not only the agreement on the summit. It also explains the lack of exact information about this crucial event. The absence of interpreters was less important – relevant exchanges took place in English which both Giscard and Schmidt spoke fluently – than the absence of note-takers, which accounts for persistent ambiguity about what precisely was agreed at Helsinki.

Schmidt, in a 'private memorandum' prepared before the Helsinki meeting and given to the other leaders, argues that:

> [b]efore the end of this year [1975] a summit conference should be covered to discuss questions of the world economy and the world monetary system. As I see it, the participants would be the United States, Great Britain, France, Japan, the Federal Republic [of Germany] and possibly also Italy. The Conference should be prepared by the personal representatives of the heads of State and Government. I suggest that at the luncheon of the Four in Helsinki the proposal of Giscard d'Estaing to convene a summit conference be adopted.

---

5   References to records in official archives follow the form suggested by those archives.

He adds: 'what is important for us now is to agree on concrete steps to stabilize the world economic situation' ... [by reactivating private investment, regaining a satisfactory rate of growth, and co-ordinating interest rate policies, among other steps]. On exchange rates, Schmidt expresses doubt that the US and France would reach agreement on a system: 'we should therefore not attempt to find a solution to this problem at the IMF Annual Assembly ... we should put this down as an item for discussion at the planned economic summit conference'. (Private Memorandum on International Concertation of Economic Action, by Helmut Schmidt [July 1975; exact date unknown]; Ford Library, Box 14, National Security Adviser, Memoranda of Conversations, July 27-28, 1975 – Ford, Kissinger, FRG Chancellor Helmut Schmidt, Foreign Minister Hans-Dietrich Genscher.) (See also Putnam and Bayne 1984: 16.)

Schmidt relates in his memoirs that he, Giscard, Wilson and Ford, at Helsinki, 'arrived at arrangements for an international economic conference of the heads of government of the major industrial democracies. The idea had originally come up in a conversation between Giscard and myself. We had been thinking about a kind of continuation of the old Library Group on a higher level.' He adds that, having overcome Ford's initial hesitation, 'on a bright summer afternoon, sitting around a garden table in Helsinki, ... we made plans for the first summit; so as to keep it from falling into the hands of the bureaucrats, we agreed to have all preparations made by people we would personally charge with the task'. He notes, as well, that the four leaders agreed on the necessity of Japan's participation (Schmidt 1989: 173-74).

Callaghan, present at the Helsinki luncheon as Foreign Secretary of the UK, remarks in his memoirs that:

> Gerry Ford had seemed rather unenthusiastic about Giscard's proposal, and as we sat in the garden of the British Embassy drinking our after-lunch coffee in the warm July sun, it was to him that Giscard mainly addressed his ideas. Helmut Schmidt too had previously sent us a paper prepared by him [see previous paragraph], containing a plea for the United States to be less domestic-orientated, urging it to take into account the international repercussions of its policies and suggesting a summit attended by the four of us plus Japan and Italy. Harold Wilson backed the idea and with Henry Kissinger also speaking in favour, the United States President agreed. We decided that each Head of Government should appoint a personal representative to prepare for the conference, and asked France to act as host.

Callaghan implies that the invitation to Italy was agreed, and adds that at Helsinki the Italians, on hearing 'a rumour' that they would not be invited, 'uttered a cry of pain which was only stilled by our reassurance that they would be there' (Callaghan 1987: 478-79). This differs from other accounts of Italy's late invitation to the first summit. Both the Schmidt and the Callaghan accounts make it clear that it was at the Helsinki luncheon that Ford agreed to the summit.

In a memorandum from Kissinger to Ford, drafted just before the Helsinki luncheon, Kissinger reviews the economic issues to be discussed at the luncheon (that was the agenda for the second hour of the luncheon, as indicated above): the current economic situation, North-South relations, energy, and international monetary issues. In his 'talking points' for Ford, Kissinger proposes for the President to say:

'(Only if Giscard presses proposal for a monetary summit to resolve outstanding issues): We do not think it would be wise to try to negotiate these complex issues at a summit meeting, although we would give a formal proposal, when and if it arrives, serious consideration.' (Memorandum, Henry A. Kissinger to President Ford, [26?] July 1975; Ford Library, Box 10, National Security Adviser, Trip Briefing Books and Cables of Gerald Ford, July 26-August 4, 1975, copy 1(1).) In fact, Kissinger favoured the summit while US Treasury Secretary Simon opposed it at that point (see also Putnam and Bayne 1984: 16-17).

Prime Minister Takeo Miki of Japan (which was not a participating country in the CSCE) told Ford on 5 August 1975: 'I agree with your remarks, Mr. President, on Giscard's proposal for a five-power economic conference, and did so publicly for the press, that is that a preliminary conference would be required to establish an agenda.' Ford's response: 'I think we should proceed on an informal basis, rather than formal. … I think an informal arrangement – for discussions by a person you would name, and persons named by Giscard, Wilson and Schmidt – would be a better way to lay the groundwork.' (Memorandum of Conversation: President's [Ford's] Tête-à-Tête with Prime Minister [Miki], 5 August 1975; Ford Library, Box 14, National Security Adviser, Memoranda of Conversations, 1973-1977, August 5, 1975 – Ford, Japanese Prime Minister Takeo Miki.) These 'persons named' did just that, and their successors have remained the personal representatives – later called 'sherpas' – of the leaders (for more information on the sherpas' role, see Chapter 6).

The Road to Rambouillet

The US attitude to the summit was finally resolved when President Ford sent George Shultz, whom he had chosen as his personal representative to prepare for the summit, on a visit to Bonn, London and Paris. After his return, a conversation took place in the Oval Office of the White House on 17 September 1975, among Ford, Kissinger, Shultz and Brent Scowcroft (National Security Adviser). This throws so much light on the US thinking on the impending Rambouillet summit and on the dynamics of prominent personalities that it is worth reproducing here *in extenso*:

> Schultz: I met with Schmidt for about 10 hours, and Giscard. Wilson thinks the burden should be on those who say there shouldn't be a meeting, not vice versa. They are interested in a personal and deep discussion rather than a very broad one.
> President: What participants will there be? What about Italy and Canada?
> Shultz: They are thinking just of the five. They asked about Canada and I said it is our biggest trading partner. I would leave Italy to the Europeans. If they want it out, I would support that. Italy would just clutter the landscape. With three people per country, that is about the maximum for the useful meeting. I said we needed the Secretary of State and the Secretary of Treasury. They agreed on three, but just who, they want to think about. On timing, I said it had to be this year. It looks like mid-November is about the latest possible.
> Kissinger: It almost would have to be before Thanksgiving.
> Schultz: On the location…
> President: From a political point of view, it would be better to have it here. I am getting criticism from being out of Washington, but it is not serious.

Kissinger: I doubt if Giscard would be willing to come here.

Shultz: If it happens, it would mark the reentry of France into the councils.

Kissinger: I don't say it has to be in France, but with Giscard coming here next year, it would be tough.

Shultz: I tried the US on them. Wilson will come of course; Schmidt is a bit reluctant and Giscard is negative.

President: We would have a joint announcement so there isn't one invitor. Let's get the schedule cleared.

Schultz: I need someone within the government to work with. Henry suggested Sonnenfeldt.

Kissinger: It is interesting how much time they spent with George. It shows how seriously they take it. (Memorandum of Conversation, President Ford, George Shultz, Henry Kissinger, Brent Scowcroft; Ford Library, Box 15, National Security Adviser, Memoranda of Conversations, September 17, 1975 – Ford, Kissinger, George Shultz.)

Italy received a late invitation to Rambouillet. Agreement to invite the Italians was reached on 25 September, before the first preparatory meeting on 5-6 October at the Carlton Hotel, New York, which they attended. Callaghan's remarks, quoted above, again illustrate the lack of precise information following a meeting without note-takers. All other sources suggest that the Helsinki luncheon meeting agreed to invite Japan but not Italy. One reason for the change of heart on the part of the G5 was that Italy occupied the European Council of Ministers' presidency at the time, and Italy's acceptance was 'employed in an effort to justify exclusion of the European Community' (Garavoglia 1984). (The EU began participating in summits starting with 1977; see also Chapter 4 for more detailed discussion of Canada, Italy and the EU in the G7.)

In contrast with the publicity that now accompanies each summit – as well as the preparations and follow-up of each summit – there was an effort to keep news of the first summit from the public until the official announcement.

In response to a press inquiry in flight from Helsinki to Bucharest on August 2, 1975, the President [Ford] stated …: 'I am not going to discuss whether there will or won't be an economic conference.' … [But o]n September 1st, *Business Week* reported that George P. Shultz, President of Bechtel Corporation, will represent the U.S. at a meeting of eminent economic statesmen from industrial nations exploring the usefulness of a summit meeting at which President Ford and his British, French, West German and Japanese counterpart[s] would meet to address mutual economic problems. Then, on October 5th, *The New York Times* reported that agreement in principle has been reached for an economic meeting of the heads of government (US, France, West Germany, Japan and the UK) in France before the end of this year. (Memorandum, Bob Evers to Roger Porter, 7 October 1975; Ford Library, Box 312, L. William Seidman Files, 1974-1977: International Economic Summit, November 15-17, 1975 – Memoranda of Conversations and Notes of Discussions (1).)

Also, the 21/22 September issue of *Le Monde* indicates that French finance minister Jean-Pierre Fourcade had told that newspaper that there would be a summit before the end of the year. The *Financial Times* of 29 September gives the names of all those attending the first preparatory meeting (whose outcome was also widely and accurately reported several days before the official announcement).

The G5 formally announced the Rambouillet meeting on 10 October 1975. The announcement states that Germany, France, Italy, Japan, the UK and the US will meet in France 'to discuss economic issues of mutual interest, including promotion of recovery in the world economy, trade and monetary policy, developments in energy and other raw material markets, and relations with other developed and developing nations'. (Memorandum, Ivan L. Head to Prime Minister Trudeau, 10 October 1975; Library and Archives Canada, P. E. Trudeau Fonds, MG 26 O, Staff Series, O19, Volume 139, File 17: 1975-1977, Ivan Head – Subject Files – Economic Summit 1975-1976.)

Conclusion

Giscard and Schmidt, as former finance ministers, understood monetary and other economic issues well and were eager to discuss such issues with their opposite numbers from other major industrialized countries. The subsequent generations of G7 leaders, for the most part, did not share this background; some of them were, therefore, more inclined to broaden the scope of their discussions to political and other non-economic topics and to entrust economic issues to their finance ministers. In later years, with the various financial crises, contentious issues of world trade, and other economic imperatives, the leaders' concentration on economic issues was renewed.

Nicholas Bayne enumerates three justifications for the summit as seen by leaders of the summit countries. The first is that the leaders, through their political leadership, would be able 'to launch new ideas and resolve disputes that had persisted at lower levels'. Secondly, due to 'their capacity to reconcile domestic and international pressures [italics removed] on policy-making'. And thirdly, that 'they could introduce a system of collective management [italics removed], where Europe, North America and Japan would share responsibilities hitherto exercised by the United States alone' (Bayne 2005b: 4).

The five major democracies – France, West Germany, the UK, the US and Japan (later joined by Italy) recognized their vulnerability to economic shocks and other major international developments. They also saw the need to find solutions to these problems in a co-ordinated fashion. Existing international institutions could not cope adequately with these changes. Hence, a new forum arose in the 1970s, first in the form of periodic meetings of the finance ministers of these countries, and eventually as summit meetings of the countries' leaders.

In sharp contrast with later summits, these early meetings unfolded with a limited agenda and a restricted number of participants, amid a high degree of secrecy. Nonetheless, they laid the foundation on which were built later summits and an expanded system of ministerial and other meetings. These later meetings proceeded in a generally more transparent manner, with a steadily broadening agenda, and much greater participation by other countries, international organizations, civil society, and the private sector.

References

Note on internet addresses (URLs): Websites tend to appear, change or disappear, often without warning. Addresses cited in this source list were accurate and active at the time of writing (June 2006) unless otherwise noted.

Bayne, Nicholas (2005b), *Staying Together: The G8 Summit Confronts the 21st Century*, Ashgate, Aldershot, UK.

Callaghan, James (1987), *Time and Chance*, Collins, London.

Funabashi, Yoichi (1989), *Managing the Dollar: From the Plaza to the Louvre*. 2nd, rev. ed., Institute for International Economics, Washington, DC.

Garavoglia, Guido (1984), 'From Rambouillet to Williamsburg: A Historical Assessment', in *Economic Summits and Western Decision-Making*, 1-42, Cesare Merlini (ed.) Croom Helm; St. Martin's Press in association with the European Institute of Public Administration, London; New York.

Giscard d'Estaing, Valéry (1988), *Le pouvoir et la vie* [*Power and Life*], Compagnie 12, Paris.

Healey, Denis (1989), *The Time of My Life*, Michael Joseph, London.

Kenen, Peter B., et al. (2004), *International Economic and Financial Cooperation: New Issues, New Actors, New Responses*, Centre for Economic Policy Research, London.

'La Lutte contre la récession passe par une solution monétaire' (1975), *Le Monde*, 9 July, 24.

Putnam, Robert D. and Nicholas Bayne (1984), *Hanging Together: Cooperation and Conflict in the Seven-Power Summits*, Harvard University Press, Cambridge, Mass.

Putnam, Robert D. and Nicholas Bayne (1987), *Hanging Together: Cooperation and Conflict in the Seven-Power Summits*, rev. ed., Harvard University Press, Cambridge, Mass.

Schmidt, Helmut (1989), *Men and Powers: A Political Retrospective*, Random House, New York.

Chapter 3

The Summit Meetings

The annual summit meetings of the leaders of the G7 and G8 countries are at the apex of the steadily broadening G7 and G8 system. This chapter surveys these meetings as they have unfolded over 32 years, discusses the role of the G7 and G8, and illustrates the personal reflections and perspectives of leaders on the summit process. The evolving agenda of the summits is the subject of Chapter 5; the various fora of G7 and G8 ministers, the leaders' personal representatives (sherpas), and the network of task forces, expert groups and working groups set up over the years by the leaders or by their ministers, are discussed in Chapter 6.[1]

The G7 and G8 Summits

The first summit was held in Rambouillet, France, near Paris, on 15-17 November 1975. That year there were only six participants: the leaders of the G5 countries (France, the US, the UK, Germany, and Japan) plus Italy. The G5 had been meeting at the finance ministers' level since 1973 when the 'Library Group' first convened, to be followed by a series of periodic meetings of the ministers.[2]

Harold Wilson, UK Prime Minister at the time, describes the Rambouillet summit which met following the:

> characteristically imaginative proposal of [French President Valéry] Giscard d'Estaing, even though it had inevitably upset EEC [European Economic Community] leaders at Helsinki [the Helsinki Conference on Security and Co-operation in Europe where Giscard had suggested to his UK, US and German peers to hold the summit, with Japan also to be invited]. It took place … at Francis I's magnificent palace at Rambouillet … . A great deal of care had been taken with its preparation, each Head of Government nominating a very senior official to join in meetings to work on the agenda and administrative arrangements.

Wilson then gives a detailed account of the actual discussions as well as the atmosphere at Rambouillet (Wilson 1979: 184-88).

Although the Rambouillet summit was seen by its participants as important and positive for the six countries, it was not yet certain that there would be a follow-up meeting, let alone an ensuing annual series of summits. In a conversation in the White House Oval Office on 17 May 1976, US President Ford told Giscard:

---

1   For detailed assessments of summitry and individual summits see especially Putnam and Bayne (1987); Bayne (2000); and Bayne (2005b).

2   See Chapter 2 for a history and analysis of the Library Group and the G5, and the negotiations leading up to the convening of the summit.

'the American reaction to Rambouillet I was highly positive. We discussed there the possibility of a follow-up meeting ... . George Shultz [the President's special representative or sherpa] has taken soundings for another meeting in late June or July [1976]. There have been economic developments and many developments in Europe that we should discuss.' Giscard responded: 'I have no objections in principle ... . I think it is important to have results if we have a meeting. It is not apparent to me what results we could announce ... . We could discuss the recovery, and measures against inflation. But I am not sure if those are dramatic enough for a meeting.' (Memorandum of Conversation, President Ford, President Valéry Giscard d'Estaing, Secretary of State Henry Kissinger, [French] Minister of Foreign Affairs Jean Sauvagnargues, Assistant to the President for National Security Affairs Brent Scowcroft, 17 May 1976; Gerald R. Ford Library [referred hereafter as Ford Library], Box 19, National Security Adviser, Memoranda of Conversations, 1973-1977.)[3]

Ford did call for a follow-up summit (with the consent of his five counterparts). The second summit, with Canada joining for the first time, met in San Juan, Puerto Rico, 27-28 June 1976. Canadian Prime Minister Pierre Elliott Trudeau stated at a press conference at the end of the Puerto Rico summit: 'No ... decision was taken on ... [whether there would be another summit]. There will or will not be other summits ... depending on the appreciation that each country has of when it is necessary and what can be obtained from it ... . Il faut éviter, je crois, d'institutionnaliser ces sommets, il ne faut pas en faire des rencontres purement artificielles, if faut que le besoin se fasse sentir... [I think that we must avoid institutionalizing these summits, we must not make them purely artificial, there must be a felt need].' (Text of the Prime Minister's Remarks to Press Following the Economic Summit in Puerto Rico, June 28, 1976; Library and Archives Canada, P. E. Trudeau Fonds, 1968-1978 PMO Priority Correspondence Series, MG26 O7, Volume 536, File 1203: 1975-1977, 1976 Files.)

In a letter to President Ford dated 20 December 1976, Giscard proposed that a third summit be held in 1977, in Europe. Giscard also kept president-elect Jimmy Carter posted on this proposal. (Letter, President Valéry Giscard d'Estaing to President Ford, 20 December 1976; Ford Library, Box 1, National Security Adviser, Presidential Correspondence with Foreign Leaders, 1974-1977; France – President Giscard d'Estaing (3).) Thus, in 1977 the G7 forum had still not been firmly established as an annual event but was to be reconvened by the leaders if they saw the need for it. These conferences, nonetheless, became regular annual summits, taking place in strictly determined rotation among the G7 countries: France, US, UK, Germany, Japan, Italy, Canada. The 1977 London summit brought in the EC as a participant.[4] As discussed later in this chapter, Russia, after becoming a full member of the club, entered the rotation with its first-time G8 presidency in 2006.

The 1978 Bonn summit's communiqué ended with this statement: 'We have instructed our representatives to convene by the end of 1978 in order to review

---

3   References to records in official archives follow the form suggested by those archives.

4   For the history and evolution of EC/EU involvement in the G7/G8, see Bonvicini and Wessels (1984); Ullrich and Donnelly (1998); Hainsworth (1990).

this Declaration. We also intend to have a similar meeting among ourselves at an appropriate time next year' (G7 1978). On that occasion, the leaders felt ready to commit themselves to holding a meeting in the following year. Next year, however, the communiqué of the 1979 Tokyo summit included only this indirect indication of subsequent consultation: 'Our countries will not buy oil for governmental stockpiles when this would place undue pressure on prices; we will consult about the decisions that we make to this end' (G7 1979: Section 2). There was no similar indication in the communiqués of the summits in 1980 (Venice), 1982 (Versailles), and 1983 (Williamsburg).

Ottawa (Montebello) 1981 had already gone further than Bonn 1978 in specifying not only that a similar meeting would be held next year, but also the country where it would take place. The *Declaration* of the Ottawa summit ended with this statement: 'We have agreed to meet again next year and have accepted the invitation of the President of the French Republic to hold this meeting in France. We intend to maintain close and continuing consultation and cooperation with each other.' The final sentence of the 1984 *London Economic Declaration* reads: 'We have agreed to meet again next year and have accepted the Federal Chancellor's invitation to meet in the Federal Republic of Germany.' This was done again in London 1984, Bonn 1985, Tokyo 1986, Venice 1987, and Paris 1989.

The 1988 Toronto *Economic Declaration*, for the first time in a collective G7 document, acknowledged the usefulness of the summits, detailed their value, and posited a further cycle of Summits, including the country and exact dates of the following year's meeting:

> We, the Heads of State or Government, and the representatives of the European Community, believe that the Economic Summits have strengthened the ties of solidarity, both political and economic, that exist between our countries and that thereby they have helped to sustain the values of democracy that underlie our economic and political systems. Our annual meetings have provided the principal opportunity each year for the governments of the major industrialized countries to reflect, in an informal and flexible manner, upon their common responsibility for the progress of the world economy and to resolve how that responsibility should have practical manifestation in the years ahead. We believe that the mutual understanding engendered in our meetings has benefited both our own countries and the wider world community. We believe, too, that the opportunities afforded by our meetings are becoming even more valuable in today's world of increasing interdependence and increasing technological change. We have therefore agreed to institute a further cycle of Summits by accepting the invitation of the President of the French Republic to meet in France, July 14-16, 1989. (Paragraph 34)

The 1990 *Houston Economic Declaration* gives not only the country but also the city of the following year's summit: 'We have accepted the invitation of Prime Minister Thatcher to meet next July in London.' The practice of giving exact dates or even the month of the next summit has varied since, but the host country is always specified. The 1993 *Tokyo Economic Declaration* ends with this comment on the summits:

> We have reflected on how Summits could best focus our attention on the most significant issues of the time. We value Summits for the opportunity they provide to exchange views, build consensus and deepen understanding among us. But we believe Summits should

be less ceremonial, with fewer people, documents and declarations, and with more time devoted to informal discussion among us, so that together we may better respond to major issues of common concern. We intend to conduct future Summits in this spirit. We have accepted the invitation of the President of the Council of Ministers of Italy to meet in Naples, Italy, in July, 1994. (Paragraph 16.)

The 1994 Naples *Summit Communiqué* ends with another statement of the value and format of the summits: 'Our discussions this year have convinced us of the benefits of a less formal Summit procedure, as we agreed in Tokyo last year. In Naples, we have been able to have a freer exchange of views and to forge a closer understanding between us. Next year we look forward to an even more flexible and less formal summit. We have accepted the invitation of the Prime Minister of Canada to meet in Halifax in 1995.'

The 2000 Okinawa *G8 Communiqué* added an interesting technological note: 'We have accepted the invitation of the Prime Minister of Italy to meet in Genoa next year. To enhance communications in the meantime, we have agreed to establish an e-mail network among ourselves' (Paragraph 82). And the 2002 Kananaskis *Chair's Summary* put the seal on Russia's place in summit hosting rotation: 'We welcomed the offer of the President of France to host our next Summit in June 2003. We agreed that Russia will assume the 2006 G8 Presidency and will host our annual Summit that year.' (Germany agreed to defer its G8 presidency by one year.) Kananaskis also set out the rotation through 2010.

The 2005 Gleneagles *Chair's Summary* concluded: 'We welcomed the offer of the President of the Russian Federation to host our next Summit in 2006.' The St. Petersburg *Chair's Summary* ends with: 'We welcome the offer of the Federal Chancellor of the Federal Republic of Germany to host our next Summit in 2007' (Benoit and Schierit 2006). It has since been disclosed that the 2007 summit would take place in Heiligendamm, Germany, 6-8 June.

Summits have had their individual distinctive logos since the 1983 Williamsburg summit, the only exception being the 1984 London summit which did not produce one. In recent years, the logo has often been commercialized, carrying trademark identification. Table 3.1 shows the venue and date of each annual G7 or G8 summit from 1975 to 2007.

In addition to the regular annual summits, two special summit meetings were held: in 1985 and 1996. The 1985 special summit took place in New York, without France which refused to participate. US President Ronald Reagan used the occasion to discuss arms-control proposals in preparation for the first US-USSR superpower summit (Bayne 2005b: 25; Kirton 1995: 66). The 1991 London summit held out the possibility of convening an extraordinary summit meeting later that year, if necessary, to boost the chances of a successful conclusion of the Uruguay Round of multilateral trade negotiations. That extraordinary summit was not called, even though the Uruguay Round failed to be concluded by the end of 1991.

A special Nuclear Safety and Security Summit was convened in Moscow 19-20 April 1996, at the 'political G8' (P8) level; that is, with the full participation of Russia. It was co-chaired by Russia and France (which held that year's G7 presidency). Discussion focused on the safety of civilian nuclear reactors, the question of nuclear

Table 3.1   Annual G7 and G8 Summit Meetings, 1975-2007

G7/G8 Presidency	*Summit Venue*	*Summit Date*
France	Rambouillet (G6)	15-17 Nov. 1975
United States	San Juan, Puerto Rico (first G7 summit)	27-28 June 1976
United Kingdom	London ('London I')	7-8 May 1977
Germany (Fed. Rep.)	Bonn ('Bonn I')	16-17 July 1978
Japan	Tokyo ('Tokyo I')	28-29 June 1979
Italy	Venice ('Venice I')	22-23 June 1980
Canada	Ottawa (Montebello)	20-21 July 1981
France	Versailles	4-6 June 1982
United States	Williamsburg, Virginia	28-30 May 1983
United Kingdom	London ('London II')	7-9 June 1984
Germany (Fed. Rep.)	Bonn ('Bonn II')	2-4 May 1985
Japan	Tokyo ('Tokyo II')	4-6 May 1986
Italy	Venice ('Venice II')	8-10 June 1987
Canada	Toronto	19-21 June 1988
France	Paris ('Summit of the Arch')	14-16 July 1989
United States	Houston, Texas	9-11 July 1990
United Kingdom	London ('London III')	15-17 July 1991
Germany	Munich	6-8 July 1992
Japan	Tokyo ('Tokyo III')	7-9 July 1993
Italy	Naples	8-10 July 1994
Canada	Halifax	15-17 June 1995
France	Lyon	27-29 June 1996
United States	Denver ('Summit of the Eight')	20-22 June 1997
United Kingdom	Birmingham (first G8 summit)	15-17 May 1998
Germany	Köln	18-20 June 1999
Japan	Okinawa	21-23 July 2000
Italy	Genoa	20-22 July 2001
Canada	Kananaskis, Alberta	26-27 June 2002
France	Evian-les-Bains	1-3 June 2003
United States	Sea Island, Georgia	8-10 June 2004
United Kingdom	Gleneagles, Scotland	6-8 July 2005
Russia	St. Petersburg	15-17 July 2006
Germany	Heiligendamm	6-8 June 2007

Note: The 1975 summit met as G6; 1976-1997 as G7; from 1998 on, as G8.

liability, energy-sector strategies in countries in transition to a market economy, nuclear-waste management, the security of nuclear material and the prevention of illicit trafficking in nuclear material, the control and physical protection of – and accounting for – nuclear material, and the safe and effective management of weapons-grade fissile material designated as no longer required for defence purposes.

Following the G7 finance ministers' and central bank governors' meeting on 14 September 1998 that promised concerted action to respond to the worldwide financial turmoil, UK Prime Minister Tony Blair floated the idea of calling an emergency G7 or G8 summit late October on the financial crisis in Russia, Asia and Latin America. It was further reported that the decision on whether or not to call the special summit would be made in light of a report by G7 officials to be submitted to the G7 leaders (World Leaders... 1998: 1; Report on Russia... 1998: 2). On 30 October 1998 the G7 leaders, having consulted one another without meeting for a summit, issued a *G7 Leaders' Statement on the World Economy* (G7 1998). According to the *Financial Times*, 'the finishing touches to the leaders' statement were apparently made in a series of phone calls between President Clinton and German Chancellor Gerhard Schröder' (Baker 1998: 2). This action, in all likelihood, obviated the need for a special summit.

The special summit of the US, Germany, the UK and France in Guadeloupe on 5-6 January 1979 was not part of the regular G7 cycle but rather a legacy of past Atlanticism. Zbigniew Brzezinski, US President Jimmy Carter's National Security Adviser, recalls a meeting with Helmut Schmidt during which the German Chancellor 'said it made him feel "uneasy" that President Carter, Giscard, Callaghan, and he never met together in informal top-level discussion of political-strategic issues. The usual venue was either the larger NATO [North Atlantic Treaty Organization] Summit or the Economic Summit of the seven leading industrial democracies ... . What was lacking was a forum where the leaders of the four countries most directly engaged in security problems could meet and discuss frankly, openly, and flexibly matters of common concern' (Brzezinski 1983: 294). Giscard subsequently invited his three peers to just such a meeting, at Guadeloupe. The four participants discussed intermediate-range missiles in Europe and arms-control negotiations with the USSR, as well as the situation in Iran (Giscard d'Estaing 1988: 109-11; Schmidt 1989: 72-72, 188-91, 212-13). G7 members Japan, Italy and Canada, as well as some other countries, resented not being invited. The Guadeloupe meeting gave those three 'a strong incentive to develop the economic summit as a more formal and visible vehicle for political discussions, going beyond spontaneous exchanges over meals. This would ensure that they would not be excluded from high-level political decisions in future' (Putnam and Bayne 1987: 105). And the G7 later duly expanded its agenda to allow for security issues; by the next G7 summit, in Venice in 1980, the Soviet invasion of Afghanistan was discussed by the Seven.

Between 1993 and 1996, the Russians joined the G7 leaders at the end of the summit, after the release of the economic communiqué, for the political discussions. Each of those summits thus had two quite distinct phases: they were G7 events up to and including the release of the communiqué but then turned themselves into P8 for the rest of the summits. At the Denver 'Summit of the Eight', the Russians participated from the beginning of the summit but with a 90-minute meeting set aside for the G7 to consider financial and other economic questions. In Birmingham in 1998, Russia finally became a full member, turning the G7 officially into the G8. Russia, having offered to host a G8 meeting as early as 1998, was given the opportunity to enter the summit hosting rotation by the 2002 Kananaskis summit. This moved them ahead of the Germans, by enabling them to assume the G8 presidency in 2006 and thus the hosting of the annual summit in St. Petersburg. The complex issue of Russian participation is discussed in detail in Chapter 4.

Nevertheless, the G7, after Birmingham, remained alive up to and including the 2002 Kananaskis summit. Starting with the 2003 Evian summit, the leaders have no longer met at the G7 level at the summit proper. The G7 finance ministers, however, have continued to meet as G7. In fact, not only did the finance ministers meet at the G7 level in London the week before the Birmingham summit, but the G7 heads themselves had their own meeting in Birmingham for two hours, before the official start of the G8 summit.[5] The G7 remained very active; during and after the fall 1998 meetings of the International Monetary Fund (IMF) and the World Bank, the G7 – both at the finance ministers' and at the leaders' level – produced important and high-profile initiatives.

Summit Chronology

Guido Garavoglia and Pier Carlo Padoan (1994: 50) distinguish four summit periods in terms of economic issues:

- 1975-1979 – a period of strong economic growth accompanied by high inflation and balance-of-payments problems. Macroeconomic co-ordination, especially in Bonn in 1978, was a major summit preoccupation;
- 1980-1984 was a time of economic recession during which the summit emphasized microeconomic issues and anti-inflationary measures;
- 1985-1989, during which macroeconomic aspects were re-emphasized, and so was economic development. This phase saw the Plaza (1985) and Louvre (1987) accords; and
- another recessionary cycle starting in 1990, during which summit interest shifted again to microeconomics and structural problems.

Writing in 1995, John J. Kirton (1995: 66) examined summit history in terms of institutional development, dividing it into three cycles: the first, 1975-1981, consisted of the annual meeting of leaders, accompanied by their foreign and finance ministers; during the second cycle, 1982-1988, stand-alone meetings of ministers arose: trade ministers, starting in 1982; foreign ministers in 1984, and finance ministers in 1986; the third cycle, 1989 to 1995, initiated annual G7 post-summit meetings with the USSR (later with Russia) in 1991; the environment ministers' meetings began in 1992; and from 1993 a number of *ad hoc* ministerial meetings convened, on assistance to Russia and Ukraine, on employment issues and the information highway, among others.

Nicholas Bayne (1997: 1), in May 1997, distinguishes four cycles by rhythm and pace of activity: the first, 1975-1980, had summits that 'were very ambitious in economic policies, arguably too ambitious'. The second, 1981-1988, saw summits paying 'much more attention ... to non-economic foreign policy issues'. The third,

---

5   The Russians professed indifference to meetings at the G7 level before and at Birmingham, saying that this was of no interest to them because the meetings had taken place before the summit proper. On the other hand, they were quick to offer to host a G8 summit in Russia in 2000 – which would have displaced Japan as holding the G8 presidency that year.

1989-1994, was the first post-Cold War cycle, focusing on Central and Eastern Europe and the USSR, then Russia, but with lively activity 'on trade and debt issues; and new work on transnational issues, especially the environment, drugs and money laundering'. The fourth cycle started with the 1995 Halifax summit, whose 'key feature [was] the focus on reforming international institutions'.

In 2005 Bayne drew a distinction among three types of summit chronologies:

- Summit cycle: the first cycle comprised all G7 summits from the first one in Rambouillet in 1975 through the Denver Summit of 1997; the second, G8 cycle began in 1998 and continues to the present;
- Summit sequence: a full run of seven summits for the G7 with rotating presidency among the member countries (first sequence: Rambouillet 1975 through Ottawa 1981; second sequence: Versailles 1982 through Toronto 1988; third sequence: Paris 1989 through Halifax 1995; the fourth was shorter: Lyon 1996 and Denver 1997. The first G8 sequence stretched from Birmingham 1998 through Sea Island 2004; and the second, eight-year sequence began with Gleneagles 2005, followed by Russia's first-time presidency in 2006); and
- Summit series: a run of summits that focused on a particular set of issues (see Bayne 2005b).

There have been seven summit series so far, each concentrating on specific issue areas:

- First series: reviving growth (1975-1978);
- Second series: holding down inflation (1979-1982);
- Third series: the rise of politics (1983-1988);
- Fourth series: the end of the Cold War (1989-1993);
- Fifth series: institutions for globalization (1994-1997);
- Sixth series: globalization and development (1998-2000); and
- Seventh series: fighting terrorism and its causes (2002-) (Bayne 2005b: 7, 18).

It should be added that the evolution of issue groups on the summit agenda tends to proceed by incremental adjustments rather than sudden shifts. The changes in focus from series to series imply larger trends rather than sudden shifts.

The Role of the G7 and G8

Recalling the first summit, Ford (1979: 331) offers this assessment: 'In mid November, I had journeyed to Rambouillet, France, to attend an international economic summit conference. My sessions with President Giscard, West German Chancellor Schmidt, British Prime Minister Wilson and other leaders had been very productive, and all our countries would benefit from our agreements on monetary policy, trade and our relations with the developing world.' Ford's successor, Jimmy Carter, similarly asserts the significance of private, confidential interaction among the leaders:

There is a strong inclination at the summit meetings to evolve a unanimous report, either by compromises or by using more general language in order to avoid unresolved specific issues. Also, with an opportunity to discuss complicated matters personally, in private, rather than to depend on subordinates or diplomatic messages – or the news media – it is easier to resolve many differences. Finally, it is not politically dangerous to approve a controversial point if six other leaders do the same. (Carter 1982: 538-39)

Former British Prime Minister Margaret Thatcher quotes German Chancellor Helmut Schmidt on the advantages and disadvantages of the G7 summits:

They helped the West to avoid what he called 'beggar my neighbour' policies – the competitive devaluations and protectionism which had inflicted such economic and political harm during the 1930s. On the other hand, he thought that too often the summits had been tempted to enter into undertakings which could not be kept … . There was always pressure, to which some governments were all too ready to bend, to come up with forms of words and ambitious commitments which everyone could accept and no one took seriously. (Thatcher 1993: 67)

Joe Clark (1995: 215), who participated in summits first as prime minister and later as foreign minister of Canada, remarks:

[S]ummits are extremely constructive. They focus the attention of governments and leaders and often allow breakthroughs that would not occur in the more cumbersome traditional system. Precisely because heads of government are so busy now, they can become locked into patterns of dealing only with the most urgent issues and the most familiar allies. Summits free leaders of those patterns and allow both a wider experience of international issues and a real opportunity for initiative and co-operation. They rescue multilateralism from its inherent bureaucracy and caution.

Former Canadian government official and summit participant Wendy Dobson (1995: 6) observes that:

[s]ummit participants are quick to note two enduring values of Summits that are next to impossible to quantify. First, there is great value in leaders' meeting for the purpose of getting to know one another and one another's views on current issues … . Second, the complexity and range of issues with which leaders must deal is such that Summits provide opportunities to identify issues where cooperative action might be possible, delegate authority to analyze and respond, and provide for accountability by the delegates. In effect, Summits are less and less forums for initiatives, and more and more forums for issue identification and delegation.

In his memoir, Boris Yeltsin illustrates the informality of the leaders at G8 summits by relating two episodes. During one of the discussions at the 1998 Birmingham summit host Tony Blair suddenly 'slammed his file down and announced, 'All right! It's 4 P.M. I won't make it to the stadium, but at least I can watch the football match on TV. It's Arsenal against Newcastle today – the English Cup finals!' Everyone in the room understood. The prime ministers of Italy, Canada, and Japan; the presidents of Russia and France; and the chancellor of Germany all stood up in unison and moved toward the TV, chatting with one another as they walked out of the room.' And commenting on the advantages of the casual atmosphere among leaders, Yeltsin recalls that during a recess at the 1997 Denver summit he, along with Clinton, Chirac, Schröder, Blair, Hashimoto, Prodi and Chrétien, 'discussed our joint proposals and plans – two of us, three, four. We would go out onto the lawn; the sun shone; it was summertime. Chirac would come up to me, and we would have a fleeting conversation about future global agreements. Important international issues were brought up here, often in the space of two minutes. Such informal discussions are simply impossible in the framework of official state visits' (Yeltsin 2000: 129-30, 140-41).

There is a lighter side to the leaders' meetings. Many summits include a large entertainment component staged for the visiting heads, their spouses and delegations, but also for the attending media. These vary from the popular to the elaborate, and they are used by the host leader to showcase his or her country. A particularly lavish event occurred during the 1989 Summit of the Arch which coincided with the bicentenary of the French revolution. Thatcher notes that 'the G7 in Paris ... had largely been overtaken by the hugely expensive – and for Parisians wildly inconvenient – celebrations of the Bicentennial of the French Revolution. ... The G7 summit itself definitely took second place to this pageantry' (Thatcher 1993: 752-54).

The preceding paragraphs illustrate the perspective of leaders and other government officials. There has also been a fair amount of academic discussion of the role of the summits. According to John J. Kirton (1995: 66), perhaps the central role of the G7 is 'to create consensus among its members, at the highest political level, on the major global issues of the moment. It does so ... through the G7's *deliberative* function of forcing the leaders to get acquainted, listen and learn about one another's national constraints, priorities and goals ... [leading] to effective ongoing relationships ...[;] the *directional* function of setting the agenda [and] defining the priorities ... [and] the *decisional* function of reaching concrete agreements on specific subjects ... .' More recently, Kirton (2006b: 6) added two more elements of the role of the G7 and G8: domestic political management, and global governance.

Differing from Kirton, Cesare Merlini (1994: 22) holds that '[t]he summit is not a decision-making forum ... . [It] does not play; it conducts the orchestra, interpreting the score, assigning the instruments and giving the starting note.' Hisashi Owada (1994: 96) distinguishes three major purposes of the summit: '[p]olicy convergence through the process of an exchange of views and discussion ...; [p]olicy cooperation through the process of agreeing to a common strategy ...; [and p]olicy coordination through the process of concerted action undertaken ...'. And a study by the Atlantic Council (1980: 38-39; in Silvestri 1994) highlights the G7 function 'to link together political, economic and security issues which might otherwise be dealt with in highly compartmentalized contexts, without any overall strategy or set of objectives'.

Bayne (2005b: 213) identifies the three major objectives of the original G7 summit: '*political leadership* of heads of government to launch new ideas and overcome deadlock at lower levels; ... *[reconciliation of] domestic and international pressures* ... generated by growing interdependence; [and] ... *collective management* among Europe, North America, and Japan, to replace original US hegemony'. A fourth objective, *integrating international economics and politics*, entered into summitry later.

Conclusion

Over the 32-year history of the G7/G8, the leaders' summits have evolved from the first meeting which was then considered a one-time event to an elaborate annual occasion, central to the foreign policy endeavours and priorities of the host country, providing many opportunities ranging from substantive joint and bilateral and other meetings to photo sessions and entertainment for delegates, their spouses and the attending media. The informality and flexibility of the summits have allowed the relatively like-minded leaders of major democratic, market-economy countries to exchange views freely and in confidence, as G7 from 1975 to 1997 and as G8, with Russia, since 1998. Such candid and private interaction would be unlikely in larger, more cumbersome, and economically and politically more diverse formal organizations with large bureaucracies.

The role of the G7 and G8 embraces deliberation, direction-giving, and decision-making as well as global governance and domestic political management functions. The summit allows the attending heads of state and government to exercise political leadership, reconcile domestic and international concerns, develop collective management, and integrate economics and politics in their negotiations and decisions. Present and former leaders and other high officials of the G7 and G8 appreciate the value of this forum and invest considerable political, financial and personal resources in preparing, conducting and following up the summits.

References

Note on internet addresses (URLs): Websites tend to appear, change or disappear, often without warning. Addresses cited in this source list were accurate and active at the time of writing (June 2006) unless otherwise noted.

Atlantic Council of the United States (1980), *Summit Meetings and Collective Leadership in the 1980's*, Charles Robinson and William C. Turner, co-chairmen; Harald B. Malmgren, rapporteur, Atlantic Council of the United States Policy Papers, Working Group on Political Affairs, Washington, DC.

Baker, Gerald (1998), 'G7 Attempts to Restore Calm to World Finance', *Financial Times*, 31 October/1 November, 2.

Bayne, Nicholas (1997), 'Changing Patterns at the G7 Summit', *G7 Governance*, 1, May, www.g8.utoronto.ca/governance/gov1/.

Bayne, Nicholas (2000), *Hanging in There: The G7 and G8 Summit in Maturity and Renewal*, Ashgate, Aldershot, UK, The G8 and Global Governance Series.

Bayne, Nicholas (2005b), *Staying Together: The G8 Summit Confronts the 21st Century*, Ashgate, Aldershot, UK.

Benoit, Bertrand and Mark Schieritz (2006), 'Germany Plans to Shake Up G8 Agenda', *Financial Times*, 27 July.

Bonvicini, Gianni and Wolfgang Wessels (1984), 'The European Community and the Seven', in *Economic Summits and Western Decision-Making* 167-91, Cesare Merlini (ed.), Croom Helm; St. Martin's Press in association with the European Institute of Public Administration, London; New York.

Brzezinski, Zbigniew (1983), *Power and Principle: Memoirs of the National Security Adviser, 1977-1981*, Farrar Straus Giroux, New York.

Carter, Jimmy (1982), *Keeping Faith: Memoirs of a President*, Bantam Books, New York.

Clark, Joe (1995), 'The PM [Prime Minister] and the SSEA [Secretary of State for External Affairs]: Comment 2', *International Journal*, 50:1, 213-15, Winter.

Dobson, Wendy (1995), 'Summitry and the International Monetary System: The Past as Prologue', *Canadian Foreign Policy*, 3:1, 5-15, Spring.

Ford, Gerald R. (1979), *A Time To Heal: The Autobiography of Gerald R. Ford*, Harper & Row, New York.

G7 (1978), *Declaration*, 17 July, Bonn.

G7 (1979), *Declaration*, 29 June, Tokyo.

G7 (1998), *G7 Leaders' Statement on the World Economy*, 30 October, www.g8.utoronto.ca/finance/g7_103098.html.

Garavoglia, Guido and Pier Carlo Padoan (1994), 'The G-7 Agenda: Old and New Issues', in *The Future of the G-7 Summits*, 49-65, *The International Spectator* 29:2 April/June, Special Issue.

Giscard d'Estaing, Valéry (1988), *Le pouvoir et la vie [Power and Life]*, Compagnie 12, Paris.

Hainsworth, Susan (1990), *Coming of Age: The European Community and the Economic Summit*, Country Study No. 7, University of Toronto, Centre for International Studies, www.g8.utoronto.ca/scholar/hainsworth1990/index.html.

Kirton, John J. (1995), 'The Diplomacy of Concert: Canada, the G7 and the Halifax Summit', *Canadian Foreign Policy* 3:1, 63-80.

Kirton, John J. (2006b), 'A Summit of Significant Success: The G8 at St. Petersburg 2006', 19 July, (Appendix A), www.g8.utoronto.ca/evaluations/2006stpetersburg/kirton_perf_060719.pdf.

Merlini, Cesare (1994), 'The G-7 and the Need for Reform', in *The Future of the G-7 Summits. The International Spectator*, 29:2, 5-25, April/June, Special Issue, www.library.utoronto.ca/g7/italiano/merlini_i1.html (Italian).

Owada, Hisashi (1994), 'A Japanese Perspective on the Role and Future of the G-7', in *The Future of the G-7 Summits*, 95-112, *The International Spectator*, 29:2, April/June, Special Issue.

Putnam, Robert D. and Nicholas Bayne (1987), *Hanging Together: Cooperation and Conflict in the Seven-Power Summits*, rev. ed., Harvard University Press, Cambridge, Mass.

'Report on Russian Crisis Prepared for G7' (1998), *Financial Times*, 15 September, 2.

Schmidt, Helmut (1989), *Men and Powers: A Political Retrospective*, Random House, New York.

Silvestri, Stefano (1994), 'Between Globalism and Regionalism: The Role and Composition of the G-7', in 'The Future of the G-7 Summits', 27-48, *The International Spectator*, 29:2, April/June, Special Issue.

Thatcher, Margaret (1993), *The Downing Street Years*, Harper-Collins, London.

Ullrich, Heidi and Alan Donnelly (1998), 'The Group of Eight and the European Union: The Evolving Partnership', *G8 Governance*, 5, www.g7.utoronto.ca/governance/gov5/intro.html.

Wilson, Harold (1979), *Final Term: The Labour Government, 1974-1976*, Weidenfeld and Nicolson, and Michael Joseph, London.

'World Leaders Back Joint Action in Face of Financial Turmoil' (1998), *Financial Times*, 15 September, 1.

Yeltsin, Boris (2000), *Midnight Diaries*, Weidenfeld & Nicolson, London.

Chapter 4

The Players: Members, Potential Members, and Unofficial Associates

This chapter discusses the members and potential members of, as well as other countries' association with, the G7 and G8. It reviews the evolution of the club's composition from the initial G6 of 1975 through the years of the G7 and (from 1998) the G8; examines the contentious issue of Russia's membership; and outlines the case for and against other candidates. Other aspects of the role of non-members and potential members of the G7 and G8 are examined in Chapter 12.

The G6 and the G7

The five countries (France, Germany, the UK, the US and Japan) whose finance ministers had been meeting, initially without Japan, since 1973 (see Chapters 2 and 6) were the founding members of the G7, with Italy somewhat reluctantly admitted into the club in time for the inaugural G6 summit held at Rambouillet in 1975. Chapter 2 provides more detail about the background of that reluctance which goes back to the beginnings of the series of meetings of G5 finance ministers' forum before the inception of the summits.

Italy's invitation to the second summit in 1976 in Puerto Rico was again uncertain. US President Gerald R. Ford's telephone conversation with West German Chancellor Helmut Schmidt, for which [Assistant to the President for National Security Affairs] Brent Scowcroft drafted Ford's 'talking points', would have Ford say:

> Mr. Chancellor, I am calling to ask your advice and assistance in resolving the question of how Italy's participation should be treated in the announcement [of the 1976 summit]. [Italian] Prime Minister Moro has advised that the language we most recently circulated – ... words to the effect that the five countries favouring Italy's participation would examine with Italy whether it believed it was able to take part – would be totally unacceptable ... May I invite you to get in touch with [French] President [Valéry] Giscard d'Estaing and to reach agreement today on language acceptable from the European viewpoint regarding Italy's participation? (Telephone conversation [of President Ford] with FRG Chancellor Schmidt, Wednesday, June 2, 1976; Gerald R. Ford Library [hereafter referred to as Ford Library], Box 6, National Security Adviser, Presidential Country Files for Europe and Canada; Germany (11).)[1]

The G5 leaders held their own meeting 'on the margins' of the Puerto Rico summit. At that limited-participation meeting the G5 decided to extend a large loan to Italy,

---

1   References to records in official archives follow the form suggested by those archives.

conditional upon excluding the Italian Communist Party from participation in the government. The way then became clear to allow Italy's summit participation. Disclosed by Schmidt to some US reporters a few weeks after Puerto Rico, this incident revealed for the first time 'the habit of holding behind-the-curtains meetings on issues not included in the summit agenda' (Garavoglia 1984: 11).

Canada strongly wished to be a member of the club from the very first summit, but this was not possible due mostly to French opposition. Giscard's letter of 13 November 1975 to Canadian Prime Minister Pierre Elliott Trudeau recalls that he [Giscard] and Ford had envisaged a very restricted meeting of five countries and that it was for very particular political reasons that Italy was added, but any further increase in the number of participants would change the restricted character of the meeting necessary for success. Trudeau's reply to Giscard, dated 19 November 1975, expressed his satisfaction at the success of the Rambouillet summit and his understanding of Giscard's reasons not to invite Canada, but he argued that Canada's economic weight, international role and contributions in the areas of energy, international trade, and other issues of common interest to the G6 would justify its inclusion in that restricted group. He added: 'nous ne puissions accepter d'être exclus de conférences qui réunissent tous nos principaux partenaires économiques' [we could not accept being excluded from conferences that bring together all our principal economic partners]. Trudeau also wrote on 19 November 1975 to Ford, Schmidt, UK Prime Minister Harold Wilson and Japanese Prime Minister Takeo Miki, thanking each for supporting Canada's desire to participate in the Rambouillet summit. (Library and Archives Canada [hereafter referred to as LAC], MG26019, Vol. 139, File 17: 1975-1977, P. E. Trudeau Fonds, Staff Series, Ivan Head – Subject Files – Economic Summit 1975-1976.)

The matter of Canada's participation made its way into US official archives as well, with a report of Trudeau's 19 November 1975 letter to Ford, thanking the President warmly for his 'vigorous support' for Canada's desire to participate in the Rambouillet summit and for Ford's statement that the US 'would insist on Canada's being involved in any follow-up to Rambouillet.' (Memorandum, Brent Scowcroft to President Ford, 12 January 1976; Ford Library, Box 32, WHCF-Subject File, FO 6-1, Letter from Prime Minister Trudeau.)

French opposition to treating Canada (and Italy) identically to the other G7 countries was clear even after the invitation to these two countries to the 1976 Puerto Rico summit became firm. A memorandum to Prime Minister Trudeau, sent by his personal representative, Ivan L. Head on 4 June 1976, reports that the French asked that the original text of the invitation, listing the participating G7 countries alphabetically, be changed to distinguish Canada and Italy as special cases. In the event, host President Ford insisted on the alphabetical listing of the seven as equal participants, and he prevailed. (LAC, P. E. Trudeau Fonds, 1968-1978 PMO Priority Correspondence Series, MG26 O7, Volume 536, File 1203: 1975-1977, 1976 Files – Foreign Affairs – Conferences – Documents RB – Economic Summit.)

This disagreement carried through to the draft communiqué. In a memorandum to Prime Minister Trudeau, dated 15 June 1976, Secretary of State for External Affairs Allan J. MacEachen comments on continuing attempts by France to treat Canada differently from the other G7 countries in the French version of the draft communiqué of the 1976 Puerto Rico summit, and compares it with the US draft communiqué which made no such distinction. (LAC, MG26 O7, Vol. 536, File 1203.)

In the following year, President Ford, as host of the Puerto Rico summit, was in a strong position to invite Canada, and he did so. His announcement begins with this statement:

> At the invitation of the President of the United States, the Heads of States and Governments of France, the Federal Republic of Germany, Italy, Japan, the United Kingdom ... and the United States will meet June 27 and 28 in Puerto Rico. In addition, given the close ties and cooperation between the United States and Canada and the fact that the meeting is being held in the Western Hemisphere, the President of the United States has invited Canada to participate. ('Joint Announcement of the International Summit, Puerto Rico, June 27-28, 1976', June 3, 1976 [White House Press Release], Folder 'Economic Summit – Puerto Rico'; Ford Library, Box 7, Vernon C. Loen and Charles Leffert Files)

The European Communities (EC; later European Union, EU) was first represented in a G7 summit in London in 1977. It has occupied an unusual position in the G7 and G8. Unlike the member states, the EU does not have the right to host a summit; therefore, it does not have the opportunity to shape the summit agenda that the G8 presidency provides to leaders of member states. But in all other respects the EU has been a full member of the G7 and G8; it has its own sherpa and takes part in the preparation and conduct of the summits, participating in all discussions including political topics. It also participates in the meetings of ministerial fora and other subsidiary G7 and G8 bodies, with the exception that it was absent from the meetings of G7 finance ministers before 3 October 1998 (see Chapter 6). The EU is particularly active on issues where its members act collectively and when either its Commission (for example, in trade matters) or its Presidency (for example, on the environment) act as spokesmen.[2]

Up to and including the 1997 Denver Summit of the Eight, delegations of each summit country included the head of state or government, the foreign minister, the finance minister, and the 'sherpa', a term that originates from the name (or, rather, nationality) of the mountain guides in the Himalayas and denotes the senior official who is the leader's personal representative (see Chapter 6 for a detailed explanation and discussion of the sherpas and their role). There are some variations: France, the US and Russia are the only three G8 countries that are represented at the level of head of state (although at the 1996 Lyon summit Russia was represented in President Boris Yeltsin's absence by Prime Minister Viktor Chernomyrdin); Germany and Japan, traditionally having coalition governments, sent the minister of economy (in Germany's case) and minister of international trade and industry (for Japan), in addition to their foreign and finance ministers; and France, during its period of 'cohabitation' (1986-87) sent both its president (then François Mitterrand) and its prime minister (then Jacques Chirac); during a later period of 'cohabitation' that began in June 1997, Prime Minister Lionel Jospin did not accompany President Chirac.

---

2   For the history and evolution of EC/EU involvement in the G7 and G8, see the following analyses: Bonvicini and Wessels (1984); Ullrich and Donnelly (1998); and Hainsworth (1990).

The EU is represented by the President of the Commission, the vice-presidents for external relations and for economic and financial affairs, and the president's personal representative. The President of the European Council is also represented in years when that office is held by a non-G7 European country. This occurred, for example, in 1982 (Belgium), 1986 (Netherlands), 1987 (Belgium), 1991 (Netherlands), 1997 (Netherlands), 2005 (Portugal) and 2006 (Finland). But the European Council President takes part in the actual summit and ministerial meetings only, while only the Commission takes part in the preparation.

The 1998 Birmingham G8 summit changed this pattern: Birmingham was a leaders-only summit, with foreign and finance ministers meeting separately in London a week before the summit, on 8-9 May, to prepare for the leaders' agenda and to deal with issues not on the agenda of the summit itself. This format made it possible to achieve a long-desired but never-before-fulfilled informality, enabling the leaders to spend considerable time together and to focus personally on topics that they wished to discuss. This was further enhanced by an all-day retreat at the beautiful, secluded 17th-century Weston Park estate on the border of Staffordshire and Shropshire, away not only from bureaucrats but, more importantly, from the prying eyes of the media. At the end of the summit, the leaders expressed great satisfaction with this format, which has prevailed ever since.

Russia's Membership

On 14 July 1989, Soviet President Mikhail Gorbachev sent a letter to President Mitterrand expressing the Soviet Union's wish to be associated with the summits. Although that did not happen immediately, Russia has played an increasingly important, albeit controversial, role ever since. The event that dominated the 1991 summit was Gorbachev's historic visit to London. He did not attend the summit *per se* but met with G7 leaders individually and collectively, and discussed in detail the plans for Soviet economic and political reform. Although attitudes among the G7 varied about how and how much to help the Soviet Union, the leaders 'all agreed to work together to promote the integration of the Soviet Union into the world economy' (Joint Press... 1991). It was at their meeting in London on 17 July 1991 that Presidents Gorbachev and Bush tackled the last impediment to the Strategic Arms Reduction Treaty (START). They subsequently signed the treaty on 31 July 1991, during their bilateral meeting in Moscow. But then the unsuccessful coup that took place a month after the summit led to the demise of the Soviet Union and the end of Gorbachev as leader of his country.

The following year, Russian President Yeltsin's visit to Munich took the spotlight. Although formally outside the summit framework, he held bilateral meetings as well as joint sessions with the G7 leaders, and returned home not only with a greater show of goodwill but also a more concrete aid package (some US$4.5 billion) than had his predecessor. The idea was even floated by Bush (but not taken up then by other summit leaders) of turning the G7 into a G8 with the formal participation of Russia. The leader of the USSR and then Russia had been invited to meet with the G7 heads after the official ending of the 1991, 1992 and 1993 summits.

It was only at the 1994 Naples summit that Russia participated for the first time as a full partner in the political discussions. Russia itself referred to a new 'political G8', but the preferred Western term, at least until the 1997 Denver summit, was P8 ('Political 8'). At Denver, Russia joined the G7 (except for certain financial and other economic issues), to form the Summit of the Eight (Freeland and Kaminski 1997: 1). In Birmingham in 1998, the G7 became officially the G8, with Russia as a full member, although the G7 continued to coexist with the G8, both at the summit and ministerial levels. G7 leaders met in Birmingham for two hours on 15 May, before the official start of the G8 summit. The G7 continued to meet annually up to and including the 2002 Kananaskis summit.

Russia's full membership has changed the institution. The G8 is more representative than the G7, and reflects greater diversity. At the Denver Summit of the Eight in 1997 the host leader, President Bill Clinton stated: 'we believe we are stronger because we now have Russia as a partner ... – evidence of Russia's emergence as a full member of the community of democracies' (US 1997: 1-2). Going one step further, Prime Minister Blair, the chairman of the 1998 Birmingham G8 summit, affirmed: 'The contribution that Russia has made to the G8 has already been very evident ... we appreciate very well that without the voice of Russia being heard in the G8 councils, it is far more difficult for us to deal with the serious international issues that confront us' (UK 1998). Blair cited nuclear energy and the millennium bug as examples of areas where Russia had made contributions.

Zbigniew Brzezinski, while accepting the necessity of Russia's membership, inserted a note of realism into this debate. He noted in 1996: the G7's 'membership is no longer representative of power or of principle, and it needs to be expanded. Russia ... cannot now be excluded. ... China, India and Brazil are as entitled to participation as Russia, and in some respects much more so'. Thus, he advocated a G11 (Brzezinski 1996: A11). In 2004, he recalled the rationale for the original G7: 'to provide an opportunity for the heads of the leading and economically most powerful democracies to consult one another'. But he qualified this: 'The inclusion of Russia ... was motivated by the political desire to give the troubled post-Soviet Russia – though it is neither a genuine democracy nor a leading economy – a sense of status and belonging.' And with Russia a member, China and India should also be added, turning the G8 into a G10 both in the economic and political spheres (Brzezinski 2004: 123).

Russia's newfound democratic credentials, economic reforms and commitment to free markets were cited prior to Birmingham as justification for full G8 membership. Many, however, questioned – right from the beginning, given the chaotic Russian economy and politics in late 1998 – how much Russia could contribute to economic policy co-ordination, notwithstanding its contributions on other issues, and how strong its democracy really was. It is more plausible that the decision to integrate Russia was driven to a large extent by geopolitical, strategic considerations rather than by recognition of Russia's status as an advanced democracy and a major market-based industrial power. The stated desire of the G7 to integrate Russia into political, global and other areas of co-ordination went hand-in-hand with the recognition of a *quid pro quo*: Russia's acquiescence (after earlier strenuous opposition) to North Atlantic Treaty Organization (NATO) expansion. Another element of the calculation was the recognition that Russia continued to play a major role among nuclear powers. And there was the G7's desire to 'socialize' Russia into democratic ways.

In his memoir, Clinton (2005: 750, 758) gives this account of his conversation with Yeltsin in Helsinki in the spring of 1997, during Clinton's year of G7 presidency: 'I told Yeltsin that if he would agree to NATO expansion and the NATO-Russia partnership, I would make a commitment not to station troops or missiles in the new member countries prematurely, and to support Russian membership in the new G-8, the World Trade Organization, and other international organizations. We had a deal.' At the Denver summit that year, 'we voted to take Russia in as a full member of the new G-8, but to allow the finance ministers of the other seven nations to continue to meet on appropriate matters. Now Yeltsin and I had both kept our Helsinki commitments.'

Belonging to the club was important to Russia from the very beginning of their relationship. Yeltsin (2000: 137), under whose presidency Russia became a G8 member, sees the circumstances of NATO expansion as a completely separate issue from Russia's acceptance into the group. 'Russia is one of the most influential countries in the world. Its makeup is unique. We have huge reserves of natural resources, advanced technology, an unbelievable internal market, a highly qualified labor market, and a dynamic society. That is why we were included in the Eight.'

Scrutiny of Russia's G8 role intensified in the lead-up to Russia assuming its first-time G8 presidency for 2006.[3] Even before the 2005 Gleneagles summit, a *Financial Times* article called the prospect of Russian presidency 'a travesty of leadership by example' and argued that Russia was moving against the trend of freer markets and democratization. It stated: 'Moscow's leadership of the G8 reduces the credibility and the relevance of the group to zero' and 'even by the low standards that the G8 has set in the past, when the baton is passed to Moscow, it will be a gigantic step backwards' (Garten 2005: 23). Also in 2005, US senators Joe Lieberman and John McCain called for the suspension of Russia's membership in the G8 until democratic and political freedoms are ensured in that country.

In its G8 year 2006, Russia's recent political, economic and social developments, and its suitability to be a G8 member, were questioned even more closely. For example, the Foreign Policy Centre in the UK commented that Russia was behind the other G8 members (and also behind China and India) on important economic indicators such as GDP per capita and share of world GDP. Moreover, the Foreign Policy Centre, while acknowledging the great strides made by Russia since Soviet days as well as the richness of its natural resources and the resulting strong economic growth, argues that Russia is 'still only a junior partner [in the G8 in respect of] ... democracy, rule of law, open society, free media' and that it has 'doubtful credentials as a responsible energy supplier'. Based on the 'scorecard' the Centre concludes that: the size of Russia's economy does not justify its inclusion in the G8; Russia is not free politically or economically; Russia's G8 presidency is therefore anomalous;

---

3   Russian President Boris Yeltsin expressed his wish at the 1998 Birmingham summit to host the 2000 summit, but giving up Japan's 2000 G8 presidency was rejected by Prime Minister Ryutaro Hashimoto (Bayne 2005: 38).

and the other G8 members 'must develop a concerted policy to force Putin to live up to his international obligations' (Barnes and Owen 2006: 14-19, 50).

The UK think tank Chatham House, in a March 2006 report, discusses and analyzes recent developments and trends in Russia's strategic thinking. The report's author, Yury E. Fedorov (2006: 4), notes: the leadership's optimism on economic growth due to high oil and gas export revenues, the foreign policy aim of restoring Russia's global great power status; and using the status of major energy exporter as a foreign policy tool, particularly in Russia's strategic partnership with China and in dominating former Soviet republics. Fedorov cautions, however, that overestimation of national resources and setting unattainable goals may well result in failures and then greater hostility toward the West and greater isolation. But in 2006, Russia is 'ready for cooperation with the Western countries in fighting terrorism and is looking for a "special relationship" with the European Union. In particular, the Kremlin is especially interested in the success of the G8 Summit in St. Petersburg in July 2006, seeing it as a matter of personal importance for President Putin.'

In the US, the Council on Foreign Relations (2006: 7, 73) issued a report of an independent bipartisan task force on US policy toward Russia, co-chaired by former Senator John Edwards and former Congressman Jack Kemp. The report notes significant economic progress in Russia (for example, lower unemployment and fewer people living below the poverty line) but laments a steadily more authoritarian political system, claiming that over the last five years the country had become less open, less pluralistic, less subject to the rule of law, and more restrictive toward political opposition and the independent media. Among the report's recommendations is the following: 'To protect the credibility of the G8 at a time when many are questioning Russia's chairmanship, the United States should make clear that this role does not exempt Russian policies and actions from critical scrutiny. Keeping the G8 a viable international forum will require a *de facto* revival of the Group of Seven (G7). Without creating a new forum, the United States and its democratic allies have to assume a stronger coordinating role within the old one.'

The Washington-based Institute for International Economics produced a policy brief on Russia's presidency of the G8. The study argues that Russia is indisputably a market economy, with a strong position in international trade and on budget surpluses, though not on other economic indicators. On the other hand, it states that Putin 'has systematically dismantled Russia's nascent democracy', that Russia has shown more authoritarianism in its foreign policy, and that 'it is evident that the G7 has failed in its objective to secure Russian democracy'. In addition, there are institutional impediments to Russia's full authority on macroeconomic and trade issues, given that it is not a member of the WTO. Nor is Russia a member of the International Energy Agency, though it is a major power in the energy sector. The study presents five options for the US and the other G7 countries to handle this situation: full or partial boycott of the St. Petersburg summit; accepting the summit as mostly a photo opportunity; taking Russia's central agenda item, energy security, at face value, since in this area Russia has much to contribute; focusing on issues where Russia clearly has competence; and subcontracting traditional G7 matters to other organizations and groups that are more competent. The study concludes with recommending: that the G7 convene a mini-summit in a Baltic country just before the St. Petersburg G8;[4] that the US, Canada, and the four European G8 countries, and Russia (that is, the G8 minus Japan) work to revive the European Energy Charter; that China, India, Brazil and South Africa be invited as full members of the G8; and that the International Energy Agency be expanded by including China, India and possibly other large energy consuming countries (Åslund 2006: 2-3, 5-7).

In a 2006 study funded by the US Army War College External Research Associates Program, Richard J. Krickus (2006: v-vi, 54) asserts that the Russian government, through its energy assets, is using what he terms 'Iron Troikas' to reassert its influence on Eastern and Central Europe.[5] He argues that the US should 'demand [that Russia] subscribe to the rules that govern membership in both' the G8 and the WTO.

The G7 mini-summit in a Baltic country did not materialize. But it was in the Baltic, in the Lithuanian capital Vilnius, that US Vice-President Dick Cheney pointedly chose on 4 May 2006 to launch into sharp public criticism of Russia, arguing that Russia was using its considerable energy resources as 'tools of intimidation or blackmail' in conducting its foreign policy, a reference to the New Year's Day temporary cutoff of gas flows to Ukraine. He also criticized that country's growing repression against civil society, warning that this trend 'could begin to affect [Russia's] relations with other countries.' But the criticism is one-sided, ignoring that Russia has become a stable and confident society, running budget surpluses and investing more generously in social needs (Handelman 2006: F1, F6).

In a February 2006 report prepared for the US Congress, the Congressional Research Service reviews the context and implications of Russia's energy position and policies, particularly in light of the cutoff of natural gas to Ukraine at the beginning of 2006. The report states that some argue that US-Russian co-operation in fighting terrorism and addressing global issues such as nuclear proliferation in Iran and North Korea should not be jeopardized by concerns about Russia's reliability as energy supplier; others see the use of energy supplies as an economic and political tool in a way that is illustrative of Russian neo-imperialism. Shortly after the gas cutoff, US Secretary of State Condoleezza Rice first expressed concerns about Russia's suitability to chair the G8 in 2006, but she later urged that engagement with Russia should continue. Some members of Congress, notably Senator John McCain, in early February 2006, called for the G8 leaders to boycott the St. Petersburg summit (Nichol et al. 2006: 506). Such extreme measures, however, were not taken by the US administration.

It is not only the US and UK that have voiced such misgivings. Significantly, Andrei N. Illarionov (2006: A17), dismissed for his outspokenness by President Putin

---

4   In a demonstration of US public displeasure with Russia, and perhaps as an intentional slap on Russia's face, Bush's Vice President Dick Cheney, at a meeting of European leaders (Russia was not invited) in Vilnius, Lithuania on 4 May 2006, delivered 'the Bush administration's strongest rebuke of Russia to date'. Cheney criticized Russia's restrictions of people's rights, its use of its natural resources as 'tools of intimidation and blackmail' of its neighbours, and so forth (Myers 2006: A1, A10).

5   Krickus's 'Iron Troikas' consist of the *siloviki*, men of power; economic warlords, rogue military personnel and the Russian mafia; and the old *nomenklatura* and new oligarchs. These troikas, according to Krickus, represent a 'new threat from the East' to the East Baltic Sea Region (Poland and the three Baltic countries).

as his sherpa in early 2005 (followed on 27 December 2005 by Illarionov's resignation as Putin's economic advisor), is sharply critical of Russia's recent antidemocratic political tendencies and economic and social decisions. Recalling the traditional G7 criteria for membership in that forum – democratic political regime, large economy, convertible currency, high level of economic and institutional development, and membership in key economic institutions – he argues that meeting only some of those criteria is not sufficient for membership, regardless of possessing other assets such as high GDP or nuclear-power status. Russia, in his view, meets only one criterion of membership: being a large economy. Its per capita GDP is low, its inflation rate is high, and it is no longer free politically. Illarionov then writes that 'idealists' in G7 capitals have proposed a boycott of the St. Petersburg summit, while 'pragmatists' recommend reasons for participating. Russian patriots are in favour of their country's G8 membership but would like their country to be free, prosperous and democratic. He is pessimistic about the future of the G8 regardless of the outcome of the St. Petersburg summit: it will cease to exist as a club of advanced democratic countries, to be replaced, perhaps, by the G7, G4, G3, or some other entity – without Russia.

On the other hand, voices have been raised in support of Russia's role and membership in the G8. President Chirac (2006: A17) is unequivocal in acknowledging Russia's place in the G8: 'Responding to President Vladimir Putin's invitation means putting aside out-of-date Cold War arguments and moving toward a future together based on peace and co-operation. It means recognizing Russia's progress and its place in Europe. Hosting the G8 in St. Petersburg also commits Russia, since a common future implies shared values: democracy, the rule of law, human rights, freedom – everything that contributes to progress and dignity for mankind.'

Nicholas Bayne, former UK government official and later eminent G8 scholar, states that the St. Petersburg summit's 'focus on energy means that Russia has got a legitimate point of entry'.[6] And John Kirton (2006b: 2) makes a case for the G7 countries' positive role in helping the development of Russian democracy. He also relates that 'Russians responded with bewilderment and anger at … harsh reaction to their effort to follow the market principles long preached by the West … Russia's presidency of the G8 forced … both sides to … learn more about the other's faults and achievements, about … their interdependence and shared vulnerabilities, and about how best to induce the other to pull together for the common cause.'

Potential Members

There have been other, unsuccessful, candidates for membership: Belgium and the Netherlands in the early years of summitry; in the late 1970s and early 1980s Australia was in this category, as were Spain in 1992 and Indonesia in 1993 (Kirton 1995: 65). As noted above, however, Belgium was represented at the summits of 1982 and 1987, the Netherlands in 1986, 1991 and 1997, Portugal in 2005 and Finland in 2006, all by virtue of these countries holding the presidency of the European Council when those summits met.

---

6   Quoted in Beattie (2006).

Writing in 1995, Bayne (1995: 497) observes that there is a mismatch between current summit structure and real economic geography, and that this will have to be faced. Another former high official argues 'that the G7 is no longer representative of the range of countries active in the international system. In particular, large, populous countries, like China, India, Mexico and Brazil, deserve more weight as they open up their large, internal markets', but then cites the counterargument that the 'present G7 membership provides the best opportunity for exerting reciprocal pressure between the highly developed countries of Europe, North America and Japan, which would be lost if the composition were changed'.

Jeffrey Sachs (1998: 23-25), writing in 1998, argues that the time has come for a G16 instead of a G8. This would consist of the G8 and eight major countries of the developing world, all satisfying the common standard of democratic governance. Sachs sees Brazil, India, South Korea and South Africa as the four core developing-country members in the G16, soon to be joined by a more democratic Nigeria, as well as '[s]maller democratic countries that carry disproportionate credibility in the world, such as Chile and Costa Rica'. He does not indicate which country might be the sixteenth member.

China has had many advocates for membership.[7] C. Fred Bergsten (1998: 1-2) noted in June 1998 the World Bank's estimate that 'China has already passed Germany to become the third-largest economy on the globe' and adds: 'China will obviously play an increasingly central role in the world economy. Hence, it must also play a central role in global economic management ... [It] should shortly begin participating in the "finance G-7" the club of finance ministers and central bank governors of the seven largest industrial democracies.' Bergsten acknowledges, however, that '[i]n light of China's continued failure to democratize, its inclusion in the G-7 summits ... would ... be premature'. *The Economist* disagrees: 'China seems to some to be an island of stability, perhaps a new economic leader in the region, worthy of a seat at the G7's top financial table' (Welcome... 1998: 17). Hodges (1999: 71) argues that 'China is a major player, not only in the regional context of the 1997-8 Asian crisis, but also in the world economy as a whole. China may not be a suitable candidate for membership in a new G9. However, it may be useful to extend formalised links between the G7 or G8 and China, given the growing importance of China to the global economy.'

Writing in 2005, Bayne (2005b: 8) argued that '[w]hile China was identified as the next potential member of the group, on both economic and foreign policy grounds, it did not meet the democracy test of summit membership. The G8 was in no hurry to take a decision on further expansion and China itself was not pressing.' China, indeed, has expressed no particular interest in joining the club, preferring to associate itself with developing countries. Shortly after the St. Petersburg summit, the Chinese foreign ministry stated: 'China is deeply satisfied with Russia's actions as part of its G8 presidency, during which it made an important contribution to successful dialogue between the G8 and the leaders of developing nations.'[8]

---

7   For an analysis of the G8/China connection see Kirton (1999).

8   Quoted on the official Russian government website for the 2006 St. Petersburg summit, http://en.g8russia.ru/news/20060726/1257643.html.

And yet, China's non-membership highlights a paradox. True, it fails the democracy criterion for membership. But in the economic arena, in addition to the relative weight of China in the world proven by various indicators alluded to above, it is difficult to discuss contemporary exchange rate without China, a key actor in the fate of the US dollar. China's membership in the G20 (that group is discussed in Chapter 11) and its frequent guest status at recent meetings of the G7 finance ministers and central bank governors (about which see Chapter 6) may point to the increasing importance of those two fora, as opposed to the leaders' G8, when negotiating economic and financial matters.

Media comments around the time of the 2005 Gleneagles summit reflected increasing frustration with the current membership of the G8. The *Financial Times* called the G8 'increasingly an anachronism' and added: 'No one today would propose an annual meeting that includes Canada (population of 31 m[illion], gross domestic product of $870 b[illio]n ..., Italy (58m and $1,200bn) and Russia (144m and $615bn) but not China (1.3bn and $1,650bn) and India (1.1bn and $650bn)' (Haas 2005: 19). More significantly, British Prime Minister Tony Blair (2006: A19) has expressed a strong preference for the 'G8+5' formula, stating in late May 2006: 'the G8 now regularly meets as the G8+5. That should be the norm.'[9]

Invited Countries

President Mitterrand, holder of the G7 presidency in 1989, invited the leaders of fifteen developing countries to dinner on the eve of the Summit of the Arch. This pre-summit dinner was not a true G7 outreach but rather Mitterrand's own initiative; the rest of the G7 leaders did not join the 15 guests. These countries subsequently formed their own Group of 15 (G15). Several years later, in 1996, Ukraine was represented at the Moscow Nuclear Safety and Security Summit.

In what was the first instance of agreed G8 outreach to developing countries, the Japanese government hosted a pre-summit dinner in Tokyo in 2000, prior to that year's Okinawa summit. The guests were the following leaders: Presidents Thabo Mbeki of South Africa (as Chair of the Non-Aligned Movement, NAM), Olusegun Obasanjo of Nigeria (as Chair of the Group of 77), Abdelaziz Bouteflika of Algeria (as Chair of the Organization of African Unity, OAU) and Prime Minister Chuan Leekpai of Thailand (as Chair of both the Association of Southeast Asian Nations, ASEAN and of the United Nations Conference on Trade and Development, UNCTAD).

The 2002 Kananaskis summit introduced a qualitative change in G8 relations with the 'outreach countries'; there, the same leaders were actual participants in certain portions of the summit. The four African leaders (from South Africa, Nigeria, Algeria and Senegal) represent the first and longest strand in G8 outreach; they were always invited to summits from Kananaskis to Gleneagles in 2005, and can be expected to return at Heiligendamm in 2007.

---

9   See also a press briefing on 26 May 2006 by Blair's spokesman in which he quotes the Prime Minister: 'the G8+5, which had been on an informal basis at Gleneagles, should become the norm', www.pm.gov.uk/output/Page9550.asp.

The second strand of outreach began in 2003 at the Evian summit, where the 'enlarged dialogue' (or 'extended dialogue') included major developing countries: the four Presidents (Bouteflika of Algeria, Obasanjo of Nigeria, Mbeki of South Africa and Wade of Senegal), plus the Presidents of China (Hu Jintao), Brazil (Luiz Inacio Lula da Silva), Mexico (Vicente Fox Quesada), and the Prime Minister of India (Atal Bihari Vajpayee). With Evian located so near the Swiss border, the President of Switzerland (Pascal Couchepin) also participated. The King of Morocco did not come and the President of Egypt (Hosni Mubarak) left before the G8/Africa meeting. Also present were the Crown prince of Saudi Arabia (Abdallah bin Abdulaziz al Saoud), the Prime Minister of Malaysia and President of the Non-Aligned Movement (Mahathir bin Mohamad). The following administrative heads of international organizations also participated: UN Secretary-General Kofi Annan, President of the World Bank James Wolfensohn, Managing Director of the IMF Horst Koehler, and WTO Director General Supachai Panitchpakdi. The G8-NEPAD (New Partnership for African Development) dialogue included the G8 heads plus the Presidents of Algeria, Nigeria, South Africa, and Senegal (as noted above, Mubarak left before this meeting).

The third strand may have been an anomaly, since it has not yet been repeated. At Sea Island in 2004, the invitees attending (Egypt declined) included several leaders from the 'broader Middle East': the Presidents of Algeria (Bouteflika), Iraq (Ghazi Mashal Ajil al-Yawer), Afghanistan (Hamid Karzai), Yemen (Ali Abdallah Salih); the King of Jordan (Abdallah II); and the Prime Minister of Turkey (Recep Tayyip Erdogan). The African contingent comprised the Presidents of Ghana (John Agyekum Kafuor), Uganda (Yoweri Museveni), Nigeria (Obasanjo), South Africa (Mbeki) and Senegal (Wade).

The second strand has resumed with the 'G8+5' meeting at the 2005 Gleneagles summit, which established the closest association in summit history with invited leaders from Africa, the Middle East, Latin America and Asia, as well as heads of international organizations. These leaders participated actively in several meetings and working lunches, and played an important part, associating themselves with some of the summit's declarations. These 'outreach leaders' clearly played a greater role in the deliberations and in the policy and decisional process than comparable invitees at any previous summit.

The first full day of the Gleneagles summit, 7 July, began with a G8 working session, followed by a working lunch of G8 leaders with the leaders of Brazil, China, India, Mexico and South Africa, and the administrative heads of the International Energy Agency (IEA), International Monetary Fund (IMF), United Nations (UN), World Bank and World Trade Organization (WTO), from 12:15 to 1:15 PM. The deliberations, concentrating on climate change, were affected – though not derailed – by the terrorist bomb attacks in London that morning. The leaders of the G8 and of the other participating countries, together with the heads of the international organizations present at the session, condemned the attack in a joint statement, in what was a new precedent in the history of the summits. The leaders of the other G8 countries and the President of the European Commission also made individual statements condemning the terrorist attacks.

The second day of the summit, 8 July, with Africa at the core of discussions, began with the third working session of the G8 leaders, after which those leaders met with leaders of Algeria, Ethiopia, Ghana, Nigeria, Senegal, South Africa and Tanzania, and the administrative heads of the AU Commission, the IMF, the UN and the World Bank. It was originally planned to continue with an afternoon session but the summit wrapped up about 1 PM. At the conclusion of the session the leaders issued and signed the communiqué – the first time this happened in the summits. In another summit first, the G8 leaders and the G8 and AU issued another joint statement on the Sudan.

Although this was not the Russians' initial plan for the 2006 St. Petersburg summit, the hosts could not resist (as had the US in 2004) pressure from their other G8 counterparts to continue the 'G8+5' trend. Thus the following leaders participated at St. Petersburg: the Presidents of South Africa (Mbeki), Mexico (Fox), Brazil (Lula da Silva), China (Hu), and the Prime Minister of India (Manmohan Singh). Two other leaders represented not their own countries but international organizations: the President of Kazakhstan, Nursultan Nazarbaev, in his capacity as Chairman of the CIS [Commonwealth of Independent States]; and the President of the Republic of the Congo, Denis Sassou-Nguesso, in his capacity as Chairman of the African Union (see Chapter 7 for a discussion of international organizations vis-à-vis the G7 and G8).

These 'outreach' meetings have constituted the response of the G8 leaders to demands for greater engagements with other countries, particularly the major developing and emerging-economy countries. For a related discussion, in the context of initiatives for G8 reform, see Chapter 12.

Concluding Remarks

Examination of the 32-year evolution of the membership of the institution reveals the difficult and contentious incremental increase from the original G6 through the many years of the G7 to the G8 of 1998 and 2006. Several potential trajectories for further development can be envisioned. But the question remains: What is the likeliest scenario of the G8's evolution: into a 'G8+5' or a larger group? A smaller core group? A looser grouping based on the agenda of each summit? An expanded-membership institution? Discussion and analysis of various proposals presented over the years for expanding, contracting or otherwise reforming the G7 and G8 are found in Chapter 12.

References

Note on internet addresses (URLs): Websites tend to appear, change or disappear, often without warning. Addresses cited in this source list were accurate and active at the time of writing (August 2006) unless otherwise noted.

Åslund, Anders (2006), *Russia's Challenges as Chair of the G-8*, Policy Briefs in International Economics, PB06-3, Institute for International Economics, Washington, DC, www.iie.com/publications/pb/pb06-3.pdf.
Barnes, Hugh and James Owen, comp[ilers] (2006), *Russia in the Spotlight: G8 Scorecard*, Foreign Policy Centre, London, http://fpc.org.uk/fsblob/686.pdf and http://fpc.org.uk/events/past/224.

Bayne, Nicholas (1995), 'The G7 Summit and the Reform of Global Institutions', *Government and Opposition*, 30:4, 492-509.

Bayne, Nicholas (2005b), *Staying Together: The G8 Summit Confronts the 21st Century*, Ashgate, Aldershot, UK.

Beattie, Alan (2006), 'G8 Legitimacy Queried as Russia Plays Host', *Financial Times*, 13 July.

Bergsten, C. Fred (1998), 'The New Agenda with China', *International Economics Policy Briefs*, 98-2, May.

Blair, Tony (2006), 'Our Values Are Our Guide', *The Globe and Mail*, 27 May, A19.

Bonvicini, Gianni and Wolfgang Wessels (1984), 'The European Community and the Seven', in *Economic Summits and Western Decision-Making* 167-91, Cesare Merlini (ed.), Croom Helm; St. Martin's Press in association with the European Institute of Public Administration, London; New York.

Brzezinski, Zbigniew (1996), 'Let's Add to the G-7', *The New York Times*, 25 June, A11.

Brzezinski, Zbigniew (2004), *The Choice: Global Domination or Global Leadership*, Basic Books, New York.

Chirac, Jacques (2006), 'The G8's Raison d'être', *The Globe and Mail*, 13 July, A17.

Clinton, Bill (2005), *My Life*, Vintage, New York. (Originally published by Knopf in 2004.)

Council on Foreign Relations (2006), *Russia's Wrong Direction: What the United States Can and Should Do*, Task Force Report, 57, CFR, New York, March.

Fedorov, Yury E. (2006), '*Boffins' and 'Buffoons': Different Strains of Thought in Russia's Strategic Thinking*, REP BP 06/01, Chatham House, Lodnon, March, www.chathamhouse.org.uk/pdf/research/rep/BP0306russia.pdf.

Freeland, Chrystia and Matthew Kaminski (1997), 'Helsinki Talks Reach Nuclear Breakthrough', *Financial Times*, 22-23 March.

Garavoglia, Guido (1984), 'From Rambouillet to Williamsburg: A Historical Assessment', in *Economic Summits and Western Decision-Making*, 1-42, Cesare Merlini (ed.), Croom Helm; St. Martin's Press in association with the European Institute of Public Administration, London; New York.

Garten, Jeffrey (2005), 'Russia's Leadership of the Group of Eight Will Be Farcical', *Financial Times*, 28 June, 23.

Haas, Richard (2005), 'Leaders Have a Flawed Gleneagles Agenda', *Financial Times*, 1 July, 19.

Hainsworth, Susan (1990), *Coming of Age: The European Community and the Economic Summit*, Country Study No. 7, University of Toronto, Centre for International Studies, www.g8.utoronto.ca/scholar/hainsworth1990/index.html.

Handelman, Stephen (2006), 'They're Back!', *The Globe and Mail*, 3 June, F1, F6.

Hodges, Michael R. (1999), 'The G8 and the New Political Economy', in *The G8's Role in the New Millennium*, 69-73, Michael R. Hodges, John J. Kirton and Joseph P. Daniels (eds), Ashgate, Aldershot, UK.

Illarionov, Andrei (2006), 'Moscow and the G8: Membership Has Its Privileges', *The Globe and Mail*, 18 April, A17.

'Joint Press Conference Given by the Prime Minister, Mr John Major and the Soviet President, Mr Mikhail Gorbachev' (1991), London, 17 July, www.g8.utoronto. ca/summit/1991london/joint.html.

Kirton, John J. (1995), 'The Diplomacy of Concert: Canada, the G7 and the Halifax Summit', *Canadian Foreign Policy* 3:1, 63-80.

Kirton, John J. (1999), *The G7 and China in the Management of the International Financial System*, paper prepared for the Forum 'China in the 21st Century and the World', Shenzen, China, 11-12 November, www.g8.utoronto.ca/scholar/ kirton199903/index.html.

Kirton, John J. (2006b), *A Summit of Significant Success: The G8 at St. Petersburg*, G8 Research Group, Toronto, 19 July, www.g8.utoronto.ca/evaluations/ 2006stpetersburg/kirton_perf_060719.pdf.

Krickus, Richard J. (2006), *Iron Troikas: The New Threat from the East*, Strategic Studies Institute, US Army War College, Carlisle, PA, www.strategicstudiesinstitute. army.mil/pubs/display.cfm?pubID=643.

Myers, Steven Lee (2006), 'Strong Rebuke for the Kremlin from Cheney', *The New York Times*, 5 May, A1, A10.

Nichol, Jim, Steven Woehrel and Bernard A. Gelb (2006), *Russia's Cutoff of Natural Gas to Ukraine: Context and Implications*, CRS Report for Congress, RS22378, Washington, DC, 15 February.

Sachs, Jeffrey (1998), 'Global Capitalism: Making It Work', *The Economist* 348:8085, 23-25, September 12.

Ullrich, Heidi and Alan Donnelly (1998), 'The Group of Eight and the European Union: The Evolving Partnership', *G8 Governance*, 5, www.g7.utoronto.ca/ governance/gov5/intro.html.

United Kingdom, Prime Minister's Office (1998), Press Conference Given by the Prime Minister, Birmingham, 17 May, www.g8.utoronto.ca/summit/ 1998birmingham/blaira.html and www.g8.utoronto.ca/summit/1998birmingham/ blairb.html.

United States, White House, Office of the Press Secretary (1997), *Press Conference of the President*, 22 June, Denver, www.g8.utoronto.ca/summit/1997denver/ clint22.htm.

'Welcome to China, Mr Clinton' (1998), *The Economist*, 347:8074, 17, June 27.

Yeltsin, Boris (2000), *Midnight Diaries*, Weidenfeld & Nicolson, London.

Chapter 5

The G7 and G8 Summit Agenda

This chapter discusses the process of G7 and G8 agenda setting, traces the evolution of the agenda through the 32-year history of summitry, and outlines the effects of unexpected major events that occur just before, or during, summit meetings. For a detailed analysis and history of the summit meetings themselves, see Chapter 3.

Agenda-Setting

Because the G7 and G8 is a forum of the leaders of member countries, '[o]nly intractable international problems, which cannot be settled at lower levels, come up to the summit' (Bayne 2005b: 3). It is the host leader's prerogative to set the thematic focus for the summit and, even after the agenda is set, the leader can modify, add or delete agenda items. As well, certain major issues call for negotiation over several years, so continuity is also at work as those agenda items are carried over to subsequent summits. Africa is a case in point: G8 involvement has been strong for several years and was a topic of the leaders' discussions at Sea Island summit in 2004 even though it had not been a central theme for the US host government; the UK host leader of the 2005 Gleneagles summit placed Africa in the centre of his agenda (along with climate change). At the Russian-hosted 2006 St. Petersburg summit the hosts did not put Africa specifically on the agenda but it became clear that the subject would have to be discussed in conjunction with practically all issues officially on the agenda.

It is the task of the leaders' personal representatives – known as sherpas – to develop and flesh out the agenda before each summit meeting. They accomplish this in a series of meetings with their counterpart sherpas in the lead-up to the summit and in co-ordination with their leaders and other G8 officials (Hajnal and Kirton 2000: 7-8). (For more information on the role of the sherpas see Chapter 6.)

The Evolution of the G7 and G8 Agenda

In the early years of summitry, in the 1970s, the leaders were concerned mainly with 'management of international economics ... [-] the future of the international monetary order; ... the enhancement of international economic growth through further liberalisation of world trade, macroeconomic policy coordination among the major industrialised countries and measures to alleviate the situation of the poor developing countries; and ... the containment of oil insecurity and instability.' But all in all, economic and financial issues 'have left the most significant imprint on the G7/G8 process' from the first summit in Rambouillet in 1975 to the Genoa summit of 2001. In the 1980s 'the emphasis shifted away from economic policy coordination ... towards broader political issues and transnational problems such as the global environment, international terrorism and drugs' (Maull 1994: 120; Sherifs and Astraldi 2001: 199).

The evolution of the political agenda can be seen to have unfolded in three stages:

- 1975-1981, when France opposed the extension of political and security discussions beyond itself, Great Britain and the US, and when Japan remained reluctant to commit itself in what had traditionally been the competence of the Atlantic Alliance;
- 1982-1988, when political, security and other non-economic issues became increasingly important for the summits; and
- From 1989 onward, with the emergence of global issues such as democratisation, the environment, drugs and terrorism (Garavoglia and Padoan 1994: 50-53).

Summit agenda has, by and large, responded to the global economic and political context and challenges while centring on the host leader's priorities. Global, transnational issues became prominent in the 1990s and have continued to the present: the benefits and risks of globalization as well as the problems of countries and populations marginalized by it; the challenges of development; climate change and other environmental issues; terrorism and transnational organized crime; migration; food safety; and diverse other global topics. Dealing with regional and other crises and conflicts, too, has come into the purview of the G8 (Sherifs and Astraldi 2001: 208-14).

Macroeconomic policy co-ordination, international trade, the monetary system and North-South relations have been of concern to the G7 and G8 from the beginning. East-West economic issues and energy have also been recurrent preoccupations. Later additions have included microeconomic topics such as employment and the global information infrastructure; other global, transnational issues such as the environment, crime, drugs, and AIDS; and political and security issues such as human rights, migration, regional security, arms control, terrorism, nuclear safety, and the effects of globalization. Still later, the G7 and G8 turned its attention to global issues: the environment, crime, drugs and AIDS, among others.

Although the evolution of the summit agenda often proceeds by incremental adjustments, it is useful to highlight the larger trends of the evolution of issues. Nicholas Bayne examines the progression of agenda expansion and divides the history of summits into seven series, each focusing particularly strongly on specific issue areas:

- Reviving economic growth, from 1975 to 1978;
- Holding down inflation, from 1979 to 1982;
- Gradually adding political issues, from 1983 to 1988;
- Responding to the end of the Cold War, from 1989 to 1993;
- Scrutinizing and reforming institutions for globalization, from 1994 to 1997;
- Tackling the issues and linkages of globalization and development, from 1998 to 2000; and
- Fighting terrorism and its causes, starting with 2002 (Bayne 2005b: 7, 18; see also Hajnal and Kirton 2000).

The main topics at Rambouillet in 1975 were exchange rates, inflation, economic growth, oil prices and supplies, unemployment, and trade including the Tokyo Round of the General Agreement on Tariffs and Trade (GATT) negotiations. The final communiqué – known as the Declaration of Rambouillet – reflected these concerns.[1] The communiqué – the only public document of Rambouillet – gives no hint of the informal exchanges of views among the leaders at the summit: on Spain's prospects following Franco's death; the prospects of the US-Soviet SALT negotiations; the West's relations with China; and public expenditures in the UK.[2]

The 1976 San Juan summit added to the agenda balance-of-payments problems and reaffirmed the G7 commitment to the completion of the Tokyo Round. Energy, especially the use of nuclear energy, and North-South relations were added in London in 1977. The key issues of the 1978 Bonn summit were economic growth, energy, and trade. A non-economic issue, aircraft hijacking, entered the agenda as well. This summit earned the highest rating in Putnam and Bayne's ranking of summits (for summit evaluations, including the Putnam and Bayne ranking, see Chapter 10).

Energy was the paramount concern of the Tokyo summit in 1979. The final communiqué included specific undertakings by summit countries to curb their oil imports. Hijackings and Indochinese refugees were also discussed. Energy continued to be at the top of the agenda in Venice in 1980, with the Soviet invasion of Afghanistan and the occupation of the US Embassy in Tehran as additional issues. The 1981 Ottawa summit (also known as the summit of Montebello where, in the 'world's largest log cabin', the delegations held their meetings away from the media waiting for news in Ottawa and Canadian Prime Minister Pierre Elliott Trudeau, as summit host, flew back to Ottawa by helicopter to brief journalists following each afternoon session) discussed the usual economic issues, along with aid to developing countries, East-West economic relations, and terrorism. It also established the Trade Ministers' Quadrilateral (see Chapter 6 for a discussion of G7- and G8-related bodies).

The Versailles summit of 1982 reviewed the whole gamut of economic concerns, concentrating on East-West trade and setting the stage for more effective multilateral surveillance of monetary policies and exchange rates, to be co-ordinated by the IMF. The Israeli invasion of Lebanon also received attention. At Williamsburg, Virginia in 1983 the summit participants discussed the usual economic issues, including the growing debt crisis, but the principal subject was arms control and the stationing of US cruise and Pershing II missiles in Europe to counter the threat from Soviet missiles, reflected in the political declaration. Debt was again a central concern at the 1984 London summit. Democratic values, terrorism, East-West security relations, and the Iran-Iraq conflict were discussed as well.

The most important issue at Bonn in 1985 was trade, but the summit failed to agree on a starting date for the Uruguay Round of multilateral negotiations. That summit was, however, notable for introducing the topic of the environment to the agenda. It also commemorated the fortieth anniversary of the end of the Second World War. The 1986 Tokyo summit, considered to be one of the more successful summits, called for

---

1 These and other documents of the G7 and G8 summits are accessible at the G8 Information Centre website, <www.g8.utoronto.ca/summit/index.htm>.

2 These informal negotiations are outlined in Callaghan (1987: 480).

an overhaul of agricultural policies of summit countries, established the Group of Seven finance ministers, and agreed to launch (through GATT) the Uruguay Round. Action against terrorism – following the US raid on Libya – was a key issue that year in Tokyo. The leaders there were also concerned with the Chernobyl nuclear-reactor accident. Terrorism, the Iran-Iraq war, AIDS, and narcotic drugs were the non-economic agenda items in Venice in 1987.

The 1988 Toronto summit produced the so-called 'Toronto terms' for relieving the debt burden of the poorest developing countries.[3] Toronto also reaffirmed the Uruguay Round, and dealt with the Middle East, South Africa and Cambodia. Debt relief also played an important part in the 'Summit of the Arch' of 1989, with the adoption of the Brady Plan. Other topics included the environment, the strengthening of GATT, and economic efficiency, as well as human rights, China and the Tiananmen Square massacre, democratization in Eastern and Central Europe and help for that region, money laundering, and terrorism.

The 1990 Houston summit addressed not only the usual range of economic issues but also a number of specific environmental problems; democratization in Europe and elsewhere in the world; Soviet economic reforms; liberalization of export controls; drug abuse; and the non-proliferation of nuclear, biological, and chemical weapons. The most contentious issues at Houston were agricultural trade subsidies, aid to the Soviet Union, and global warming or climate change.

The official theme of the 1991 London summit was 'building world partnership and strengthening the international order'. UK Prime Minister John Major, the host leader, highlighted eight main achievements: proposals to strengthen the United Nations (UN) and to improve the regulation and control of conventional arms sales by means of a UN arms register; commitment to sustained economic recovery and price stability; personal commitment of the leaders to work for the conclusion of the Uruguay Round of trade negotiations by the end of 1991;[4] support for political and economic reform in Central and East European countries; financial and technical assistance to developing countries, including debt relief to the poorest, beyond the Toronto terms; support for the June 1992 United Nations Conference on Environment and Development (UNCED or the 'Earth Summit'); and stepping up the fight against drug abuse and drug trafficking. Help for the USSR was an important concern for the leaders, and a post-summit meeting with Gorbachev was held at the summit site.

The theme of the 1992 Munich summit was 'working together for growth and a safer world'. The communiqué noted the end of the East-West conflict and covered the world economy, focusing on growth, interest rates, unemployment and trade. The leaders at Munich gave another boost to the stalled Uruguay Round. The communiqué praised the Earth Summit as a landmark event; and devoted special sections to Central and Eastern Europe and the new independent states of the former Soviet Union, and to the problems of safety of nuclear power plants in those two areas. In addition, the leaders addressed nuclear non-proliferation, and the further strengthening of the UN.

---

3   The 'Toronto terms' called for a one-third reduction of the official debt (debt owed to governments) of the poorest developing countries.

4   Despite this 'personal commitment', the Uruguay Round was concluded successfully and ratified only at the end of 1994.

The main economic theme of the 1993 Tokyo summit was 'a strengthened commitment to jobs and growth'. The communiqué confirmed a $3 billion fund to aid Russian privatization. A major achievement was the agreement (actually reached on the eve of the summit by the US, Canada, Japan, and the EC trade ministers' quadrilateral meeting) on market access to manufactured goods – this was a catalyst for the completion of the stalled Uruguay Round. The communiqué reiterates that 'our highest priority is a successful conclusion to the Uruguay Round'.

The involvement of Russia in the leaders' political deliberations ('Political 8' or P8) was the most important issue for the 1994 Naples summit. The rest of the Naples agenda included jobs and economic growth; trade, including a call for ratification of the Uruguay Round agreements and the establishment of the World Trade Organization (WTO) by January 1, 1995. The leaders also addressed the environment; progress in developing countries; nuclear safety in Central and Eastern Europe and the former Soviet Union; the economic and security situation in, and aid to, Ukraine; political and economic reform in Russia; countries in transition; and transnational crime and money laundering. In addition to these issues, the Naples communiqué included – at Canada's initiative – a call for a conference on Ukraine. (The conference took place in Winnipeg in October 1994.)

The Naples summit set out the centrepiece of the agenda for the following year's Halifax summit; namely, the role of international financial and economic institutions. The leaders in Naples forecast 'an even more flexible and less formal summit' in Halifax. Writing on the eve of the 1995 Halifax summit, Bayne and Putnam (1995: 4) stated that 'inaugurating a review of the international system ... is intended to give new momentum to the summit process as it enters its fourth seven-year cycle'.[5]

At the 1995 Halifax summit, the leaders had more time for informal, unstructured discussion than had been the case for many years, and the centrality of the reform of international institutions was evident in the deliberations and documentation. The review of international institutions (the Bretton Woods institutions and the UN system in general – especially the United Nations Conference on Trade and Development and the United Nations Industrial Development Organization – as well as the regional development banks) was the main item on the agenda, reflecting host Canadian Prime Minister Jean Chrétien's wish to reform the financial institutions, and illustrating the leaders' role in focusing on selected agenda items. Other concerns at Halifax were growth and employment, open markets, economies in transition, and nuclear safety. A separate background document set out details of the desired review of international financial institutions and issued a call for co-ordination among the WTO, the International Monetary Fund (IMF), the World Bank, the Organisation for Economic Co-operation and Development (OECD), and trade-related UN bodies. The political agenda at Halifax ranged from Bosnia and the Israeli-Palestinian agreement through North Korea and Rwanda to the role of the UN and the Conference on Security and Co-operation in Europe (CSCE).

---

5   Later, Bayne recast the history of summits into a single G7 cycle from 1975 to 1997, and a new cycle for the G8 beginning in 1998; 7-year (for the G7) and 8-year (for the G8) sequences; and summit series, a multi-year run of summits focusing on a particular set of issues. (See Bayne 2005b: 7, 18.)

The main theme of the 1996 Lyon summit was 'making a success of globalization for the benefit of all'. The economic agenda ranged from growth, trade and investment to unemployment, North-South economic relations, and the integration of Russia and the countries of Central and Eastern Europe into the world economy. Building on the Halifax initiatives of the previous year, the Lyon summit called for enhancing the effectiveness of the UN, the international financial institutions, the regional development banks and the WTO. The host leader, President Jacques Chirac, pressed for meaningful discussion of development issues. A major achievement at Lyon was on debt relief and the endorsement of the Heavily Indebted Poor Countries (HIPC) initiative.

The political and global-issue agenda of the Lyon summit centred on security and stability, and encompassed the strengthening and further reform of the UN system; human rights, democratization, and humanitarian emergencies; non-proliferation, arms control and disarmament; nuclear safety and security; environmental protection; and the information society. It also included the 'Human Frontier Science Program', HIV/AIDS and other infectious diseases, illegal drugs, transnational organized crime; regional security and stability in various parts of the world including Central and Eastern Europe, the Middle East, Iran, Iraq, Libya, and the two Koreas.

The 1997 Denver Summit of the Eight resumed discussion of economic and social issues including globalization and its effects, the problem of aging populations, and the potentials and problems of small and medium-size enterprises. Global issues of concern ranged from environmental topics to infectious diseases; nuclear safety; transnational organized crime; illicit drugs; terrorism; UN reform; and a partnership for development in Africa. On the political agenda at Denver were the growth of democracy and the protection of human rights; nuclear non-proliferation, arms control and disarmament; and potential or actual problem areas (Hong Kong, the Middle East, Cyprus, and Albania). The host leader, US President Bill Clinton, emphasized that Africa was a priority for him.

Prime Minister Tony Blair was determined to shorten the agenda at Birmingham in 1998, which thus focused on three themes: promoting sustainable growth in the global economy; employability and social inclusion; and combating drug trafficking and other forms of transnational crime. Particular attention was paid to the Asian financial crisis and its impact on the poorest and most vulnerable sectors of society. The leaders also confirmed their wish to see developing and emerging economies participate fully in the multilateral trading system. The G8 pledged support for developing countries to build democracy and good governance. Summit undertakings on the HIPC initiative fell far short of the expectations of over 50,000 demonstrators (some forming a human chain around the summit site, others rowing small coracles along Birmingham's canals) during the summit who presented a 'Jubilee 2000 petition' urging complete debt forgiveness for all poor countries by the year 2000. Blair, on behalf of the G8 leaders, responded to the petition in a separate document.

The G8 leaders at Birmingham expressed support for WHO initiatives on fighting malaria and AIDS. They made commitments on the development of energy markets and supported the enhancement of the safety of nuclear power plants. As well, they discussed drugs and transnational crime, non-proliferation of weapons of mass destruction, the Millennium Bug, and various regional conflicts. Remaining G7 issues were: economic policies of the seven countries, and proposals for further reform of the IMF, the World Bank and other international financial institutions (building on the Halifax initiatives to reform international institutions).

At the Köln (Cologne) summit of 1999 debt relief for the poorest countries was a major topic. Host leader Chancellor Gerhard Schröder was persuaded by his colleagues to change his position on this issue, resulting in the important Cologne Debt Initiative. This, and the international financial architecture, remained G7 issues at Köln. The main G8 issues were economic assistance for Russia, employment, international crime, terrorism, trade, development, the environment, education and social protection. The pressing political issues of Kosovo and the Balkans were also on the agenda.

The Japanese hosts of the 2000 Okinawa summit grouped their large agenda under three main rubrics:

- greater prosperity (including the world economy, information and communication technology, development, debt, health, education, trade, and cultural diversity);
- deeper peace of mind (this embraced such diverse topics as crime and drugs, the challenges of an aging population, biotechnology and food safety, the human genome, and nuclear safety); and
- greater world stability (conflict prevention, disarmament and arms control, and terrorism).

Thus, a number of global issues, in addition to economic and political concerns, figured prominently in the deliberations of the summit at the G8 level. G7 issues in Okinawa included economic growth, the international financial architecture, the enhanced HIPC initiative, fight against abuses of the global financial system, and nuclear safety (with particular reference to Ukraine). The Korean Peninsula, other regional issues, and the Global Information Society merited separate summit declarations. Information technology and infectious diseases were a personal priority for host leader Keizo Obuchi, again illustrating the leaders' role in the development and focusing of agenda items.

Economic issues discussed at the Genoa summit of 2001 included trade, development and development assistance, poverty reduction, employment and education. Global issues on the agenda were: the environment, renewable energy, information and communication technology, food safety, drugs and transnational organized crime. Political concerns included conflict prevention in the Middle East and other regions, and disarmament. Economic issues continued to be discussed at the G7 level: the world economy, Africa, multilateral trade negotiations at the WTO, strengthening the international financial system and debt relief under the enhanced HIPC initiative.

The agenda of the 2002 Kananaskis summit was a focused one. Despite increased pressure in the aftermath of the 11 September 2001 terrorist attacks in the US, Chrétien was determined to press for G8 initiatives on Africa. Thus, the leaders concentrated on that continent (including the launching of the G8 Africa Action Plan). They also discussed the enhanced HIPC initiative, the fight against the spread of weapons of mass destruction, education, transport security, and information and communication technology. A particularly important topic was the role of Russia in the G8; it was at Kananaskis where the leaders agreed to Russia's chairing the G8 and hosting its first annual summit, in 2006.

At Evian in 2003 Africa was again a major topic; the leaders met with invited African leaders, as they had at several previous summits. Economic issues discussed included trade, debt relief, corruption and transparency. Corporate and public governance were central themes, reflecting a French proposal 'to strengthen corporate responsibility and build a responsible market economy' (Fratianni et al. 2007). One related G8 declaration was entitled *Fostering Growth and Promoting a Responsible Market Economy*. Political and global agenda items were terrorism, non-proliferation, sustainable development, health, water resources and other topics.

The Sea Island summit of 2004 introduced the topic of the 'Broader Middle East and North Africa'. It also discussed the world economy, trade, terrorism, non-proliferation, and various development issues including health, HIV/AIDS, debt relief, famine, among others. Africa, particularly peacekeeping, was also on the agenda, as were regional conflicts (Sudan, North Korea, Iraq, and Israel/Palestine).

UK Prime Minister Tony Blair first indicated in 2004 that his focus for the 2005 Gleneagles summit would be Africa and climate change. He confirmed and fleshed out this agenda at the World Economic Forum in Davos on 27 January 2005 (UK 2005d). The British hosts kept this focus at the summit itself, although they left room on the agenda for other issues as well: counter-terrorism, nonproliferation of chemical, biological, radioactive and nuclear weapons, and support for reform in the broader Middle East and North Africa. As the summit approached, energy questions (especially fast-rising oil prices) gave rise to G8 concern. And the terrorist attacks on London on the first morning of the summit (7 July) naturally intruded upon the agenda of the meetings. Nevertheless, Africa and climate change remained the centrepieces. This was in keeping with the G8 tradition of the host leader setting the agenda while also being influenced by peer pressure from fellow leaders, momentum from the previous summit, and, of course, unexpected events occurring just before or during the summit.

The three main agenda items of the 15-17 July 2006 St. Petersburg summit were energy security, health/infectious diseases and education. Other topics included intellectual property piracy, the fight against corruption, trade, terrorism, post-conflict stabilization and reconstruction, non-proliferation, the Middle East and Africa.

German Chancellor Angela Merkel originally planned to concentrate on global trade imbalances, energy and intellectual property rights for the 2007 Heiligendamm summit. But, on 18 October 2006, German officials announced an expansion of the agenda by adding development and climate change. They also indicated that the overall theme of the summit would be 'growth and responsibility', and that priority would be placed on African development and the globalized economy. Discussion on African development would include HIV/AIDS, encouraging democracy and good governance, fighting corruption, and supporting growth and investment in Africa[6] (McHugh 2006; Benoit 2006; German G8... 2006).

---

6   I thank Laura Sunderland of the G8 Research Group for this information.

The Unexpected

From time to time during summit history, major unexpected events have intruded on the summits' approved agenda. When this occurs, the leaders are obliged to discuss these developments. Here are some examples:

- The Chernobyl nuclear reactor explosion before the 1986 Tokyo summit, leading to a summit statement on the implication of this event;
- North Korean leader Kim Il Sung's death the day before the 1994 Naples summit;
- Intensification of fighting in Bosnia in 1995, before the Halifax summit, causing a change (advocated by Chirac) in the agenda of the first working dinner of the leaders;
- A terrorist truck bombing against the US military base in Dhahran, Saudi Arabia before the 1996 Lyon summit, prompting a summit declaration on terrorism; and
- India's nuclear tests and the Indonesian political crisis around the time of the 1998 Birmingham summit (followed shortly after the summit by Pakistani nuclear tests).

The leaders were able to discuss these events in the first evening of the summit, enabling them to move on to negotiations on the agreed-upon agenda during the rest of the summit (Hajnal and Kirton 2000: 8). The violent demonstrations, including the tragic death of a protester, around the time of the 2001 Genoa summit, were also acknowledged and regretted by the leaders.

Two more recent incidents, however, were sufficiently grave to intrude seriously on summit proceedings. The terrorist suicide bomb attacks against the London underground on the first morning of the 2005 Gleneagles summit (7 July), forcing the host leader, Tony Blair, to leave the summit for London for a good part of the day to deal with the crisis, compelling the leaders to discuss the attacks and cutting into the time allotted for the regular agenda. Several important events took place just before and during the 2006 St. Petersburg summit: the death of Chechen warlord Samil Basayev (Russia claimed to have assassinated him but the cause of death may have been an explosion of his car which was carrying weapons); the terrorist attacks on trains in and around Mumbai, India; and – more than anything – the flare-up of violence in the Middle East, first between Israel and Gaza, then the Israeli-Hezbollah war. The Middle East dominated the summit discussions, so that Russia's priority themes received less attention than would otherwise have been the case.

Concluding Remarks

It is the G7 and G8 leader hosting a particular summit whose prerogative it is to set the agenda for the summit, but this occurs in the context of global economic and political realities and the force of continuity, all reflected in the topics to be discussed. In view of those changing realities – and to input from other G7 and G8 countries

– the agenda undergoes numerous changes, additions or deletions by the time the summit is reached. In addition to the leader and his peers, the leaders' personal representatives (sherpas) have a crucial role in honing and completing the agenda, through an intensive process of year-round negotiations with their counterparts and with other G7 and G8 officials.

From the original focus of the summits on economic and financial issues, the G7 and G8 agenda has evolved over 32 years to embrace more and more topics: political concerns, and later a great number of diverse transnational, global issues from the environment to terrorism and infectious diseases. As well, major unexpected events that occur just before or during summits inevitably make an impact on the actual agenda.

In addition to the publicly announced agenda items, the leaders tend to discuss various other issues privately, as they see fit. This is part of the dynamics of the informal, confidential forum that is the leaders' summit.

References

Bayne, Nicholas (2005b), *Staying Together: The G8 Summit Confronts the 21st Century*, Ashgate, Aldershot, UK.

Bayne, Nicholas and Robert D. Putnam (1995), 'Introduction: The G-7 Summit Comes of Age', in *The Halifax G-7 Summit: Issues on the Table*, 1-13, Sylvia Ostry and Gilbert R. Wynham (eds), Centre for Foreign Policy Studies, Dalhousie University, Halifax.

Benoit, Bertrand (2006), 'Hedge Fund Transparency Put on G8 Agenda', Financial Times, 18 October.

Callaghan, James (1987), *Time and Chance*, Collins, London.

Fratianni, Michele, Paolo Savona and John J. Kirton (forthcoming 2007), 'Governance amid Globalisation: Corporations, Governments, and the G8', in *Corporate, Public, and Global Governance: The G8 Contribution*, Michele Fratianni, Paolo Savona, and John J. Kirton (eds), Global Finance Series, Ashgate, Aldershot, UK.

Garavoglia, Guido and Pier Carlo Padoan (1994), 'The G-7 Agenda: Old and New Issues', in *The Future of the G-7 Summits*, 49-65, *The International Spectator* 29:2 April/June, Special Issue.

'German G8 Presidency to Focus on Hedge Funds, Product Piracy, Africa' (2006), *BBC Monitoring European*, 18 October.

Hajnal, Peter I. and John J. Kirton (2000), 'The Evolving Role and Agenda of the G7/G8: A North American Perspective', *NIRA Review* 7:2, 5-10.

Maull, Hanns W. (1994), 'Germany at the Summit', in *The Future of the G-7 Summits*, 112-39 (*The International Spectator*, 29:2 Special Issue).

McHugh, David (2006), 'Germany Sets Agenda for Next Year's G-8', *The Associated Press*, 18 October, Berlin.

Sherifis, Rossella Franchini and Valerio Astraldi (2001), *Il G7/G8 da Rambouillet a Genova = The G7/G8 from Rambouillet to Genoa*, FrancoAngeli, Milano.

Sunderland, Laura (2006), *The Prospective Agenda for the 2007 G8 Heiligendamm Summit*, G8 Research Group, www.g8.utoronto.ca/evaluations/2007heiligendamm/ 2007agenda.html.

United Kingdom, Prime Minister's Office (2005d), *Special Address by Tony Blair, Prime Minister of the United Kingdom at the World Economic Forum in Davos*, 27 January, www.g8.gov.uk/servlet/Front?pagename=OpenMarket/Xcelerate/Sh owPage&c=Page&cid=1078995903270&a=KArticle&aid=1106749656900.

Chapter 6

The G7 and G8 System

This chapter surveys and comments on the various components of the G7 and G8 system: the expanding panoply of ministerial fora; the sherpas and personal representatives for Africa; and Task Forces, Working Groups and Expert Groups. For ease of reference, these bodies are summarized in the Appendix. The leaders' summits are analyzed in Chapter 3, and the G20 in Chapter 11. See Chapter 14 for a discussion of the documentation of ministerial fora, task forces, working groups and expert groups.

Ministerial Fora

In the course of the thirty-two year history of the G7 and G8, these institutions have created or initiated a large number of diverse G7 and G8 ministerial fora – some of these hold regularly scheduled meetings, while others have been *ad hoc* affairs (and several *ad hoc* meetings later became a regular series). The following section introduces many of these fora. Because the finance and foreign ministers have been integral to the summit process all along, they are discussed first; other ministerial fora follow alphabetically.

G5 Finance Ministers

The Group of Five (G5) finance ministers (France, Germany, the UK, the US and Japan), dates back to the Library Group (March 1973) and its aftermath – thus preceding the leaders' summits which did not begin until November 1975. This G5 forum first ran parallel with, and then was subsumed by, the G7 finance ministers' forum. The last meeting of the G5 occurred at the Louvre in Paris on 21 February 1987, a day before the Louvre meeting of the G7 finance ministers minus Italy. The Plaza Accord of 22 September 1985, which began the 'managed floating' of exchange rates, was a notable achievement of the G5. Chapter 2 presents a detailed discussion and analysis of the G5 finance ministers' forum.

G7 and G8 Finance Ministers[1]

G7 finance ministers met annually at the summit site from 1975 (as G6 that year) until 1997. In fact, a US government memorandum written just before the

---

1   Andrew Baker's *The Group of Seven* (2006) explores in detail the role of the G7 finance ministers and central bank governors in global financial governance.

Rambouillet summit, in presenting two options for a summit follow-up mechanism, states that such follow-up could either be achieved by co-ordination with the OECD [Organisation for Economic Co-operation and Development], or by constituting the G7 finance ministers (Canada was included in this proposal) 'as an autonomous, informal group with loose connection to the IMF [International Monetary Fund] through its Group of 10 and the Interim Committee of 20'. (Economic Summit: A Follow-On Mechanism, [undated, 1975]; Gerald R. Ford Library, Box 46, Council of Economic Advisers Records, 1974-1977, [Chairman of the Council] Alan Greenspan Files: International Economic Summit (Paris), November 15-17, 1975.)[2] Beginning with the 1998 Birmingham summit, the leaders have been meeting without their finance and foreign ministers, so that separate pre-summit meetings of these ministers have since taken place, to feed into the summits themselves.

It was the 1986 Tokyo summit that officially set up the G7 finance ministers' group as a separate entity meeting four or more times a year, usually attended also by the governors of the central banks of the Seven and often by the Managing Director of the IMF. Some of these periodic meetings take place at the time of the semiannual joint meetings of the World Bank and the IMF. The finance and foreign ministers' joint pre-summit meeting that took place for the first time in 1998 is discussed in more detail below. The G7 finance ministers' and central bank governors' meetings on 3 and 30 October 1998 (especially the latter) developed a series of far-reaching proposals to deal with the 1997-98 Asian financial crisis and to enable the Bretton Woods institutions to play a greater role in addressing this crisis and preventing or mitigating future ones.

With the establishment of the European Central Bank (ECB) and the launching of the euro as the common European Union (EU) currency, the president of the ECB became a regular participant of the meetings of the G7 finance ministers and central bank governors, starting with the 3 October 1998 Washington meeting with the appearance of ECB President Willem Duisenberg. This was the first time that the EU was able to participate in the G7 finance ministers' forum. But because EU member states and even euro area member states continue each to control their fiscal policies and affairs, there is little likelihood at present that the G7 finance ministers meetings would change into a format similar to that of the Trade Ministers' Quadrilateral (see below). At the 'Quad', the EU spoke with one voice in trade matters.

For the first time in their history, the G7 finance ministers invited China to participate in their meeting on 1 October 2004, 'in recognition of the country's growing economic clout' (Scares Ahead 2004: 11). This was not just a one-time phenomenon; for example, Brazil, China, India, Russia, and South Africa took some part at the G7 finance ministers' and central bank governors' meeting on 23 September 2005 – significantly, the G7 lumped Russia with the other 'outreach countries', implying the continuation of this forum as a G7 rather than a G8 gathering. A G7 finance ministers' meeting, held unusually on 2-3 December 2005 – quite possibly to avoid the difficulty of holding a G7 rather than a G8 finance ministers' meeting early in 2006 with Russia holding the year's G8 presidency – continued pushing

---

2   References to records in official archives follow the form suggested by those archives.

China to make its exchange rate system less rigid. In addition to the finance minister of China, his counterparts from Brazil and India – all three being economically very important developing countries – also met with the G7 finance ministers at that meeting. As further indication of expanding outreach by the G7 finance ministers, they met as well with Israeli finance minister (now Prime Minister) Ehud Olmert and then Palestinian Authority finance minister Salam Fayyad, plus the Middle East Quartet's special envoy, James Wolfensohn, to discuss economic development in the West Bank and Gaza. Still, there was a G8 finance ministers' meeting on 10-11 February 2006 in Moscow, but the G7 finance ministers and central bank governors met again on 21 April 2006 in Washington. The pre-summit G8 finance ministers' meeting in 2006 took place in St. Petersburg on 9-10 June; the ministers also met there with their counterparts from Australia, China, India, Nigeria and South Korea. The G8 finance ministers' meetings, unlike the G7 finance ministers' meetings, occur without the participation of the central bank governors.

Nonetheless, Russia is not fully integrated into the G7 finance ministers' forum. This follows the understanding reached at the 1997 Denver summit, the first to be called 'Summit of the Eight' where it was decided that Russia would be fully included in the leaders' club 'but the finance ministers opposed the move because of Russia's economic weaknesses. Since Russia depended on the financial support of the international community, they felt it shouldn't be in on the G-7's financial decision making' (Clinton 2005: 758). But this, too, may change; just before the 2006 St. Petersburg summit, the German ambassador to Russia expressed his country's support for Russia joining the finance ministers' forum as a full member (although he conceded that the matter was still open and opinions varied on this) (German Ambassador... 2006).

Foreign Ministers

G7 (now G8) foreign ministers also met annually at the summit site from 1975 to 1997. In addition, they have, since 1984, met each year for a working dinner in New York in September, around the time of the opening of the UN General Assembly. A special meeting of G7 foreign ministers, with Russian participation, was held as a Conference on Partnership for Economic Transformation in Ukraine in Winnipeg, Canada in October 1994. Another special meeting, of G8 foreign ministers and the EU representative, took place on 12 June 1998 to discuss the Indian and Pakistani nuclear tests conducted at that time. This resulted in a collective commitment of the G8 to use their votes in the international financial institutions to block loans to India and Pakistan (G8 to Step... 1998: 3). Having talked since 9:30 that morning, at 11:30 the meeting transformed itself, unusually, into a (non-G8) Contact Group meeting on the Kosovo crisis. In addition to Contact Group members US, UK, France, Germany, Russia and Italy, the meeting, on that occasion, also included Canada and Japan – presumably a function of the vagaries of timing rather than a decision to expand the Contact Group. At 2 PM there was an informal lunch that, again unusually, included representatives of Argentina, Brazil, China, the Philippines, South Africa, and Ukraine, in addition to ministers and representatives of the Contact Group plus Canada and Japan.

G7 foreign and finance ministers, with Russia also present, assembled in Tokyo on 15 April 1993 in preparation for the 1993 Tokyo summit, to discuss support for reform in Russia. As noted above under 'G7 finance ministers', starting with the 1998 Birmingham summit, the leaders have met without their finance and foreign ministers, and those ministers have since met separately from the leaders just before each summit. G8 foreign and finance ministers held their pre-summit meeting in London on 9 May 1998 to prepare for the Birmingham summit a week later and to deal with issues not on the agenda of the Birmingham 'heads only' summit. Starting with 1999, the pre-summit meetings of G8 foreign and finance ministers have been held separately. The pre-summit G8 foreign ministers' meeting in 2006 took place in Moscow on 29 June.

Development Ministers

G8 development ministers have met in Windsor, Ontario, Canada on 26-27 September 2002 and in Paris on 23-24 April 2003. They met, together with their environment minister colleagues, in Derbyshire, UK on 17-18 March 2005.

Education Ministers

Following an initiative of the 1999 Cologne summit, the G8 education ministers met in Okinawa, Japan on 1-2 April 2000. As education was one of the three main agenda items for the St. Petersburg summit, a meeting of education ministers took place in Moscow on 1-2 June 2006.

Employment and Labour Ministers

The employment or labour ministers' first meeting was the 'Jobs Conference' in Detroit on 14-15 March 1994, with ministers of labour, industry, trade and finance participating. Subsequent employment or labour ministers' meetings have occurred annually since 1996:

- A 'Jobs Ministerial Conference' in Lille, France on 1-2 April 1996;
- A 'Jobs Conference' in Kobe, Japan, on 28-29 1997;
- A 'G8 Conference on Growth, Employability and Inclusion' in London on 21-22 February 1998 (which brought together ministers for economic, financial and employment issues);
- A conference of G8 labour ministers, with representatives from the ILO, OECD, and IMF as well as labour and business leaders, in Washington on 24-26 February 1999;
- A G8 labour ministers' meeting in Turin, Italy on 10-11 November 2000;
- A G8 labour and employment ministers' meeting in Montreal, Canada on 26-27 April 2002;
- G8 labour ministers' meetings in Stuttgart, Germany, on 15-16 December 2003;
- A G8 employment ministers' meeting in London on 11 March 2005; and
- A G8 labour and employment ministers' meeting on 9-10 October 2006 in Moscow.

Energy Ministers

G8 energy ministers' meetings (see also under 'environment ministers' below) took place in Moscow on 31 March-1 April 1998 and in Detroit on 2-3 May 2002. G8 energy and environment ministers met with ministers of 12 other countries in London on 1 November 2005. In addition, the UK chair of the G8 held an international energy and environment ministers' roundtable in London on 15-16 March 2005. With energy security at the top of the agenda of the St. Petersburg summit, energy ministers met in Moscow on 15-16 March 2006.

Environment Ministers

The impetus for the G7 (now G8) environment ministers to form their own forum began around the time of the United Nations Conference on Environment and Development (UNCED, or the Earth Summit) in 1992. The ministers first met formally in Germany just before the 1992 Munich summit. Beginning with 1994, the environment ministers have met annually in the country whose turn it is to host the G8 summit. In 2005, the G8 environment and development ministers held a joint meeting on 17-18 March. On 1 November there was a larger meeting of environment and energy ministers and senior officials of the G8 and from Australia, Brazil, China, India, Indonesia, Mexico, Nigeria, Poland, South Africa, South Korea, and Spain, and senior officials from the World Bank, UN Framework Convention on Climate Change, Intergovernmental Panel on Climate Change, International Energy Agency, and the United Nations Environment Programme. This 1 November meeting was the first session of the Dialogue on Climate Change, Energy and Sustainable Development, launched by the G8 at Gleneagles. See also above, under energy ministers.

Global Information Society

A G7 ministerial conference on the 'global information society' was held in Brussels on 24-26 February 1995, with the participation of relevant ministers; for example, Canada was represented by the ministers of industry and of heritage, and the Secretary of State for Science, Research and Development; the US delegation was led by the Secretary of Commerce, but the Vice-President delivered the keynote speech. For the first time in a G7 meeting, industrial leaders participated alongside government representatives. The conference adopted eight core policy principles and set out several pilot projects. The 1995 Halifax summit welcomed these results and the proposal that a follow-up information society conference be held in South Africa in the spring of 1996 (G7 1995: para 10). This 'Information Society and Development Conference' met in Midrand, South Africa on 13-15 May 1996, but as a much larger gathering, with representatives from forty countries as well as the EU and seventeen other international organizations. A conference on the global marketplace for small and medium-sized enterprises (SMEs) took place in Bonn, Germany, on 7-9 April 1997, as one of the joint projects stemming from the 1995 Brussels G7 ministerial conference on the global information society, followed by regional conferences; for example, one held in Manchester, UK, on 8-9 September 1998.

Health Ministers

G7 (now G8) health ministers met, with Mexico and the representative of the European Commission, in Ottawa, Canada, on 7 November 2001, in London on 14 March 2002 and in Mexico City on 6 December 2002 under the name 'Global Health Security Initiative'. The group, with the same composition, met in Berlin on 6-7 November 2003 (from that date on incorporating bioterrorism concerns in their deliberations), in Paris on 10 December 2004, in Rome on 17-18 November 2005, and in Moscow on 27-28 April 2006 (infectious diseases constituted one of three main agenda items of the 2006 St. Petersburg summit).

Justice Ministers

Ministerial meetings on terrorism took place in Ottawa, Canada, on 12 December 1995 and in Paris, France, on 30 July 1996. A G7 + Russia justice ministers' meeting on crime was held in Washington, DC on 10 December 1997. On 15 December 1998 the G8 justice and interior ministers conducted a 'virtual meeting' on organized crime and terrorist funding – the first time the G8 ministers 'met' via videoconference (which lasted three hours). There were:

- G8 ministerial meetings on crime in Moscow on 19-20 October 1999 and in Tokyo on 7-9 February 2000;
- G8 justice and interior ministers meetings in Milan on 26-27 February 2001 and in Mont-Tremblant, Canada on 13-14 May 2002;
- Justice and home affairs ministers' meetings in Paris on 5 May 2003, in Washington on 10-11 May 2004;
- A meeting of European interior ministers (with European G8 members France, Germany, Italy and the UK, plus Spain) in Florence on 17-18 October 2004;
- A G8 justice and interior ministers' meeting in Sheffield, UK on 16-17 June 2005;
- A G8 home affairs ministers' meeting in London on 9-10 November 2005; and
- A meeting of G8 interior and justice ministers and attorneys-general in Moscow on 15-16 June 2006.

Related expert groups, dealing with various aspects of transnational organized crime and terrorism, are described in the section 'Task Forces, Working Groups and Expert Groups.'

Science Ministers

The 'Carnegie Group' of G7, later G8, science ministers started in 1991. Unlike the other G7 and G8-related ministerial fora mandated by the leaders' summits (with the exception of the G5 finance ministers' forum which preceded the G7 summits themselves), this group met at the initiative of the Carnegie Commission on Science, Technology, and Government, to allow science ministers of G8 countries (plus EU representatives) and their advisors to meet informally to exchange views and experiences on issues of science and technology, and to develop mutual understanding of national perspectives on these issues. These meetings take place twice a year. In Russia's year of G8 presidency, the G8 science ministers met on 3-4 June 2006 in St. Petersburg. For information on a related expert group see below, under 'Task Forces, Working Groups and Expert Groups'.

Trade

G7 trade ministers first met at the 1978 summit. The 1981 Ottawa summit created the Trade Ministers Quadrilateral ('the Quad'), bringing together ministers from the US, Canada, Japan and the EU.[3] Starting in 1982, the Quad generally met three or four times per year. The Quad meeting held just before the 1993 Tokyo summit was especially important because it hammered out an agreement on market access to manufactured goods – an agreement that was a catalyst for the completion of the stalled Uruguay Round of multilateral trade negotiations and the resulting establishment of the World Trade Organization (WTO). The Quad's meeting in Tokyo in May 1999 appears to have been the last one on the ministerial level, but Quad officials met several times in preparation for the WTO's Doha Development Round of multilateral trade negotiations (the WTO Doha ministerial meeting took place on 9-13 November 2001) (Cohn 2002: 259). During the 2005 Hong Kong WTO ministerial a new group emerged: the Five Interested Parties (FIP), consisting of Australia, Brazil, the EU, India and the US. The FIP 'appear … to have formally replaced the Quad … as the decision-making core' (Wilkinson 2006: 2).

Meetings of Sherpas and Personal Representatives for Africa

In addition to the leaders' summit meetings and the various ministerial meetings, the G7 and G8 system has a third component: the leaders' personal representatives, known as sherpas. The sherpas, as personal representatives, actually constitute the oldest element of the G7 and G8 system, even predating the summits themselves as discussed in Chapter 2. They meet several times a year as part of their function to prepare for the forthcoming summit, and they play a special role at the summit itself: in formal sessions, they are the only people in the meeting room apart from the leaders themselves, they serve as note-takers, and they transmit any decisions that the heads make. They also follow up after the summit.

National sherpa teams generally include, in addition to the sherpa, two sous-sherpas. The finance sous-sherpa comes from his or her country's finance ministry and the foreign affairs sous-sherpa from the foreign ministry. Foreign affairs sous-sherpas tend to handle those economic issues that are outside the responsibility of finance ministries (such as trade and environment). Most 'foreign affairs' matters are looked after by the political directors, officials from each foreign ministry. Finance deputies report directly to their finance ministers; although part of the G7 and G8 system with their ministers, they are not on the sherpa teams. There are also 'Finance Deputies' Deputies' who may act as finance sous-sherpas.

---

3 For a detailed study of the Trade Ministers' Quadrilateral see Cohn (2002).

The 2001 Genoa summit created the position of Personal Representatives for Africa (APRs). APRs and their assistants have met regularly ever since. For example, between Sea Island and the end of 2005 (which was the year of the UK's G8 presidency), the following sherpa, APR and related meetings took place:

- Foreign affairs sous-sherpa meeting (last under the US presidency of the G8), Washington, DC, 4-5 October 2004;
- Sherpa meeting, Washington, DC (last under US presidency), 15 October 2004;
- APR meeting (UK presidency), London, 10-11 January 2005;
- G7 finance sous-sherpa meeting, London, 4 February 2005;
- First sherpa meeting under the UK presidency, Lancaster House, London, 18-19 February 2005;
- Second APR meeting, Johannesburg, South Africa, 28 February 2005;
- First foreign affairs sous-sherpa meeting under the UK presidency, Chevening, UK, 10-11 March 2005;
- Second sherpa meeting, Lancaster House, London, 23-24 March 2005;
- Political Directors' meeting, London, 6 April 2005;
- G8 finance sous-sherpa meeting, London, 9 May 2005;
- Second foreign affairs sous-sherpa meeting, Lancaster House, London, 10-12 May 2005;
- Third sherpa meeting, Lancaster House, London, 25-26 May 2005;
- APR meeting, London, 26 May 2005;
- G8 finance sous-sherpa meeting, London, 31 May 2005;
- Political Directors' meeting, London, 6 June 2005;
- Third foreign affairs sous-sherpa meeting, Gleneagles, Scotland, 13-14 June 2005;
- Fourth sherpa meeting, Gleneagles, 14-16 June 2005;
- Fourth foreign affairs sous-sherpa meeting, London, 30 June-1 July 2005;
- Fifth sherpa meeting, London, 1-2 July 2005;
- Fifth foreign affairs sous-sherpa meeting, London, 25-26 October 2005; and
- Sixth sherpa meeting, London, 9-10 November 2005.

Former Canadian sherpa Robert Fowler (2003: 221) describes the sherpas' role thus: 'The Sherpas' task is to act and take decisions in the name of heads of government, and in their interests, in all matters relating to the organization and substantive preparation of these meetings. Sherpas do not act on any kind of *ad referendum* basis but, rather, settle issues as they arise based on an understanding of their principals' views and objectives. It is diplomacy at the sharp end.'

Sherpa activity is not necessarily confined to summit preparation, intensive work at the summits, and technical follow-up after each summit. The G7 leaders' consultation process in September and October 1998 (culminating in the 30 October *G7 Leaders' Statement on the World Economy*) was conducted principally through the sherpa network, beginning with the year's sherpa chairman (the UK sherpa, since 1998 was the UK's year of G8 presidency) contacting his counterparts in other G7 countries each of whom, in turn, consulted his leader. Sherpas have also been actively involved in consultations with representatives of civil society, starting with the 2002 Kananaskis summit (see Chapter 9 for more details of civil society interaction with the G7 and G8). Another interesting example is French sherpa Jacques Attali's initiative in launching the idea of the European Bank for Reconstruction and Development at the final sherpa meeting he chaired in late 1989 (the Bank was established in 1991) (Attali 1995: 315, 317, 318, *passim*).

The sherpas do not release public statements on their invariably confidential meetings, but other writings throw light on the summit preparatory process. Two short writings, François Camé's (1989) 'Comment les sherpas avaient ficelé le sommet' and Estelle Ardouin's (1996) *Sherpas et sommets des 7*, add interesting perspectives.

Most leaders depend on and highly appreciate, the role and work of their sherpas, but the closeness and warmth of the actual relationship varies greatly from leader to leader, even within the same country. Jacques Attali, French President François Mitterrand's sherpa from 1982 to 1990, was perhaps closer to the thinking of his leader than any other sherpa in summit history. His *Verbatim* (Attali 1993-95) is a lively and candid account of his years working with Mitterrand; it includes fascinating insights into the inside story of those summits, notwithstanding the fact that some of his assertions have been disputed, for example by Pierre Favier and Michel Martin-Roland (1990-91) in their *La décennie Mitterrand*.

US President Jimmy Carter thanked his sherpa for his performance at the 1977 London summit: 'You did a superb job on the Summit meeting in London. Your tremendous talents really paid off. Thank you for letting me take the credit for your good work.' (Note, President Carter to [sherpa] Henry Owen, May 17 1977; Jimmy Carter Presidential Library, Box FO-43, WHCF-Subject File.) By contrast, in early 2005, Russian President Vladimir Putin dismissed his sherpa Andrei N. Illarionov for commenting critically and publicly on Russia's various economic, political and environmental decisions. Illarionov remained as an economic advisor to Putin until 27 December 2005, when he resigned, after stepping up his criticism of recent Russian policies and asserting that his country had not only changed its basic economic model but had also 'ceased to be politically free' (Outspoken Silenced 2005: 47; Outspoken Putin... 2005: A1).

Task Forces, Working Groups and Expert Groups

Regular and *ad hoc* task forces, working groups and expert groups are also part of the G7 and G8 system. Over the years, the summits or ministerial meetings have established a number of such groups. What follows is a brief survey of selected groups.[4] The website of the Civil G8 (2006) lists several such groups at <http://en.civilg8.ru/g8_group/1651.php>. John J. Kirton (2005a: 21-22) provides a more complete list of G8 bodies.

At the 2003 Evian summit, the G8 and invited African leaders agreed on a long-term programme to strengthen the partnership between Africa and the developed

---

4   For another listing and description see Sherifis and Astraldi (2001: 192-94).

world. The result was the Africa Partnership Forum, a major venue for the discussion and monitoring of policies, strategy and priorities to support Africa's development. The partners of the forum are senior officials of African countries, the G8, the OECD and other development agencies. At the 2005 Gleneagles summit G8 and African leaders acknowledged the important role of the forum and of the G8's Africa Personal Representatives, and agreed that the forum should be strengthened. The forum has met, twice a year, beginning with 10 November 2003; one meeting each year takes place in Africa. The latest meeting convened on 26-27 October 2006 in Moscow.

The Global Fund to Fight AIDS, Tuberculosis and Malaria was launched by the G8 at the 2001 Genoa summit, building on earlier initiatives including plans by the UN. Associated with the Global Fund is the Partnership Forum which brings together various categories of stakeholders to discuss the Fund's performance and make strategic and other recommendations. The Forum first met in Bangkok in 2004 and again in Durban, South Africa on 1-3 July 2006.

It was announced about a week before the 2006 St. Petersburg summit that the auditing agencies of the G8 countries would monitor the implementation of programmes following that summit. Sergei Stepashin, chairman of the Russian Audit Chamber, was quoted as saying: 'We decided to establish supervision of programs, especially those that involve budget funds, after the summit. This will first of all apply to energy security.' Stepashin reported that this was a Russian initiative, dating back to 2002 (G8 Auditing... 2006).

The Chemical Action Task Force was mandated by the 1990 Houston summit to monitor the movement of chemical precursors used in the manufacturing of illegal drugs. Its membership was broader than the G7 and it functioned until 1991 or 1992.

The 1995 Halifax summit charged the Counter-terrorism Experts' Group (also known as Terrorism Experts' Group) to report to a ministerial-level meeting on counter-terrorism measures and instructed that the appropriate meetings take place prior to the 1996 summit. The 1996 meeting of the ministerial forum endorsed 25 counter-terrorism measures and asked the Experts' Group to follow up on those measures. Meetings of the group took place in Washington, DC on 14-15 April 1997, in Berlin on 15-17 February 1999 and on 17-18 November 1999, and in Rome on 7-9 March 2001.

The Counter-Terrorism Action Group was set up in 2002. It is known to have met as early as on 17 November 2003, in Paris. The St. Petersburg summit refers to this group and its continuing important activities (G8 2006l).

The Senior Experts' Group on Transnational Organized Crime was established by the G8 foreign ministers at the 1995 Halifax summit; after the 1996 Lyon summit it became known as the 'Lyon Group'. It met in Ottawa on 12-14 October 1995; in Paris on 12 April 1996 as the P8 Senior Experts' Group on Transnational Organized Crime (the P8 stands for 'Political 8', the G7 and Russia – a designation used until the G8 was fully established at the 1998 Birmingham summit); in Washington, DC on 16-18 April 1997; then as the G8 Experts' Group on Transnational Crime in London on 2-5 November 1998; and in Tokyo on 22-24 May 2000.[5]

---

5   A discussion of transnational organized crime and the G8 can be found in Amandine Scherrer (2005).

In addition, an expert group on financial crime was set up by the 1997 Denver Summit of the Eight. At the initiative of the Lyon Group, a G8 Conference on Dialogue between the Public Authorities and Private Sector on Security and Trust in Cyberspace was held in Paris on 15-17 May 2000, with senior government officials participating. Another group, the G8 Subgroup on High-tech Crime, was established in January 1997. The subgroup, in turn, has set up a G8 Network of 24-Hour High-tech Points of Contact to fight cybercrime, including bomb threats, fraud, child pornography and other crimes. The network has since grown to include a number of countries in addition to the G8.

The Carnegie Group of G8 science ministers and advisors established an Expert Group on Misuse of International Data Networks to evaluate the misuse of such networks and to suggest recommendations for potential solutions. The expert group held meetings in Bonn from 27 to 29 November 1996, in Paris from 26 to 27 June 1997, and in Rome from 16 to 17 October 1997.

The Digital Opportunities Task Force (DOT force) was created in 2000 on the basis of the Okinawa Charter on Global Information Society, adopted at the Okinawa summit. Its mandate was to examine concrete steps to bridge the international digital divide. It completed its task in 2002. The DOT force is one of the rare examples of successful multi-stakeholder approaches, productively involving governments, the private sector and civil society in the provision of public goods.

Russia, host of the 2006 St. Petersburg summit, proposed the establishment of an expert group on education, with a mandate 'to develop criteria and procedures for evaluating educational outcomes and qualifications'. This would potentially be a multi-stakeholder group, including government, business, and civil society representatives (G8 2006a).

The Financial Action Task Force (FATF) was established by the 1989 Paris Summit of the Arch to co-ordinate efforts to fight drug-related money laundering. The mandate of FATF is to develop and promote national and international policies to combat money laundering and terrorist financing. The mandate is renewed every five years.[6] FATF monitors the progress of its members in the implementation of appropriate measures, reviews money laundering and terrorist financing activities and counter-measures against such activities, and promotes global adoption and implementation of the required counter-measures. It collaborates with other international bodies in fighting money laundering and the financing of terrorism. It considers itself a policy-making body. Its membership has become broader than the G7 and G8. For the first time, China attended the FATF meeting in Paris from 9-11 February 2005 as an observer.

The Financial Stability Forum (FSF) was established by the G7 Finance Ministers and central bank governors in February 1999 to improve the functioning of financial markets and to reduce systemic risk. The FSF has 43 members and meets twice a year. The members are: 26 senior officials of national authorities charged with ensuring financial stability in 11 major international financial centres; six senior officials of four international financial institutions (IFIs); seven senior members

---

6   For an analysis of the work of the Financial Action Task Force see Rudich (2005); see also Gilmore (1992).

of three international supervisory/regulatory bodies; two representatives of central bank expert committees; a representative of the European Central Bank; and the chair of the FSF (Kenen et al. 2004: 20; see also Porter 2000; Culpeper 2003).

Speakers of the parliaments of G8 countries have held annual meetings since the 2002 Kananaskis summit, forming the G8 Parliamentarians' Group. Beyond a few web pages, and scant media and wire service reports, not much public information is available about the meetings of this group.

The first meeting of the G8 Parliamentarians took place in Kingston, Ontario, Canada, on 8 September 2002, focusing on democracy and terrorism. The second meeting, in Paris, on 9 September 2003 had on its agenda parliamentary scrutiny and the funding of political activities. The third occurred in Chicago on 11-12 September 2004, with two main agenda items: ensuring the uninterrupted work of parliaments during terrorist attacks, military actions and other crises; and strengthening institutions that support the activity of parliaments. The fourth meeting, called G-8 International Parliamentarians' Conference on Development in Africa, was quite different from its predecessors; it met in Edinburgh, Scotland on 6-7 June 2005, shortly before the Gleneagles G8 summit. Expanding far beyond parliamentary speakers, its participants included some 80 parliamentarians from the G8 and a number of other countries, as well as representatives of international organizations and civil society groups. It was expanded and timed to influence the summit, representing as it did very large numbers of constituents. The conference produced the Edinburgh Declaration, and some 40 of the assembled parliamentarians signed a personal appeal to Prime Minister Tony Blair and President George W. Bush to take action on Africa at Gleneagles (France 2003; Gryzlov 2004; Inter-European 2005). The latest meeting of speakers of parliaments of G8 countries was held in St. Petersburg, Russia, on 15-17 September 2006, two months after the Russian-hosted G8 summit in the same city.

John J. Kirton (2005d) analyzes the role of parliamentarians vis-à-vis the G8 in a 2005 paper, focusing on commitments made on Africa at the Gleneagles summit. He advocates a stronger role for parliamentarians in pushing the G8, international organizations and their own governments toward full implementation of the promises made at Gleneagles.

At their meeting in London on 8-9 May 1998, the G8 foreign ministers launched a G8 Action Programme on Forests. Another initiative on a similar issue had been the Brazil Pilot Program on Tropical Forests, established in 1990.

The Forum for the Future was established under the 'Broader Middle East' (BMENA) initiative, originated by the 2004 Sea Island summit. It aims to be an important part of the G8 'Partnership for Progress and a Common Future with the Region of the Broader Middle East and North Africa'. This multi-stakeholder forum has met thus far in Rabat, Morocco on 10-11 December 2004 and in Manama, Bahrain on 11-12 November 2005.

The G8 Renewable Energy Task Force was established by the 2000 Okinawa summit, with a mandate to promote the supply, distribution and use of renewable energy in developing countries. The task force, co-chaired by an official of the Italian government and the chairman of the Shell Group of companies, reported to the 2001 Genoa summit (which did nothing to follow it up). The emergence of a more recent entity was indicated in the St. Petersburg summit's declaration on *Global Energy Security*. In this declaration, the G8 leaders instructed their experts to examine and make recommendations on securing energy infrastructure, and to report to the Russian presidency by the end of 2006. They also instructed their experts to facilitate technology transfer, in order to assist developing countries to reduce 'energy poverty' (G8 2006g: paras 42 and 50).

The St. Petersburg summit created a group of experts to enhance international co-operation in the stabilization and reconstruction of post-conflict and other vulnerable states. The group is to examine the feasibility and implementation of measures in peace support operations, conflict prevention, co-ordination, awareness of capabilities, pre-positioning of resources, strengthening regional organizations, and interoperability (G8 2006d).

The Support Implementation Group (SIG) on assistance to Russia was established by the 1993 Tokyo summit. Japan chaired the SIG briefly and temporarily, and was then succeeded by the US as chair of the group, located in Moscow. The group's mandate was troubleshooting rather than administering actual aid programmes (Hodges 1994: 156). SIG facilitated the implementation of G7 assistance to Russia through information sharing and co-ordination among the G7, and through consultation with Russian organizations, international financial institutions and non-G7 countries. SIG had a secretariat whose role was to co-ordinate G7 action concerning taxation aspects of assistance; to serve as an information source on external assistance to Russia; to be a research centre on problems of assistance implementation; and to facilitate the co-ordination of assistance, bringing together Russians and external donors. On 31 December 1997, SIG ceased functioning as a secretariat to G7 embassies on assistance to Russia. SIG was a rare example of the G7 actually creating a bureaucratic structure.

The Global Partnership against Weapons and Materials of Mass Destruction was formed at the initiative of the 2002 Kananaskis summit. (The 1998 Birmingham summit communiqué refers to an earlier group of experts on export controls to prevent proliferation of weapons of mass destruction.) The Partnership's role is acknowledged in the 2004 Sea Island summit's G8 Action Plan on Nonproliferation. Under the Global Partnership there is a Global Partnership Working Group (GPWG). Reference has also been made to a Senior Group on Weapons of Mass Destruction, established in 2004.

Conclusion

The annual summit meetings form the basis of the G7 and G8 but, in addition, an elaborate system of related fora has evolved over the years. Many meetings take place each year to discuss and make decisions on issues of concern to the G7 and G8 and in preparation and follow-up of each annual summit.

The leaders' summits themselves are at the apex of the G7 and G8 system. The second layer consists of the progressively intensifying and increasingly widespread meetings of ministers. A number of these ministerial meetings take place on a regular basis, while others are *ad hoc* affairs, with some *ad hoc* meetings subsequently becoming regular events. The system has a third component consisting of the leaders' personal representatives or sherpas, who meet several times a year as part of their function to prepare for each summit; at the initiative of the 2001 Genoa summit, yet another layer has been added at a similar level: the leaders' Personal Representatives for Africa – in some cases the same individuals act in both capacities: as sherpa and as APR. As well, there is a fourth component: an intricate network of task forces, working groups and expert groups established by the G7 and G8 leaders and by the ministerial fora.

Not everyone sees the G7 institution as a true system. According to W. R. Smyser (1993: 20), '[d]uring the 1980s, the G-7 system split into two separate structures related more in name than in reality ... . The summits became political and representational. Economic coordination moved back to the finance ministers.' Hodges (1994: 142) concurs, stating that '[t]he summit is perceived in the UK as separate from the finance ministers' process'. De Guttry (1994: 72), on the other hand, comments that 'the degree of institutionalization, bureaucratization and formalization of ... [the G7 system's] new structures is ... higher and more sophisticated than that of the summit itself'.

Nicholas Bayne (2005b: 5, 9), too, notes the increased autonomy of some of the ministerial fora. He argues that during the 1980s, with the rising predominance of political over economic issues at the leaders' summits, '[m]uch of the economic agenda returned to the finance ministers'. He points out that although the ministerial fora and the various task forces and official groups 'originated from a summit decision, they steadily detached themselves from the summit and pursued their own agendas, only rarely seeking endorsement or decisions from the heads. ... [As well,] while these subsidiary groups retained the G8 as a nucleus, they were much freer than the summit itself to invite other countries to join them if the theme of their meeting justified it.'

The advent of the new, leaders-only summit format in 1998 again brought the relationship between G7 leaders and finance and foreign ministers closer together at least in the immediate lead-up to the summits, with these ministers meeting just before each summit and preparing their reports to the heads. For example, the pre-summit meeting of G7 finance ministers in Frankfurt on 11-12 June 1999 prepared documents on debt relief for poor countries and on new financial architecture. The Cologne summit, which convened a week later, welcomed those statements, and the G7 meeting there (which still took place then, ahead of the G8 summit), revealed the 'Cologne Debt Initiative' (Bayne 2005: 50). And in the aftermath of the 11 September 2001 terrorist attacks, there has been sustained G8 interest in combating the financing of terrorism, which has remained on the agenda of the finance ministers and the leaders' summits alike.

Sherifis and Astraldi group the G7 and G8 system into 'circuits'. According to their classification, the leaders, the sherpas (with their supporting apparatus) and the foreign and finance ministers comprise the principal circuits. Other circuits are termed 'derived groups'; these include ministerial fora established later (the trade ministers' 'quad', the environment, labour, education, interior and other ministers, as well as the various expert working groups and task forces) (Sherifis and Astraldi 2001: 185-94). Sherifis and Astraldi point out that many of these fora have taken on a more or less independent existence from the leaders' summits.

Appendix

The G7 and G8 System

Annual summits of leaders
1975- (see Table 3.1 for details of G7 and G8 summits)

Special summits of leaders
New York 1985 (G7 minus France), Moscow 1996 (G8)

Ministerial meetings (regular)
G8 development ministers   Annual or less frequent, 2002-

G8 education ministers   1999, 2006

G7 and G8 employment or labour ministers   1994; usually annual, 1996-

G8 energy ministers   1998, 2002, 2005, 2006

G7 and G8 environment ministers   1992; annual, 1994-

G5 finance ministers   1973-1987 (irregular; see Chapter 2 for detailed list)

G7 and G8 finance ministers and central bank governors   Annual (G7) on summit site 1975-1997; stand-alone meetings 4 or more times a year (usually G7), 1987-; annual pre-summit meeting (G7 or G8), 1998- (includes EU, 1998-)

G7 and G8 foreign ministers   Annual (G7) on summit site 1975-1997; once or more yearly as stand-alone meeting (G7 or G8), 1984-; annual pre-summit meeting (G8), 1998-

Global Information Society   1995 (G7); 1996 (broader than G7 and G8); related meetings (broader than G7 and G8); for example, on small and medium-sized enterprises, irregular, 1997-

G7 and G8 health ministers (with Mexico and EU)   Annual, 2001-

G7 and G8 interior, justice and other ministers (on terrorism, organized transnational crime, etc.)   Usually annual or more frequent, 1995-

G7 and G8 science ministers (Carnegie Group)   Twice a year, 1991-

Trade ministers' quadrilateral (Canada, EU, Japan, US)   3 or 4 times a year, 1978-1999?

Ministerial meetings (ad hoc)
Examples: Aid to Russia (finance and foreign ministers): 1993; Economic aid to
　　Ukraine: 1994

Sherpa meetings (G7 and G8)
4-5 times a year

Personal Representatives for Africa (APR) meetings (G8)
Several times a year, 2001-

Task Forces, Working Groups and Expert Groups (selective list)
Africa Partnership Forum (broader than G8): 2003-
Chemical Action Task Force (broader than G7): 1990-1992?
Counter-Terrorism Action Group: 2002-
Counter-Terrorism Experts' Group: 1995-
Digital Opportunities Task Force (DOT force): 2000-2002 (broader than G8)
Expert Group on Financial Crime: 1997-(?) and its G8 Network of 24-Hour High-
　　tech Points of Contact (broader than G8)
Expert Group on Misuse of International Data Networks: 1996-1997
Financial Action Task Force (FATF): 1989- (broader than G8)
Financial Stability Forum: 1999- (broader than G8)
Forum for the Future (under the 'Broader Middle East' initiative): 2004-
G8 Parliamentarians' Group: 2002-
G8 Subgroup on High-tech Crime: 1997-
G8 Renewable Energy Task Force: 2000-2001
Global Partnership against Weapons and Materials of Mass Destruction: 2002-; and
　　its Global Partnership Working Group
Group of Experts to Enhance International Co-operation in the Stabilization and
　　Reconstruction of Post-Conflict and Other Vulnerable States: 2006-
Senior Experts' Group on Transnational Organized Crime: 1995- (Lyon Group,
　　1996-)
Senior Group on Weapons of Mass Destruction: 2004-
Support Implementation Group (on assistance to Russia): 1993-1997

Funds, Programmes and Other Initiatives (selective list)
Action Programme on Forests: 1998-(?)
Brazil Pilot Program on Tropical Forests: 1990-(?)
G8 Action Plan on Nonproliferation: 2004-
G8 Africa Action Plan: 2002-
Gleneagles Plan of Action: Climate Change, Clean Energy and Sustainable
　　Development: 2005-; and the related Dialogue on Climate Change, Energy and
　　Sustainable Development (broader than G8): 2005-
Global Fund to Fight AIDS, Tuberculosis and Malaria (broader than G8): 2001-
St. Petersburg Plan of Action on Global Energy Security: 2006-

Based on research by Peter Hajnal, John Kirton and other members of the G8 Research Group

References

Note on internet addresses (URLs): Websites tend to appear, change or disappear, often without warning. Addresses cited in this source list were accurate and active at the time of writing (June 2006) unless otherwise noted.

Ardouin, Estelle (1996), *Sherpas et sommets des 7* [Sherpas and Summits of the 7], Institut d'Etudes Politiques, Lyon.

Attali, Jacques (1993-95), *Verbatim*, Fayard, Paris. [Tome 1: Chronique des années 1981-1986; Tome 2: Chronique des années 1986-1988; Tome 3: Chronique des années 1988-1991].

Baker, Andrew (2006), *The Group of Seven: Finance Ministries, Central Banks and Global Financial Governance*, Routledge/Warwick Studies in Globalisation, 10, Routledge, London; New York.

Bayne, Nicholas (2005b), *Staying Together: The G8 Summit Confronts the 21st Century*, Ashgate, Aldershot, UK.

Camé, François (1989), 'Comment les sherpas avaient ficelé le sommet [How the Sherpas Had Wrapped Up the Summit]', *Libération*, 8-15, 17 juillet.

Clinton, Bill (2005), *My Life*, Vintage, New York. (Originally published by Knopf in 2004.)

Cohn, Theodore H. (2002), *Governing Global Trade: International Institutions in Conflict and Convergence*, The G8 and Global Governance Series, Ashgate, Aldershot, UK.

Culpeper, Roy (2003), 'Systemic Reform at a Standstill: A Flock of "Gs" in Search of Global Financial Stability', in *Critical Issues in International Financial Reform*, 203-36, Albert Berry and Gustavo Indart (eds), Transaction Publishers, New Brunswick, N.J.; London.

Favier, Pierre and Michel Martin-Roland (1990-91), *La décennie Mitterrand*, 3 vols, Seuil, Paris.

Fowler, Robert (2003), 'Canadian Leadership and the Kananaskis G-8 Summit: Towards a Less Self-centred Foreign Policy', in *Coping with the American Colossus: Canada among Nations 2003*, 219-41, David Carment et al. (eds), Oxford University Press, Don Mills, Ontario.

France, Assemblée Nationale, Douzième Legislature (2003), *Second Meeting of the Parliamentary Presidents of the G8 Countries*, 9 September, www. assembleenationale.fr/12/rap-dian/dian018-2004-english.asp#P58_1649.

G7 (1995), *Halifax Summit Communiqué*, Halifax, June 16, in United States, Department of State, Bureau of Public Affairs, *US Department of State Dispatch* 6:4, 6, July, www.g8.utoronto.ca/summit/1995halifax/communique/growth.html and www.g8.utoronto.ca/summit/1995halifax/communique/challenge.html.

G7 Finance Ministers (2005), *Statement by G7 Finance Ministers on Assisting Countries Devastated by the Indian Ocean Tsunami*, www.g8.utoronto.ca/finance/fm050107.htm.

G8 (2006a), *Chair's Summary*, http://en.g8russia.ru/docs/25.html and www. g8.utoronto.ca/summit/2006stpetersburg/summary.html.

G8 (2006d), *G8 Declaration on Cooperation and Future Action in Stabilization and Reconstruction*, http://en.g8russia.ru/docs/19.html and www.g8.utoronto.ca/summit/2006stpetersburg/stabilization.html.

G8 (2006e), *G8 Statement on Strengthening the UN's Counter-Terrorism Program*, http://en.g8russia.ru/docs/18.html and www.g8.utoronto.ca/summit/2006stpetersburg/counterterrorism-un.html.

G8 (2006g), *Global Energy Security*, http://en.g8russia.ru/docs/11.html and www.g8.utoronto.ca/summit/2006stpetersburg/energy.html.

G8 (2006l), *Report on the G8 Global Partnership*, http://en.g8russia.ru/docs/22.html and www.g8.utoronto.ca/summit/2006stpetersburg/gp_report.html.

'G8 Auditing Agencies to Monitor Implementation of Programs' (2006), http://en.g8russia.ru/news/20060707/1169602.html and www.ach.gov.ru/psp/in/12.php.

'G8 to Step Up Pressure on India and Pakistan' (1998), *Financial Times*, 3, June 13-14.

'German Ambassador for Russia's Full Membership of G8 Financial Forum' (2006), 5 July http://en.g8russia.ru/news/20060705/1167611.html.

Gilmore, William C. (ed.) (1992), *International Efforts to Combat Money Laundering*, Cambridge International Documents Series, 4, Grotius Publications in association with the Commonwealth Secretariat, Cambridge.

'Gryzlov to Meet Parliamentarians in Chicago' (2004), *RIA Novosti* [wire service report], 10 September.

Guttry, Andrea de (1994), 'The Institutional Configuration of the G-7 in the New International Scenario', in *The Future of the G-7 Summits*, 67-80, (*The International Spectator* 29:2; April/June, Special Issue).

Hodges, Michael R. (1994), 'More Efficiency, Less Dignity: British Perspectives on the Future Role and Working of the G-7', in *The Future of the G-7 Summits*, 141-159, (*The International Spectator* 29:2, April/June, Special Issue).

Inter-European Parliamentary Forum on Population and Development (2005), *Outcome of the G-8 International Parliamentarians' Conference on Development in Africa.* www.iepfpd.org.

Kenen, Peter B. et al. (2004), *International Economic and Financial Cooperation: New Issues, New Actors, New Responses*, Centre for Economic Policy Research, London.

Kirton, John J. (2005a), 'From Collective Security to Concert: The UN, G8 and Global Security Governance', paper prepared for the conference 'Security Overspill: Between Economic Integration and Social Exclusion', Centre Études Internationales et Mondialisation, Université de Québec à Montréal, Montreal, Appendix A, 27-28 October.

Kirton, John J. (2005d), 'A Promising Push: Complying with the Gleneagles G8 Africa Commitments and Parliamentarians' Role', Paper prepared for the conference 'Partnership Beyond 2005: The Role of Parliamentarians in Implementing NEPAD Commitments', 19-22 October, London. www.g8.utoronto.ca/scholar/kirton2005/kirton_london2005.pdf.

'Outspoken Putin Aide Quits, Scolding Kremlin' (2005), *The New York Times*, A1, 28 December.

'The Outspoken Silenced' (2005), *The Economist*, 374:8408, 47, 8 January.

Porter, Tony (2000), 'The G-7, the Financial Stability Forum, the G-20, and the Politics of International Financial Regulation', paper prepared for the International Studies Association Annual Convention, Los Angeles, March 15, www.g8.utoronto.ca/g20/g20porter/index.html.

Rudich, Denisse V. (2005), 'Performing the Twelve Labors: The G8's Role in the Fight against Money Laundering', *G8 Governance*, 12, www.g8.utoronto.ca/governance/rudich_g8g.pdf.

'Scares Ahead: Can the World Economy Sustain its Stunning Pace of Growth?' (2004), *The Economist*, 373:8395, 11, 2 October.

Scherrer, Amandine (2005), 'Le G8 face au crime organisé' [G8 and organized crime], *G8 Governance*, 11, www.g8.utoronto.ca/governance/scherrer_g8g.pdf.

Sherifis, Rossella Franchini and Valerio Astraldi (2001), *Il G7/G8 da Rambouillet a Genova = The G7/G8 from Rambouillet to Genoa*, FrancoAngeli, Milano.

Smyser, W.R. (1993), 'Goodbye, G-7', *The Washington Quarterly*, 16:1, 15-28.

Wilkinson, Rorden (2006), 'Ghost of a Chance: ACUNS in Hong Kong', *ACUNS* [Academic Council on the United Nations System] *Informational Memorandum*, 65.

Chapter 7

G7 and G8 Relations
with International Organizations

This chapter outlines the nature and evolution of the relationship of international organizations with the G7 and G8. For a related discussion of the role of non-member countries and potential members see also Chapters 4 and 12. For a more detailed treatment of international organizations versus the G7 and G8, covering the years 1975-1998, see Hajnal (1999). Chapter 8 of the present work looks at connections of the G7 and G8 with the business sector, and Chapter 9 analyzes the role of non-profit civil society.

The G7 and G8 system does not and could not exist in isolation from other international events and organizations. The summits have made it clear from their beginning that 'the G7 intends to make use of existing [international organizations] to achieve certain objectives, but absolutely does not intend to replace them' (Guttry 1994: 73). Initially, the G7 was cautious toward global international governmental organizations (IGOs), but after 1989 it began to urge United Nations (UN) reform. In the international financial institutions (IFIs), in which the G7 carried more weight, the G7 influenced important decisions and prescribed relations among the IFIs' member states. And G7 (later G8) relations with the Organisation for Economic Co-operation and Development (OECD) were very close from the beginning of summitry (Guttry 1994: 74).

The significant influence of the G7 (and to a lesser extent the G8) on the IFIs is not surprising when one considers that the G8 collectively wields about one half of all votes in the IMF and the World Bank, as illustrated by Table 7.1. The table also includes, for comparison, data on the five major developing countries that have become regular partners of the G8 with the Gleneagles summit: Brazil, China, India, Mexico and South Africa.

Subsequently, the G7 and G8 took an increasingly more activist role in their relations with IGOs, particularly with IFIs. Summit documents often refer to the activities of the IMF, the OECD, the GATT and its successor the World Trade Organization (WTO), the United Nations Environment Programme (UNEP), and other international institutions. Conversely, traditional international organizations have produced official publications instigated by the summit.

The 1995 Halifax summit went further than earlier summits in proposing a number of concrete steps in the review and reform of international institutions. These proposals ranged from delineating the respective roles of the UN and the Bretton Woods institutions and clarifying the mandates of some UN agencies, through urging IGOs to focus their programmes more sharply, eliminate duplication and improve their working methods, to supporting the establishment of new institutions.

Table 7.1   G8 Voting Power in the IMF and the World Bank as of 2005

Country	% of IMF Votes	% of World Bank Votes
United States	17.08	16.39
Japan	6.13	7.86
Germany	5.99	4.49
France	4.95	4.30
United Kingdom	4.95	4.30
Italy	4.18*	2.78
Canada	3.71*	2.78
Russia	2.74	2.78
G8 TOTAL	**49.73**	**45.68**
China	2.94#	2.78
India	2.39*	2.78
Brazil	2.46*	2.07
Mexico	**#	1.18
South Africa	**	0.85

\#   *On 18 September 2006 the IMF Board of Governors approved an ad hoc quota increase for China (as well as Korea, Mexico and Turkey).*
*   *Includes a small number of votes cast on behalf of other countries.*
**   *Data for South Africa and Mexico, both part of the 'Gleneagles G8 + 5' along with China, India and Brazil, are not reported in a comparable fashion in the IMF source table. Compiled by Peter I. Hajnal (based on IMF 2005; World Bank 2005; IMF 2006b).*

In Halifax the leaders endorsed enhanced consultations of G7 ministers with the IMF. (G7 1995: para 13; US 1995: 6). Louis W. Pauly (1997: 129-30) notes that:

> in recent years the [IMF] managing director has been invited to provide finance ministers at G-7 meetings with a summary of the Fund's current views on the condition of the international system and the requirements for stability. Over time, the ministers and their deputies have relied on the senior staff of the Fund for an increasing amount of technical assistance, particularly related to the use of comparable economic indicators to monitor and evaluate policy trends across the G-7.

Bayne (1995: 501-502, 508) comments that in undertaking the review of Bretton Woods institutions and other IGOs '[f]or the first time, the leaders decided to work not from outside international institutions but from inside them'.

At the 1996 Lyon summit, the administrative heads of four major international organizations (the Secretary-General of the UN, the Managing Director of the IMF, the President of the World Bank and the Director General of the WTO) had a working session and lunch with the summit leaders. The summit welcomed the progress in the implementation of the Halifax proposals, in particular the enhanced surveillance capacities of the IMF, the establishment of standards for the provision of economic and financial information to the markets, and the creation of an emergency financing mechanism. The G7 leaders at Lyon gave direct guidance to IGOs: '[T]he IMF should remain an institution based on quotas providing the [necessary] resources ... The IMF should continue to reflect on the role of Special Drawing Rights within the international monetary system ... We strongly urge the OECD to vigorously pursue its work ... aimed at establishing a multilateral approach' in limiting tax competition between States (G7 1996b: para 12, 13, 16).

On UN reform, the Lyon communiqué stated categorically that the 'UN must clarify its role and comparative advantages ... must enhance the efficiency of its Secretariat and operational framework ... [and must] ensure genuine coordination' (G7 1996b). The Lyon *Chairman's Statement*, issued on behalf of the P8 and thus reflecting the views of the G7 and Russia, includes, as a Halifax summit follow-up, a review of UN reforms in the economic and social fields (G7 1996a).

At the Denver Summit of the Eight, the leaders noted progress in economic and social fields since Lyon, welcomed UN Secretary-General Kofi Annan's reform proposals, and expressed continuing commitment to work with all UN members to accomplish these and other proposed UN reforms. The Denver communiqué states that 'financial reform should proceed together with necessary reform measures in other areas ... the UN system must be placed on a firm financial footing ... [and affirms that] robust oversight mechanisms and sound personnel policies are essential for success' and emphasizes the need for the UN to streamline its subsidiary bodies and improve its working relationship with international financial institutions and the WTO. The communiqué calls for 'a thorough and urgent review of the UN's funds and programs, as well as a system-wide review of the roles and mandates of specialized agencies and commissions' (G7 1997a).

In their statement issued at the G7 rather than G8 level, the leaders at Denver reaffirmed their support for reform of the international financial institutions, and welcomed the IMF's progress in strengthening surveillance and improving transparency, as well as the World Bank's 'Strategic Compact'. They called for amending the IMF Articles of Agreement to allow for capital account liberalizations, and urged 'the IMF and the World Bank to finalize governance policies, consisting of principles and guidelines on best governance practices' (G7 1997b).

Just before the 1998 Birmingham summit, the IMF Managing Director, the World Bank President and the WTO Director-General participated in the pre-summit joint meeting of finance and foreign ministers on 8-9 May 1998 in London. The Birmingham *G7 Chairman's Statement* endorses the report of the G7 Finance Ministers, *Strengthening the Architecture of the Global Financial System*. This report deals with proposed further reforms of the IMF, the World Bank, the Bank for International Settlements (BIS) and other international financial institutions.

In the *G8 Birmingham Summit Communiqué*, the G8 leaders expressed confidence in the ability of IMF programmes to restore stability in countries affected by the financial crisis in Asia, but they also recognized the impact of the crisis on the poorest and most vulnerable sectors of society, and pointed to the need to protect these groups with the support of the World Bank, the Asian Development Bank and bilateral donors. They reaffirmed their commitment to trade and investment liberalization within the multilateral framework of the WTO; expressed strong support for widening the WTO's membership and encouraged greater transparency in the WTO and in other international organizations. The leaders endorsed the Heavily Indebted Poor Countries (HIPC) initiative on debt relief; supported the WHO initiative to 'Roll Back Malaria' by 2010 as well as the continuing efforts to fight AIDS; stated their willingness to share their principles and experiences with other members of the ILO, OECD and the international financial institutions in matters of growth, employability and inclusion; and agreed to wide-ranging action on transnational organized crime (G8 1998a).

Later in his G8 presidency year, in September 1998, Prime Minister Tony Blair called for major reforms of the Bretton Woods institutions, including better supervision and regulation of the world's financial system, greater transparency and accountability of the World Bank and the IMF and possibly even a partial merger of those two institutions. In criticizing the Bretton Woods institutions he stated: 'The existing system has not served us terribly well' in the current financial crisis (Peston 1998: 1). Around the same time, President Clinton presented his initiative to step up World Bank aid to Asia, create an IMF emergency fund to combat economic contagion in Latin America, to establish an emergency line of credit and to adopt other robust international measures to develop a new international financial architecture (Sanger 1998: A1, A16).

During the annual meetings of the World Bank and the IMF held in Washington on 6-8 October 1998 (plus related meetings that began 29 September) the financial crisis dominated the agenda. The flurry of meetings engaged not only the World Bank's Development Committee, the IMF Interim Committee and other bodies of the two institutions but other groups as well, including a meeting on 3 October of the G7 finance ministers, a meeting of the Group of 10 and a meeting of the Intergovernmental Group of Twenty-Four on International Monetary Affairs. Although the meetings addressed many aspects of the financial crisis, the G7 was dissatisfied with the way the results reflected or failed to reflect G7 understandings that had already been reached. Hence the two statements issued on 30 October by the G7: *Declaration of G7 Finance Ministers and Central Bank Governors*, and *G7 Leaders' Statement on the World Economy* (G7 1998a; G7 1998c). The IMF and the World Bank, both much criticized in the media in September 1998 for their handling (some said mishandling) of the financial crisis, were given detailed guidelines by the G7.

The finance ministers and central bank governors took steps to address the situation at hand and specified detailed reforms of the international financial system in general and the international financial institutions in particular. The G7 set these specific goals: to increase the transparency and openness of the international financial system; identify and disseminate international principles, standards and codes of best practice; strengthen incentives to meet these international standards; and strengthen official assistance to help developing countries reinforce their economic and financial infrastructures. The ministers and governors also set out longer-term goals for the IMF: to monitor the implementation of the new codes and standards; to publish systematically and in a timely fashion a transparency report showing the results of its surveillance of member countries' compliance with transparency and disclosure codes and standards; and to develop a formal mechanism for systematic evaluation, with external input, of the effectiveness of its operations, programmes, policies and procedures. The ministers and governors committed themselves to monitor progress and to meet as necessary to develop further measures.

The 30 October 1998 statement of the G7 heads of state and government not only endorsed the work of their finance ministers but also welcomed such specific developments as: the agreement to increase IMF quotas and 'New Arrangements to

Borrow', yielding additional IMF resources of US$90 billion; and the reduction of interest rates in the US, Japan, Canada, the UK, Italy and other countries; and the progress made in several Asian countries for economic recovery. Among the most important direct results of G7 initiatives was the agreement to establish an IMF precautionary line of credit to be made available to countries that follow strong IMF-approved policies, so that those countries can avoid financial crises; and the agreement to establish a new World Bank emergency facility to provide support to the most vulnerable groups in times of crisis. The leaders also made specific reference to their willingness to support Brazil, in co-operation with the broader international community. The *Financial Times* commented editorially that the set of the 30 October G7 initiatives 'was, in effect, an agenda to avert future financial crises' and that the longer-term proposals were intended to tackle the problems of uneven financial risk-taking, and of the 'obscurity of corporate accounting and national financial statistics in some emerging countries'. An early measure of the potential success of these recent G7 initiatives was the fact that 'shares in New York and London rose again in response to the G7 announcement' (The G7... 1998: 6).

As an indication of the seriousness of G7 commitments concerning the IMF, the representatives of the seven countries in the IMF Executive Board sent a memorandum, also dated 30 October 1998, to the IMF Managing Director and to members of the Executive Board, entitled 'Work Program on Strengthening the Architecture of the International Monetary System'. The memorandum proposes a number of priority reforms in light of the G7 leaders' and finance ministers' statements. These reforms embrace standards and codes of good practice, transparency and accountability, and terms and conditions of IMF loans (IMF 1998).

The 1999 Cologne summit asked the OECD to prepare a study on biotechnology and other aspects of food safety for the 2000 Okinawa summit. In response, several reports were duly produced; for example, the *Report of the Task Force for the Safety of Novel Foods and Feeds* (OECD 2000a); and the *Report of the Working Group on Harmonization of Regulatory Oversight in Biotechnology* (OECD 2000b).

The 2000 Okinawa summit's communiqué states: 'We must engage in a new partnership with non-G8 countries, particularly developing countries, international organisations and civil society, including the private sector and non-governmental organisations (NGOs). This partnership will bring the opportunities of the new century within reach of all' (G8 2000a: para 4). This statement explicitly recognizes the need for multistakeholder partnerships; in that spirit, this summit launched such an initiative, the DOT Force. The leaders at Okinawa also continued to call for reform of the IMF and the multilateral development banks, and acknowledged the work of the IMF and the World Bank on poverty reduction and the HIPC initiative. The communiqué commented on OECD's progress on development aid, on food safety, and the Anti-Bribery Convention arrived at under its aegis. The leaders expressed support for the UN and the WHO in the fight against HIV/AIDS.

The 2001 Genoa summit revisited some of these issues. It also expressed support for the aims of the UN Millennium Development Goals. The leaders pledged to provide bilateral assistance on developing standards, legislation and customs systems required for membership in the WTO. They called on the WTO and the World Intellectual Property Organization (WIPO) to promote compliance by the poorest developing countries with international rules governing intellectual property rights; and they welcomed the establishment of the joint FAO/WHO Global Forum of Food Safety Regulators. After a hiatus at Okinawa, the heads of four international organizations were present again in Genoa: Kofi Annan of the UN, James Wolfensohn of the World Bank, Renato Ruggiero of the WTO, and Gro Harlem Brundtland of the WHO. On 20 July, the first day of the summit, UN Secretary-General Kofi Annan addressed the leaders in a statement on the global fight against AIDS, thanking the G8 countries for their support.

Kofi Annan was also present (without his counterparts from other IGOs) at the 2002 Kananaskis summit. The *Chair's Summary* reports on the leaders' meeting with him, along with the presidents of Algeria, Nigeria, Senegal and South Africa, 'to discuss the challenges faced by Africa and the G8's response to the *New Partnership for Africa's Development* (NEPAD)'. The summit's response was the G8 Africa Action Plan. In addition, the leaders pledged additional funding for the enhanced HIPC initiative, and expressed support for WTO's Doha trade negotiations.

In 2003, the leaders at the Evian summit invited the heads of the UN, IMF, World Bank and WTO. The summit revisited the Doha trade round, urged the IMF to step up its surveillance activities, agreed to strengthen the Global Fund on HIV/AIDS, Malaria and Tuberculosis (Global Fund), and reiterated support for the Millennium Development Goals and for the HIPC initiative. The leaders launched an action plan on capacity building against terrorism and created a Counter-Terrorism Action Group to support the UN Counter-Terrorism Committee. They welcomed UN Security Council resolution 1483 on Iraq.

The 2004 Sea Island summit proceeded without invited IGO heads. The leaders welcomed UN Security Council resolution 1546 on Iraq. They referred to the G8 Action Plan on Nonproliferation and the G8 Global Partnership against the Spread of Weapons and Materials of Mass Destruction, which, among other measures, calls for strengthening the International Atomic Energy Agency (IAEA). Within the framework of the summit's 'Broader Middle East Initiative', they called on the Quartet (UN, European Union [EU], US and Russia) to step up efforts to implement the Middle East road map. And, once again, the summit revisited Doha.

The 2005 Gleneagles summit acknowledged the essential role of international organizations as partners and collaborating or implementing institutions. The administrative heads of the African Union (AU), the International Energy Agency (IEA), the IMF, the UN, the World Bank and the WTO took part, along with invited leaders of five major countries, in some of the summit's deliberations. The Africa communiqué relies heavily on the UN, the AU, the World Bank, the IMF and regional development banks. The climate change communiqué calls upon the World Bank and the IEA in a similar manner. The document on reducing Intellectual Property Rights (IPR) piracy promises to work with the WIPO, Interpol, the WTO and the World Customs Organization. The progress report on the Secure and Facilitated International Travel Initiative cites the International Civil Aviation Organization as essential to the project. It is clear that the G8 needs a broader international and institutional context to achieve the goals of its initiatives. In another summit first, the G8 leaders and the AU issued another joint statement on the Sudan. Blair's final press conference at the end of the Gleneagles summit refers to OECD as more than just a consulting body: on the increased aid figures committed by the G8, 'the reason that we put the OECD imprimatur on it was precisely in order to make it clear that this is not just our estimate' (UK 2005).

The Gleneagles summit passed on many unresolved issues to major meetings under the aegis of IGOs during the second half of 2005: among others, the UN's Millennium Development Goals review summit on 14-16 September 2005, the World Bank/IMF Executive Board meeting on 24-26 September, the Dialogue on Climate Change, Clean Energy and Sustainable Development in London, 1 November, the meeting of states parties to the Kyoto Protocol in Montreal, 28 November-9 December, and the WTO Ministerial meeting in Hong Kong, 13-18 December. Some of these conferences failed to achieve meaningful advances on the issues left pending by Gleneagles.

The millennium review summit produced a watered-down outcome document that suffered from the prevailing geopolitical context; nevertheless, there were some advances, particularly in the areas of the Canadian-championed Responsibility to Protect, the establishment of the Peacebuilding Commission, and the allocation of significant additional resources for the Office of the Human Rights Commissioner (Evans 2005: A19; see also The Lost UN … 2005). On a more positive note, the World Bank and the IMF endorsed the G8 initiative of forgiveness of debt owed by the poorest countries to multilateral financial institutions. And the results of the Hong Kong WTO meeting were, as had been widely predicted, meager, although the door remained open to further progress, particularly in the agreement to eliminate agricultural export subsidies by 2013 and the offer of technical assistance for developing country exports. (By August 2005 it was clear that the Doha round had collapsed.)

The following heads of international organizations participated in the 2006 St. Petersburg summit: Nursultan Nazarbaev, Chairman of the Commonwealth of Independent States (CIS); Denis Sassou-Nguesso, Chairman of the AU; Kofi Annan, Secretary-General of the UN; Mohamed Elbaradei, Director-General of the IAEA; Koichiro Matsuura, Director-General of Unesco; Claude Mandil, Executive Director of the IEA; Paul Wolfowitz, President of the World Bank; Pascal Lamy, Director-General of the WTO; and Anders Nordström, Acting Director-General of the WHO.

The St. Petersburg *Chair's Summary* reported on the G8's discussion with the invited heads of the AU, CIS, IEA, IAEA, UN, Unesco, the World Bank, the WHO and the WTO on the summit's priority themes. On infectious diseases, it emphasized the role of the WHO. On trade, it referred to the WTO. On the proliferation of weapons of mass destruction, on counter-terrorism and on post-conflict stabilization, it expressed support for the UN Security Council and IAEA. On the Nagorno-Karabakh situation it supported the work of the OSCE.

Other IGOs mentioned in St. Petersburg documents include material on a number of IGOs, international conferences and other intergovernmental groups, and international agreements; for example, the Conference on Disarmament, the WTO, WIPO, Interpol, the World Customs Organization, the Council of Europe, ICAO, IMO, the AU, the IAEA, the EU, the Quartet, the Chemical Weapons Convention and, of course, the UN. In addition, the summit issued a separate document devoted to the UN: the *G8 Statement on Strengthening the UN's Counter-Terrorism Program*. Many summit documents refer to OECD and its work; for example, *Combating IPR Piracy and Counterfeiting*. Putin's end-of-summit press statement reaffirms the essential role of IGOs.

OECD's website is a good example of an IGO giving space to relations with the G8. The site has a page dedicated to its connection with the G8, at <www.oecd. org/g8>. It affirms that '[t]he G8 and OECD work very closely together. Top OECD officials meet periodically with the [sherpas and sous-sherpas] of the G8 leaders ... to discuss current and future OECD work related to G8 issues. It has also become a tradition that the OECD holds its annual ... [Council of Ministers'] meeting four to six weeks before the Summit meeting to promote the best possible co-ordination.' For the St. Petersburg summit, OECD and the related IEA co-operated closely with the Russian presidency on all major agenda items.

Conclusion

The G7 and G8 have always recognized the essential role of international organizations, and have continually widened and deepened their links with them. There has been increasing IGO participation in and around the summits themselves, although the same organizations are not consistently involved in each summit. Issues dealt with by the G7 and G8 are routinely remitted to IGOs for action within the competence of those bodies.

References

Note on internet addresses (URLs): Websites tend to appear, change or disappear, often without warning. Addresses cited in this source list were accurate and active at the time of writing (August 2006) unless otherwise noted.

Bayne, Nicholas (1995), 'The G7 Summit and the Reform of Global Institutions', *Government and Opposition*, 30:4, 492-509, Autumn.

Evans, Gareth (2005), 'UN Missed the Chance of a Lifetime', *The Globe and Mail*, 11 October, A19.

G7 (1995), *Halifax Summit Communiqué*, Halifax, June 16, in United States, Department of State, Bureau of Public Affairs, *US Department of State Dispatch* 6:4, 6, July, www.g8.utoronto.ca/summit/1995halifax/communique/growth.html and www.g8.utoronto.ca/summit/1995halifax/communique/challenge.html.

G7 (1996a), *Chairman's Statement*, Lyon, 29 June, www.g8.utoronto.ca/summit/ 1996lyon/chair.html.

G7 (1996b), *Economic Communiqué*, Lyon, 28 June, www.g8.utoronto.ca/summit/ 1996lyon/communique.html.

G7 (1997a), *Communiqué*, Denver, 22 June, www.g8.utoronto.ca/summit/ 1997denver/g8final.htm.

G7 (1997b), *Confronting Global Economic and Financial Challenges: Denver Summit Statement by Seven*, Denver, 21 June, www.g8.utoronto.ca/summit/1997denver/confront.htm.

G7 (1998a), *Declaration of G7 Finance Ministers and Central Bank Governors*, 30 October, www.g8.utoronto.ca/finance/fm103098.htm.

G7 (1998b), *G7 Chairman's Statement*, Birmingham, www.g8.utoronto.ca/summit/1998birmingham/chair.htm.

G7 (1998c), *G7 Leaders' Statement on the World Economy*, 30 October, www.g8.utoronto.ca/finance/g7_103098.html.

G8 (1998a), *G8 Birmingham Summit Communiqué*, Birmingham, www.g8.utoronto.ca/summit/1998birmingham/finalcom.htm.

G8 (2000a), *G8 Communiqué Okinawa*, 23 July, www.g8.utoronto.ca/summit/2000okinawa/finalcom.htm.

'The G7 Lays Its Plans' (1998), *Financial Times*, 31 October/1 November, 6.

Guttry, Andrea de (1994), 'The Institutional Configuration of the G-7 in the New International Scenario', in *The Future of the G-7 Summits*, 67-80, (*The International Spectator* 29:2; April/June, Special Issue).

Hajnal, Peter I. (1999), *The G7/G8 System: Evolution, Role and Documentation*, Ashgate, Aldershot, UK.

International Monetary Fund (1998), 'Work Program on Strengthening the Architecture of the International Monetary System', (Office Memorandum), 30 October, www.imf.org/external/np/g7/103098ed.htm.

International Monetary Fund (2005), *Annual Report of the Executive Board for the Financial Year Ended April 30, 2005*, IMF, www.imf.org/external/pubs/ft/ar/2005/eng/index.htm.

International Monetary Fund (2006b), *IMF Board of Governors Approves Quota and Related Governance Reforms*, Press Release 06/205, 18 September.

'The Lost U.N. Summit Meeting' (2005), *The New York Times*, editorial, 14 September.

Organisation for Economic Co-operation and Development (2000a), *Report of the Task Force for the Safety of Novel Foods and Feeds*, OECD Council document C(2000)86/ADD1, 17 May.

Organisation for Economic Co-operation and Development (2000b), *Report of the Working Group on Harmonization of Regulatory Oversight in Biotechnology*, OECD Council document C(2000)86/ADD2, 25 May.

Pauly, Louis W. (1997), *Who Elected the Bankers? Surveillance and Control in the World Economy*, Cornell University Press, Ithaca, NY; London.

Peston, Robert (1998), 'Blair To Urge Full Overhaul of IMF and WB', *Financial Times*, 21 September, 1.

Sanger, David E. (1998), 'Clinton Presents Strategy To Quell Economic Threat', *The New York Times*, 15 September, A1, A16.

United Kingdom, Prime Minister (2005a), *British Prime Minister Tony Blair Reflects On 'Significant Progress' Of G8 Summit*, Press Conference at the Conclusion of the Gleneagles Summit, 8 July, www.g8.gov.uk/servlet/Front?pagename=OpenMarket/Xcelerate/ShowPage&c=Page&cid=1078995903270&a=KArticle&aid=1119520262754.

United States, Department of State, Bureau of Public Affairs (1995), *US Department of State Dispatch* 6, Supplement No. 4, July.

World Bank (2005), *The World Bank Annual Report*, World Bank, Washington, DC.

Chapter 8

G7 and G8 Relations
with the Business Sector

This chapter discusses the nexus of the G7 and G8 with an important group of stakeholders, the private (business) sector. For an analysis of the role of other stakeholders vis-à-vis the G7 and G8, see Chapter 4 (non-member countries and potential members), Chapter 7 (international organizations) and Chapter 9 (non-profit civil society).

Business and the G7 and G8 have been mutually cognizant of each other for a number of years. An example of interaction with business in the earlier years of the G7 is the informal two-day 'Pre-Venice Mini-Summit' that was convened in London on 26-27 March 1980. At this meeting, a group of 20 business, financial and economic leaders from the G7 countries and the EC reviewed various issues to be discussed at the Venice summit later that year: inflation, economic growth, tax and regulatory systems, energy conservation, imbalances of international payment flows, among other matters. The group appealed to the G7 leaders to use and expand the facilities of the International Monetary Fund (IMF), the World Bank and other International Financial Institutions (IFIs), and to develop investment instruments. (Memorandum, [Carter's sherpa] Henry Owen to [Chairman of the Council of Economic Advisers] Charles L. Schultze, April 10, 1980; Jimmy Carter Presidential Library, Box 90, JC-CEA, Records of the Council of Economic Advisers.)[1]

The International Chamber of Commerce (ICC), which calls itself 'the world business organization' that speaks on behalf of enterprises from around the world, has long followed the G7 and G8 summits, sought input into the summits and related G7 and G8 meetings, and issued policy statements and messages to the leaders. For example, in 1999 the ICC (ICC 1999) addressed a statement on behalf of world business to the leaders attending the Cologne summit, highlighting four key issues: international trade; international financial stability; innovation, technology and jobs; and the fight against bribery and extortion. The 2000 statement (ICC 2000) to the Okinawa summit emphasized that the global economy was the most powerful force for raising living standards around the world; the support of business for research and innovation as main engines of economic growth and job creation; advocated the launching of a new round of multilateral trade negotiations following the failure of the Seattle ministerial conference of the WTO; recommended that non-trade issues should be dealt with in the UN system; highlighted electronic business opportunities afforded by technological advances; urged G8 governments to examine the

---

1 References to records in official archives follow the form suggested by those archives.

economic, social and environmental implications of the legally-binding targets for emission reductions contained in the 1997 Kyoto Protocol; expressed opposition to government-mandated business codes of conduct at the international level; and called for improving the quality of financial information.

In 2001, the ICC statement (ICC 2001) to G8 leaders meeting in Genoa addressed international trade policy; the relationship of the G7 and G8 with developing countries; global financial stability; the relationship of globalization, technology and development; the function of business in society; and sustainable development. In 2002, the themes of the statement to the Kananaskis summit were the global economy as an opportunity for all; international trade policy following the Doha ministerial meeting of the WTO; innovation, technology and development; and public-private partnerships in Africa (ICC 2002). The statement to the 2003 Evian summit focused on trade policy in the year of the Cancún WTO meeting; the role of business in society; technology, investment and development; and security and an open world economy (ICC 2003).

The themes of the 2004 ICC statement (ICC 2004) to the G8 leaders at Sea Island were: managing the global economy; multilateral trade policy after Cancún; security and cross-border business; and the protection of intellectual property. The statement to the 2005 Gleneagles summit concentrated on the ingredients of economic development (particularly applied to Africa); the Doha trade negotiations at a crossroads; intellectual property and innovation; and climate change (ICC 2005).

Gleneagles made very little progress on trade, particularly on the prickly issue of the elimination of agricultural subsidies, passing this issue on to the WTO for its ministerial conference in Hong Kong in December 2005. On the very same day the summit ended, the WTO Director-General said pessimistically: '[I]t is sobering to pass from the high level of expectations and hopes that I have encountered in Scotland to the reality of the negotiating process … in Geneva' (Beattie 2005b: 8). A month after the summit, the WTO process was still stalled. Six business groups from four continents issued a joint statement, remarking that '[t]he great hopes for global economic growth and development promised by this trade round are now at serious risk', and urged the leaders 'to get negotiations back on track' (Chase 2005: B1-2).

The 2006 St. Petersburg ICC (ICC 2006a) statement covers global energy security, the Doha trade negotiations, and intellectual property protection and economic progress. Shortly after the St. Petersburg summit, the ICC urged a strong follow-up to the summit's commitments on the protection of intellectual property (ICC 2006b). Thus, the ICC approach to the G8 tends to be rather closely tailored to at least parts of the G8 agenda.

Significantly, Blair chose to unveil his full twofold agenda for the 2005 Gleneagles summit at the World Economic Forum (WEF) at Davos early in the year before a heavily business-oriented audience. The business sector then continued to use its various contacts with the British host government during the year.

The WEF was not new to summitry. It has had an interest in the G7 and G8 for several years. Leaders and their ministers or other officials appeared at annual meetings of the Forum as guests or participants. In 2005 the UK government invited the WEF to contribute input into a Gleneagles Dialogue on Climate Change, a major initiative of the Gleneagles summit. The dialogue involves periodic meetings to develop policy recommendations on climate change for the period 2008-2012 and beyond. A year later, at the 2006 annual meeting of the WEF, UK Chancellor of the Exchequer Gordon Brown 'called for the G8 to formally designate tuberculosis a top priority at its next meeting in July, and urged G8 member countries to pledge immediate new funding to implement the Global Plan' (WEF 2006a; WEF 2006b).

Wendy Dobson (2001) has suggested that regular CEO fora, linked to the G8 summits, should be held. These could be along the lines of similar adjuncts to other IGOs; for example, the business advisory council established by the UN Secretary-General and the CEO forum at APEC summits. As well, she has cited the precedent of the CEO forum organized by Japan as the host of the Okinawa G8 summit.

The Business Action for Africa (2005), a campaign of 330 African and international companies from 36 countries, was formed to support Africa's development. It held a 'summit' conference in London just before the Gleneagles summit, on 5-6 July 2005, co-sponsored by the G8 and NEPAD, and organized by the Commission for Africa and the Commonwealth Business Council. The conference issued a communiqué in which it expressed support for the G8 Africa Action Plan and made recommendations to the G8 leaders on: trade reform; improving aid; governance; the AU/NEPAD Investment Climate Facility and the Global Fund. As well, it had recommendations for African governments on African leadership; the role of the private sector; market access and economies of scale; and corporate and public accountability. It also presented its own action plan to carry on the work of the Africa Commission until the 2005 WTO Ministerial Meeting in Hong Kong (see also Aid to Africa 2005: 24-26).

The G7 and G8 have, for a long time, acknowledged the role of the business sector in a variety of ways. The G8 gave explicit recognition to the WEF. In the 2000 *Okinawa Charter on Global Information Society*, the G8 leaders 'welcome contributions from the private sector, such as those of the Global Digital Divide Initiative of the World Economic Forum (WEF) ...' (G8 200b). In the lead-up to the St. Petersburg summit, the Russian hosts met with several business groups and accepted communications from them. For example, on 13-14 March, a few days before the G8 energy ministers' meeting, an International Energy Forum focusing on the future structure of global energy security was held in Moscow. It was attended by some 300 representatives of G8 governments, business groups, scientific and research organizations, and international organizations. On 11 July a G8 Business and University Leaders Symposium on Innovation convened in Moscow, with the participation of executives of large innovative corporations from a number of countries and rectors of the major technical universities of G8 countries. They adopted a statement addressed to the G8 leaders, expressing their views on how to stimulate innovative developments and promote public-private partnerships. (See G8 Business... 2006.)

Two examples of business-sector participation are the multi-stakeholder Digital Opportunities Task Force (DOT Force) which included representatives of the corporate sector, along with government, international organization and civil society representatives; and the Global Fund. The DOT Force functioned from 2000 to 2002, but the Global Fund, voted for by the UN General Assembly in 2001 and endorsed by the G8 at the 2001 Genoa summit, continues to expand its activities and programmes. The Global Fund has a Partnership Forum, bringing together a variety of stakeholders: government, business, civil society. For more information on these two bodies see Chapter 6; for the Global Fund, see also its website at <www.theglobalfund.org>.

Summit documents often refer to the private sector; and the concept of partnerships has been part of G7 and G8 initiatives. In his St. Petersburg *Chair's Summary*, Putin refers to the role of business on several St. Petersburg issues. On education, the leaders agreed to 'promote cooperation with the private sector to foster diverse, efficient, sustainable education institutions'. In the fight against infectious diseases, they undertook to 'promote research and development of new drugs and vaccines, through building public-private partnerships'. They welcomed the outcome of the 26-28 June ministerial Conference on Drug Trafficking Routes from Afghanistan, including the initiative to call, later in 2006, a forum on co-operation between states and the business community in fighting terrorism. On the issue of energy security, the centrepiece of Putin's agenda, paragraph 37 of the *St. Petersburg Plan of Action: Global Energy Security* (an annex to the G8 statement *Global Energy Security*) states: 'We will work in partnership with the private sector to accelerate market entry and utilization of innovative energy technologies by supporting market-led policies that encourage investments in this area' (G8 2006g: para 37). The main collective G8 document of the summit on education, *Education for Innovative Societies in the 21st Century*, makes references to the business sector under 'Developing a Global Innovation Society' and 'Building Skills for Life and Work through Quality Education'. And on the third main agenda item, infectious diseases, the statement *Fight against Infectious Diseases*, the G8 leaders call for working with pharmaceutical companies on increasing the production of antiviral drugs, developing a new generation of influenza vaccines, and promoting a comprehensive approach – prevention, treatment and care – to tackling HIV/AIDS. G8 documents on other agenda items (intellectual property piracy, counter-terrorism) also call for participation of the private sector.

Another facet of G7 and G8 relations with business is in the area of corporate responsibility and governance. The 1995 Halifax summit represented the first significant instance of the G7 focusing on these issues. There, the leaders called for 'private pension plans to bear more of the burden of an aging society, welcomed private sector participation in the Global Information Society, and concentrated on the supervision of IFIs, especially in the field of banking and securities'. Later, as the 1997/1999 financial crisis unfolded, the concern of the G7 and G8 with corporate governance expanded, addressing the behaviour of large multinational corporations and the need for the rule of law for companies. The 1999 Cologne summit and the 2000 Okinawa summit emphasized transparency and accountability. The 2002 Kananaskis summit's G8 Africa action plan called for 'developing an effective corporate governance framework'.

At the 2003 Evian summit, corporate and public governance 'took centre stage' and the 2004 Sea Island summit made further advances on this (Fratianni et al. 2007). Building on this, the main documents on one of the two central agenda items of the 2005 Gleneagles summit, *Africa*, stresses that '[E]nhancing governance and the rule of law will attract more and broader private investment … which is the basic condition for inclusive growth'.[2] At St. Petersburg in 2006 the leaders, in their action plan accompanying the statement *Fighting High Level Corruption*, commit themselves to 'work with all the international financial centers and our private sectors to deny safe haven to assets illicitly acquired by individuals engaged in high level corruption'. And in their statement *Combating IRP Piracy and Counterfeiting;* they stress the necessity for government authorities, civil society and the business community to uphold laws and regulations governing intellectual property rights and to promote the fight against intellectual property piracy and counterfeiting.

At times, business-related groups are lumped together with non-profit groups as part of civil society. The 2005 G8 stakeholder consultation project, organized by the UK's Chatham House and several partner institutions, included representatives of the business sector along with civil society, government and other groups. The Civil G8, which was active during Russia's G8 presidency in 2006, also brought together civil society and business sector representatives (Chapter 9 discusses the civil society nexus with the G7 and G8, including the Chatham House Project and the Civil G8, in detail). This is a questionable practice; the aims, priorities, methods, and resources of NGOs and other nonprofit civil-society coalitions and organizations are quite different from those of business. That said, it is crucial to bring government, civil society and business together, the better to accomplish complex global goals that no single-sector stakeholder group can accomplish alone.

Conclusion

The private sector has long been recognized as an essential interlocutor of the G7 and G8. This recognition is mutual, as reflected by G7 and G8 statements and other documents, and by papers and analysis originating from business organizations. Several summits of recent years have produced initiatives to promote corporate responsibility. Moreover, both parties have come to value multi-stakeholder approaches and have, on occasion, followed this by establishing working partnerships.

References

Note on internet addresses (URLs): Websites tend to appear, change or disappear, often without warning. Addresses cited in this source list were accurate and active at the time of writing (August 2006) unless otherwise noted.

'Aid to Africa: The $25 Billion Question' (2005), *The Economist*, 376:8433, 24-26, July 2.
Beattie, Alan (2005b), 'G8 Mood and Doha Talks "Show Disconnect"', *Financial Times*, 9/10 July, 8.

---

2 Texts of summit documents are available at the G8 Information Centre website, at www.g8.utoronto.ca.

Business Action for Africa (2005), *Conference Statement*, 5-6 July, London.

Chase, Steven (2005), 'Alarm Bells Raised over WTO Talks', *The Globe and Mail*, 6 September, B1-2, Toronto.

Dobson, Wendy (2001), 'Broadening Participation in G-7 Summits', in *Toward Shared Responsibility and Global Leadership: Recommendations for the G-8 Genoa Summit from the G-8 Preparatory Conference, 23-29.* [Turin, Italy: G-8 Preparatory Conference].

Fratianni, Michele, Paolo Savona and John J. Kirton (forthcoming 2007). 'Governance amid Globalisation: Corporations, Governments, and the G8', in *Corporate, Public, and Global Governance: The G8 Contribution*, Michele Fratianni, Paolo Savona, and John J. Kirton (eds), Global Finance Series, Ashgate, Aldershot, UK.

G8 (2000b) *Okinawa Charter on Global Information Society*, Okinawa, 22 July, www.g8.utoronto.ca/summit/2000okinawa/gis.htm.

G8 (2006g), *Global Energy Security*, St. Petersburg, www.g8.utoronto.ca/summit/2006stpetersburg/energy.html.

G8 Business and University Leaders Symposium on Innovation (2006), *Working Meetings Summit 2006*, Moscow, 11 July, http://en.g8russia.ru/page_work/27.html.

International Chamber of Commerce (1999), *Business and the Global Economy: ICC Statement on Behalf of World Business to the Heads of State and Government Attending the Cologne Summit*, www.iccwbo.org/home/statements_rules/statements/1999/g7_statement.asp.

International Chamber of Commerce (2000), *Business and the Global Economy: ICC Statement on Behalf of World Business to the Heads of State and Government Attending the Okinawa Summit*, www.iccwbo.org/home/statements_rules/statements/2000/g8_statement.asp.

International Chamber of Commerce (2001), *Business and the Global Economy: ICC Statement on Behalf of World Business to the Heads of State and Government Attending the Genoa Summit*, www.iccwbo.org/home/statements_rules/statements/2001/genoa_summit_trade.asp.

International Chamber of Commerce (2002), *Business and the Global Economy: ICC Statement on Behalf of World Business to the Heads of State and Government Attending the Kananaskis Summit*, www.iccwbo.org/home/statements_rules/statements/2002/G8kananskis.asp.

International Chamber of Commerce (2003), *Business and the Global Economy: ICC Statement on Behalf of World Business to the Heads of State and Government Attending the Evian Summit*, www.iccwbo.org/home/statements_rules/statements/2003/G8.asp.

International Chamber of Commerce (2004), *Business and the Global Economy: ICC Statement on Behalf of World Business to the Heads of State and Government Attending the Sea Island Summit*, www.iccwbo.org/home/statements_rules/statements/2004/G8_statement.asp.

International Chamber of Commerce (2005), *Business and the Global Economy: ICC Statement on Behalf of World Business to the Heads of State and Government*

Attending the Gleneagles Summit, www.iccwbo.org/uploadedFiles/ICC/policy/economic/Statements/G82005.pdf.

International Chamber of Commerce (2006a), *Business and the Global Economy: ICC Statement on Behalf of World Business to the Heads of State and Government Attending the St. Petersburg Summit*, www.iccwbo.org/uploadedFiles/ICC_G8_St_Petersburg_statement.pdf.

International Chamber of Commerce (2006b), *ICC Urges Strong Follow Up to G8 Statement on Intellectual Property*, 26 July, www.iccwbo.org/iccicij/index.html

World Economic Forum (2006a), 'Developing the Future Framework for Climate Change and Energy Policy with the G-20', *The World Economic Forum on East Asia: Initiative Activity*, www.weforum.org/en/events/eastasia/InitiativeActivity/InitiativeActivityAsia.

World Economic Forum (2006b), 'Obasanjo, Brown and Gates Call on Leaders To Fund New TB Plan', *Annual Meeting 2006*, www.weforum.org/en/events/annualmeeting/AnnualMeetingContent.

Chapter 9

The Role of Civil Society[1]

Introduction

In today's interdependent, globalized world, no institution – whether governmental, intergovernmental, business, or civil society organization – can exist in isolation. Governance implies complex, ever-changing interaction between and among various actors. This chapter examines the evolving relationship of nongovernmental organizations (NGOs) and other civil society organizations (CSOs) and coalitions with the G7 and G8, identifies various modes of this interaction, and concludes with a review of lessons learned and factors contributing to a more successful relationship.

In sharp contrast with the United Nations (UN), the G7/G8, as described in Chapter 1, is a more informal, flexible and by-and-large nonbureaucratic forum that lacks the two main characteristics of more structured international governmental organizations (IGOs): a constitutive intergovernmental agreement, and a secretariat. It follows, therefore, that civil society relations with the G7 and G8, too, are largely informal in nature, unlike the long-established, well-defined NGO relations with formal international organizations such as the UN. Practices and structures vary from country to country among G7 and G8 members, and there are different government departments that have administrative units responsible for continuous monitoring, co-ordination and follow-up of G7- and G8-related activities and issues, both at the summit level and at lower (ministerial and task-force) levels of the broader G7 and G8 system. All this has implications for civil society's interaction with the G8 system and with individual G8 member governments. The history of this interaction may be divided into four phases as outlined in the following section.

G7 and G8 Interaction with Civil Society: A Brief History

Phase 1 (1975-1980): Limited Interaction between Civil Society and the G7

As implied above, the G7/G8 has seen itself from the very beginning of G7 summitry in 1975 as an informal, nonbureaucratic forum of the leaders of the most advanced market-economy countries with a democratic system of governance. Public recognition of civil society groups as interlocutors seems not to have entered the consciousness of the G7 leaders and their support apparatus. On the other side, the power and importance of the G7 as a discrete entity does not appear to

---

1   For an earlier, more detailed discussion of the civil society-G7/G8 nexus see Hajnal (2002); see also Hajnal (2006b).

have been widely recognized during this phase by most NGOs and broader civil society, although some academic CSOs, notably the Trilateral Commission, started discussing the summit as early as 1978 (Sauzey 1978), and certain trade unions and other NGOs, especially in the United States, made approaches to their own government on issues that they wished conveyed to the summit. Possibly the earliest example of this can be seen in a letter by Nicolás Nogueras Rivera, president of the Puerto Rico Free Federation of Labor, to President Gerald Ford, 23 June 1976, in which the writer expresses 'hope [that] the Almighty God enlighten the distinguished representatives of England, France, Italy, West Germany, Japan, Canada and you, Mr. President' and the belief that in addition to co-ordinating economic recovery the summit would 'have to confront the realities that emerge from the situation in Angola, Rhodesia and South Africa and the uneasiness and challenge of the growing forces of communism that represent a potential menace not only to the North Atlantic Treaty Organization but to the preservation of peace, of democracy and prosperity' (Rivera 1976). Another instance is revealed in a 1978 memorandum by Henry Owen, the US sherpa, to President Jimmy Carter:

> I recently sent you a memo asking whether you want to hold separate meetings with labor and business leaders, in line with Mike Mansfield's suggestion, to consult about the upcoming Summit. Last night a businessman who favors such a meeting suggested an interesting format: The [labor and business] leaders would meet first among themselves and with your subordinates (Blumenthal, Strauss, Cooper, Owen, etc.) at some length to hear the Administration's plans and to think through their reactions. Then you would join the meeting to hear the conclusions that they had reached. (Owen 1978)

These initiatives are interesting early evidence of business and the labour segment of civil society wishing a pre-summit dialogue. Thus, at least some G7 governments were already aware of civil society concerns but there was little publicity or apparent impact on G7 leaders and their support apparatus.

Phase 2 (1981-1994): Civil Society Recognizes the G7

As the summit agenda expanded to embrace many issues beyond the early focus on macroeconomic policy co-ordination,[2] civil society began to see the G7 as a legitimate target both for lobbying and for opposing. Many of these new G7 issues have been crucial to a wide variety of NGOs and civil society coalitions. Moreover, it was becoming common public knowledge that the G7 was indeed a powerful group that had evolved into a major global institution.[3]

In addition to pre-summit lobbying of individual G7 governments by business, labour and agricultural representatives, initial civil society reaction to the G7 took rather an undifferentiated form: the alternative summits. For some years, these counter-summits generally went by the name 'The Other Economic Summit' (TOES), and sometimes 'people's summit' or 'citizens' summit'. The first alternative summit,

---

2 For an account of the evolution of G7 and G8 agenda, see Hajnal and Kirton (2000).

3 Kirton has termed the G7/G8 'a centre of global governance'. Some disagree with this characterization. See, for example, Baker (2000), 165-189.

called the 'Popular Summit', met in Ottawa on 18-19 July 1981. It was well attended, featured workshops and speeches by prominent 'disarmament spokesmen [including Lord Philip Noel-Baker], left-wing professors and representatives for African and South American revolutionary groups', called for disarmament, criticized the conservative economic policies of Western countries, and supported revolutionary struggle in El Salvador and Namibia (Evans 1981a; 1981b).

The first TOES proper was organized by the London-based TOES/UK – later called New Economics Foundation – and took place simultaneously with the 1984 London G7 summit (Schroyer 1997: x). TOES described itself as 'an international non-governmental forum for the presentation, discussion, and advocacy of the economic ideas and practices upon which a more just and sustainable society can be built – "an economics as if people mattered"'.[4] In 1985, 1986 and 1987 TOES sent delegations to the G7 summits; starting with 1988, TOES met in an event parallel with the summit. Its prominence then declined in favour of more focused, issue-oriented civil society approaches to the G7 (and later to the G8). Each year's TOES featured a civil society coalition with varying membership meeting in the G7 and G8 summit city. These counter-summits ran workshops and demonstrations, and produced press releases and often a counter-communiqué critical of the official G7 and G8 communiqué (see People's Summit 1995). Harriet Friedmann (2001: 88) states that '[i]n the 1990s, TOES morphed into teach-ins and similar gatherings under the rubric of the International Forum on Globalization' but at least one national TOES, TOES/USA, reappeared at the time of the 2004 Sea Island summit. A much stronger people's summit (discussed below) was to emerge later.

In many instances, civil society adopted issue-specific approaches. For example, the environmental movement lobbied the G7 as early as 1988. In 1990, at Houston, a coalition of NGOs led by the World Wildlife Fund issued its report card on compliance with G8 environmental commitments, and in 1991 an 'Enviro-summit' met in London a few city blocks from the official G7 summit site. A more recent example is the robust advocacy on climate-change and other environmental issues by a number of environmental NGOs and CSOs before and during the 2005 Gleneagles summit on whose agenda climate change figured prominently.

Phase 3 (1995-1997): The G7 Recognizes Civil Society

The G7, on its part, was slower to acknowledge civil society formally. The terms 'civil society' and 'NGO' were not used in official G7 documents until the 1995 Halifax summit. The Halifax communiqué refers to NGOs and civil society in the context of promoting sustainable development and the reform of international financial institutions, adding that the UN and the Bretton Woods institutions should 'encourage countries to follow participatory development strategies and support governmental reforms that assure transparency and public accountability, a stable rule of law, and an active civil society'. In the same document, the G7 makes this undertaking: '[t]o increase overall coherence, cooperation and cost effectiveness we

---

4   An account of the first two TOES can be found in Ekins (1986). Two more recent works are Mander and Goldsmith (1996) and Schroyer (1997).

will work with others to encourage ... improved coordination among international organizations, bilateral donors and NGOs' (G7 1995: Sections 26, 37).

The Halifax reference to civil society was only the beginning. The 1996 Lyon summit, which began the fourth seven-year cycle of summitry, spoke out even more strongly about the positive role of civil society. In its economic communiqué, it underlined the need for 'a strengthened civil society' in that partnership (G7 1996b: Section 34). The communiqué of the 1997 Denver Summit of the Eight went further, 'reaffirm[ing] the vital contribution of civil society' to the environment, democratic governance and poverty eradication (G7 1997a: Section 13). Subsequent summits have similarly acknowledged – at least in the language of their official documents – the increasingly important role of civil society in a number of sectors.

Other levels of the G7 and G8 system also took up the civil society nexus. By 9-10 May 1996, when G7 environment ministers met in Cabourg, France, they chose as one of their main themes the mobilization of civil society; the Cabourg communiqué has several references to NGOs (G7 Environment Ministers 1996). Later, more ministerial fora (the G8 environment ministers, the Trade Ministers Quadrilateral and others), as well as various G7 and G8 task forces and expert groups, have expressed their willingness to engage civil society and their appreciation of the importance of engaging all stakeholders.[5] This marks a clear trend: the G7 and G8 system has openly recognized the increasing importance of civil society. This developing relationship reflects the evolution and maturing of both civil society and the G7 and G8.

Phase 4 (1998-): Civil Society Grows Stronger and More Sophisticated

Birmingham 1998 through Okinawa 2000   The 1998 Birmingham summit was a watershed in G7 and G8 interaction with civil society. It was there that the Jubilee 2000 coalition lobbied for debt relief and organized a spectacular human chain of 70,000 peaceful demonstrators who surrounded the summit site and presented a petition to the leaders, asking for debt cancellation. This prompted an unprecedented G8 reaction: British Prime Minister Tony Blair, on behalf of the G8, responded to the petition in a separate document of the summit (G8 1998). In an additional statement, Blair paid tribute to the Jubilee 2000 campaign, for the 'dignified manner in which it demonstrated in Birmingham, and for making a most persuasive case for debt relief.' (See Dent and Peters 1999: 188.) Jubilee and its successor organizations have been supported by celebrities ranging from the Irish rock star Bono and former boxing champion Muhammad Ali to Pope John Paul II, the Dalai Lama and Archbishop Desmond Tutu.

The Jubilee movement has displayed impressive tactical and strategic savvy. It understands the workings of the G7 and G8 system very well. For example, during the year 2000, leading up to the Okinawa summit, Jubilee followed and publicized the host leader's customary pre-summit visits by Japanese Prime Ministers Keizo Obuchi, then Yoshiro Mori, to the other summit countries. It staged demonstrations

---

5   For a case study of the interaction between G8 environment ministers and civil society, see Risbud (2006).

at G7 and G8 ministerial meetings. Jubilee is familiar with the sherpa and sous-sherpa process. It monitors and publicizes the performance of G8 governments and demands that those governments implement their past commitments.

All this has given the debt issue a high public profile that governments and IGOs often find difficult to match. The idiom could not be more different from that customarily used by governments, IGOs and the G7 itself. Although it is impossible to measure the precise impact of Jubilee 2000 on G7 governments, there is a strong perception that it is influential. A spokesperson for the World Bank stated: Jubilee 2000 'has managed to put a relatively arcane issue – that of international finance and development – on the negotiating table throughout the world. The pledges Clinton and [UK Chancellor of the Exchequer Gordon] Brown have made [to debt relief] would not have happened without Jubilee 2000. It's one of the most effective global lobbying campaigns I have ever seen.' (See Hanlon and Garrett 1999.) And the *Financial Times* wrote on 17 February 1999: 'When a plea for debt relief becomes the common cause of a coalition that embraces both the Pope and the pop world, creditors should take notice' (Hanlon and Garrett 1999: 6).

The trend of largely peaceful demonstrations continued before and during the 1999 Cologne and 2000 Okinawa summits. But demonstrations and street theatre are just one aspect of civil society action, although they tend to attract the most media attention. Year-round lobbying and advocacy, as well as preparing and disseminating policy papers, are among other facets of work by NGOs and other CSOs. In the course of such activities, NGOs often consult governments, international organizations, academic experts, businesses and other stakeholders. In many cases, this type of action has opened up space for civil society for making a real impact on official policy.

In the lead-up to the Okinawa summit the Japanese government made clear its determination, as G8 Chair for 2000, to reach out beyond the G8 to developing and other countries, IGOs, the private sector and civil society:

- Ahead of the summit the Japanese government appointed an official to provide regular liaison with CSOs during the summit planning process. (Kirton 2000).
- The government sponsored a pre-summit international symposium on the role of NGOs in conflict prevention.
- There was dialogue between the Japanese government and civil society leaders, both in Europe prior to the summit, and in Japan on the opening day of the summit. Prime Minister Mori's meeting with representatives of nine NGOs (selected on a first-come-first-served basis) on 21 July was presented by the Japanese government as a new initiative. In fact, it was at the 1998 Birmingham summit that civil society had its first official dialogue with the G8 as represented by British Prime Minister Tony Blair, and where Secretary of State for International Development Clare Short, on behalf of Blair, accepted the 1.4 million signatures amassed by the Jubilee campaign (Dent and Peters 1999: 36). Although Okinawa reconfirmed the validity of consultation and dialogue, G8 governments other than the Japanese host did not reach out to civil society sufficiently in 2000.

Genoa 2001   The 2001 Genoa summit was a more ominous milestone in G8-civil society relations.[6] It was characterized by massive protests and marred by violence. Summit venues and activities were severely restricted by the protests outside. Out of concern for security the local hosts of the G8 hired a luxury cruiser, the *Spirit of Europe*, to house all but one of the G8 leaders (George W. Bush). The prefecture of Genoa took various security measures: setting up a red zone, a surrounding yellow zone, and closing most transportation access to the city. Steps taken went as far as deploying antiaircraft batteries along the runways of Genoa's Cristoforo Colombo airport. This seemed excessive at the time, but later in 2001, in the wake of the 11 September attacks against the World Trade Center in New York and the Pentagon in Washington, President Hosni Mubarak of Egypt and Italian Deputy Prime Minister Gianfranco Fini reportedly said that Osama bin Laden's terrorist network had threatened to kill President Bush and other G8 leaders (Sanger 2001: B1).

Ahead of the summit, responsible civil society groups had made clear their intention to demonstrate and protest peacefully against economic globalization and for more progress on debt relief. They expressed concern that anarchist and other potentially disruptive or violent groups would jeopardize peaceful, lawful, democratic protest. The Genoa Social Forum (GSF), an umbrella organization of some 700 international, Italian and local Genoa-based NGOs and civil society coalitions included Drop the Debt but also *Ya Basta*, an Italian anarchist (but essentially nonviolent) organization (Beattie 2001b).

It was unclear from the start how this kind of contradiction could be resolved, especially in light of the announcement by GSF that some of its member groups 'would attempt peacefully to invade the red zone during the planned "day of civil disobedience" on Friday July 20', the first day of the summit (Beattie 2001b). GSF as a whole planned three sets of demonstrations in the officially permitted area. The Jubilee movement's Drop the Debt met Italian national and local government representatives in June to negotiate plans for peaceful demonstrations.

In the event, the demonstrations of 20 July were marred by anarchist violence (including instances of anarchists turning against peaceful demonstrators) and a similarly violent police response. The resulting death of Carlo Giuliani, the many injuries, and concern for the safety of their supporters led Drop the Debt and other groups, including the World Development Movement (WDM), to stage a vigil alongside the peaceful demonstrations still held on 21 July (WDM 2001).

During the night of 21 July, Italian police stormed one of the buildings used by GSF without a warrant, smashing computers, confiscating computer disks, arresting about 90 people including members of the violent anarchist 'Black Bloc' or 'Tute Nere' (Black Overalls, to be distinguished from the generally nonviolent 'Tute Bianche' or White Overalls), and reportedly beating up protesters (many of whom were asleep) and some journalists. (See Picking Up... 2001: 49-50.) Worse, there were eyewitness accounts of police complicity with the Black Bloc (George 2001: 6; See also La Presse... 2001; Neslen 2001: 20).

---

6   For a more detailed account, see Hajnal (2001). For a journalistic treatment of 'anti-globalist' dissent and protest from Seattle 1999 to Genoa 2001, see Klein (2002).

G8 leaders and most NGO groups deplored the clashes (Drop the Debt 2001c, MSF 2001). In a special statement issued on 21 July (the first official document of the Genoa summit), the G8 leaders recognized and praised the role of peaceful protest and argument, but condemned unequivocally the violence and anarchy perpetrated by a small minority. And the final communiqué of 22 July reaffirmed the right of peaceful protesters to have their voices heard and again deplored the violence and vandalism of those who seek to disrupt discussion and dialogue (G8 2001a: para 35).

Predictably, the media paid closest attention to the violence. Several leaders expressed their frustration at this disproportionate news coverage to the detriment of reporting the actual deliberations of the G8.

A whole spectrum of issues was represented in Genoa by a variety of NGO groups, ranging from the environment to women's rights. This brief assessment focuses on just three issues: debt, health, and education. The dire consequences of unsustainable debt burdens on developing countries continued to be a major campaign objective for the Jubilee movement. But new linkages emerged as these groups added other issues to their long-standing concern with debt: education, and HIV/AIDS and other infectious diseases. This transition led to the formation of new alliances with organizations fighting against such diseases (notably Médecins Sans Frontières (MSF)) and with those promoting universal education (such as Oxfam). Civil society members of this new alliance have stressed that developing countries need deeper debt relief in order to fight the HIV/AIDS pandemic more successfully and to benefit from better educational opportunities.

The tradition of host government dialogue with civil society continued before and during the Genoa summit. In the preparatory phase, the Italian government made a serious effort to communicate with NGOs, especially in the areas of development aid and poverty reduction. Four research institutes were directed to consult NGOs and solicit their recommendations in what was termed the Genoa Nongovernmental Initiative (Zupi 2001: 59). The mayor of Genoa confirmed his intention, shared with Italian Prime Minister Berlusconi, 'to open a dialogue with the movements that intend to demonstrate ... critically but peacefully during the summit'. Italy's Interior Minister Scajola concurred (G8 2001c).

Consultations with Italian and other G8 government leaders and ministers took place on several occasions during the summit. In a news conference on 20 July, Bono, Bob Geldof and Lorenzo Jovanotti, pop music stars and strong supporters of the Jubilee/Drop the Debt campaign, talked of a series of meetings they had had with the British, German, Canadian, European Union and Russian leaders, as well as with George W. Bush's national security advisor Condoleezza Rice, but they expressed frustration at the Italian host's refusal to facilitate meetings with leaders from the South. The three rock musicians found the Millennium Action Plan for Africa (later called NEPAD, for New Partnership for African Development) encouraging, and they welcomed the debt-forgiveness commitments of Canada and Italy as particularly praiseworthy. Nonetheless, they added that even some countries whose debt had been cancelled still had to continue to pay their rich creditors (Drop the Debt 2001a).

This kind of dialogue is no less important for the leaders of the G8. But dialogue, to be meaningful, must not consist of empty words and promises. A representative of MSF expressed disappointment at what she saw as just that kind of inadequate dialogue at Genoa, in contrast with the more upbeat assessment of Bono, Geldof and Jovanotti. In a paper prepared for the Shadow G-8 before the Genoa summit, Wendy Dobson (2001: 23-29) proposed that there should be an appropriate mechanism for regular pre- or post-summit meetings with civil society representatives.

As at other summits starting with Halifax, NGOs and civil society were reflected in several Genoa G7 and G8 documents; for example, the *G7 Statement* of 20 July, in the section concerning the launching of the new Doha round of trade negotiations, stated that '[t]he WTO should continue to respond to the legitimate expectations of civil society, and ensure that the new Round supports sustainable development'; and the final G8 *Communiqué* of 22 July, making several references to NGOs and civil society, undertook to 'promote innovative solutions based on a broad partnership with civil society and the private sector' (G8 2001b: para 8; G8 2001a: para 2).

Civil society's verdict on the Genoa summit was rather negative. The Jubilee movement expressed disappointment at 'the failure of the richest nations to once again tackle the global debt crisis that is worsening the impoverishment of over two billion people in severely indebted countries' (Jubilee Plus 2001).

MSF criticized the global health fund, noting that pledges of $1.2 billion were 'nowhere near what is required ..., [they] are shamefully low. Governments call upon multinationals and the private sector to contribute. Among these are the pharmaceutical companies whose pricing policies are a fundamental part of the problem.' Oxfam (OI 2001) was equally critical of the Genoa summit's record on debt and the health fund, stating: 'The G8 did nothing meaningful on debt relief, and announced a global AIDS fund that still needs much more resources and does nothing about the cost of drugs in poor countries. It's unacceptable that these promises remain unmet. ... Education breaks the cycle of poverty, and is essential in building democracy and fighting AIDS. Last year the G8 promised a global plan for education. In Genoa they said how to accomplish it. ... The world can't afford another unmet promise.'

A significant concern was expressed by Drop the Debt (2001b) about the shifting priorities of the G8: 'This year the G8's big idea is to fight disease in the poorest countries. But most people are sick to death of G8 initiatives that never quite get delivered. In 1999, it was debt. Last year [in 2000], it was computers. This year it is health. Next year, we know it will be education. Every unfinished initiative is another blow to the credibility of the G8.' The G8 would do well to reflect on this perception of shifting attention to and away from crucial issues and policy initiatives. Civil society, for its part, could temper its criticism by recognizing that the G7 and G8 have been able to deal with several issues simultaneously and has at times achieved results by an iterative process, a case in point being the conclusion of the Uruguay Round of multilateral trade negotiations – it took several years of G7 deliberation to achieve success (Bayne 2000: 200-201).

Only a few months after the turbulent Genoa G8 summit came the terrorist attacks on New York and Washington. In this new, more dangerous atmosphere, questions were raised about the way G8 meetings are conducted, as well as about the activities and tactics of civil society and other protester groups. And in the security-conscious post-9/11 era, the 2002 and subsequent G8 summits have met at remote locations; this has made it difficult for civil society to interact directly with the G8 leaders.

Kananaskis 2002 Various forms of civil society action continued before and during the 2002 Kananaskis summit. The Canadian host government actively promoted dialogue with civil society representatives and conducted additional consultations with citizen groups. A high-level dialogue, under the aegis of the Montreal International Forum/Forum international de Montréal (FIM; a civil society think tank), took place on 21-23 May 2002 in Montreal and Ottawa; it brought together civil society representatives from Brazil, Canada, Colombia, France, The Netherlands, the Philippines, Senegal, the UK, Uruguay, the US and Zimbabwe with representatives of the governments of Canada, France, Japan and the UK. The three topics of discussion were: the global democratic deficit and civil society engagement; the NEPAD consultative process; and future G8/civil society dialogue building on multi-stakeholder experiences (Montreal International Forum 2002). The government also provided generous funding for the G6B ('Group of 6 Billion') People's Summit, held at the University of Calgary. 1,400 people attended, and heard excellent presentations. But the only connection with the official G8 summit occurred during the open session on the final day of the G6B, with then Foreign Minister Bill Graham and then International Co-operation Minister Susan Whelan present. Minister Graham accepted the G6B's recommendations and later transmitted them to the summit host, Prime Minister Jean Chrétien. Interestingly, the proceedings of G6B influenced the media greatly, due to the fact that the G8 leaders themselves were not very accessible.

There were small, and largely peaceful, street demonstrations. The three main themes of the Kananaskis summit (Africa, the economy, and terrorism) lent themselves to meaningful civil society participation. Amnesty International (AI) expressed the conviction that in all three summit issues the discussion and outcome should be infused with human rights concerns and perspectives. The global economy should be strengthened in a manner that is centred on human rights. The fight against terrorism raises human rights concerns. And human rights should be a crucial aspect of NEPAD and the G8 Africa Action Plan (AI 2002).

As for G8 documents, the Kananaskis *Chair's Summary* did not mention civil society. The *Statement by G7 Leaders* concentrated on the achievements and shortcomings of the Heavily Indebted Poor Countries (HIPC) initiative (G8 2002a). It, too, made no reference to civil society, even though the Jubilee movement and other CSOs had been instrumental in keeping the debt issue front and centre, and were continuing their thrust for greater and more meaningful debt relief than had hitherto been achieved. The *Africa Action Plan* (the G8's response to NEPAD) included several explicit references to civil society; other aspects of the Plan imply civil society involvement (G8 2002b). At the ministerial level, the *Chair's Summary* of the post-Kananaskis G8 Development Ministers' Meeting points to the need for greater engagement of civil society in development strategies, especially as regards Poverty Reduction Strategy Papers (PRSPs) for developing countries (G8 Development Ministers 2002).

Many CSOs were represented in Calgary by North American (Canadian and US) affiliates rather than people from international headquarters. This can be attributed to various causes but the cautious (perhaps over-cautious) approach of immigration and police authorities after September 11 was one major factor. Civil society reaction to Kananaskis tended to be rather critical, though some NGO groups acknowledged certain achievements of the G8. The reaction of African NGOs to NEPAD was particularly significant. There remained considerable opposition to a plan that many in African CSOs see as lacking in civil society involvement, as well as other limitations. The 50 Years Is Enough network asserted that '[b]oth NEPAD and the [G8] action plan on Africa were devised in a vacuum, with no input from civil society organizations. Scores of prominent African civil society and academic networks have criticized NEPAD for its faithfulness to status quo "neo-liberal" economic policies and for its claim to "African ownership" in the absence of consultation beyond the inner circles of the presidents of South Africa, Nigeria, Senegal, and Algeria'[7] (50 Years is Enough 2002). Other segments of African civil society acknowledged that the G8, by consulting with African CSOs, was showing greater openness, and African civil society chose to engage the G8 in a reciprocal manner. Yet, the G8 Africa Action Plan caused 'hurt surprise' among African CSOs because the financial commitments were far lower than expected.[8]

Evian 2003   Before and during the 2003 Evian-les-Bains summit there was again host government dialogue with civil society; for example, a series of meetings that President Chirac held with CSOs including some groups critical of the G8. On 30 April he met with representatives of more than 30 CSOs (Tagliabue 2003: YT13).[9]

A counter-summit, called Sommet pour un autre monde [Summit for Another World], was held in Annemasse, France, 29-31 May 2003, with about 4,500 participants. It benefited from facilities near Evian provided by French authorities (Graham 2003). It was based on the premise that although the individual heads of state or government of G8 countries are legitimate actors in their own countries and have the right to meet, the G8 summit has no place in a democratic 'global governance'; rather it is the UN that should be strengthened and reformed. The counter-summit held a number of round table discussions from a civil society perspective, touching on issues many of which were also dealt with by the G8 summit: NEPAD; corporate, social and environmental responsibility; global taxes for financing development; local and global effects of globalization; rules for a global environmental governance; debt, trade and development; arms transfers and human rights; AIDS; anti-terrorism and human rights; and water. The counter-summit ended with a 'debt and reparation tribunal', a concert on the theme 'for another world, drop the debt', and a communiqué entitled 'un G8 pour rien! [a G8 for nothing!]'.

Yet another parallel event, 'the poor people's summit', was organized by the Mali chapter of Jubilee 2000 and took place in the village of Siby in that country. The 400 attendees included members of NGOs, farmers, herders, women's groups, teachers

---

    7   Njoki Njoroge Njehû, the director of 50 Years Is Enough, reiterated these concerns in an interview with G8 Online during the Kananaskis summit www.g7.utoronto.ca/g8online/2002/english/features/address4.html.

    8   Remarks by L Muthoni Wanyeki, Executive Director of the African Women's Development and Communications Network (FEMNET) at the Global Governance 2002 conference, Montreal, 15 October 2002.

    9   See also CRID website, www.crid.asso.fr/g8/ong_gus.htm.

and students from six African and four non-African countries. One participant, Mohamed Thiam, a representative of Transparency International in Mali, had this message for the G8 leaders attending the Evian summit: 'You leaders of G8, you have many riches, we have nothing. I think you can help us, not by giving money, but by being honest and equal.' He added that 'debt, unfair trade and good governance [were] themes in Siby just as ... in France', and that 'the leaders of the world have to hear the voice of African civil society' (Baxter 2003). This counter-summit issued a declaration entitled 'Appel du Forum des Peuples: Consensus des peuples face au consensus du g8 [Appeal of the Peoples' Forum: Peoples' Consensus versus G8 Consensus], Siby 2003' (Appel du Forum 2003).

Demonstrations around the Evian summit site were large, with some violent confrontations. Inevitably there were clashes between some radical groups and moderate, peaceful demonstrators. The large demonstrations were generally peaceful but, once again, the media paid much attention to the violence.

Almost all official meetings of the Evian summit acknowledged civil society. Many summit documents, with exceptions notably including the Chair's Summary, refer to civil society or NGOs: the Implementation Report by Africa Personal Representatives to Leaders on the G8 Africa Action Plan; the action plans on water, on health, on famine in Africa; and the declaration on Fostering Growth and Promoting a Responsible Market Economy.

Civil society once again evaluated the Evian summit rather unfavourably. The Sommet pour un autre monde, in its communiqué 'Un G8 pour rien!', passed a negative verdict while acknowledging that the G8 leaders recognized the growing gap between rich and poor as well as the deterioration of social conditions and the environment. The Jubilee Debt Campaign, a successor of the Jubilee 2000 coalition, reached conclusions along similar lines on debt forgiveness, adding that the worldwide struggle of debt campaigners had not been in vain, 'for the issue of poor country debt remains formally on the agenda of the rich world ... [, and a] movement has been created which remains motivated to tackle the gross injustice of debt [and to] offer a clear critique of what is going wrong-and how that can be readily rectified' (Greenhill 2003: 25).

Amnesty International urged the G8 leaders to fulfil the promises made in Kananaskis in 2002, and address the sources of conflict plaguing Africa: arms trade and trade in natural resources used for wars. AI had published a report, *A Catalogue of Failures: G8 Arms Exports and Human Rights Violations*, in which it accused five G8 countries (US, Russia, France, UK and Germany) for supplying three quarters of all global arms transfers during the period 1997-2001. AI also called on G8 governments to promote moves toward corporate accountability, notably by supporting the UN's draft norms on the responsibilities of transnational corporations (AI 2003a; 2003b). Greenpeace lamented that 'all controversial environment issues were either absent or diluted to nothingness at the Group of Eight (G8) summit in Evian ...' (Agence France-Presse 2003). Friends of the Earth echoed Greenpeace's dim view, asserting that the environmental outcome of the Evian summit was weak, and that the G8 pulled back from commitments it had agreed to in Johannesburg, for example as regards corporate voluntarism (contrasted with stronger measures called for in paragraph 45.ter of the Johannesburg plan of implementation).

Sea Island 2004   The 2004 Sea Island summit followed the post-9/11 pattern (although earlier precedents of holding summits in secluded locations had been set at the very first summit, at Rambouillet in 1975 and at the Montebello (Ottawa) summit of 1981. The US-hosted summit was held in the resort of Sea Island, off the coast of the state of Georgia, with delegations housed on nearby St. Simon's Island and in Brunswick, across the water in mainland Georgia. Journalists covering the event had to content themselves with being based at the International Media Center in Savannah, some 80 miles from Sea Island.

Sea Island turned out to be something of an aberration in G8/civil society relations. Bayne (2004) reports that the US hosts 'made no attempt to engage civil society organizations', provided no facilities for CSOs in Savannah or elsewhere and, breaking with long-standing summit tradition, did not permit even major, respected NGOs such as Oxfam and Greenpeace to distribute their literature in the media centre. Even those NGOs whose representatives are normally legitimately accredited to summits as journalists were unable to do so in Savannah. Nonetheless, some CSOs managed to communicate their views and literature through the good offices of friendly journalists. As well, Oxfam and Debt AIDS Trade Africa (DATA) held a press conference outside of the media centre, and Greenpeace and other NGOs linked up with local grassroots organizations in Savannah. Other NGOs submitted articles to Georgia newspapers. So, the ability of CSOs to get their message out may have been hindered but could not be suppressed. Notably, there was a strong and very capable African civil society presence in the US before and during the Sea Island summit.

The very tight security in Sea Island as well as in Brunswick and Savannah turned out not to be needed against demonstrators, of whom there were very few in the streets. Kirton (2004) estimates that the total number of participants at various summit-related demonstrations plus the TOES counter-summit in Brunswick, was only 500, with only 15 arrests on minor charges, and no injury or physical damage. Demonstrators and parallel-summit participants were vastly outnumbered by some 20,000 security personnel. Partly motivated by fear of terrorist threats, the disproportionate presence of security forces nonetheless seemed to be overkill.

On 8 June, the first day of the summit, a peaceful protest march was organized by the International Festival for Peace and Civil Liberties to oppose the Iraq war and the Patriot Act. Estimates of turnout ranged from 100 to 500. Among the reasons for the very low participation was a new Georgia law, initiated by Governor Sonny Perdue, which enabled the halting of protest at the discretion of the police or the National Guard. There was concern that the pre-emptive state of emergency in effect until 20 June, requiring a permit issued by the state for any assembly of more than six people in the streets of Georgia, was curtailing civil liberties. The main organizer of the protest, Kellie Gasink of Savannah had applied for the required permit eight months in advance but received it just the day before the march (Smith and Burnett 2004).

The counter-summit organized by TOES-USA was a disappointment. Trent Schroyer and Susan Hunt stated that 'efforts ... to continue the TOES tradition of facilitating a critical discourse about G8 policies were systematically blocked by the Bush administration and their sycophants in Georgia. ... Virtually every conference venue and lodging was either placed off-limits "for security reasons" or booked by the federal government to house the over 20,000 CIA, FBI, Homeland Security, Secret

Service, Army National Guard, state and local police' (Schroyer and Hunt 2004). It was only five days before the conference that Governor Perdue gave permissions for access to a venue, at Coastal Georgia Community College in poor and badly-polluted Brunswick. In addition, Schroyer and Hunt assert that the local population was intimidated by authorities and sensationalist media. The result was that despite a good intellectual lineup of speakers, the audience at the conference numbered no more than 75 for each of the 24 sessions held over three days. Ironically, according to Schroyer and Hunt, the G8 summit was held on land to which General Sherman, at the end of the American Civil War, gave title to the Gullah Geechee people, former slaves whose descendants today live in near-Third World conditions.

One forceful speaker at the TOES meeting was Barbara Kalema. She outlined some achievements by Africans, such as the peer review mechanism for NEPAD and greater regional integration, but criticized the G8 for failing to take real steps toward market access for Africa and for the decline of development assistance. She also noted that the late invitation to the six African heads of state (only a week before the summit) showed that Africa was not on the real agenda (Lugo 2004).

As for Sea Island summit documents, there is no reference to civil society in the 'Chair's Summary' (from which French President Jacques Chirac publicly disassociated himself). Some other Sea Island documents, however, do mention NGOs and civil society. For example, the action plan on 'Science and Technology for Sustainable Development' encourages co-operation among various stakeholders, including NGOs and communities. The declaration and action plan on 'Fighting Corruption and Improving Transparency' calls on G8 governments to foster civil society engagement, and in the associated 'national transparency and anti-corruption compacts', the governments of Nicaragua, Georgia, Nigeria and Peru undertake to consult with, or promote participation by, their civil society in some aspects of this project. The statement on 'Ending the Cycle of Famine in the Horn of Africa' points up the importance of building civil society capacity and greater involvement of CSOs in rural development. The action plan on 'Applying the Power of Entrepreneurship to the Eradication of Poverty' similarly asks for dialogue with civil society.

The 'Broader Middle East' initiative, the centrepiece of the US agenda for the Sea Island summit, acknowledges civil society a number of times. The declaration on 'Partnership for Progress and a Common Future with the Region of the Broader Middle East and North Africa' welcomes reform declarations from the region's civil society and commits G8 governments to a multi-stakeholder partnership in various programmes including the proposed 'Forum for the Future'. The 'G8 Plan of Support for Reform' in the area calls for multi-stakeholder approaches including, among other suggestions, civil society-to-civil society dialogue and civil society participation in the 'Forum for the Future' and the proposed 'Democracy Assistance Dialogue'.

Civil society evaluation of the Sea Island summit was again mixed. The trade-union movement voiced strong criticism; the International Confederation of Free Trade Unions (ICFTU) stated that '[f]or the first time in 27 years the host broke with tradition and refused to meet with leaders of the international labour movement'. ICFTU (2004) characterized Sea Island as 'a few modest steps but a wasted opportunity in key areas. Little was achieved as regards the much needed task of re-building multilateralism to serve the needs of the people, especially the world's poorest and most marginalized.'

Oxfam acknowledged some positive results, especially the joint G8 statement on the Sudan crisis and the Global Peacekeeping Initiative by which the US 'has shown at least the intent to fulfil its part of the Africa Action Plan'. But, although the leaders 'spoke welcome words, ... [they] made little progress on fulfilling the lofty promises they made ... at Kananaskis' especially on African debt relief, AIDS, trade reform and aid' (OI 2004).

In the lead-up to Sea Island, DATA produced a policy paper with recommendations to the G8 on Africa, the debt crisis, the HIV/AIDS crisis, the trade crisis, and democracy, accountability and transparency. In his summing up after Sea Island, DATA Executive Director Jamie Drummond was more upbeat than some other CSOs. He welcomed the G8 initiatives on the AIDS vaccine, on ending famine in Ethiopia, on eradicating polio, on fighting corruption and on African peacekeeping, but he expressed disappointment at the G8 leaders' failure to commit to the complete cancellation of poor countries' debt (DATA 2004a; 2004b).

African CSOs had a small but well-prepared presence around the Sea Island summit. At the conclusion of the summit African NGOs and trade unions issued a joint statement largely critical of the G8 performance but acknowledging some achievements. The statement commented on debt cancellation (HIPC had failed to reduce sufficiently the debt of eligible countries); trade justice (the summit failed to achieve a breakthrough on agricultural subsidies and continued to advocate trade liberalization which marginalizes Africa's trade position); HIV/AIDS (the group welcomed the G8's support for a global HIV vaccine enterprise but noted the continued underfunding of the Global Fund to Fight AIDS, Tuberculosis and Malaria and the G8's failure to recognize the urgency needed to deal with the pandemic); and financing for development (the statement noted that this was likely the first time that the G8 and African leaders acknowledged the contribution of remittances by the African diaspora but asserted that these private contributions should not be viewed as an alternative to sufficient development assistance) (The 2004 Summit of the G8 2004).

The Gleneagles Summit[10]

What unfolded in the lead-up to, and during, the 2005 Gleneagles summit was an unprecedented and many-faceted citizen participation. In addition to dialogue, demonstrations, alternative events, and potential for partnership something new emerged: the hugely successful series of music events called Live 8, massive demonstrations going well beyond NGOs and civil society coalitions to embrace very large numbers of concerned citizens in various countries; and a major role played by celebrities.

Consultations

The British hosts took up dialogue with civil society early in the process of preparing for Gleneagles. This fitted well with the UK government's agreement with the voluntary

---

10   For a more detailed account, see Hajnal (2006a).

and community sector, known as 'the Compact' (<www.thecompact.org.uk>). The two central themes of Gleneagles – Africa and climate change – had great resonance for civil society, and many NGOs were determined and well-qualified to convey their views and had the expertise and skill to do so, thereby giving the G8 governments valuable insights – as well as exerting pressure – on these crucial issues. African NGOs, for their part, have been increasingly active on the international scene and there are those among them who have participated in previous dialogue with officials of G8 countries. As for climate change, the environmental movement is among the oldest and most varied components of civil society, on local, national, regional and international levels. There is a long history of involvement with governments and international institutions including the G7 and G8 on environmental issues, ranging from productive, fruitful exchanges to confrontations.

The seriousness of British interest in Africa was demonstrated by Tony Blair's Commission for Africa which, in its report of 11 March 2005, took an integrated approach to the multitude of African problems. The report was communicated to G8 governments as well as NGOs and the private sector (Commission for Africa 2005). The relationship of this report to the NEPAD project and the G8 Africa Initiative launched at the 2002 Kananaskis summit is complex, but the Commission for Africa's findings are consistent with the G8 Africa Initiative and are intended to reinforce, not rival, NEPAD (Wickstead 2005). A knowledgeable African civil society activist characterized this relationship as follows: NEPAD, in a sense, was an exchange between Africa and the rich developed world – 'this is what Africa can do and these are the developed world's responsibilities'; the Africa Initiative was the G8's response to NEPAD; and the Commission for Africa's report is not only a good document but also a means to leverage NEPAD at the Gleneagles summit and beyond (Wanyeki 2005). The UK G8 presidency provided a useful comparison between the recommendations of the report of the Commission for Africa and G8 commitments at Gleneagles, in areas corresponding to the major sections of the Commission for Africa report: governance and capacity-building; peace and security; 'leaving no-one out'; growth and poverty reduction; trade; resources; and 'how to make it happen' (A Comparison... 2005).

Chatham House (Royal Institute of International Affairs) launched a useful and productive G8 stakeholder consultation project early in 2005, in partnership with FIM, the Green Globe Network, Climate Action Network, and LEAD International. For FIM, this dialogue built on its initiative prior to Kananaskis and continuing with Evian in 2003 (only to encounter a hiatus at Sea Island in 2004).[11]

The G8 stakeholder consultation involved a series of meetings throughout 2005. Two expert group meetings convened on 21 March, each devoted to one of the central Gleneagles agenda items: Africa and climate change. The recommendations from these two meetings fed into a consultation on 23 March in which 18 civil society representatives met with five sherpas (and four sherpa assistants for G8 members that did not have their sherpas represent them at the session). This consultation was the first such event in which all G8 governments were represented, showing an increasing

---

11 A brief analysis of the rationale, process and constraints of G8-FIM consultation can be found in Martin (2005).

realization of the benefits of the dialogue process. Civil society representatives included participants from Africa, Europe, the Middle East, Asia and North America, bringing together expertise on Africa and climate change. Trade unions and business organizations were not as well represented as nonprofit civil society was, and youth groups were not present. Topics of discussion included debt relief; meeting the aid target of 0.7% of GNI; trade; governance; and climate change. A number of specific recommendations were presented to the sherpas. A workshop called Post Gleneagles Opportunities was held at Chatham House on 21 July, at which UK government officials gave civil society representatives an overview of climate change and Africa issues and of the UK G8 presidency's plans to continue moving these issues forward for the rest of the year 2005. A workshop and panel discussion scrutinized the Africa Partnership Forum on 3 October, and another workshop and panel discussion on 10 October dealt with the climate change dialogue. Finally, on 7-8 November a conference, Delivering the G8 Agenda, was held, also at Chatham House, to discuss implementation of the Gleneagles commitments. At that conference, the British and (significantly) Russian sherpas consulted with representatives of the private sector and non-profit CSOs.[12]

Immediately before, as well as during, the Gleneagles summit, host Tony Blair met with some representatives of civil society, and so did some of the other G8 leaders. These meetings included talks with Bob Geldof and Bono, who, unlike regular CSOs and the media, had the run of the Gleneagles Hotel and were able to 'buttonhole' leaders and talk with them. Another instance of the British hosts' receptivity to civil society was the granting of media accreditation to a number of civil society representatives, and designated worktables for them in the media centre.

The Live 8 Concerts

Bob Geldof, Bono and many other stars of popular music staged the 'Live 8' concert series, recalling their 'Live Aid' concert to help relieve the Ethiopian famine twenty years earlier, but this time with the aim of raising awareness and giving voice to people, rather than asking for their money (Live 8 Launched 2005). Ten rock and pop concerts were held around the world on 1 July, attracting huge audiences ranging from 200,000 fans in London's Hyde Park and 250,000 in Philadelphia to 8,000 in Johannesburg.[13] The final, 11th concert took place in Edinburgh on 6 July on the eve of the summit. The reported total number of those watching the concerts on television the world over differed wildly, ranging from 3 billion (Geldof's announcement from the Live 8 stage Saturday), to 5 billion (*Independent on Sunday*) and 5.5 billion (Rod Liddle in the *Sunday Times*) (Jha 2005). The majority of people at the concerts were presumably there for the free music, but they were now exposed to major global issues before the G8 – issues they would not likely have heard or cared about before.

---

12 For an overview of the G8 stakeholder consultation, see the Chatham House website at www.chathamhouse.org.uk/index.php?id=345. This web page has links to all related documents.

13 Based on various reports in *The Sunday Telegraph*, 3 July 2005.

The Role of Celebrities

The role of celebrities in the campaign and during the summit is a fascinating phenomenon. At Gleneagles, Geldof and Bono were much in evidence at the Live 8 concerts, many public events, the Gleneagles Media Centre and the Gleneagles Hotel itself. They held a press conference on 6 July at the Media Centre. Participants included Kenyan environmentalist and Nobel Peace Prize laureate Wangari Maathai, British screenwriter Richard Curtis (one of whose films is *The Girl in the Café*, the plot of which centres around a semi-fictional account of the 2005 G8 summit taking place in Iceland), and a few other fellow celebrities. Kumi Naidoo, chair of the Global Call to Action against Poverty (GCAP), was also there, representing civil society coalitions. Bono and Geldof talked articulately, knowledgeably and passionately (if at times undiplomatically) about their conversations with Blair, Bush, Martin and Schröder.[14] Later during the summit, the two rock stars also met with Chirac and Putin. At the end of the summit, immediately following Blair's final press conference, Bono, Geldof and fellow celebrities held their own press conference in the same briefing room as the host leader. The two rock stars, acknowledging that the G8 did not do as much as it should have, nevertheless expressed satisfaction at the $50 billion aid pledged. Geldof said: 'This has been the most important summit there ever has been for Africa … Africa and the poor of that continent have got more out of the last three days than they have ever got in any previous summit. They got that because 3 billion people demanded that it should be so' (Leaders Boost… 2005; Beattie 2005). Canadian Prime Minister Paul Martin stated: 'the work that Bono is doing is tremendous … This is bringing a fundamental issue that the whole world should be concerned about in a way that none of the G-8 leaders can do' (Nelson 2005; Bono, Geldof… 2005). Dignitaries, including Kofi Annan and Nelson Mandela, used the occasion of the Live 8 concerts to add their voices to the mass appeal for greater debt relief, more and better aid, and fairer trade. Mandela appealed to G8 leaders for action, not words.

Praise for Geldof and Bono was not shared universally, and the G8 Alternatives Summit (discussed below) was not alone in its criticism. Stephen Lewis (2005: 26), former Canadian diplomat, well-known humanitarian and the UN Secretary-General's special envoy for HIV/AIDS in Africa, asserts that Geldof's 'incestuous proximity' to the UK government, his membership in Blair's Commision for Africa and his success with the Live 8 concerts made him 'an inescapable member of the Blair team … [and] a cheerleader for the G8'. [Bono fares better.] In his passionate advocacy for Africa, Lewis (2005: 146-47) was critical of broader civil society reaction to the outcome of Gleneagles, asserting that civil society was effectively co-opted by Tony Blair: 'Its normally tough, analytic appraisals were replaced by adoring complicity; the principled NGO community suddenly found itself basking in the … aura of power…. Most of the major NGO players knew that they'd been had, but … [in their post-summit press releases t]hey could barely summon a twitch of indignation, let alone a spasm of outrage. They congratulated the G8 on progress made, overstated that progress, and then uttered only the most plaintive pleas for more.'

---

14 For a detailed story and assessment of Bono's political and social involvement, see Traub (2005).

Celebrities who communicated with summit officials also included several religious leaders, led by the Dalai Lama who, along with representatives of the Russian Orthodox Church, the World Council of Churches, the Central Conference of American Rabbis, the Latin American Council of Churches and the Interreligious Council of Mexico, signed a 'joint declaration on climate change and the defense of life'. The declaration called upon 'all the people of our world for a critical common effort to preserve and promote life on this planet Earth' to respect and protect the environment, and to reduce emissions and other pollutants. It was given to a UK summit representative on 5 July (Office of the Dalia Lama 2005a; 2005b). Pope Benedict XVI added his voice to those supporting the Live 8 ideals. On 3 July, in his Sunday address to tourists and pilgrims in the Vatican's St. Peter's Square, he called for success of the Gleneagles summit in reducing debt, working to end poverty, and promoting African development (Pope Takes up... 2005).

Other prominent personalities called upon the G8 for meaningful action. They included UN Secretary-General Kofi Annan, Gro Harlem Brundtland (former Director-General of WHO and chair of the World Commission on Environment and Development) and Michel Camdessus (former Managing Director of the IMF and President Chirac's Africa Personal Representative) (Annan 2005; Brundtland and Camdessus 2005).

The Make Poverty History (MPH) March

This large and almost entirely peaceful demonstration took place in the Scottish capital, Edinburgh, on 2 July, with 225,000 people on the streets. Various NGO groups and coalitions participated, led by MPH (a coalition of some '400 charities, campaigns, trade unions, faith groups and celebrities who are united by a common belief that 2005 offers an unprecedented opportunity for global change'), Dissent (an anti-G8 'network of resistance'), G8 Alternatives and other groups. MPH itself is under the overall umbrella of the Global Call to Action against Poverty (GCAP). MPH marchers, as well as their numerous supporters around the world, wore white wristbands calling for ending poverty. Even Gordon Brown, Chancellor of the Exchequer, and Hilary Benn, Secretary of State for International Development (and Blair's Africa Personal Representative), associated themselves with the march, as did some prominent British clergy from both the Anglican and Roman Catholic faiths.

The G8 Alternatives Summit

This parallel summit in Edinburgh began with an opening rally on 1 July, but staged its main events as an all-day programme on 3 July consisting of eight plenary sessions plus 60-odd workshops and seminars. Its stated objective was to do ideological battle with the G8, rather than co-operating with it. Reportedly, 5,000 tickets were sold to this event (G8 Information Centre 2005). Two of the counter-summit's principal themes mirrored those of the G8 summit itself: Africa and climate change. The counter-summit followed the 'altremondiste' tradition, and many of the presenters were socialists and communists from Scotland, England, Italy, the US, France, Africa and Asia. The themes of the plenaries were: 'Resisting imperialism, resisting war'; 'Fighting corporate globalization and privatization'; 'Racism, asylum and immigration'; 'Africa: can Blair and Bush deliver?'; 'How do we get climate justice?', 'Militarism and nuclearism'; 'Aid, trade and debt'; and 'The attack on civil liberties and the war on terror'. The counter-summit ended with a rousing closing rally with the theme 'Visions of a better world'. The counter-summit was highly critical not only of the G8 but also of CSOs and celebrities co-operating with the G8. Compared with the Live 8 concerts and the MPH march, the G8 Alternatives Summit received relatively little coverage in the mainstream media. This despite the participation of such stars of the anti-globalization movement as Susan George of ATTAC, Walden Bello of Focus on the Global South, activist Bianca Jagger, and firebrand British Respect Party MP George Galloway. A popular book offered for sale at the counter-summit was *Arguments against the G8*, published shortly before the Gleneagles summit, with chapters by many of the activists who addressed the G8 Alternatives Summit (Hubbard and Miller 2005).

Edinburgh was the venue of two other counter-summits, attracting fewer participants (some 400 for each) and very little media coverage. One was the Global Warming 8 (GW8) conference on 5 July, hosted by a coalition of aid and environment agencies, the Working Group on Climate Change and Development. 'It offered a "reality check" to the G8 heads of state as people from eight developing nations outline[d] the devastating impact to be expected if climate change goes unchecked.' Speakers had come from Tanzania, Nigeria, Kenya, Zambia, India, Colombia, Honduras and the Philippines (Indymedia UK 2005). The other, held on 3 July, was called the 'Corporate Dream/Global Nightmare G8 Counter-Conference'.

Other Events, Fora and Demonstrations

Two related fora involved children and young people. Just before the Gleneagles summit, the J8 (a secondary-school global-citizenship initiative across the UK), held a three-day forum in Edinburgh with some 100 young people from G8 countries participating. They discussed African trade and poverty, and climate change; their communiqué (available at www.j8changetheworld.com), was presented to Tony Blair on the first day of the G8 summit. There was also a 'C8 children's forum' supported by UNICEF, which met at Dunblane with 17 delegates aged between 11 and 18 from several (including some very poor) countries. The meeting made recommendations on poverty, education, violence against children, governance, HIV/AIDS, child labour, the environment, health and nutrition. Child delegates to the forum appeared at the final Live 8 concert in Edinburgh, and the C8's recommendations were passed on to Tony Blair (Nybo and Dollarhide 2005; Unicef UK 2005).

Other actions included a relatively small and peaceful anti-war, anti-nuclear demonstration at the Faslane nuclear facility on 4 July, and demonstrations in support of asylum-seekers at the Dungavel Detention Centre on 5 July. A less benign event took place in Edinburgh on 4 July when unauthorized protests by anarchists ranging from peaceful groups to the Black Bloc disrupted the centre of the city. The mixed group included a 'Rebel Clown Army' staging a 'Carnival for Full Enjoyment', and various anarchists including the more violent kind that confronted police, resulting in a number of injuries and 70 to 100 arrests. Closer to the Gleneagles summit site, on 6 July, at Stirling and Auchterarder, groups of anarchists caused massive delays by blocking roads leading to Gleneagles and disrupting train services. There were some violent clashes with police, perpetrated mostly by the Black Bloc, particularly in Auchterarder where several hundred anarchists split off from a larger peaceful march. A few protesters managed to breach a steel fence around the Gleneagles complex; police brought in reinforcements and repaired the damage. (This was a 5½-mile long, 6-foot high double steel fence. The seven-day security operation cost £100 million.) A peaceful demonstration did take place later in the afternoon; the marchers were allowed to approach as close as 15 feet from the fence (Day of Hope... 2005).

Civil Society Reaction to the Gleneagles Summit

A glance at the titles or headlines of end-of-summit press releases of a sample of NGOs and other civil society coalitions and organizations indicates their clearly critical tone:

- 'Justice for Africa Postponed: The Campaign Continues' (ActionAid);
- 'G8 Summit Agrees More Talk, No Action' [on Climate Change] (Friends of the Earth International);
- 'The People Have Roared But the G8 Has Whispered' (Global Call To Action against Poverty);
- 'A Major Missed Opportunity To Tackle Dangerous Climate Change' (Greenpeace, 7 July 2005, based on the leaked version of the Climate Change communiqué);
- 'Bush Prevents Better Deal on Climate at G8' (Institute for Public Policy Research, UK);
- 'G8 Outcome on Debt Cancellation: Still No Giant Leap' (Jubilee Debt Campaign);
- 'This Is a Step Forward by Eight Men, Not Yet a Giant Leap for Children' (Save the Children UK);
- 'G8 Failure To Act on Climate Change Puts Millions of Lives at Risk' (Tearfund);
- 'G8 Turn Their Backs on the World's Poor' (War on Want);
- 'G8 Condemn Africa To Miss Millennium Development Goals' (World Development Movement); and
- 'G8 Fails To Set Climate Action Agenda' (WWF International).

Nevertheless, a closer reading reveals a more nuanced reaction, with many NGOs and CSOs noting several significant and praiseworthy achievements of the Gleneagles summit. Generally, civil society reaction to the Gleneagles outcome on the major issues on the agenda tended to be negative, although several civil society groups acknowledged and even praised progress in certain areas. For example, Kumi Naidoo, Chair of GCAP, acknowledged some G8 progress on aid and on debt cancellation, but stated that even this moderate progress 'would probably not have been achieved had it not been for years of civil society mobilization around these issues' (GCAP 2005a; see also GCAP 2005b).

MPH, in its response to the Gleneagles communiqué, praised the aid increase as a step forward that will save lives, but called for the G8 to do much more to improve the amount and the quality of aid. On HIV/AIDS, MPH gave credit to the Gleneagles summit's success 'by responding courageously to the scale of the AIDS emergency', but pointed out that insufficient new aid would undermine this delivery target. On debt, MPH characterized as a positive step the principle of 100% cancellation of debt owed to international financial institutions by some countries but criticized the Gleneagles action as 'an inadequate response to the global debt crisis'. On climate change, MPH expressed the view that the G8 'has missed the opportunity to make progress' (MPH 2005).

OI was more positive in its reaction to the outcome of Gleneagles. It noted with approval that the G8's commitment to an extra $50 billion of aid by 2010 could save the lives of 5 million children but cautioned that '50 million children's lives will still be lost because the G8 didn't go as far as they should have'. It was also critical of the G8 on debt and trade (OI 2005a; see also OI 2005b).

Friends of the Earth International (FOE) lamented that the small steps on debt relief and aid for Africa would be undermined by the summit's failure to address climate change. FOE welcomed Tony Blair's leadership in putting climate change on the agenda and working to move forward on this crucial issue, but blamed the Bush administration for its lack of progress. By contrast, FOE noted with approval the separate statement on the threat of climate change, issued at Gleneagles by Brazil, China, India, Mexico and South Africa (FOE 2005; G8 2005).

Civil Society's Impact at Gleneagles

One indicator of civil society's impact on the G8 is acknowledgement in collective documents as well as by the G8 chair and other G8 leaders; and the space opened up by the leaders for possibilities of civil society participation in the implementation of summit undertakings. Significantly, the Gleneagles final document on Africa makes no reference to civil society or NGOs, raising the question of whether civil society had insufficient impact for the leaders to acknowledge its influence in the most important collective consensus document of Gleneagles. Other Gleneagles documents, however, do acknowledge civil society and NGOs, and call for engagement and participation: the *Gleneagles Plan of Action: Climate Change, Clean Energy and Sustainable Development*; the document *Partnership for Progress and a Common Future with the Broader Middle East and North Africa Region*; the *G8 Response to the Indian Ocean Disaster, and Future Action on Disaster Risk Reduction*; the *Progress Report by the G8 Africa Personal Representatives on Implementation of the Africa Action Plan*; and the *G8 Statement on Counter-Terrorism*.

Another indicator can be found in the chair's comments. At his final press conference at the end of the summit, Tony Blair acknowledged that not everything he and the anti-poverty campaigners had wanted of Gleneagles was achieved, but added that this was 'a beginning, not an end…. All of this does not change the world tomorrow' (Blitz 2005; UK 2005a). But he paid tribute to the positive contributions of civil society, mass demonstrations, and celebrities, congratulating MPH: 'I can't think of a campaign that has been so brilliantly organised or struck such a chord with such a large number of people worldwide' (UK 2005a).

Sir Nicholas Bayne (2005a), former British diplomat and current scholar of G8 summitry, asserted in his evaluation of Gleneagles that the two defining features of Gleneagles were the London terrorist bombings and the solidarity of the leaders spurred by those deadly attacks; and the 'widespread positive involvement of civil society'. Some media accounts also credit the role of civil society in pressuring the G8 particularly on the debt forgiveness and in influencing the leaders' commitment to double aid to African and other poor countries.

When assessing civil society's impact on the official G8, it must be kept in mind that consultations with sherpas or other G8 officials, even when transmitted to the leaders, do not necessarily translate into G8 policy and practice as they unfold. This does not detract from the value of consultations, parallel summits and peaceful demonstrations. These interactions result in greater mutual appreciation: host governments gain an understanding of civil society voices and priorities, and civil society develops an awareness of the realities of political negotiations and their limits.

Markedly stronger participation of others outside the G8 members was a significant feature of Gleneagles. The series of Live 8 concerts, the MPH march, and fruitful dialogue between the leaders and civil society were at an unprecedented high level, and generated greater-than-ever global public awareness of the G8's work, role and influence. The leaders acknowledged the impact of civil society and broader citizenry around the world on the work and continuing objectives of this summit. The role of celebrities was striking. On the negative side, the 'uncivil society' of disruptive anarchists and, on the far end of the spectrum, terrorists marred the proceedings but their actions were perhaps a backhanded acknowledgement of the G8's importance on the part of such extremist groups.

Gleneagles Follow-up

Civil society's continued involvement in issues that were on the Gleneagles agenda did not stop at the end of that summit. The Gleneagles meeting was no more than one (however central) event in a series of conferences held both before and after the summit and, in some cases, in subsequent months and perhaps years. Having voiced their sometimes converging, sometimes diverging views on the results of Gleneagles, CSOs affirmed that their campaigns for greater debt relief, more and better aid, and trade justice would continue past the G8 summit. This played out at major international meetings between Gleneagles and the end of 2005 at the UN, the WTO and other fora. Some of these conferences failed to achieve meaningful advances on the issues left pending by Gleneagles. Thus, the record of Gleneagles follow-up is mixed.

Further consultations between G8 countries and civil society representatives took place after Gleneagles. Consultations intensified in 2006, Russia's year of G8 presidency (see below), and are set to continue in future, including the 6-8 June 2007 summit in Heilingendamm, Germany. Of particular concern, increasingly voiced, is the monitoring of the implementation of summit commitments, and ways of influencing G8 leaders to hear and heed the voices and accommodate the concerns of civil society.

The 2006 St. Petersburg Summit

The main agenda items for the 15-17 July 2006 St. Petersburg summit were energy security, health/infectious diseases, and education. Civil society had much to offer in all three areas for the consideration of summit leaders and their teams. In the lead-up to the summit, during 2005 and 2006, Russia sent out mixed signals on civil society relations. On the positive side, the Russian sherpa participated at the Chatham House G8 stakeholder consultation project (at both the 23 March and the 7-8 November 2005 meetings with civil society and other stakeholder representatives) where he affirmed his government's desire to continue the dialogue.

On the other hand, new legislation was passed by the Russian Duma (lower house of Parliament) on 21 December 2005 (with 376 votes for and 10 against) that would curtail the freedom of activity within Russia of NGOs with links to international or foreign NGOs – although the legislation as passed is less severe than the original draft had called for, the government having dropped provisions forcing foreign NGOs to register as purely Russian ones. President Putin's supporters in the Duma claimed that the new legislation would serve national security purposes, but his critics complained that this was an attempt to control one of the few remaining sectors not yet controlled by the state (Myers 2005; Russia's... 2005). The law was signed by Putin before the end of 2005 and went into effect in April 2006. It is to be hoped that the new legislation would not affect adversely the functioning of indigenous Russian NGOs as long as they work within Russian rules and legislation.

Dialogue

In an encouraging development, in the lead-up to St. Petersburg, Ella Pamfilova, chair of the Civil Society Institutions and Human Rights Council under the President of the Russian Federation (which had been established in 2002), announced at a 2005 year-end press conference that major Russian NGOs had initiated the formation of a 'Civil G8 2006' 'to support the Russian leadership's expressed willingness to co-operate with Russian and international civil society organisations during its G8 presidency'. The Civil G8's aim was to have an impact on the dialogue and to help bring the G8 agenda closer to the public (Teslenko 2005).

The Civil G8 mounted an ambitious programme, designed to develop proposals based on NGO positions on the three main topics of the G8's St. Petersburg agenda, but also to allow for input on additional issues of civil society interest; to organize national and international discussions in order to set civil society priorities and approaches vis-à-vis the official 2006 G8; to evaluate projects, ideas and recommendations of social significance for the G8; and to develop ideas and recommendations for subsequent G8 summits.

A series of conferences, seminars and round table discussions were held throughout 2006 (most of them in Moscow). A round table discussion of NGO experts on global energy security, education and infectious diseases took place on 16 February, and culminated in an international NGO forum on 9-10 March, called 'The Contribution of Civil Society Institutions to the G8 Agenda'. The forum coincided with a meeting of G8 sherpas, and, for the first time in civil society relations with the G8, all nine sherpas (from each of the G8 countries plus the European Union) participated, assembled on the stage facing the more than 300 Russian and international participants whose representatives posed a number of questions. Each sherpa, in turn, addressed the participants, though not all questions from the floor were answered. Participants could not reach consensus by the end of the two-day forum, but a week or so later the final recommendations – on energy, global pandemics, education, human security, trade and development (including African development), and intellectual property – were transmitted to the Russian sherpa.

On 3-4 July an international 'Civil G8 – 2006' forum was held in Moscow with more than 600 Russian and international participants. The forum transmitted its recommendations to G8 leaders on topics coinciding with, but also going well beyond, the official summit agenda: genetically modified organisms (GMOs) (crops and food); mechanisms of interaction of business and society; infectious diseases; global security and the interests of society; energy security; education; biological diversity; human rights; and the strengthening of global social and economic policies for sustainable human development. In a significant precedent in summit history, Putin addressed the forum and made a statement in which he included this promise: 'I want to assure you that everything that you expound will, in essence, reach the G8 countries' heads, and that not only will we study them attentively, but we will also analyse them most critically, and will take them into account in making ultimate decisions.' He singled out for special attention the NGO proposal concerning systematic mechanisms, consultation, and monitoring the implementation of summit undertakings. Having delivered his statement, he answered a number of questions from the forum's representatives, showing openness and readiness to engage in discussion, and demonstrating that he was well briefed on most issues that came up.

After the summit, the Civil G8 focused on the implementation and monitoring of G8 summit decisions, on evaluating the results of the consultative process, and on preparing recommendations for officials of the German-hosted 2007 summit. The final event was a conference of Russian and international NGOs on 2 December, called 'Delivering the 2006 G8 Agenda'.[15]

Apart from the Civil G8, heads and delegates of Christian, Jewish, Muslim, Buddhist, Shinto and Hindu religious communities from 49 countries met in Moscow 3-5 July for a 'World Summit of Religious Leaders'. They sent an appeal to the G8 leaders, to their religious communities and to people of good will everywhere, calling for dialogue and partnership among civilizations for a democratic, participatory decision-making process, placing high value on human life, condemning terrorism, emphasizing the importance of religious freedom, upholding ethical values, and maintaining responsible stewardship of the earth's resources (G8 2006n).

A month before the summit, the national science academies of the G8 countries and Brazil, China, India and South Africa signed two joint statements: one on energy sustainability and security and the other on avian influenza and infectious diseases.

---

15 For details of the Civil G8's activities see <www.civilg8.ru> (Russian) or <http://en.civilg8.ru> (English). See also Pamfilova (2006).

These address two of the main agenda items of the St. Petersburg summit from the perspective of the scientific community.[16]

The Russian hosts also used other tracks for dialogue with civil society, involving smaller select groups of representatives rather than large groups. The J8 youth forum that was active before the Gleneagles summit, participated around St. Petersburg as well.[17] Sixty-four young people (eight from each G8 country) between the ages of 13 and 17 participated in the 'Junior 8 Summit' on 7-18 July in Pushkin, near St. Petersburg. They discussed issues on the summit agenda (energy, education and infectious diseases) but also questions of tolerance and violence. In a further instance of consultation with the host government, participants shared their ideas with the Russian minister of health and development, as well as with the Russian sherpa. They presented an *Address to the Leaders* when, in another G8 'first', eight youth representatives met with the G8 leaders on 16 July in the Konstantinovskii Palace in Strelnya, near St. Petersburg (the site of the leaders' meetings). Putin addressed the J8 on 14 July and answered questions from representatives (Junior 8 2006).

A dialogue with trade union leaders – following a long G8 tradition of such meetings – was also part of the St. Petersburg process. Representatives of Russian and international trade union leaders met with Putin on 6 July for 75 minutes. The trade unionists presented the host G8 leader with their *Trade Union Statement to the G8 Saint-Petersburg Summit*, approved at their 5-6 July meeting. The statement addressed questions on the official summit agenda and issues beyond it, all from a labour perspective: respect for workers' fundamental rights; financing development; action on health; the need for a genuine development round in the multilateral trade negotiations; energy security, environmental protection and job competitiveness; achieving G8 aims in the field of education; and migration and international mobility of labour (G8 2006m). Putin promised that he would take all the proposals to his fellow leaders.

A three-hour meeting was convened at the presidential residence in Novo-Ogaryovo near Moscow, in the evening of 4 July between Putin and heads of the following international NGOs: Greenpeace, WWF, AI, Oxfam, Social Watch, CIVICUS, ActionAid, Consumers International, Human Rights Watch, Global Campaign for Education, GCAP, International Council of Women, and Transparency International. The Russian sherpa and Ella Pamfilova also participated. The NGO heads presented a wide-ranging communiqué to Putin, addressing these issues: climate change, energy and energy security; poverty and development objectives for the G8 (including aid, debt, education and health, conditionality and IFI governance reform, trade and livelihoods); and human security including proliferation issues. After the meeting, Kumi Naidoo, the head of GCAP, stated: 'We hope the G8 leaders will take into account the main ideas, and that such meetings will become regular, and the governments of G8 countries will cooperate with NGOs on a permanent

---

16 Accessible on The Royal Society website, at <www.royalsoc.ac.uk/displaypagedoc. asp?id=20741> and <www.royalsoc.ac.uk/displaypagedoc.asp?id=20740>. These statements follow on the academies' statement on the global response to climate change issued in the lead-up to the 2005 Gleneagles summit, <www.royalsoc.ac.uk/displaypagedoc.asp?id=20742>.

17 See J8 [youth forum] website at www.j82006.com.

basis' (G8 2006h). Putin, on his part, said that he did 'not rule out permanent dialogue between G8 and NGOs' (G8 2006j).

In the context of the broader G8 system, there were meetings of energy, education, health, science, as well as finance and foreign ministers before and after the St. Petersburg summit. Most such meetings can be useful venues for productive interaction, including dialogue, with civil society.

Counter-summits and Demonstrations

An alternative summit, 'The Other Russia', was held in Moscow on 11-12 July by civil society advocacy groups and Russian opposition figures. In some respects, this meeting followed the 'altremondiste' tradition, after the pattern of the World Social Forum and some earlier counter-summits; it wished to speak with a voice other than that of the Russian government.

Participants numbered in the hundreds and included prominent human rights campaigners, among them Lyudmila M. Alekseyeva and Sergei A. Kovalyov, as well as former Russian Prime Minister Mikhail M. Kasyanov, chess master and opposition politician Garry Kasparov, and former Russian sherpa Andrei N. Illarionov. They advocated the rule of law in Russia and expressed opposition to increasingly arbitrary and antidemocratic measures of the government under Putin. It was reported that more than 40 prospective participants had been arrested while travelling from other parts of Russia to the conference. Russian officials, including Putin's sherpa, criticized those western diplomats who attended. These included the UK ambassador and two senior US diplomats (Chivers 2006: A3). It should be noted, however, that the fact the counter-summit was held openly showed that the Russia of 2006 was not a totalitarian country. Moreover, members of certain mainstream opposition parties refused to attend a meeting in which former hard-line communists participated.

The agenda of 'The Other Russia' included civil rights, 'inner war', 'violation of society and nature', and 'authority and society'. Participants sent a letter to the G7 (not G8) leaders, voicing their concern over the 'full-scale campaign of political repression … in Russia' and detention and physical abuse of Russian opposition figures. They called upon 'the leaders of the free world to demand from Russian President Vladimir Putin the immediate release of all the victims of this campaign of repression and to cease all unlawful actions against the political opposition' (The Other Russia 2006; see also Kasparov 2006: A21). Putin used his end-of-summit press conference to support his claim to growing Russian democracy when he answered a reporter's question regarding 'The Other Russia': that forum 'is another sign that democratic processes are developing normally here and that we have a functioning opposition. … [I]f the opposition says some constructive things, it is really our duty, in my view, to take these opinions into account' (G8 2006i).

As was the case for four previous summits, 'The Poor People's Summit', was organized for the fifth time in Mali, this time in the town of Gao, more than a thousand kilometres from the capital Bamako. The 500 participants from 60 NGOs (mostly from Africa but some from Europe and North America) discussed debt and privatization, and voiced strong disappointment at the scant attention that the St. Petersburg summit paid Africa and the inadequate follow-up to previous G8 commitments to alleviate poverty on the continent (Counter G8... 2006; Poor People's... 2006).

A few small demonstrations and protests took place around the time of the summit.. Some were staged by an odd assortment of communist opposition figures and other groups including the far-right, white supremacist Anti-Globalization Movement of Russia, along with human rights activists, environmental campaigners and a few anarchists. On 14 July anti-globalization activists (estimates of their number ranged from 100 to 300) gathered for a two-day rally called the Russian Social Forum, on the grounds of the Kirov stadium in the outskirts of St. Petersburg and 20 kilometres from the summit site. Respected human rights figures, for example Lyudmila Alekseyeva and Vladimir Soloveichik, took part, but many would-be participants were detained by Russian authorities before they could reach the stadium. Participants planned to have a demonstration in the centre of St. Petersburg but the authorities refused to issue a permit and prevented them from leaving the stadium (Blomfield 2006; Activists Keep... 2006; Finn and Baker 2006: A13; Page 2006).

Nevertheless, a small protest group of about 250 people, organized by the Communist Party, gathered in central St. Petersburg. Several participants were detained by riot police after they defied the ban to carry flags or shout slogans. Both at the stadium and in central St. Petersburg there were many more Russians than foreign demonstrators.

Civil Society in Summit Documents

In his end-of-summit press conference, Putin, reporting on the summit, stated:

> our discussions took into account recommendations made by two very important forums that took place in Moscow at the beginning of July – the World Summit of Religious Leaders and the International Forum of Non-Governmental Organisations, the Civil G8 2006. These two forums were organised on the Russian presidency's initiative. The summit's discussions resulted in the substantial outcome of a whole range of agreements that are reflected in the corresponding documents. (G8 2006i)

If this was indeed so, it would indicate substantial civil society impact on the outcome. So, it is worth asking: how is civil society reflected in the public documents of the summit which are the main vehicle of communicating summit results?

The twin documents on energy security, the centrepiece of the St. Petersburg agenda – the G8 statement, *Global Energy Security* and its annex, the *St. Petersburg Plan of Action on Global Energy Security* – make no reference to civil society or NGOs. But a few other St. Petersburg documents do; for example, the statement *Education for Innovative Societies in the 21st Century*; the *G8 Summit Declaration on Counter-Terrorism*; and the *Report of the Nuclear Safety and Security Group*.

Civil Society Reaction to the St. Petersburg Summit

The generally critical tone of civil society views of the St. Petersburg summit are illustrated by the press releases during and after the summit of a sample of NGOs and other civil society organizations:

- AI, in a statement issued on 18 July, 'deplored the failure of G8 member states to put the protection of civilians above politics in their discussions of the conflict and condemned continuing attacks on civilians by both Israel and Hizbullah ... [In the aftermath of the escalation in the Hezbollah-Israel conflict,] the G8 leaders have failed conspicuously to uphold their moral and legal obligation to address such blatant breaches of international humanitarian law' (AI 2006).
- DATA's media release of 24 July was entitled 'DATA Calls on G8 and EU Political Leaders to Make Good on Their Promise to Make Trade Work for Africa' (DATA 2006).
- FOE stated on 14 July, on the basis of a leaked draft document: the 'G8 plans to address global energy security are dirty, dangerous and will continue to fuel climate change. Despite G8 pledges to take action against climate change, the draft plan currently includes backwards proposals for major investment in finding new oil and gas reserves, for increased oil refining capacity and for greater reliance on nuclear power' (FOE 2006).
- An OI spokesperson asserted on 17 July: 'By downplaying the fight against poverty, the G8 ignored the world's most critical crisis, one that will kill 11 million children by the time they next meet. Next year Chancellor Merkel must put the fight against poverty at the heart of the G8 agenda. Ending poverty is a race against time. This year the G8 were jogging in circles; Chancellor Merkel must make sure they are sprinting for the finish line in Germany next year' (OI 2006). On the summit's pledge to increase funding for the Global Fund, an OI advisor said: 'we have stronger words than Gleneagles but [are] still seriously short on the cash' (Campaigners... 2006).
- On 17 July, Greenpeace rejected the G8's claims on energy security: 'Once again the G-8 has failed to develop a strategy for real and sustainable energy security. The G-8 needs to get serious on these issues or it will drift into irrelevance' (GI 2006).
- Also on 17 July, Transparency International stated: 'The G8's statement on Fighting High-Level Corruption points to a maturing understanding of corruption and numbered days for impunity of public officials. The statements on oil and on Africa contain nods to the requisite initiatives, but are short on detail and lack concrete commitments' (TI 2006).

Modes of Civil Society Interaction with the G7 and G8

This survey and analysis of civil society interaction with the G7 and G8 shows that civil society actions have been of four main types: First, consultation with summit country leaders and officials. This is an important means of exchanging useful ideas, sharing common positions, and giving both G8 governments and responsible civil society groups greater legitimacy in the political process. Dialogue or consultation implies willingness to co-operate, though not necessarily to agree, with G8 governments. In recent years, G8 governments – particularly those hosting the summits – have, for the most part, welcomed and accommodated dialogue with civil society.

Second, demonstrations, advocacy and compliance monitoring. Peaceful demonstrations are a democratic right and the governments of democratic countries should not only permit but also facilitate such demonstrations, regardless of whether or not they agree with particular groups or their objectives. Provision of the appropriate level of public security is also a government responsibility, but it should be done in a professional, non-confrontational manner. Demonstrations can feature the whole gamut of civil society, from advocacy groups that prefer the co-operative mode of interaction through protester groups that do not wish to co-operate, to the violence-prone minority that tend to take advantage of the opportunity presented by such events and can hurt the cause of the peaceful majority of civil society groups. Advocacy and compliance monitoring has been and will remain essential roles for civil society.

Third, parallel summits or people's summits. These, too, are a legitimate democratic activity of citizen and NGO groups, and summit host governments should support rather than hinder this activity. These events attract both co-operative and non-co-operative groups, and the predominance of the former or the latter affects the tenor of each counter-summit. Ideally, the summit host government should provide premises (a meeting room of sufficient size) at a central location, with telephone, internet, food and other usual conference facilities. Constructive proposals of these parallel summits can then be transmitted to the G8 heads for consideration. A related point is the provision of working space for civil society groups. During some past summits (for example in Genoa in 2001), civil society groups arranged for premises where they could meet, discuss, prepare documents and interact with journalists and government officials. In one case (Okinawa 2000) the host government actually provided such an NGO centre.

Fourth, civil society partnership in G7/G8-initiated multi-stakeholder groups or task forces. Multi-stakeholder groups, including appropriate NGOs, are excellent examples of mutually useful partnerships. As with dialogue, partnerships imply willingness to co-operate, though not necessarily agree, with G8 governments and private-sector stakeholders. Both the G8 and civil society groups need a multi-stakeholder approach, productively involving governments, the private sector and civil society in the provision of public goods. Two good examples of such a multi-stakeholder partnership are the DOT Force (Digital Opportunities Task Force), which was active between 2000 and 2002; and the still active and important Global Fund. Notably, the 'Broader Middle East' initiative, the centrepiece of the US agenda for the Sea Island summit, acknowledges civil society a number of times. The declaration on 'Partnership for Progress and a Common Future with the Region of the Broader Middle East and North Africa' welcomes reform declarations from the region's civil society and commits G8 governments to a multi-stakeholder partnership in various programmes including the 'Forum for the Future'. The 'G8 Plan of Support for Reform' in the area calls for multi-stakeholder approaches including, among other suggestions, civil society-to-civil society dialogue and civil society participation in the 'Forum for the Future' and the also-proposed 'Democracy Assistance Dialogue'. Multi-stakeholder partnerships should flow logically from the constellation of NEPAD/G8 Africa Action Plan/ Commission for Africa report, but the decisions of the Gleneagles summit lack sufficient commitment to such a partnership.

Concluding Remarks

There has been a fair amount of examination and re-examination of the state and future of the civil society nexus with the G7 and G8, particularly after the September 11, 2001 terrorist attacks on the US. Former Canadian foreign minister Bill Graham (2006: 367, 370) said this at a conference in 2003: '[a]t all levels of governance, the support of civil society is vital for ensuring the integrity and soundness of policy making'. He added that 'international institutions must move beyond secret meetings of experts if they are to be recognized as legitimate and effective'.

It is now widely recognized that civil society is an increasingly important and powerful actor locally, regionally, nationally and globally. At its best, civil society gives voice to those who have been marginalized or left behind by globalization and it fights for the universal extension of the benefits of globalization. What are some of the factors that have contributed to civil society's success (and whose absence at times has mitigated against success) in interacting with the G7 and G8?[18]

First, NGOs and CSOs have been most successful when working in co-ordination or coalition with like-minded groups. The greater impact of networks and coalitions is not merely the function of larger numbers; the whole tends to be more than a sum of its parts.

Second, civil society has been most effective when it recognized and exploited linkages of G7 and G8 issues, as was the case with the interconnectedness of education, health and debt relief. Although it is natural for NGOs and CSOs to concentrate their energies on what they know best, it is important to avoid the 'single-issue' trap.

Third – and related to the previous point – an important factor is the realization that the G8 summit is part of a continuum of international meetings that advance or fail to advance on issues where the G8 summit is unable or unwilling to make progress. This was especially clear in 2005 and 2006 – as was civil society's awareness of the implications for continuing attention and action around these other international fora.

Fourth, thorough knowledge of the G7 and G8 system and process is crucial. There still are many myths and misconceptions about the nature and global governance role of the G7 and G8. NGOs and other CSOs have found themselves well positioned to succeed in ensuring fruitful dialogue with the G8 when they mastered the structure and workings of the whole G8 system, including ministerial, task force and sherpa meetings and their timing and agenda, as well as the G8 member governments' summit-supporting institutions.

Fifth, starting the dialogue and lobbying early in the summit process is essential. G8 agenda-building is at least a year-long process, being formulated and honed gradually from one summit to the next. The main agenda items are generally set by the host of the next summit soon after the previous summit, although host governments have had to heed other G8 governments' priorities as well as persistent, multi-year G8 issues. If CSOs hope to have any influence on the evolving summit agenda, they can do so more realistically if they get involved in the process early.

---

18 For a counterpart set of ideas – addressing what G8 governments can do to improve their interaction with civil society – see Kirton (2006a: 320-33).

Sixth, flexibility contributes to effectiveness. More successful CSOs have shown their readiness to be reactive or proactive, according to need. This implies, for example, taking advantage of issues that the G8 is seized of that are also important to CSOs, as well as lobbying to try to get other civil society concerns on the G8 agenda.

Seventh, it has been a continuing challenge for civil society to isolate potentially violent or disruptive elements. Seattle, Quebec City, Genoa, Evian/Geneva/Lausanne and Gleneagles showed that violence and anarchy could do immense harm to the vast majority of civil society activists who use peaceful and democratic methods. After September 11, it has become even more crucial for civil society to distance itself from, and isolate, the 'uncivil society' of violent anarchists and others of similar bent. CSOs have shown that they can succeed in this, but they must remain vigilant and step up self-patrolling and other efforts at events such as G8 summits.

Eighth, certain NGOs and other CSOs may choose on the grounds of principle or ideology not to participate in dialogue or other constructive interaction with the G8. In view of their limited human and material resources, CSOs also need to reflect on whether it is worth expending time and energy on dialogue and other interaction with G8 governments before, at and after summits and ministerial meetings. However, it is important to weigh carefully the costs and benefits of self-inclusion and self-exclusion and to recognize that the price of self-exclusion is lack of influence on the G8.

Ninth, information and communication technology (ICT) has played a crucial role in transforming and empowering civil society. It has increased the scope and the speed of CSO activity exponentially. For many NGOs, ICT is the tool of choice. They have been able to use the internet and other communication technologies strategically in fundraising, research, advocacy, service delivery, and networking and coalition-building. On the other hand, ICT can be used against civil society, or misused by mischievous or irresponsible elements within civil society itself.

Tenth, when a host country is unwilling to interact with civil society (as at Sea Island in 2004), NGOs and other CSOs were able to resort to other options to influence the G8: advocacy including the drafting and dissemination of policy papers, dialogue with receptive non-host G8 governments, and staging parallel events – in another country if necessary. Moreover, national NGOs in G8 countries are in a strong position to lobby their own government.

Finally, the record of civil society activism shows that while government initiatives toward nonstate actors are important, civil society does not have to take its cues from government. CSOs have been more successful when they developed strategies on their own terms.

The four dimensions of civil society action – dialogue, demonstrations, parallel summits and partnerships – have played an important role in the evolving relations with the G8. The usefulness of productive dialogue, forceful but peaceful demonstrations and creative parallel summits has been clearly shown. As well, multi-stakeholder partnerships can produce public good in ways that a single type of actor (governments, civil society or the private sector) cannot accomplish alone.

References

Note on internet addresses (URLs): Websites tend to appear, change or disappear, often without warning. Addresses cited in this source list were accurate and active at the time of writing (June 2006) unless otherwise noted.

'Activists Keep up Pressure on G-8 Leaders to Alleviate Poverty' (2006), Associated Press, 15 July.

Agence France-Presse (2003), 'Greens Glum as World Environment Day Heads for 30th Anniversary', 4 June, Paris.

Amnesty International (2002), Telephone Interview, 30 August.

Amnesty International (2003a), *A Catalogue of Failures: G8 Arms Exports and Human Rights Violations*, 19 May, IOR 30/003/2003, http://web.amnesty.org/library/Index/ENGIOR300032003?open&of=ENG-366.

Amnesty International (2003b), *G8: No Trade Off for Human Rights*, Press release, 2 June, POL 30/002/2003, http://web.amnesty.org/library/Index/ENGPOL300022003.

Amnesty International (2006), *UN: Security Council Must Adopt Urgent Measures to Protect Civilians in Israel-Lebanon Conflict*, Press release, 18 July, http://news.amnesty.org/index/ENGIOR410122006.

Annan, Kofi (2005), 'Here is What the G8 Leaders Should Do', *The Globe and Mail*, 6 July, A15.

Appel du Forum des Peuples, (2003), 'Consensus des peuples face au consensus du g8', Siby. www.attac.info/g8evian/index.php?NAVI=1016-114297-14fr.

Baker, Andrew (2000), 'The G-7 as a Global 'Ginger Group': Plurilateralism and Four-Dimensional Diplomacy', *Global Governance: A Review of Multilateralism and International Organizations*, 6:2, 165-89.

Baxter, Joan (2003), 'Poor People's Summit Held in Mali', BBC News, 1 June, http://news.bbc.co.uk/1/hi/world/africa/2957372.stm.

Bayne, Nicholas (2000), *Hanging in There: The G7 and G8 Summit in Maturity and Renewal*, The G8 and Global Governance Series, Ashgate, Aldershot, UK.

Bayne, Nicholas (2004), *Impressions of the 2004 Sea Island Summit*, 29 June, www.g7.utoronto.ca/evaluations/2004seaisland/bayne2004.html.

Bayne, Nicholas (2005a), *Overcoming Evil with Good: Impressions of the Gleneagles Summit, 6-8 July 2005*, Gleneagles and London: G8 Research Group, 18 July, www.g8.utoronto.ca/evaluations/2005gleneagles/bayne2005-0718.html.

Beattie, Alan (2001a), 'Aid Groups Could Miss G8 Talks', *Financial Times*, 2 July.

Beattie, Alan (2001b), 'Protests Aim to Breach G8 Cordon', *Financial Times*, 5 July.

Beattie, Alan (2005), 'Campaigners Divided on Aid Promises for Africa', *Financial Times*, 9/10 July, 8.

Blitz, James (2005), 'Blair Contrasts G8 with "Politics of Terror"', *Financial Times*, 9/10 July, 4.

Blomfield, Adrian (2006), 'Far-Right Racists Join the Protests', *The Daily Telegraph*, 14 July.

'Bono, Geldof Win Ear of Bush' (2005), *Toronto Star*, 7 July, A7.

Brundtland, Gro Harlem and Michel Camdessus (2005), 'The World Expects Bold Action', *Toronto Star*, 23 June, A25.

'Campaigners Say G8 AIDS Pledge Not Enough' (2006), Reuters Health E-Line, 17 July.

Chivers, C.J. (2006), 'Rights Activists Gather to Call for Russian Evolution', *The New York Times*, A3, 12 July.

Commission for Africa (2005), *Our Common Interest: Report of the Commission for Africa*, London, www.commissionforafrica.org/english/report/thereport/english/11-03-05_cr_report.pdf.

'Counter G8 Summit Disappointed at Little Attention Paid to Africa' (2006), Agence France Presse, 17 July.

A Comparison between the Recommendations of the Commission for Africa Report and the G8 Commitments (2005). www.number-10.gov.uk/output/Page7894.asp. No longer accessible.

DATA (2004a), *Disappointment, but Door Left Open to Progress on Debt Relief*, 10 June, www.data.org/archives/000527.php.

DATA (2004b), *G8 and African Leadership in the War on AIDS and Extreme Poverty*. June, www.data.org/archives/G82004report.pdf.

DATA (2006), *DATA Calls on G8 and EU Political Leaders to Make Good on Their Promise to Make Trade Work for Africa*, Media release, 24 July, www.data.org/archives/000798.php.

'Day of Hope Turns to Day of Violence' (2005), *The Scotsman*, 7 July, 1-5.

Dent, Martin and Bill Peters (1999), *The Crisis of Poverty and Debt in the Third World*, Ashgate, Aldershot, UK.

Dobson, Wendy (2001), 'Broadening Participation in G-7 Summits', in *Toward Shared Responsibility and Global Leadership: Recommendations for the G-8 Genoa Summit from the G-8 Preparatory Conference, 23-29*, G-8 Preparatory Conference, Turin.

Drop the Debt (2001a), *Bono, Bob Geldof and Lorenzo Jovanotti Meet G8 Leaders in Genoa*, Press Release, 20 July, www.dropthedebt.org. No longer accessible.

Drop the Debt (2001b), *Drop the Debt Response to the G7 Communiqué*, Genoa, 20 July, www.dropthedebt.org. No longer accessible.

Drop the Debt (2001c), *Verdict on Genoa Summit*, Press Release, 22 July, www.dropthedebt.org. No longer accessible.

Ekins, Paul (ed.) (1986), *The Living Economy: A New Economics in the Making*, Routledge & Kegan Paul, London & New York.

Evans, David (1981a), '"Popular Summit" Calls for World Disarmament', *Ottawa Citizen*, 20 July, 3.

Evans, David (1981b), 'Summit Security Noose Tightens around Ottawa Core', *Ottawa Citizen*, 21 July.

50 Years is Enough (2002), 'Activists Disappointed, But Not Surprised, As G7 Africa Decisions Affirm Economic Status Quo', www.50years.org/cms/updates/story/9.

Finn, Peter and Peter Baker (2006), 'At Carefully Staged G-8, Dissenters Kept in Wings', *The Washington Post*, A13, 16 July.

Friedmann, Harriet (2001), 'Forum: Considering the Quebec Summit, the World Social Forum at Porto Alegre and the People's Summit at Quebec City: A View from the Ground', *Studies in Political Economy: A Socialist Review* 66, 85-105.

Friends of the Earth International (2005), *G8 Summit Agrees More Talk, No Action*, Final G8 Media advisory, 8 July, www.foei.org/media/2005/0708.html.

Friends of the Earth International (2006), *G8 to Feed Oil Addiction, Fuelling Climate Change*, Media advisory, 14 July, www.foei.org/media/2006/0714.html.

G7 (1995), *Halifax Summit Communiqué*, 16 June, Halifax, www.g8.utoronto.ca/summit/1995halifax/communique/index.html.

G7 (1996b), *Economic Communiqué*, 16 June, Lyon. www.g8.utoronto.ca/summit/1996lyon/communique/eco4.htm.

G7 Environment Ministers (1996), *Chairman's Summary*, 9-10 May, Cabourg, www.g8.utoronto.ca/environment/1996cabourg/summary_index.html.

G7 (1997a), *Communiqué*, 22 June, Section 13, www.g8.utoronto.ca/summit/1997denver/g8final.htm.

G8 (1998), *Response By the Presidency on Behalf of the G8 to the Jubilee 2000 Petition*, 16 May, Birmingham, www.g8.utoronto.ca/summit/1998birmingham/2000.htm.

G8 (2001a), *Communiqué*, 22 July, paras. 2, 35, Genoa, www.g8.utoronto.ca/summit/2001genoa/finalcommunique.html.

G8 (2001b), *G7 Statement*, 20 July, para. 8, Genoa, www.g8.utoronto.ca/summit/2001genoa/g7statement.html.

G8 (2001c), *Genoa, City of Dialogue*, Genoa, www.genoa-g8.it/eng/attualita/primo_piano/primo_piano_2.html. No longer accessible.

G8 (2001d), *Terrorism: Statement by the Leaders of the G8 over Last Week's Terrorist Attacks in New York and Washington*, 19 September, www.g8.utoronto.ca/terrorism/sept192001.html.

G8 (2002a), *G8's Africa Action Plan*, 27 June, Kananaskis, www.g8.utoronto.ca/summit/2002kananaskis/africaplan.html.

G8 (2002b), *The Kananaskis Summit Chair's Summary*, 27 June, Kananaskis, www.g8.utoronto.ca/summit/2002kananaskis/summary.html.

G8 (2005), *Joint Declaration of the Heads of State and/or Government of Brazil, China, India, Mexico and South Africa Participating in the G8 Gleneagles Summit*, www.g8.utoronto.ca/summit/2005gleneagles/plusfive.pdf.

G8 (2006h), *NGO Leaders Pleased with Meeting with Putin, Hope Their Dialogue with G8 Leaders Will Become Regular*, St. Petersburg, http://en.g8russia.ru/news/20060704/1167339.html.

G8 (2006i), *Press Statement Following the G8 Summit*, St. Petersburg, 18 July, http://en.g8russia.ru/podcast/001/246/115/putin4_en.mp3.

G8 (2006j), *Putin Does Not Rule Out Permanent Dialogue Between the G8 and the NGOs*, St. Petersburg, http://en.g8russia.ru/news/20060704/1166906.html, http://en.g8russia.ru/news/20060717/1246115.html (transcription).

G8 (2006m), *Trade Union Statement to the G8 Saint-Petersburg Summit*, St. Petersburg, 6 July, http://en.g8russia.ru/news/20060706/1169801.html.

G8 (2006n), *World Summit of Religious Leaders. Message*, http://en.g8russia.ru/news/20060712/1174296.html.

G8 Development Ministers (2002), *Chair's Summary*, 27 September, Windsor, www. g8.utoronto.ca/development/09-2002-chair.html.

G8 Information Centre (2005), www.g8.utoronto.ca/evaluations/csed/CIVIL/events. html.

George, Susan (2001), 'L'ordre libéral et ses basses oeuvres', *Le Monde diplomatique* 48:569, 6.

Global Call to Action against Poverty (2005a), *Reflections on the G8 Summit*, by Kumi Naidoo, CIVICUS Secretary General and Chair of the Global Call to Action against Poverty, 13 July, www.civicus.org/new.

Global Call to Action against Poverty (2005b), *Statement by the Global Call to Action against Poverty Marking the End of the G8 Summit*, 8 July.

Graham, Bill (2006), 'Civil Society and Institutions of Global Governance', in *Sustainability, Civil Society, and International Governance: Local, North American, and Global Contributions*, 367-74, John J. Kirton and Peter I. Hajnal (eds), Ashgate, Aldershot, UK.

Graham, Robert (2003), '"Enlarged Dialogue" May Fall on Deaf Ears', *Financial Times*, 29 May.

Greenhill, Romilly et al. (2003), *Did the G8 Drop the Debt? Five Years after the Birmingham Human Chain, What Has Been Achieved, and What More Needs to Be Done?*, Jubilee Research, Jubilee Debt Campaign and CAFOD, www. jubileeresearch.org.

Greenpeace International (2006), *G-8 Fails to Develop Strategy for Energy Security*, 17 July, www.greenpeace.org/international/press/releases/g-8-fails-to-develop-strategy.

Hajnal, Peter I. (2001), 'Civil Society at the 2001 Genoa G8 Summit', *Behind the Headlines* 58:1.

Hajnal, Peter I. (2002), 'Civil Society Encounters the G7/G8', in *Civil Society in the Information Age*, 215-42, Peter I. Hajnal (ed.), Ashgate, Aldershot, UK.

Hajnal, Peter I. (2006a), *Civil Society and the Gleneagles Summit*, paper presented at the Civil G8 International Forum, Moscow, 9 March, www.g8.utoronto.ca/scholar/hajnal_060309.html.

Hajnal, Peter I. (2006b), 'Civil Society, the United Nations, and G7/G8 Summitry', in *Sustainability, Civil Society, and International Governance: Local, North American, and Global Contributions*, 279-318, John J. Kirton and Peter I. Hajnal (eds), Ashgate, Aldershot, UK.

Hajnal, Peter I. and John J. Kirton (2000), 'The Evolving Role and Agenda of the G7/G8: A North American Perspective', *NIRA Review* 7:2, 5-10.

Hanlon, Joseph and John Garrett (1999), *Crumbs of Comfort: The Cologne G8 Summit and the Chains of Debt*, Jubilee 2000 Coalition, London.

Hubbard, Gill and David Miller, (eds) (2005), *Arguments against the G8*, Pluto Press, London, Ann Arbor.

Indymedia UK (2005), *GW8 Audio: Global Warming 8 Counter Conference Recordings*, www3.indymedia.org.uk/en/2005/07/317152.html.

International Confederation of Free Trade Unions (2004), *Outcome of the Sea Island G8 Summit, 8-10 June 2004: Evaluation by the TUAC Secretariat*, www.icftu. org/displaydocument.asp?Index=991220130.

Jha, Alok (2005), 'How Many People Does it Take to be Right?', *The Guardian*, 7 July, G2:2,4

Jubilee Plus (2001), *Jubilee Movement International for Economic and Social Justice Statement on G7 Final Communiqué*, Press Release, 21 July, Genoa, www.jubileeresearch.org.

Junior 8 (2006), *J8 Delegation Meets the G8 Leaders*, St. Petersburg, 15 July, http://juniorg8.com/press/main/?page=28, http://en.g8russia.ru/news/20060718/1254740.html.

Kasparov, Garry (2006), 'What's Bad for Putin is Best for Russians', *The New York Times*, A21, 10 July.

Kirton, John J. (2000), 'Broadening Participation in Twenty-First Century Governance: The Prospective and Potential Contribution of the Okinawa Summit', paper presented at the conference 'The Kyushu-Okinawa Summit: The Challenges and Opportunities for the Developing World in the 21st Century', co-sponsored by the United Nations University, the Foundation for Advanced Studies in Development, and the G8 Research Group, Tokyo, July 17, www.g8.utoronto.ca/scholar/kirton20000717/.

Kirton, John J. (2004), *What the G8's Sea Island Summit Means for the World Ahead*, Paper prepared for a seminar at the Canadian Embassy, Tokyo, Japan, July 27, www.g8.utoronto.ca/scholar/kirton2004/kirton_040727.html.

Kirton, John J. (2006a), 'Building Democratic Partnerships: The G8-Civil Society Link', in *Sustainability, Civil Society, and International Governance: Local, North American, and Global Contributions*, 319-35, John J. Kirton and Peter I. Hajnal (eds), Ashgate, Aldershot, UK.

Klein, Naomi (2002), *Fences and Windows: Dispatches from the Front Lines of the Globalization Debate*. Debra Ann Levy (ed.), Vintage Canada, Toronto.

'Leaders Boost African Aid by $25b' (2005), *Toronto Star*, 9 July, A10.

'La Presse Internationale Conteste l'Utilité du Sommet' (2001), *Le Monde*, 24 July.

Lewis, Stephen (2005), *Race against Time*, House of Anansi Press, Toronto.

'Live 8 Launched' (2005), www.makepovertyhistory.org/2005/index.shtml.

Lugo, Chris (2004), *From the G8 to Africa to You – The Other Economic Summit*, Tennessee Independent Media Center, 10 June, www.tnimc.org/newswire/display/2189/index.php.

Make Poverty History (2005), *Response to G8 Summit Communiqué*, Press release, [8 July], www.makepovertyhistory.org/response.shtml.

Mander, Jerry and Edward Goldsmith (eds) (1996), *The Case against the Global Economy and for a Turn Toward the Local*, Sierra Club Books, San Francisco.

Martin, Nigel (2005), 'Not Representative, but Still Legitimate', *Alliance*, 10:2, June, 16-17.

Médecins Sans Frontières (2001), 'Violence Grants No Perspectives', Press Release, 20 July, Genoa.

Montreal International Forum (2002), *Civil Society and the G8*, 21-23 May, consultations in Montreal and Ottawa, www.fimcivilsociety.org/english/CivilSocietyG8.html.

Myers, Steven Lee (2005), 'Bill to Increase Russia's Control over Charities Moves Ahead', *The New York Times*, 22 December, A3.

Nelson, Fraser (2005), 'After the Revelry Comes the Cold Political Reality', *The Scotsman*, 4 July, 2-3.

Neslen, Arthur (2001), 'Mean Streets: On Location, Genoa Summit', *Now* (Toronto), No.1019, 26 July-1 August, 18-20.

Nybo, Thomas and Maya Dollarhide (2005), 'Young People at C8 Children's Summit Insist World Leaders Listen', www.unicef.org/policyanalysis/index_27604.html.

Office of the Dalai Lama (2005a), 'Inter-religious Declaration Presented to the G8 Summit Leaders', [London,] 6 July.

Office of the Dalai Lama (2005b), 'Leaders Joint Declaration on Climate Change and the Defense of Life', [Dharmasala, India?] July 2005.

The Other Russia (2006), *Closing Statement of the Participants of the Other Russia Conference*, www.theotherrussia.ru/eng/.

Owen, Henry (1978), Memorandum to President Jimmy Carter. Jimmy Carter Library, WHCF-Subject File, Box FO-44, Memorandum, Henry Owen to President Carter, May 9, 1978.

Oxfam International (2001), *Genoa Fails: Big Promise for Next Year*. Press release, 22 July, Genoa, www.oxfam.org/eng/pr010722_G8_Reaction_to_Genoa.htm. No longer accessible.

Oxfam International (2004), *Oxfam on G8 2004: More Said than Done, and Not Enough Said*, Press release, 10 June, www.oxfam.org/en/news/pressreleases2004/pr040610_G8_final.htm.

Oxfam International (2005a), *Oxfam International Reaction to the G8 Outcome*, Press release, 8 July, www.oxfam.org/en/news/pressreleases2005/pr050708_g8.htm.

Oxfam International (2005b), *What Does $50 Billion by 2010 Actually Mean?* Press release, 8 July.

Oxfam International (2006), *Oxfam Verdict on St. Petersburg G8 Summit*, 17 July, www.oxfam.org/en/news/pressreleases2006/pr060717_g8verdict.

Page, Jeremy (2006), 'Fear Silences the Voices of Russian Revolution', *The Times*, 17 July.

Pamfilova, Ella (2006), 'The Civil G8 2006', in *G8 Summit 2006: Issues and Instruments*, 23, Maurice Fraser (ed.), Newsdesk Communications, London.

People's Summit (1995), *Communiqué from the People's Summit*, 16 June, Halifax.

'Picking Up the Pieces: After the Genoa Summit' (2001), *The Economist* 360:8232, 28 July, 49-50.

'"Poor People's Summit" Slams G8 Policies' (2006), *All Africa*, 18 July, http://allafrica.com/stories/200607180812.html.

'Pope Takes up Live 8 Message' (2005), *Toronto Star*, 4 July, A7.

Risbud, Sheila (2006), 'Civil Society Engagement: A Case Study of the 2002 G8 Environment Ministers Meeting', in S*ustainability, Civil Society and International Governance: Local, North American and Global Contributions*, 337-42, John J. Kirton and Peter I. Hajnal (eds), Ashgate, Aldershot, UK.

Rivera, Nicolás Nogueras (1976), Letter to President Gerald Ford. Gerald R. Ford Library, WHCF-Subject File, FO 6-5, Box 33, Economic Summit Conference, Puerto Rico, 6/27-28/76.

'Russia's Anti-West Offensive' (2005), *The New York Times*, 27 December, A22.

Sanger, David E. (2001), 'Two Leaders Tell of Plot to Kill Bush in Genoa', *New York Times*, 26 September, B1.

Sauzey, François (ed.) (1978), *The London Summit Revisited*, T16, Trilateral Commission, Washington, DC.

Schroyer, Trent (ed.) (1997), *A World That Works: Building Blocks for a Just and Sustainable Society*, A TOES Book. Bootstrap Press, New York.

Schroyer, Trent and Susan Hunt (2004), *TOES 2004 Experience in Georgia*, www.toes-usa.org/TOESBrunswick.html.

Smith, Janel and Montana Burnett (2004). *Report on Civil Society Presence at 2004 G8 Summit*, G8 Research Group, 10 June, Savannah, www.g8.utoronto.ca/g8online/2004/english/featured-content5.html.

Tagliabue, John (2003), 'Chirac To Call for a Shift from Battling Terrorism to Helping Poorer Nations', *The New York Times*, 1 June, YT13.

Teslenko, Peter (2005), 'Press Conference on Co-operation between Civil Society and the Group of Eight during Russia's Presidency', Moscow, 20 December, [Canadian embassy official in Moscow], www.g8.utoronto.ca/whatsnew/cs051220.html.

Transparency International (2006), *The G8 Communiqué: Strong Words on Global Fight against Corruption, Treading Water on Africa and Oil*, 17 July, http://transparency.org/news_room/latest_news/press_releases/2006/2006_07_17_g8_communique.

Traub, James (2005), 'The Statesman[: Why, and How, Bono Matters]', *The New York Times Magazine*, 18 September, 80-89, 96, 98, 113, 120, 180, 187.

The 2004 Summit of the G8: Trick or Retreat? Joint Statement from African NGOs and Trade Unions at the Conclusion of the 2004 Summit (2004), www.oxfam.org.uk/what_we_do/issues/panafrica/rich_countries.htm.

UNICEF UK (2005), 'C8 Children in Urgent Plea to G8 Leaders on Murrayfields Stage To Make a World Fit for Children', Press release, [8?] July.

United Kingdom, Prime Minister (2005a), 'British Prime Minister Tony Blair Reflects On 'Significant Progress' Of G8 Summit', Press Conference at the Conclusion of the Gleneagles Summit, 8 July, www.g8.gov.uk/servlet/Front?pagename=OpenMarket/Xcelerate/ShowPage&c=Page&cid=1078995903270&a=KArticle&aid=1119520262754.

Wanyeki, L. Muthoni (2005), Remarks as Executive Director of the African Women's Development and Communications Network (FEMNET) at the conference 'Global Democracy: Civil Society Visions and Strategies', Montreal, 29 May-1 June.

Wickstead, Myles (2005), Presentation as Head of the Secretariat to the Commission for Africa, Munk Centre for International Studies, University of Toronto, 25 April.

World Development Movement (2001), *WDM Report on the G8 Summit in Genoa, July 2001*, www.wdm.org.uk/campaigns/Genoa.htm.

Zupi, Marco (2001), 'The Genoa G-8 Summit: Great Expectations, Disappointing Results', *The International Spectator* 36:3, 59.

Chapter 10

Evaluating the Summits

Critical comments were made almost as soon as the G7 summit first met at Rambouillet in 1975 (as G6 that year, before Canada joined), and they have intensified and diversified greatly in the years that followed. The media naturally gravitated toward these important meetings of the leaders of major industrialized democratic countries. This resulted in much journalistic writing about the events and the issues and personalities involved. Later, scholarly analyses of summit results started to appear, along with assessments of results by civil society and other stakeholders with interest in G7- and G8-related issues. Civil society assessments of individual summits are described and discussed in Chapter 9. The present chapter focuses on three sets of scholarly evaluations, each with its own objective and approach. Putnam and Bayne (1987), and Bayne (1997; 2005) assess summits on the basis of co-operative achievements of the leaders. George M. von Furstenberg and Joseph P. Daniels, and later John J. Kirton and Ella (Eleonore) Kokotsis evaluate compliance with measurable or verifiable commitments by the summits. Finally, the Foreign Policy Centre, a think tank based in London, uses the 'scorecard' approach to assess the record of summit host countries.

Leaders' Co-operative Achievements

Robert D. Putnam and Nicholas Bayne (1987: 270, Table 11.1), writing in 1987, assessed the leaders' co-operative agreements and other achievements at each G7 summit from 1975 to 1986, presenting a letter grade from the highest 'A' to the lowest 'E'. In 1997 Bayne updated the Putnam scale, yielding higher marks for the 1989-1994 summits than was the case for the 1981-1988 summits but lower than for the first summits from 1975 to 1980. In late 1998 Bayne had updated and revised the score to cover the years 1975 through 1998. Still later, in 2005, Bayne (2005b: 12-15) again updated the grades for all summits from 1975 to 2004 and described in detail his method of assessing summit performance, the subjects assessed, and the grading system using six criteria (previously he had used only five criteria, without 'solidarity'):

- Leadership: 'how far the G8 summit was able to exercise the political authority'.
- Effectiveness: 'the summits' ability to reconcile the tensions between different pressures on the member governments'.
- Solidarity: were 'all the G8 countries committed to the decisions taken at the summit, so that they could be fully implemented'?

- Durability: has 'the agreement reached at the summit produced a lasting solution to the problem'?
- Acceptability: have 'the solutions reached at the summit commanded the support not only of the G8 members but also of the world community as a whole'?
- Consistency: have 'G8 decisions in one policy area, such as finance, fitted in with the policies the G8 adopted on other subjects, like trade or development'?

Table 10.1 is based on Bayne's findings. His detailed 2005 assessments focus on achievement of G8 summits in the areas of: international finance, particularly as regards the new international financial architecture and debt relief for poor countries; international trade and development issues; and Africa, terrorism and non-proliferation of weapons of mass destruction (Bayne 2005b: 61-78, 105-25, 169-88).

Compliance with Summit Commitments

Writing in 1989 about summit performance, Kirton (1989a: 3) noted 'a threefold progression – from effectiveness in the period 1975-1980, to reduced effectiveness in the period 1981-1984, to a renaissance in effectiveness in the period 1985-1988'. By contrast, C. Fred Bergsten and C. Randall Henning (1996: 3-4), writing on the eve of the 1996 Lyon summit, presented quite a pessimistic assessment of G7 performance, although it focused on the G7 finance ministers rather than the summit itself. They remarked: '[t]he G-7's effectiveness has declined sharply over the last decade ... [and] that this recent paralysis is the strongest indictment of the contemporary G-7'. Kirton (1997) argued that this criticism 'comes from those who conceive the G7's central purpose as producing large package deals, embracing macroeconomic, trade and energy policy, through which governments can optimize economic performance through direct, collective intervention'.

In 1991 and 1992, von Furstenberg and Daniels examined the degree of compliance with 209 verifiable undertakings of fifteen summits (1975-1989), primarily in the areas of inflation, unemployment, economic growth, fiscal imbalances, interest rates, exchange rates, and energy policy (Furstenberg and Daniels 1991; 1992). They gave a combined score of 0.317 (simple average) or 0.280 (weighted average); that is, these undertakings were honoured only one-quarter to one-third of the time. Their findings showed a wide variation in compliance among summit countries (with Canada and Great Britain scoring higher than France and the US) as well as different rates from issue to issue. Von Furstenberg and Daniels concluded:

> the fact that undertakings remain largely unfulfilled means that the process has as yet acquired little binding force and that fuzziness and credibility have not been supporting each other in this regard. Rather, the low level of credibility may have made fuzziness indicative of a lack of commitment. If ... the economic declarations are the main institutional product of the summit process, the product has yet to prove itself as deserving of much credit with the public. (Furstenberg and Daniels 1992: 43)

Table 10.1   Co-operative Achievements of G7 and G8 Summits, 1975-2005

Year	Summit Site	Achievements	Grade
	First series	**Reviving growth**	
1975	Rambouillet	Monetary reform	A-
1976	San Juan, Puerto Rico	Nothing significant	D
1977	London	Trade, growth, nuclear power	B-
1978	Bonn	Growth, energy, trade	A
	Second series	**Holding down inflation**	
1979	Tokyo	Energy	B+
1980	Venice	Afghanistan, energy	C+
1981	Ottawa (Montebello)	Trade ministers' quadrilateral	C
1982	Versailles	East-West trade, surveillance	C
	Third series	**The rise of politics**	
1983	Williamsburg, Virginia	Euromissiles	B
1984	London	Debt	C-
1985	Bonn	Nothing significant	E
1986	Tokyo	Terrorism, surveillance, G7 finance ministers	B+
1987	Venice	Nothing significant	D
1988	Toronto	Debt relief for poor countries	C-
	Fourth series	**End of the Cold War**	
1989	Paris (Summit of the Arch)	Helping Central Europe, environment, debt	B+
1990	Houston	Trade (no net advance)	D
1991	London	Helping USSR	B-
1992	Munich	Nothing significant	D
1993	Tokyo	Trade	C+
	Fifth series	**Institutions for globalization**	
1994	Naples	Russia into political debate	C
1995	Halifax	Institutional review, IMF and UN reform	B+
1996	Lyon	Debt, development	B
1997	Denver (Summit of the Eight)	Russian participation, Africa	C-
1998	Birmingham (first G8 summit)	New format, crime	B+
	Sixth series	**Fighting terrorism and its causes**	
1999	Köln (Cologne)	Debt, Kosovo, finance	B+
2000	Okinawa	Outreach, information technology	B
2001	Genoa	Infectious diseases, Africa	B
2002	Kananaskis, Alberta	Africa, cleaning up WMD	B+
2003	Evian	Outreach, reconciliation	C+
2004	Sea Island, Georgia	Middle East	C+
2005	Gleneagles, Scotland	*Climate change dialogue, Africa	**A-

*   *Based on Bayne (2005a).*
**   *Reported by John J. Kirton as Bayne's 'preliminary grade'.*
Notes: *Adapted from (Bayne 2005b: 18 Table 2.1, 214 Table 14.1). Reproduced with Sir Nicholas Bayne's permission.*
             For details of the summits and their agenda, see chapters 3 and 5.

Building on the von Furstenberg and Daniels work, the G8 Research Group, under the leadership of Kirton, and with major research by Kokotsis, began a G7/G8 compliance study with the 1996 Lyon summit, and has continued this work on an annual as well as cumulative basis, the latest result being the 2005 Gleneagles summit's final compliance report, accessible at <www.g8.utoronto.ca/evaluations/2005compliance_final/2005-g8compliance-final.pdf>. The full text of commitments of all summits from 1975 to 2006 may be found on the Research Group's website, at <www.g8.utoronto.ca/evaluations/G8_commitments.pdf>, the methodology of the compliance studies is described by Kokotsis at <www.g8.utoronto.ca/evaluations/methodology/g7c2.htm>, and her complete compliance coding manual is accessible at <www.g8.utoronto.ca/evaluations/compliance_manual_2006.pdf> (see also Daniels 1993; Kokotsis 1999).

Kokotsis (2004) defines a commitment 'as a discrete, specific, publicly expressed, collectively agreed statement of intent, a "promise" or "undertaking" by Summit members that they will take future action to move toward, meet or adjust to an identified welfare target.' Commitments must satisfy several criteria in order to qualify: first, they 'must be discrete, in that each specified welfare target represents a separate commitment, even if a single set of actions is declared to be in support of these multiple aims'. Second, they 'must be sufficiently specific, in the future action (the instrument), or the timetable of the welfare target to be both identifiable and measurable'. Third, they 'must be future-oriented, rather than represent endorsements of previous or simultaneously unfolding action'. And fourth, 'while action by Summit members is assumed to be required in the future, this need not be specified. Verbal instructions to international institutions, issued at the time of the Summit in the passive … are included as there is an assumption that summit members will take action to move toward this result. There is also a specified actor target and welfare target.'

What constitutes compliance? According to Kokotsis (2004), '[c]ompliance requires conscious new or altered effort by national governments in the post-Summit period. Summit members must actively and consciously endeavour to implement the provisions contained in Summit communiqués.' In the work of the G8 Research group, '[c]ompliance is measured according to governmental actions designed to modify existing instruments within the executive branch to accommodate the commitments reached. A commitment can be said to have been fully complied with if a Summit member succeeds in achieving the specific goal set out in the commitment.' A five-point scale is used, assessing '[o]fficial reaffirmation', '[i]nternal bureaucratic review and representation', '[b]udgetary and resource allocations … made or changed', '[n]ew or altered programs, legislation and regulations' and '[f]ull implementation; the welfare target is substantially achieved'. Kokotsis and Kirton use the following three-level measurement:

> [f]ull or nearly full conformance with a commitment … [receives] a score of +1. A score of -1 indicate[s] complete or nearly complete failure to implement a commitment. An 'inability to commit', or a 'work in progress' … [gets] a score of 0. An 'inability to commit' refers to factors outside of the executive branch impeding the implementation of a given commitment and a 'work in progress' refers to an initiative that has been launched by a government but is not yet near completion and whose results can therefore not be judged.

Table 10.2   Compliance with G7 and G8 Summit Commitments, 1975-2006

Year	Summit Site	Number of Commitments	Compliance Score
	First hosting rotation		
1975	France: Rambouillet	14	+57.1
1976	US: San Juan, Puerto Rico	7	+08.9
1977	UK: London (London I)	29	+08.4
1978	Germany: Bonn (Bonn I)	35	+36.3
1979	Japan: Tokyo (Tokyo I)	34	+82.3
1980	Italy: Venice (Venice I)	55	+07.6
1981	Ottawa (Montebello)	40	+26.6
	Second hosting rotation		
1982	France: Versailles	23	+84.0
1983	US: Williamsburg, Virginia	38	-10.9
1984	UK: London (London II)	31	+48.8
1985	Germany: Bonn (Bonn II)	24	+01.0
1986	Japan: Tokyo (Tokyo II)	39	+58.3
1987	Italy: Venice (Venice II)	53	+93.3
1988	Canada: Toronto	27	-47.8
	Third hosting rotation		
1989	France: Paris (Summit of the Arch)	61	+07.8
1990	US: Houston	78	-14.0
1991	UK: London (London III)	53	00.0
1992	Germany: Munich	41	+64.0
1993	Japan: Tokyo (Tokyo III)	29	+75.0
1994	Italy: Naples	53	+100.0
1995	Canada: Halifax	78	+100.0
	Fourth hosting rotation		
1996	France: Lyon	128	+36.2
1997	US: Denver (Summit of the Eight)	145	+12.8
1998	UK: Birmingham (first G8 summit)	73	+31.8
1999	Germany: Köln (Cologne)	46	+38.2
2000	Japan: Okinawa	105	+81.4
2001	Italy: Genoa	58	+49.5
2002	Canada: Kananaskis, Alberta	187	+35.0
	Fifth hosting rotation		
2003	France: Evian	206	+65.8
2004	US: Sea Island, Georgia	245	+54.0
2005	UK: Gleneagles, Scotland	212	+65.0
2006	Russia: St. Petersburg	317	N/A
	Average	*80*	*+41.9*

Notes: *Based on research by John J. Kirton and Ella Kokotsis. Reproduced with Professor John J. Kirton's permission.*

Compliance scores from 1990 to 1995 measure compliance with commitments selected by Ella Kokotsis. Compliance scores from 1996 to 2005 measure compliance with G8 Research Group's selected commitments. Score for 2006 is not yet available.

Table 10.2 shows the Kirton/Kokotsis record of compliance with commitments of the summits from 1975 to 2006, but in terms of average scores rather than on the +1/-1/0 scale. These scores reflect the combined averages of G8 countries on compliance with all issues selected for the study (Kokotsis 2006: 37).

Although quantification can be problematic when it involves numerical evaluation of texts, there can, at times, be sufficient specificity; for example, documents can be skimmed for concrete, verifiable undertakings such as a commitment to increase aid to 0.7%. Other commitments can be seen as merely aspirational. Thus, the exercise is an inventory of quantifiable parts but not all parts of a particular document. Modest measures, dealing with specific undertakings, can be quantified, and credibility scores can be calculated. Moreover, when goals had been stated specifically in summit documents, compliance scores are useful measures of past performance.

Apart from quantitative assessments, it may be noted that reports by the news media generally show growing disenchantment with the summits, although certain summits, for example the 1995 Halifax summit, received rather more favourable treatment. Discussing summits from a British point of view, Michael R. Hodges (1994) commented: '[o]verall the G-7 summits are considered to be a worthwhile endeavour, although individual meetings have been of variable utility. Munich was ... not worth the time invested; Tokyo [1993] was perceived as more successful.' Writing in 1995 about implementation of summit commitments, Kirton (1995: 67) remarked: '[c]ompliance is very high in the fields of international trade and in energy (a category which has now broadened to include the global environment), very low in the monetary policy areas of foreign exchange, inflation and interest rates, and somewhat better in the Keynesian fundamentals of demand composition, fiscal adjustments, official development assistance, and Gross National Product (GNP) growth'.

The 'Scorecard' Approach

In the run-up to the 2006 St. Petersburg G8 summit, chaired by Russia, the Foreign Policy Centre in London issued its first annual 'scorecard' aimed at: presenting data on G8 commitments; monitoring the behaviour of the country holding the presidency of the G8 on implementing the principles of freedom and democracy; identifying examples of good practice among G8 members; and allowing for comparison over time. The scoring system is designed to capture key characteristics relevant to membership in the G8 and adapted from principles of the founding declaration of the G8 (then the G6) at Rambouillet in 1975: liberal democracy, a stable and growing economy, and global governance. The 12 indicators are:

- Openness and freedom of speech;
- Political governance;
- Rule of law;
- Civil society;
- Economic weight in the world;
- Inflation;

Table 10.3   Scorecard Results – Russia 2006

Indicator	Score
Open Society	5
Political Governance (elections)	4
Rule of Law	4
Civil Society (social capital)	4
Economic Growth and Stability	3
Inflation	3
Stable Exchange Rate and Market Conditions	3
Unemployment Levels	4
Trade Volume	3
Trade Restrictions (protectionism, etc.)	4
Energy Market Conditions and Policies	4
Discernable Stance on Key International Issues	4

Notes: Scoring: 1 = broad compliance
2 = moderate compliance
3 = sporadic compliance
4 = lack of compliance
5 = total failure to comply

Based on data from: Freedom House, World Bank, WHO, IMF, Russian official statistics, Economist Intelligence Unit, Energy Information Administration, Foreign Policy Centre and various print and electronic media (Barnes and Owen 2006: 18-19).

- Economic stability and solvency;
- Unemployment;
- Volume of trade;
- Protectionism;
- Energy market conditions; and
- Stance on key international issues.

For each indicator, the scorecard assesses the measure of each country's compliance with G8 norms on a five-point scale: (1) broad compliance; (2) moderate compliance; (3) sporadic compliance; (4) lack of compliance; and (5) total failure to comply (Barnes and Owen 2006: 1-8).

Russia, the subject of this first 'scorecard' fares poorly or very poorly on eight indicators and in a mediocre manner on another four. Table 10.3 shows the details of the scores.

Concluding Remarks

There has been long-running interest in evaluating summit achievements. Examining and analyzing the leaders' co-operative agreements is an important method of accomplishing this. The fact that each of these methods starts from different premises and each measures or evaluates different aspects of the subject makes them difficult to compare. Nonetheless, the studies cover the period from the inception of the summits in 1975 to 2006, yielding evaluations over a period of thirty-two years. They reveal relatively high success rates on certain issues and by some summit countries, and lower rates (in some cases, negative values) for other issues and countries. They do, however, make a good case that, over all, there has been a fairly significant degree of compliance with summit undertakings.

References

Note on internet addresses (URLs): Websites tend to appear, change or disappear, often without warning. Addresses cited in this source list were accurate and active at the time of writing (June 2006) unless otherwise noted.

Barnes, Hugh and James Owen, comp[ilers] (2006), *Russia in the Spotlight: G8 Scorecard*, Foreign Policy Centre, London, http://fpc.org.uk/fsblob/686.pdf and http://fpc.org.uk/events/past/224.

Bayne, Nicholas (1997), 'Changing Patterns at the G7 Summit', *G7 Governance*, 1, May, www.g8.utoronto.ca/governance/gov1/.

Bayne, Nicholas (2005a), *Overcoming Evil with Good: Impressions of the Gleneagles Summit, 6-8 July 2005*, Gleneagles and London: G8 Research Group, 18 July, www.g8.utoronto.ca/evaluations/2005gleneagles/bayne2005-0718.html.

Bayne, Nicholas (2005b), *Staying Together: The G8 Summit Confronts the 21st Century*, Ashgate, Aldershot, UK.

Bergsten, C. Fred and C. Randall Henning (1996), *Global Economic Leadership and the Group of Seven*, Institute for International Economics, Washington DC.

Daniels, Joseph P. (1993), *The Meaning and Reliability of Economic Undertakings, 1975-1989*, Garland Publishing, New York.

Furstenberg, George M. von and Joseph P. Daniels (1991), 'Policy Undertakings by the Seven "Summit" Countries: Ascertaining the Degree of Compliance', *Carnegie-Rochester Conference Series on Public Policy* 35, 267-308.

Furstenberg, George M. Von and Joseph P. Daniels (1992), *Economic Summit Declarations, 1975-1989: Examining the Written Record of International Cooperation*, Princeton Studies in International Finance, 72, International Finance Section, Dept. of Economics, Princeton University, Princeton, NJ.

Hodges, Michael R. (1994), 'More Efficiency, Less Dignity: British Perspectives on the Future Role and Working of the G-7', in *The Future of the G-7 Summits*, 141-159, (*The International Spectator* 29:2, April/June, Special Issue).

Kirton, John J. (1989a), '*Contemporary Concert Diplomacy: The Seven-Power Summit and the Management of International Order*', Paper prepared for the annual meeting of the International Studies Association and the British International Studies Association, London, March 29-April 1. Unpublished in print. www.g7.utoronto.ca/scholar/kirton198901/index.html.

Kirton, John J. (1995), 'The Diplomacy of Concert: Canada, the G7 and the Halifax Summit', *Canadian Foreign Policy* 3:1, 63-80.

Kirton, John J. (1997), 'Economic Cooperation: Summitry, Institutions, and Structural Change', Paper prepared for a conference on 'Structural Change and Co-operation in the Global Economy', Center for International Business Education and Center for Global Change and Governance, Rutgers University, New Brunswick, N.J., 19-20 May, www.g7.utoronto.ca/scholar/kirton199702/index.html Also in *Structural Change and Co-operation in the Global Economy* (1999), John Dunning and Gavin Boyd (eds), Edward Elgar , London.

Kokotsis, Ella (1999), *Keeping International Commitments: Compliance, Credibility, and the G7, 1988-1995*, Garland, New York, Transnational Business and Corporate Culture series.

Kokotsis, Ella (2004), *Background on Compliance Assessments: Methodology*, www.g8.utoronto.ca/evaluations/methodology/g7c2.htm.

Kokotsis, Ella (2006), *G8 Compliance Coding and Reference Manual*, G8 Research Group, Toronto, www.g8.utoronto.ca/evaluations/compliance_manual_2006.pdf.

Putnam, Robert D. and Nicholas Bayne (1987), *Hanging Together: Cooperation and Conflict in the Seven-Power Summits*, rev. ed., Harvard University Press, Cambridge, MA.

Chapter 11

The G20 and its Documentation[1]

This chapter describes the origins, mandate, membership, structure, ministerial and other meetings, and evolution of the agenda of the Group of Twenty (G20) finance ministers' and central bank governors' forum. It continues with a brief section on the G20's connections with international organizations, fora, and other actors; and discusses the documentation and publications of the G20.

Origins

Predecessors of the G20 included the Group of 22 (G22) and the Group of 33 (G33). The G22 – also known as the Willard Group after the Washington hotel where the group first met – was set up in April 1998 as a result of a US initiative. The group – which characterized itself as 'Finance Ministers and Central Bank Governors from a number of systemically significant economies' – was originally conceived as a one-time meeting to resolve global aspects of the financial crisis in emerging-market economies. It then was given an extension, and met for the second time on 5 October 1998 on the margins of the fall 1998 meetings of the World Bank and the International Monetary Fund (IMF). At that second meeting, four more countries joined the group. It submitted three reports to the IMF and the World Bank. It brought together finance ministers and central bank governors from the G7 plus Argentina, Australia, Brazil, China, Hong Kong, India, Indonesia, Korea, Malaysia, Mexico, Poland, Russia, Singapore, South Africa and Thailand (G22 1998: 1).

The G33 met on the initiative of the G7, succeeding the G22 in early 1999. Its members were the finance ministers and central bank governors of the G7 countries plus Argentina, Australia, Belgium, Brazil, Chile, China, Côte d'Ivoire, Egypt, Hong Kong, India, Indonesia, Malaysia, Mexico, Morocco, the Netherlands, Poland, Russia, Saudi Arabia, Singapore, South Africa, South Korea, Spain, Sweden, Switzerland, Thailand, and Turkey (IMF 2006a).

The G33's two meetings took place in March and April 1999, to discuss reforms of the global economy and the international financial system. 'The proposals made by the G-22 and G-33 to reduce the world economy's susceptibility to crises showed the potential benefits of a regular international consultative forum embracing the

---

1 Not to be confused with the trade ministers' G20 – unrelated to the G8 system – which was established on 20 August 2003, prior to the Cancún WTO ministerial conference, as a coalition of developing countries to address trade issues at the WTO from the perspective of the developing South and to counter agricultural trade distortions. Its membership (it now has 21 members) varies but it is led by Brazil, India and China. For more information on the 'Trade G20' see <www.g-20.mre.gov.br>.

emerging-market countries. Such a regular dialogue with a constant set of partners was institutionalised by the creation of the G-20 in 1999' (G20 [Australian Chair] 2006).

The G20 itself was established following the recommendation of the G7 finance ministers in their report to the 1999 Cologne G8 summit on strengthening the international financial architecture. It was confirmed by the G7 finance ministers and central bank governors in their joint communiqué in September 1999. (See Culpeper 2000; Helleiner 2001: 243-63; Kirton 2005b; Porter 2000.)

Paul Martin, former prime minister (previously finance minister) of Canada, writing in 2005 to advocate transforming the G20 into a leaders' level forum, the L20, reviews and analyzes the circumstances of the emergence and functioning of the finance ministers' G20 (Martin 2005: 2-6). This is discussed more fully in Chapter 12.

Mandate

The G20's inaugural communiqué states that the group 'was established to provide a new mechanism for informal dialogue in the framework of the Bretton Woods institutional system, to broaden the discussions on key economic and financial policy issues among systemically significant economies and promote co-operation to achieve stable and sustainable world economic growth that benefits all' (G20 1999: para 2). More recently, the G20 was characterized as 'an informal forum which promotes an open and constructive dialogue between finance ministers and central bank governors from systemically significant industrial and emerging market economies' (G20 [Australian Chair] 2006). In addition to dealing with key issues related to the international monetary and financial system and thus strengthening the international financial architecture, the G20 provides its members with a platform for discussing other current international economic questions.

Membership and Structure

The members of the G20 are the finance ministers and central bank governors of the following 19 countries: the G8 countries plus Argentina, Australia, Brazil, China, India, Indonesia, Mexico, Saudi Arabia, South Africa, South Korea, and Turkey. The twentieth member is the European Union, represented by the Council presidency and the President of the European Central Bank. In addition, there are the following ex-officio participants: the managing director of the IMF, the President of the World Bank, and the chairpersons of the International Monetary and Financial Committee and Development Committee of the IMF and World Bank.

The G20 represents all regions of the world. Together, its members comprise two-thirds of the world's population and generate approximately 90% of global gross domestic product. Their combined economic clout and broadly representative membership give the G20 greater legitimacy and potentially greater influence than the G8 commands. The Australian treasurer, co-chair of the group in 2006, calls the group 'the premier forum for discussion of global economic issues' (G20 [Australian Chair] 2006). Nonetheless, the fixed composition of the group as it stands has been criticized. For example, Gerald Helleiner considers the G20 flawed, since there is no representation of the poorest developing countries or of important European countries such as the Netherlands and Scandinavian countries that could 'speak on their behalf. Presumably, this is because the poorest and the smallest are unlikely ever to constitute any systemic threat.' Helleiner also comments on the lack of the G20's accountability to the broad international community, and proposes sweeping changes to the group's procedures, agenda and membership (Helleiner 2001: 253-54).

The G20 has no permanent staff. Instead, each year the country that chairs the group forms a temporary secretariat to co-ordinate activities and organize meetings.

Meetings

G20 finance ministers and central bank governors meet annually. These meetings are held in private, although the media and the public are informed afterwards of what took place and many documents are made available. The inaugural meeting was convened in Berlin, Germany on 15-16 December 1999, hosted by German finance minister Hans Eichel and chaired by then Canadian finance minister Paul Martin. The G20 remained under Canadian chairmanship; its next meeting took place in Montreal, on 24-25 October 2000. It, too, was chaired by Paul Martin who also chaired the Ottawa meeting on 16-17 November 2001.

India took over chairmanship in 2002. The meeting that year was held in New Delhi on 22-23 November and was chaired by India's finance minister Jaswant Singh.

In 2003 it was Mexico's turn to assume chairmanship, and the ministerial meeting, held on 26-27 October 2003 in Morelia, was chaired by Mexican finance minister Francisco Gil Díaz.

In January 2004 Germany assumed chairmanship. The Berlin meeting of 20-21 November 2004 was presided over by German finance minister Hans Eichel who had also hosted the inaugural meeting of the group. China was the chair in 2005; the ministerial meeting, held on 15-16 October in Xianghe, Hebei, was chaired by finance minister Zhou Xiao-chuan. In 2006, Australia chaired the G20 and the ministerial meeting, presided over by treasurer Peter Costello, was held in Melbourne on 18-19 November. South Africa has the chair in 2007; in 2008 it will be Brazil's turn.

In addition to the annual meeting of ministers and central bank governors, the finance ministers' and central bank governors' deputies hold their own meetings twice a year to prepare the agenda and content of the ministers' and governors' forthcoming meeting. The very first meeting of the deputies took place in Vancouver, Canada in November 1999 to prepare the first ministerial meeting to be held a month later. As well, beginning in January 2002, a 'troika' of current, past and future chairs of the group has played a co-ordinating role to ensure continuity of the G20's work.

Besides ministerial and deputies' meetings, the G20 has organized some technical seminars (not necessarily in countries chairing the G20) and prepared various reports and case studies. For example, three workshops were held in 2004 (Developing Strong Domestic Financial Markets, April, Ottawa, Canada; Demography and Growth, July, Paris, France; another one on Regional Economic Integration in a Global Framework, September, Beijing, China). Another workshop convened on Demographic Challenges and Migration in Sydney, Australia on 27-28 August 2005.

Agenda

The agenda of the G20 has evolved and expanded substantially from its initial financial and economic focus. This section reviews that evolution.

The first G20 ministerial meeting in Berlin in 1999 tackled questions of the group's role and objectives, particularly in addressing common vulnerabilities to their economies and the global financial system; reaffirmed trade liberalization under the aegis of the World Trade Organization (WTO); welcomed the work of the World Bank and IMF in developing international codes and standards, and undertook the preparation of G20 reports on the implementation of such codes and standards. The 2000 meeting focused on the opportunities and challenges of globalization; committed the group to improve the effectiveness of international financial institutions; agreed to implement policies to reduce vulnerability to financial crises; supported the integration of global finance; advocated support for the Heavily Indebted Poor Countries (HIPC) initiative; pledged combating financial crime; supported the fight against infectious diseases; and endorsed WTO's efforts to achieve multilateral trade liberalization.

In the wake of the terrorist attacks of 11 September 2001, that year's meeting, while continuing to focus on economic and financial issues, also addressed the fight against the financing of terrorism. The 2002 meeting dealt with economic and financial stability; questions of globalization, trade and development; and the continuing fight against terrorist financing and other abuses of the financial system. The 2003 ministerial meeting continued to concentrate on economic growth, multilateral trade, crisis prevention, and the fight against financial abuses including tax evasion. It also embraced the fight against global poverty.

The 2004 meeting proceeded along similar lines, particularly reaffirming support for the United Nations (UN) Millennium Development Goals. Expanding its agenda, it also addressed trade imbalances, regional co-operation, employment, demographic changes, and problems of international financial architecture. And in 2005, the G20 ministers expressed their concern over high oil prices and their effects on the world economy.

The theme of Australia's G20 chairmanship of 2006 was 'Building and Sustaining Prosperity'. The Australian work programme built on the 2005 G20 Accord for Sustained Growth. The meeting addressed the following issues: the global economic outlook; global energy and minerals markets; demographic change; reform of the Bretton Woods institutions; advancing economic reform; aid commitments and effectiveness; and transparency and information exchange for tax purposes.

Connections with International Organizations and Other Actors

There is close co-operation between the G20 and several international organizations and fora, particularly the Bretton Woods institutions. This flows from the participation of the World Bank's President, the Managing Director of the IMF and the chairs of the International Monetary and Financial Committee and the Development Committee. Another connection is with the Financial Stability Forum. G20 documents, depending on the agenda of particular ministerial meetings, refer to other international organizations, for instance the WTO, the UN, the Financial Action Task Force, the Organisation for Economic Co-operation and Development (OECD) and the New African Partnership for African Development (NEPAD).

In addition, the G20 enlists the expertise of selected private-sector institutions whose representatives are invited to G-20 meetings on an *ad hoc* basis. For example, G20 deputies held a roundtable discussion in Toronto on 25 August 2000 with representatives of the private financial sector.

Documentation and Publications

The principal document of each annual ministerial meeting is the communiqué, expressing the consensus of the participating ministers and central bank governors on the issues addressed by the meeting. The 2000 communiqué included an annex, *Reducing Vulnerability to Financial Crises*, detailing plans to accomplish this through exchange rate arrangements, prudent liability management, private sector involvement, and international standards and codes.

Some annual meetings produce separate declarations and action plans in addition to the core communiqué. The 2001 action plan focused on the prevention of terrorist financing by freezing terrorist assets, implementing applicable international standards, exchange of information and outreach, technical assistance, and compliance and reporting. The 2004 meeting produced: the 'G-20 Accord for Sustained Growth' which aims to achieve stability, competition, the mobilization of economic forces for long-term growth, and the empowerment of people so that poverty can be reduced; the 'G-20 Reform Agenda' which provides for actions to implement the accord; and the 'G20 Statement on Transparency and Exchange of Information for Tax Purposes' [hyphenation of 'G20' is inconsistent in the source documents]. The 2005 meeting issued separate statements on reforming the Bretton Woods institutions and on global development issues, as well as an action plan, under the G20 reform agenda, to implement the 2004 Accord for Sustained Growth. In 2006 the ministers adopted the G-20 Reform Agenda, a statement of agreed national actions to implement the G20 Accord for Sustained Growth; it takes up the 2005 declaration on the same topic.

In addition to documents, publications have also appeared, some based on G20 workshops. Examples are:

- *Globalisation, Living Standards and Inequality: Recent Progress and Continuing Challenges* (2002) <www.bundesbank.de/g20/download/public/20020916_publication_conference_2002_aus.pdf>;
- *Economic Reform in This Era of Globalization: 16 Country Cases* (2003) <www.bundesbank.de/g20/download/public/20031026_publication_economic_reform.pdf>;
- *Combating Money Laundering and Terrorist Financing: Report to G-20 Finance Ministers and Central Bank Governors* (2004) <www.bundesbank.de/g20/download/public/20041120_berlin_terrorist_financing.pdf>;
- *Case Studies – Institution Building in the Financial Sector* (2005) <www.g20.org/Public/Publications/CSInstitutionBuilding/index.jsp>;

- *G-20 Accord for Sustained Growth* (a separate brochure published in 2005) <www.g20.org/Public/Publications/Pdf/brochure_on_g20_accord_for_ sustained_growth_1.pdf>.

Each year's G20 chairing country sets up a website to publish meeting schedules, work programmes, texts of documents and information for the press. These websites vary greatly in completeness, sophistication and durability. The website also features pages reserved for G20 officials. These restricted pages include the working documents of the deputies of the finance ministers and central bank governors. In recent years, the website, although administered by the country chairing each given year's G20 activities, has retained its address: <www.g20.org>. Canada and Germany have maintained archival websites, respectively at <www.fin.gc.ca/g20/ indexe.html> and <www.bundesbank.de/g20/public>. Germany still maintains its archival website.

Conclusion

The G20 finance ministers' and central bank governors' forum arose from the need to address adequately the key issues of the international monetary and financial system, to strengthen the international financial architecture, and to serve as a platform for discussing other pressing international economic questions. Although a creation of the G7, the G20 has developed as an autonomous, informal group. Its membership embraces systemically important developing and emerging-market countries, reflecting a much broader global constituency and, thus, greater legitimacy than the limited composition of its parent, the G7. Although the G20 brings together countries that, together, account for two-thirds of the world's population and some 90 per cent of global gross domestic product, the group still excludes representation of the poorest developing countries. Its agenda has expanded considerably over its now seven-year lifespan, but it has not had the mandate and the capacity to deal with a host of global issues linked to economic and financial matters. One possible solution may lie in the proposal to convert the present G20 forum into a leaders' level group (see Chapter 12).

References

Note on internet addresses (URLs): Websites tend to appear, change or disappear, often without warning. Addresses cited in this source list were accurate and active at the time of writing (June 2006) unless otherwise noted.

Culpeper, Roy (2003), 'Systemic Reform at a Standstill: A Flock of "Gs" in Search of Global Financial Stability', in *Critical Issues in International Financial Reform*, 203-36, Albert Berry and Gustavo Indart (eds), Transaction Publishers, New Brunswick, N.J.; London.
G20 (1999), *Communiqué* (Berlin).
G20 [Australian Chair] (2006), www.g20.org/Public/index.jsp.

G22 (1998), *Summary of Reports on the International Financial Architecture* (Washington, D.C.), www.imf.org/external/np/g22/summry.pdf.

Helleiner, Gerald K. (2001), 'Markets, Politics and Globalization: Can the Global Economy Be Civilized?', *Global Governance* 7:3, 243-63.

International Monetary Fund (2006a), *A Guide to Committees, Groups, and Clubs*: *Factsheet*, IMF, Washington, DC, www.imf.org/external/np/exr/facts/groups. htm.

Kirton, John J. (2005b), 'From G7 to G20: Capacity, Leadership and Normative Diffusion in Global Financial Governance', paper presented for the annual convention of the International Studies Association, Honolulu, March 1-5, www. g8.utoronto.ca/scholar/kirton2005/kirton_isa2005.pdf.

Porter, Tony (2000), 'The G-7, the Financial Stability Forum, the G-20, and the Politics of International Financial Regulation', paper prepared for the International Studies Association Annual Convention, Los Angeles, March 15, www.g8.utoronto.ca/g20/g20porter/index.html.

Chapter 12

Reform of the G7, G8 and G20

This chapter reviews the various initiatives over a number of years to reform the G7 and G8. Reform proposals have ranged from membership changes, restructuring, rationalizing the agenda and processes of the G7 and G8, and, more radically, abolishing the G8 or replacing it by a new – more restricted or expanded – forum. For a more detailed treatment of the role on non-members and potential members of the G7 and G8, see also Chapter 4.

Pre-1998 Proposals and Initiatives

For many years, the G7 and G8 leaders had voiced their wish to stage smaller, more intimate and more focused meetings, with fewer officials in attendance and perhaps fewer media personnel around. Former British Prime Minister John Major stated his conviction, perhaps more emphatically than his G7 peers, 'that the summits have lost their original personal character, becoming institutional (or at least bureaucratic) and [he has invoked] a return to their origins. His proposal seems to have met with consensus from his colleagues ...' (Merlini 1994: 6; Hodges 1994: 146). His letter of August 1992, detailing his concerns to other G7 heads of state or government, was not released to the public but a summary of it appeared in the *Financial Times* of London (Stephens 1992: 1). The fact that his proposals have indeed found resonance with the other heads is shown by the 1993 Tokyo communiqué, and the more informal, leader-oriented summits of Naples, Halifax, Lyon, and especially Birmingham and subsequent summits.

Others have proposed various courses of action for the G7, ranging from abolition to institutional strengthening. W. R. Smyser (1993) states that although the G7 became 'for a time one of the most influential institutions of the twentieth century ..., it ... [later] evolved in ways that could not be foreseen and that no longer serve its original purpose'. Because he considers that the 'G-7 mechanism now receives a failing score ... [and] is not functioning as originally conceived ..., [he asks whether] the G-7 structure, including the ministerials and especially the summits, should be discontinued'. Nevertheless, he then acknowledges the continuing reasons for some type of summit: the usefulness of informal talks among leaders, the need to discuss post-Cold War problems on the highest level, and the need for agreement of the most important states in order to build 'a successful world order'; and goes on to suggest a different format and agenda, and a cabinet-level working committee to replace the sherpas.

William E. Whyman (1995), on the other hand, asserts that the summit has a future but must be strengthened. He presents two 'trajectories' of summit evolution:

(1) a revitalized G7 process that would refocus the agenda on core macroeconomic issues, keep membership small but develop associations with other countries or groups of countries and make the summit process simple and flexible, with closer ties with finance ministers; and (2) an incremental process that would expand the summit agenda to include more political and global issues, result in larger membership as well as association relationships, and increase the complexity of the process, with 'creeping institutionalism'. Staking out a middle ground between summit optimists and pessimists, Whyman concludes that the 'incremental' scenario is the more realistic one.

Flora Lewis (1992), writing about the summit in the early 1990s, is rather optimistic about the state of the institution, but suggests a greater role for Russia. Kuniko Inoguchi (1994: 23) is very supportive of the summits in the post-Cold War era, stating that 'periodic meetings of the leaders of major nations to discuss international problems are becoming the most realistic means of overseeing the world order and building consensus on new directions. In a sense, this format can be seen as laying the groundwork for joint management of the post-hegemonic international politics of the twenty-first century.'

Andrea de Guttry (1994: 76) envisions a greater degree of bureaucratic institutionalization; she suggests a secretariat for the G7 (either by creating one within the G7 or by using the OECD for this purpose). G. John Ikenberry (1993: 136-38) goes even further, calling for a G7 secretariat and a G7 council of ministers, composed of foreign and treasury ministers, with varying membership according to topic. Hanns W. Maull (1994: 135), by contrast, states that from a German perspective 'the answer to the idea of a G-7 secretariat is an unequivocal "no"' and that Germany would rather see other international organizations – the OECD, the IMF, the World Bank, the EBRD – assume follow-up and monitoring of summit undertakings. Writing about ideas of radical summit reform, Robert D. Putnam (1994: 86) points out that 'neither Smyser's recommendation to "abolish it" nor Ikenberry's advice to "institutionalize it" has significant official support'.

Writing on the eve of the 1996 Lyon summit, Zbigniew Brzezinski (1996: A11) noted: 'the very concept of the Group of Seven not only has become compromised but distorts global realities'. He adds that 'the group's membership is no longer representative of power or of principle, and it needs to be expanded. Russia ... cannot now be excluded. ... China, India and Brazil are as entitled to participation as Russia, and in some respects much more so.' Acknowledging the need to limit membership, he thus advocates a Group of Eleven. But in 2004, commenting on Russia's admission into membership which turned the G7 into the G8, Brzezinski (2004: 123) recalled the rationale for the original G7 which 'was meant to provide an opportunity for the heads of the leading and economically most powerful democracies to consult one another'. He added: 'The inclusion of Russia ... was motivated by the political desire to give the troubled post-Soviet Russia – though it is neither a genuine democracy nor a leading economy – a sense of status and belonging.' But given that Russia is a member, he advocates adding China and India, thus turning the G8 into an economic and political G10.

One other possible model of an expanded G8, suggested by Sylvia Ostry in late 1998, would be in the image of three concentric circles. The innermost one is the core G3: the US, Germany and Japan which, together, are capable of exercising leadership and crisis management, combining power with responsibility. The middle circle would consist of the existing G8, with the possible addition of China, a logical partner at this level. This group could deal with geopolitical, security and other global issues. The outer circle, symbolizing a more widely representative institution, would embrace major regional powers that could play an appropriate role in their own right and as representatives of their regions (for example, Brazil, India, Australia and South Africa).[1]

The 1998 Birmingham Reforms

The 1998 Birmingham summit took major steps in summit reform, producing several innovations in participation, format and agenda. Birmingham officially integrated Russia into the club, turning it into the G8 (for a detailed discussion of Russia's membership see Chapter 4). It was a leaders-only summit, with foreign and finance ministers meeting separately in London a week before the summit, on 8-9 May, to prepare for the summit and to deal with issues not on the agenda of the summits. This format made it possible to achieve greater informality than was the case at previous summit history, enabling the leaders to spend considerable time together and to focus personally on topics that they wished to discuss. And it had a more focused agenda than previous summits. The more limited agenda also reduced the volume of documentation, although this effect proved to be rather inconsistent after Birmingham (Bayne 2005b: 6, 8-10, 37).

Although the Birmingham innovation of leaders-only summits has become established practice, there continued to be much dissatisfaction with the G7 and G8. Shortly after the Birmingham summit, Jeffrey Sachs (1998) proposed a G16, instead of the G8, summit, comprising the present G8 plus eight developing countries. Democratic governance should be the major criterion of membership, and the core developing country candidates should be Brazil, India, South Korea and South Africa, joined 'soon [by] a democratic Nigeria'. Sachs suggested a 'development agenda': global financial markets and international financial reform; conditionality and foreign aid; reform of the international assistance programme; and ending the debt crisis.

In a post-Genoa leader in 2001, the *Financial Times* questions whether 'G8 summits should exist and, if so, in what form'; notes that 'summits have worked best when the leaders have had a chance to be separate from their national entourages ... and when there has been a crisis to try to sort out'; and concludes that there 'should have been ... a commitment to hold the next G8 only when there is a burning topic to discuss' (For Slimmer ... 2001: 10).

In the post-9/11 era, security for the leaders became paramount for summit host countries. So, G8 summits since Kananaskis 2002 have met at remote places (although there are early precedents of summits held far from urban centres: the very first summit in the Château de Rambouillet outside Paris in 1975 and the first

---

1   I am grateful to Dr. Sylvia Ostry for sharing her idea of this model.

Canadian-hosted summit at Montebello, well away from Ottawa, in 1981). This has had the advantage of easier security for the G8 leaders but also the disadvantage of the leaders meeting far from the media, the public and civil society. At Gleneagles in 2005, however, accredited media personnel were again located near, but still isolated from, the venue of the leaders' meetings.

The Shadow G-8

The Shadow G-8 (first called *G-8 Preparatory Conference*) is a group of distinguished private citizens from each of the G8 countries. It was originally convened by the Tokyo Foundation and the Institute of International Economics, with support from other foundations. It has been characterized as a self-motivating group, rather than one that came into being on the G8 leaders' initiative. Its aim is to educate the public about G8 issues and processes, and to provide advice to G8 governments and analytical input into the summit process. The group's members have had considerable involvement with previous summits, some as ministers, others as sherpas, still others as government officials or prominent participants in think tanks. It has a varying number of members, usually about 20, and is co-chaired by C. Fred Bergsten (Director of the Institute of International Economics) and a rotating member who is a national of a given year's summit host country. Members consult with one another frequently to exchange views and decide on the focus of each annual report. They hold one meeting annually, and then issue their report or a set of recommendations. The group usually meets with the host G8 leader and/or the host leader's sherpa, and transmits the report to the host government or all G8 governments (Shadow G-8 2003a; Shadow G-8 2004).

The first meeting of the Shadow G-8 was held in Tokyo on 10-11 April 2000, and the group presented its report to Prime Minister Yoshiro Mori as chair of the G8 for the year (and host of the Okinawa summit) the next day, 12 April. The report, entitled *Strategies for the New Century: A Report to the Leaders of the G-8 Member Countries: Recommendations for the G-8 Okinawa Summit from the G-8 Preparatory Conference*, urges the leaders to recognize dramatic changes in the world economy and the inadequacy of governing regimes to deal with those changes (G-8 Preparatory Conference 2000). It calls upon the leaders to adopt the required strategic focus to fulfil their responsibilities. It makes specific proposals on six issue areas: globalization, international financial architecture, world trade, relations with Russia, and Asian security.

The second meeting took place in Turin, Italy on 21-22 January 2001, followed by another meeting in Genoa (the venue of that year's summit) on 1-3 July. The Shadow G-8 then conveyed its observations to the leadership of the Italian government as host of the G8. Group member Renato Ruggiero, was Italian foreign minister at the time, which made communication with his government that much easier. The 2001 report, *Toward Shared Responsibility and Global Leadership: Recommendations for the G-8 Genoa Summit from the G-8 Preparatory Conference*, posits four strategic themes: reinvigorating the multilateral economic system, organizing a new structure of shared collective responsibility and leadership, addressing the threat of conflict between the US and Europe, and linking economic and security issues. The report then makes recommendations for action on trade, global governance, global poverty, aging, the world economy, and security. To support these recommendations, the report includes several background documents (G-8 Preparatory Conference 2001).

In 2002 the Shadow G-8 met in Washington, DC, on 5 April to prepare for the Kananaskis summit. Its report for that year, *Global Responses to the New Global Challenges: Recommendations for the G-8 Kananaskis Summit from the G-8 Preparatory Conference*, was later conveyed to the Canadian host government. It notes the leaders' plan to follow the kind of strategic approach at Kananaskis that was suggested in the Shadow G-8's first two reports. It then notes the impact of the terrorist attacks of 11 September 2001, and identifies the following key issues for Kananaskis: the world economy, Africa and development, and combating terrorism. The report makes several specific recommendations under each of these themes (G-8 Preparatory Conference 2002).

2003 was the turn of the French government to hold the G8 presidency. The Shadow G-8 convened on 8-9 January; then, in April, it updated its comments and analysis after the formal end of the Iraq war. The initial report was given to the sherpas, and the final report, *Restoring G-8 Leadership of the World Economy: Recommendations for the Evian Summit from the Shadow G-8*, was transmitted to the G8 heads of state or government. The final report identifies problems in relations among leading G8 countries in the wake of the Iraq war, comments on the decline of the G8 and some causes of that decline, and gives detailed analyses, with proposals, on four clusters of issues: the world economy; trade policy, energy security and the global environment; North-South issues; and the management of globalization. The report ends with an action programme for Evian (Shadow G-8 2003b).

The Shadow G-8 did not meet and did not submit a report in 2004, the year of the US-hosted Sea Island summit. Some members of the group felt that there was insufficient interest on the part of the host government; the administration was not particularly receptive to the Shadow G-8's input. In Spring 2005 the group met for two brainstorming sessions but decided that it would not produce a report that year, as the British hosts of the Gleneagles summit were already strongly focused on the two central themes of Africa and climate change. As of mid-2006, it was unclear whether the Shadow G-8 would resume its work to its full extent in 2006 (Shadow G-8 2004; Shadow G-8 2005; Shadow G-8 2006).

The InterAction Council

The InterAction Council predates the Shadow G-8. It was established in 1983 'as an independent international organization to mobilize the experience, energy and international contacts of a group of statesmen who have held the highest office in their own countries. Council members jointly develop recommendations on, and practical solutions for the political, economic and social problems confronting humanity' (InterAction Council). With more than 30 members, the council is not confined to former G8 officials; conversely, some G7 and G8 leaders have not participated – non-participants have included UK Prime Minister Margaret Thatcher and Canadian

Prime Minister Kim Campbell, as well as other women leaders, which is why the council was informally referred to as the 'old boys' summit'; this imbalance has now been corrected. Japanese Prime Minister Takeo Fukuda was the council's founder, and Canadian Prime Minister Pierre Elliott Trudeau was also a founding member. Among previous G7 and G8 leaders are former heads of state or government including French President Valéry Giscard d'Estaing, US Presidents Jimmy Carter and Bill Clinton, UK Prime Ministers James Callaghan and John Major, German Chancellor Helmut Schmidt (honorary chairman), and Japanese Prime Minister Kiichi Miyazawa (co-chair, along with former Australian Prime Minister Malcolm Fraser). As of June 2006, the Council is co-chaired by Ingvar Carlsson, former Prime Minister of Sweden, and again by Miyazawa. Fraser and Schmidt remain Honorary Chairmen. The Council's Secretary-General in 2006 is Isamu Miyazaki, former State Minister of the Economic Planning Agency of Japan.

The council had a somewhat closer connection with the G7 and G8 in earlier years than more recently. For some years it formulated and transmitted to G7 and G8 leaders various policy proposals and other recommendations.

The three priority themes of the council are: peace and security; world economic revitalization; and universal ethical standards. Ever since its establishment, the council has held annual plenary sessions (all except the 1995 plenary issued communiqués) as well as a number of expert meetings. The text of communiqués, keynote speeches delivered at the annual plenary meetings, and documents issued at expert meetings are available at the council's website, <www.interactioncouncil.org>, in English and Japanese. Here are a few examples:

- Monetary, financial and debt issues – report of a high-level expert group chaired by Schmidt, 1984;
- Interrelated problems of the environment, population and development – report of a high-level expert group chaired by Fukuda, 1985;
- Economies in transformation: limitations and potential of the transition process – report of a high-level expert group chaired by Trudeau, 1991;
- Pluralism and global governance – report of a high-level expert group chaired by Fraser, 2001;
- A universal declaration of human responsibilities – proposed by the council and prepared under the direction of Schmidt and noted theologian Hans Küng, with the participation of Canadian academic and former government official Thomas Axworthy and many other prominent personalities, 1997;
- Final communiqué of the 21st plenary session, Moscow, 2003.

The L20 Initiative

One of the most interesting reform ideas is the proposal to turn the G20 finance ministers' forum into a leaders' level group of 20, or L20. In a paper predating the L20 initiative but not dissimilar in its thrust, Wendy Dobson (2001) notes that the challenges to leaders have changed since the Cold-War days when the G7 was first established, and asserts that a 'G-3 or G-7 "directorate" is no longer acceptable....

[What is required is] consensus among a wider group.' She envisions two scenarios to build on the precedent of the G20 finance ministers' forum: convening functional groups of ministers from G20 countries on systemic problems such as climate change, North-South issues, trade and poverty alleviation; and expanding leaders' meetings to include all the leaders of the G20 countries. In the interest of efficient management, this leaders' body would require a steering committee with revolving membership. This new body would not replace the G8 but would meet periodically before or after G8 summits.

The L20 idea was taken up with enthusiasm by former Canadian Prime Minister Paul Martin (2005) who, in his previous post as finance minister, had been the first chairman of the finance ministers' G20. Writing in 2005, he succinctly made the case for a leaders' level forum of L20. He reviewed and analyzed the circumstances of the emergence and functioning of the finance ministers' G20; discussed the need for a similar forum for political leaders; and outlined the L20's possible composition, initial agenda and potential ambit, role, and relations with existing multilateral organizations.

Motivated by the need to resolve issues that have proven intractable in institutions of global governance – including summits – the Centre for International Governance Innovation (CIGI), a Canadian think tank, in co-operation with the Centre for Global Studies at the University of Victoria, Canada (CFGS), has been examining the ramifications of this potential transformation of the G20 into the L20: What are the issues? What may be the appropriate design for a successful L20 acceptable to the leaders? And what is the best route to attaining consensus to establish the L20 summit process? Such a new L20, if successful, would be more broadly representative than the G8, bringing to the table systemically important developing countries (notably China, India, Brazil, South Africa and Mexico) and countries with emerging economies. It would set and focus on priorities at the highest level, transcending national bureaucracies, and would be an institution enjoying legitimacy in promoting fiscal, social and environmentally responsible policies; it would also address the efficiency gap, and would be a catalyst for and guide to broader reforms of global governance. The 2005 book analyzing these issues, *Reforming from the Top: A Leaders' 20 Summit*, considers the wider positive and negative context of the L20 proposal, and examines the degree of receptivity for an L20 by the South. It discusses the modalities of achieving the L20: having an L20 replace the G7 and G8 through a 'giant leap', incrementally increasing the membership of the G8 through a G9 and G10 to an eventual L20; and creating an L20 that would operate alongside a continuing G8 (English 2005).

Among the contributors to the CIGI/CFGS project, John Kirton (2005e) traces and assesses the origins, mandate, membership, evolution and performance of the finance ministers' G20 and its relation to the G7 and G8, and formulates the three options for the L20 as that of the 'rejectionists' who consider that an L20 would stretch the financial G20 beyond its competence; the 'reinforcers' who would add an *ad hoc* or permanent L20 to existing institutions of global governance; and the 'replacers' who advocate an L20 that would supplant the G8. He favours an L20 that would function in parallel with the G8 rather than replace it.

Barry Carin and Gordon Smith (2005) examine the record of the G7 and G8, and draw up two alternative scenarios for the G8/L20 – one that would turn the existing G8 summit plus the finance G20 into a leaders' level L20, and the other that would see the G8 leaders continuing to meet with leaders of the South and of the emerging economies outside the UN framework. They then outline the possible machinery and membership of a legitimate, effective L20 (their preferred outcome), and the path to achieve this goal incrementally.

Colin I. Bradford (2005a) prefers a more rapid establishment of an L20 which would have an agenda aimed at: strengthening institutions of global governance; improving transparency; enhancing dialogue with emerging market economies; poverty reduction and support for the Millennium Development Goals; and incorporating cultural pluralism into the economic policy process. In an earlier paper, Bradford and Johannes F. Linn (2004) marshal three reasons for upgrading the G20 to the leaders' level: the shifting demographic and economic balance away from G7 countries and toward emerging market economies; the need for more representative global governance; and the key role of emerging market economies in the occurrence and impact of global economic crises and in responses to these crises.

Angel Gurría (2005), a former Mexican finance and foreign minister (now Secretary-General of the OECD), underlines the need for an L20 '[b]ecause the different fora that [now] deal with globalization are not working'. This L20 would function parallel with the G8, have a small secretariat, and an agenda that would concentrate on contentious or stalled issues whose successful solution requires the leaders' participation.

Richard Higgott (2005) points to structural changes in the world economy and the increasing weight of major emerging economies (China, India, Mexico, Brazil, South Korea) – even though the G8 is still dominant. He sees these changes as progressively reducing the role of the G7 and G8, and making the extension of the G7 and G8 to a leaders' level G20 rational and just, at least theoretically. This would help bridge the legitimacy gap of the current G7 and G8. How to manage this transition, though, is fraught with problems. Daniel Drache (2005) argues that there is a new challenge for L20 countries: global dynamics have moved from the former, primarily economic configuration to a more complex one, with the new dimensions of cultural power and collective identity.

Anne-Marie Slaughter (2005) surveys a variety of government networks including the G8, the Financial Stability Forum, and the G20. She proposes transforming the G20 into a more robust institution, give that enhanced G20 a presence in major international organizations, and use the advantages of other networks in which the G20 members are participants.

Among heads of state or government, former Canadian Prime Minister Paul Martin was the foremost champion of the idea of a leaders-level forum of the 20. He generated some support among some of his peers, but the position and attitude of the US remained uncertain. Higgott (2005) highlights the distinction of US and European, and US and East Asian positions on multilateralism and global governance, particularly under the current US administration. Saori Katada (2005) affirms Japan's support for the G7-led process of global financial architecture and for the finance ministers' G20 but is silent on Japanese attitudes toward an L20. Kirton

(2004a) states that 'the G8 leaders themselves ... are strongly attached to the G8, and would refuse or be reluctant to let it die'.

Support from the South, particularly from the major developing countries, for the L20 idea would be crucial for the initiative to succeed. Yoginder Alagh (2005), presenting the concerns of India, a key member of the G20, emphasizes that the restructuring of the G20 into an L20 must be based on knowledge networks and links between the local, the national and the global, in order to create a level playing field for developing countries. Ricardo Sennes and Alexandre de Freitas Barbosa (2005) assert that Brazil's position on the L20 proposals is positive though sceptical.

Ian Taylor (2005) analyzes South Africa's place in the network of coalitions and fora, and concludes that there is a need to manage both globalization and financial governance, and that there is positive potential in a G20-turned-L20 as an institution comprising both developed and emerging market economies. Yongding Yu (2005), in his discussion of China's evolving global position, with a special emphasis on its relations with the G7 and G8 and the G20, notes that China, not really wishing to become a member of the G8, has nonetheless entered into a dialogue with it. China, an active member of the financial G20, supports it as a continuing complement to the G7 and G8 and feels that transforming the G20 into an L20 is premature at present. Writing from an Egyptian perspective, Abdel Monem Said Aly (2005) underlines the need for organizational reform or new fora to deal with the challenges and promises of globalization, and argues that a reformed G20 or an L20 would help remedy the representativeness gap of the G8 and still function effectively.

The report of a high-level UN panel on 'threats, challenges and change' notes briefly that it would be helpful for policy impetus and coherence to transform the finance ministers' G20 into a leaders' group. Such a body would bring together leaders of key developed and developing countries collectively accounting for 80 percent of the world's population and 90 percent of the world's economic activity. The panel requests that, in addition to the heads of the IMF, World Bank, WTO and EU, the L20 include the UN Secretary-General and the president of ECOSOC in order 'to ensure strong support for United Nations programmes and initiatives' (UN 2004: 88). In this context, Andrew Cooper and Thomas Fues (2000) call for two complementary steps to enhance effectiveness in global governance: reforming ECOSOC, thereby enabling it to function effectively as a global forum for policy advocacy and co-ordination; and establishing the L20 based on the composition of the present G20 of finance ministers and central bank governors. The G7 and G8 could then either be dissolved or carried on as a parallel, informal network.

The CIGI/CFGS project has involved a series of conferences deliberating the concept of a G20 at the leaders' level, IMF accountability, capacity-building, and the prospects of an L20 (CIGI 2003b; CIGI 2003a; CIGI 2004). There was a stocktaking meeting on 19-20 February 2005 which concluded that a modest, low-key beginning was most likely, with a leaders' dinner or lunch on the margins of a UN General Assembly session, and the hope that the leaders would decide to meet again a year later. The guiding principles for any future meetings would be a limited agenda of issues that are already being considered but need a high-level push; informality; avoiding becoming a world directorate; and networking with other governments and nonstate actors (CIGI 2005: 1, 5). The most recent phase of the L20 project is focusing on research and advice through conferences and workshops to explore global issues for the potential L20 agenda (Centre for Global Studies; CIGI).

Thinking in mid-2006 envisioned a first, stand-alone meeting of the L20 around the time of the UN General Assembly in the fall of 2006, with a carefully selected short agenda, likely focusing on global health and terrorism. (Such a meeting did not take place at that time.) With the Asian outbreak and westward spread of avian flu and fears that its virus may mutate into more deadly form and precipitate a global pandemic, high-level political impetus in this area is becoming crucial; existing technical organizations – notably the WHO – are drawing up scenarios and several countries are working on vaccines but an L20 would bring to the process its unique combination of leadership, capacity and political will. It is worth noting that this possible initial agenda is proposed from outside the group of the 20 leaders themselves, in contrast with the agenda-setting of the G7 and G8. There, particularly in the early years of summitry, agenda-setting and evolution occurred among the G7 officials themselves, though more recently that process has, to some extent, been influenced from outside sources – non-G8 governments, civil society and other actors. If the L20 comes into being, it can be expected that the 20 leaders would take 'ownership' of their agenda, possibly in consultation with other stakeholders. It now seems quite unlikely that an L20 would supplant the existing G8.

Paul Martin, now an opposition member of Parliament in Canada, continues to champion the L20. In an interview reported on 1 June 2006, he talked about his impending trip to Germany 'to further his ambition of creating a new League of Nations – the L20, as he calls it'. The venue of this was a conference of the Development and Peace Foundation in Dresden, Germany on 8-9 June 2006, focusing on the L20 idea, where Martin was the lead speaker. It would be significant if Germany, holder of the 2007 presidency of the G8, supported the L20 initiative. Ideally, support should also come from one of the major developing or emerging-market countries. Martin emphasized that the world was 'no longer unipolar. China and India are major players. I believe the L-20 is going to happen' (Martin L. 2006: A1, A7).

In his speech to the conference – named Multilateralism in Transition: Summer Dialogue 2006 – Martin discussed the origins of the G20 finance ministers' forum, and stated that the G20 had come into being 'because we needed a body that could form the consensus required to deal on a timely basis with economic issues that had global repercussions'. Now other global issues, such as growth, aid, trade, environment, and poverty, necessitate an L20 where government leaders can deal with these problems at the highest political level.

Martin (2006) then outlined the set of questions facing the L20: criteria of membership; continuation or cessation of the G8; complementarity with the UN; initial agenda; and *modus operandi*. The L20 should bring together the existing G8 and 'other leading economies'. Criteria of membership would include 'the requisite social and political stability' and major regional powers, such as Egypt and Nigeria, should be included. With the establishment of the L20, the G8 itself should continue to play its own role. The G8+5 formula, with guest leaders invited to parts of the meeting, is no substitute for an L20. 'What is needed for successful international dialogue, is the kind of familiarity, the recognition that only comes from people who have met often as a group, who know they will continue to meet in the future and who know the dynamics of the room. That's what happens at the G8, it's what happens at the G20, and it's what should happen at the L20.' Initial agenda of the L20 would focus on issues where 'core political leadership is needed': on energy, health, environment, or trade. There should be no communiqués (but only an overview by the chair), no secretariat (except perhaps for the initial startup), and no 'set piece' speeches but rather natural discussion among the leaders who 'should break free of the briefing book syndrome'.

L20 relations with other governments, civil society, international organizations, and the business sector would have to be a major consideration in the design of this proposed new forum. The above-mentioned February 2005 stocktaking meeting noted that a 'key element ... may be creating non-governmental and governmental networks to feed in and disseminate out from the L20' (CIGI 2005: 2). A roundtable discussion held at a conference on global democracy and civil society in May 2005 grappled with the issue of how civil society could and should interact with the proposed L20 (G05 2005). Modalities of this interaction could range from civil society distancing itself from the L20 (eschewing dialogue or other engagement) to taking advantage of the opportunities that engagement would afford both to civil society and to the L20, with various combinations of action in-between. The phenomenon of civil society taking initiatives would apply; even if the L20 chooses not to engage with NGO groups, civil society would find ways to influence the L20 agenda and press for dialogue or other interaction.

Other Recent Proposals

Another interesting initiative is presented in a 2004 book published by the Centre for Economic Policy Research and the International Center for Monetary and Banking Studies. The authors, Peter B. Kenen, Jeffrey Shafer, Nigel Wicks and Charles Wyplosz, trace the evolution of international economic and financial co-operation and conclude that its machinery is becoming obsolete (although they acknowledge the G7's record of negotiating joint positions and using its influence in the Bretton Woods institutions). They offer far-reaching recommendations for putting in place new structures: make room for new players, for instance by streamlining European representation in the G7 and in the IMF Executive Board; establish a new G4 bringing together the US, the euro zone, Japan and China to deal with exchange rate problems and adjustments; convene an Independent Wise Persons Review Group to examine existing institutions and groups, including the G7 which is experiencing diminishing legitimacy and problems with representativeness; and establish a Council for International Financial and Economic Cooperation, another new body with membership not exceeding 15, which would set agenda and provide strategic direction for the international financial system and would oversee multilateral institutions of international economic co-operation. This council would include the systemically important countries, represented by their finance ministers. The heads of the UN, IMF, World Bank and WTO would be invited to the council's meetings (Kenen et al. 2004). Commenting on this book, *The Economist* agrees that the G7 today is not what it was and is now only one of an 'alphanumeric panoply of bodies' attempting to co-ordinate economic policies. (This does not address the wide range of non-economic issues that the G8's agenda has come to embrace.) *The Economist* notes with approval the book's proposal to give China its rightful place in the structure of macroeconomic diplomacy, stating that without China, 'the G7 cannot hope to achieve much' (G-Force 2004: 72).

In a somewhat similar vein, Stephen Roach (2004) of Morgan Stanley, noting that the global economy, in 2005, needs major steps of rebalancing, recommends a new architecture for economic policy co-ordination. One of these steps would be to replace the G7 with a new G5 consisting of the US, the euro zone, Japan, the UK and China. Roach argues that the G7 is a creature of a different era and he finds it particularly odd that it excludes China while giving the EU euro-zone three votes (Germany, France and Italy). His G5 would be a full-fledged organization based on a charter that would embrace in its mandate all aspects of global economic imbalances. It would have a permanent staff. It would hold semiannual meetings based on consultations of the finance ministries and central banks of the member states with the G5's staff of experts. The staff would produce semiannual reports to serve as agenda for the formal meetings. Like the proposal by Kenen and his colleagues, Roach's ideas do not account for the non-economic agenda of the present G8 – the environment, security, global health, and other transnational issues.

In a 2005 paper, Bradford argues that the existing 'institutional framework for dealing with contemporary global challenges does not match the scope, scale and nature of the challenges themselves', notably those embodied in the Millennium Development Goals and the Millennium Declaration. One aspect of this mismatch is the G8 and the broader G8 system as now constituted. Given considerable reluctance to major reform and expansion of the G8 into a true L20, Bradford suggests adding a few regular core members (the leading candidates being China, India, Brazil and South Africa) to the G8 – turning it into a G12 – and allocating six additional places to other countries that would participate on a rotating basis, depending on particular issues on the agenda. This formula would enhance both the representativeness and the legitimacy of the summit mechanism and would provide top-level strategic leadership to the whole international system (Bradford 2005b: 5, 20, 23-25).

Edwin Truman (2004: 20) of the Institute for International Economics would wish to see disbanding the G7 and G8 and moving many of the latter's policy co-ordination functions to the G20 (which he does not call 'L20'). He argues that this strengthening of the G20 would be a major step in rationalizing the institutions of international economic co-operation. In addition to representation at the level of leaders, ministers of finance and central bank governors, he calls for *ad hoc* working groups as well. He sees the US and the euro area as leaders of this strengthened G20. At the same time, he envisions as well informal policy co-ordination of the US and the euro area as an 'informal G2'. The 'finance G2' concept is explored by C. Fred Bergsten (2004a: 1, 9-10), who argues that 'Euroland' and the US need a new G2 mechanism not only to monitor and consult on the evolution of the dollar-euro exchange rate but, more ambitiously, also to develop a new G2 monetary regime. This 'finance G2' would not be a substitute for the G7 and would function informally and without even public announcement of its existence and activities.[2] In another article, Bergsten (2004b: 99) paints an additional scenario under which the G2 operated and the G7 could become the G3 (the US, the EU and Japan) 'or, eventually, the G-4 (when China is ready to join)'.

As for the non-economic agenda, it has been reported that Klaus Schwab, the president of the World Economic Forum, proposed a 'P21' meeting of heads of government, focusing on security issues. He is further reported to have said 'that the creation of the P21 should mean the end of the G8' (CIGI 2003a: 13).

In a comment piece in the *Financial Times* just before the 2005 Gleneagles summit, Richard Haas (2005: 19) contrasts the weaker G8 members, Canada, Italy and Russia, with China and India, both of which have huge populations and high gross domestic product figures. He adds: 'The G8 needs to become the G10. Both China and India deserve a seat.... It would be a concession to reality that would benefit everyone.' Another article in the same newspaper suggests, along somewhat similar lines, that restructuring the G8 should be considered, eliminating the membership of Canada and Italy, and stating: [n]or should Russia have membership when China, India and Brazil do not'. Moreover, Africa and the Islamic world should be represented (Garten 2005: 23).

The idea of expanding the G8 was raised again in early 2006, by the Institute of International Economics, with the proposal that China, India, Brazil and South Africa be invited as full members, thus transforming the G8 into a more representative G12. The inclusion of non-democratic China would make sense since with Russia's presidency of the G8 it is evident that a democratic form of government is no longer a criterion for membership in the club (Åslund 2006: 7).

George Haynal (2005) makes the case for a 'G-XX' – a more comprehensive and representative summit process, where 'XX' does not stand for 'twenty' but implies that the number of members of such a new group is an open question. He argues that such a more inclusive summit 'would express the changing nature and balance of power and assist our shared institutions to function better by providing them with the appropriate political direction'. Haynal outlines the weaknesses of the existing international system of institutions: the UN Security Council, General Assembly, specialized agencies including the Bretton Woods institutions; the WTO. He suggests that new global issues, as well as linkages among international institutions now missing could be addressed by a 'G-XX'. He identifies the core membership of the G-XX: the existing G8; China, India, South Africa, Brazil and possibly Mexico; and representation from Africa, the Middle East, Southeast Asia, the Americas and the former Soviet bloc. He sees the G-XX as functioning alongside the G8, not replacing it. Differing from the L20 initiative, he considers that transforming the G20 finance ministers' forum into a leaders' level summit would overburden the G20; nonetheless, he would proceed from the existing composition of the G20. Finally, he recommends starting with a 'one-off' process of the leaders, meeting perhaps on the margins of the General Assembly, and focusing on global security as the initial agenda.

Other proposals presented in 2006, along with rising criticism of Russia's antidemocratic tendencies, include reviving the G7 while preserving the G8 as well.

---

2   The G2 concept is explored more fully in Bergsten and Koch-Weser (2004).

This G7 would again be a forum of the core democratic countries, and could usefully address issues on which Russia has little to contribute; for example, on trade, given the fact that Russia is not yet a member of the WTO (see CFR 2006; Åslund 2006).

Another possible trajectory is the steady evolution and expansion of the agenda of the G20 finance ministers' forum. Should further major agenda expansion move the G20 beyond the competence of finance ministers and central bank governors, this could hasten the transformation of the G20 into an L20.

Conclusion

There is a widespread (though not universal) perception of the structural, procedural, democratic and other shortcomings of the present G8 and the need to reform or replace it. This perception is not restricted to the news media, academia and civil society but has also been expressed by some former and even present officials of various G8 governments associated with summit preparation, conduct and follow-up. There is no shortage of reform proposals ranging from abolishing the G8 altogether to expanding or reducing its membership, rationalizing its agenda and processes, increasing its legitimacy and representativeness, replacing it with a new body, or supplementing it with additional bodies. Many of these proposals have merit, and some have high-level advocates. The ultimate outcome may be promoted by various constituencies, but will have to be endorsed and agreed by the leaders of the present G8 (and perhaps G20).

Thus, there are many possible trajectories that the G8 could take. It could continue – but for how long? – with fixed membership but a flexible agenda and dynamic processes that would allow involving other important countries without absorbing them as members. It could carry on but function in parallel with a revived G7. It could expand and become more representative, more responsive to global issues, and bring together greater capacity to deal with those issues, by continuing to invite key countries (particularly China, India, Brazil, South Africa and Mexico). It could be turned into a more representative (but perhaps less efficient) L20, or continue as G8 but work alongside with an L20. It could disappear. Or it could evolve in ways unforeseen by anyone today.

References

Note on internet addresses (URLs): Websites tend to appear, change or disappear, often without warning. Addresses cited in this source list were accurate and active at the time of writing (June 2006) unless otherwise noted.

Alagh, Yoginder K. (2005), 'On Sherpas and Coolies: The L20 and Non-Brahmanical Futures', in *Reforming from the Top: A Leaders' 20 Summit*, 169-86. English et al. (eds), Centre for International Governance Innovation; United Nations University Press, New York; Tokyo.

Åslund, Anders (2006), *Russia's Challenges as Chair of the G-8*, Policy Briefs in International Economics, No. PB06-3, Washington, DC, www.iie.com/publications/pb/pb06-3.pdf.

Bayne, Nicholas (2005b), *Staying Together: The G8 Summit Confronts the 21st Century*, Ashgate, Aldershot, UK.

Bergsten, C. Fred (2004a), 'The Euro and the Dollar: Toward a "Finance G-2"?', paper prepared for the conference on 'The Euro at Five: Ready for a Global Role', 26 February, www.iie.com/publications/papers/bergsten0204.pdf.

Bergsten, C. Fred (2004b), 'Foreign Economic Policy for the Next President', *Foreign Affairs*, 83:2, 88-101, March/April.

Bergsten, C. Fred and Caio Koch-Weser (2004), 'The G-2, a New Conceptual Basis and Operating Modality for Transatlantic Economic Relations', in *From Alliance To Coalitions: The Future of Transatlantic Relations*, 237-49, Werner Weidenfeld et al. (eds), Bertelsmann Foundation Publishers, Gütersloh, Germany.

Bradford, Colin I. (2005a), 'Anticipating the Future: A Political Agenda for Global Economic Governance', in *Reforming from the Top: A Leaders' 20 Summit*, 46-62. English, et al. (eds), Centre for International Governance Innovation; United Nations University Press, New York; Tokyo.

Bradford, Colin I. (2005b), 'Global Governance for the 21st Century', prepared for the Brookings Institution/Centre for International Governance Innovation Governance Project, Spring, Washington, DC, www.brookings.edu/views/papers/20051024bradford.pdf.

Bradford, Colin I. and Johannes F. Linn (2004), 'Global Economic Governance at a Crossroads: Replacing the G-7 with the G-20', *Brookings Institution Policy Brief* No. 131.

Brzezinski, Zbigniew (1996), 'Let's Add to the G-7', *The New York Times*, 25 June, A11.

Brzezinski, Zbigniew (2004), *The Choice: Global Domination or Global Leadership*, Basic Books, New York.

Carin, Barry and Gordon Smith (2005), 'Making Change Happen at the Global Level', in *Reforming from the Top: A Leaders' 20 Summit*, 25-45. English, et al. (eds), Centre for International Governance Innovation; United Nations University Press, New York; Tokyo.

Centre for Global Studies, *L20: The G20 at the Leaders' Level*, www.l20.org.

Centre for International Governance Innovation, *L20 Project*, www.cigionline.org/research/l20_events.php.

Centre for International Governance Innovation (2003a), *The G-20 at Leaders' Level?: Record of the Discussion at Bellagio, 9-11 December*, www.cigionline.ca/publications/docs/Bellagio.pdf.

Centre for International Governance Innovation (2003b), *The G-20 at Leaders' Level?: Report of a Meeting Hosted by the Centre for International Governance Innovation and the Centre for Global Studies, Waterloo, Ontario, 26-27 October*, www.cigionline.ca/publications/docs/G-20 Conference Report November 2003.pdf.

Centre for International Governance Innovation (2004), *CFGS/CIGI Report: 'The G-20 at Leaders' Level?'*, www.cigionline.ca/publications/docs/G20 Feb 2004 Report.pdf.

Centre for International Governance Innovation (2005), *Report on L-20 Stocktaking Conference*, Ottawa, 19-20 February.

Cooper, Andrew F. and Thomas Fues (2000), 'L20 and ECOSOC Reform: Complementary Building Blocks for Inclusive Global Governance and a More Effective UN', *Briefing Paper* 6/2005, Deutsches Institut für Entwicklungspolitik, Bonn.

Council on Foreign Relations (2006), *Russia's Wrong Direction: What the United States Can and Should Do*, Task Force Report, 57, CFR, New York, March.

Dobson, Wendy (2001), 'Broadening Participation in G-7 Summits', in *Toward Shared Responsibility and Global Leadership: Recommendations for the G-8 Genoa Summit from the G-8 Preparatory Conference, 23-29.* [Turin, Italy: G-8 Preparatory Conference].

Drache, Daniel (2005), 'The Political Economy of Dissent: Global Publics after Cancún', in *Reforming from the Top: A Leaders' 20 Summit*, 121-40. English, et al. (eds), Centre for International Governance Innovation; United Nations University Press, New York; Tokyo.

English, John, Ramesh Thakur and Andrew F. Cooper, (eds) (2005), *Reforming from the Top: A Leaders 20 Summit*, Centre for International Governance Innovation; United Nations University Press, New York; Tokyo.

'For Slimmer and Sporadic Summits' (2001), *Financial Times*, 10, 23 July.

G-8 Preparatory Conference (2000), Strategies for the New Century: A Report to the Leaders of the G-8 Member Countries: Recommendations for the G-8 Okinawa Summit from the G-8 Preparatory Conference, [1st report] [Tokyo]. www.iie.com/publications/papers/g8-2000.pdf.

G-8 Preparatory Conference (2001), Toward Shared Responsibility and Global Leadership: Recommendations for the G-8 Genoa Summit from the G-8 Preparatory Conference, [2nd report] [Turin]. www.iie.com/publications/papers/g8-2001.pdf.

G-8 Preparatory Conference (2002), Global Responses to the New Global Challenges: Recommendations for the G-8 Kananaskis Summit from the G-8 Preparatory Conference, [3rd report] [Washington, DC]. www.iie.com/publications/papers/g8-2002.pdf.

G05 (2005), *Global Democracy: Civil Society Visions and Strategies Conference*, Montreal, 31 May, www.g05.org.

'G-Force: The G7 No Longer Governs the World Economy: Does Anyone?' (2004), *The Economist*, 373:8396, 72, October 9.

Garten, Jeffrey (2005), 'Russia's Leadership of the Group of Eight Will Be Farcical', *Financial Times*, 23, 28 June.

Gurría, Angel (2005), 'A Leaders' 20 Summit?', in *Reforming from the Top: A Leaders' 20 Summit*, 63-71. English et al. (eds), Centre for International Governance Innovation; United Nations University Press, New York; Tokyo.

Guttry, Andrea de (1994), 'The Institutional Configuration of the G-7 in the New International Scenario', in *The Future of the G-7 Summits*, 67-80 (*The International Spectator*, 29:2 Special Issue).

Haas, Richard (2005), 'Leaders Have a Flawed Gleneagles Agenda', *Financial Times*, 19, 1 July.

Haynal, George (2005), 'Summitry and Governance: The Case for a G-XX', in *Setting Priorities Straight: Canada among Nations 2004*, 261-74. David Carment, Fen Osler Hampson and Norman Hillmer, (eds), McGill-Queens University Press, Montreal.

Higgott, Richard (2005), 'Multilateralism and the Limits of Global Governance', in *Reforming from the Top: A Leaders' 20 Summit*, 72-96. English, et al. (eds), Centre for International Governance Innovation; United Nations University Press, New York; Tokyo.

Hodges, Michael R. (1994), 'More Efficiency, Less Dignity: British Perspectives on the Future Role and Working of the G-7', in *The Future of the G-7 Summits*, 141-159 (*The International Spectator*, 29:2 Special Issue).

Ikenberry, G. John (1993), 'Salvaging the G-7', *Foreign Affairs*, 72:2, 132-39.

Inoguchi, Kuniko (1994), 'The Changing Significance of the G-7 Summits', *Japan Review of International Affairs*, 8:1, 21-38.

InterAction Council, www.interactioncouncil.org.

Katada, Saori N. (2005), 'Balancing Act: Japan's Strategy in Global and Regional Financial Governance', in *Reforming from the Top: A Leaders' 20 Summit*, 97-120. English, et al. (eds), Centre for International Governance Innovation; United Nations University Press, New York; Tokyo.

Kenen, Peter B. et al. (2004), *International Economic and Financial Cooperation: New Issues, New Actors, New Responses*, Centre for Economic Policy Research, London.

Kirton, John J. (2004a), *Getting the L20 Going: Reaching out from the G8*, paper prepared for a workshop on 'G20 to Replace the G8: Why Not Now?', sponsored by the Brookings Institution, Institute for International Economics and the Centre for Global Governance, Washington, DC, September 22. www.g7.utoronto.ca/scholar/kirton2004/kirton_040922.html.

Kirton, John J. (2005e), 'Toward Multilateral Reform: The G20's Contribution', in *Reforming from the Top: A Leaders' 20 Summit*, 141-68. English, et al. (eds), Centre for International Governance Innovation; United Nations University Press, New York; Tokyo.

Lewis, Flora (1992), 'The 'G-7½' Directorate', *Foreign Policy*, 85, 25-40.

Martin, Lawrence (2006), 'Miles to Go before Martin Sleeps', *The Globe and Mail*, A1, A7, 1 June.

Martin, Paul (2005), 'A Global Answer to Global Problems: The Case for a New Leaders' Forum', *Foreign Affairs*, 84, 2-6, May/June.

Martin, Paul (2006), *Speaking Notes for the Right Honourable Paul Martin P.C., M.P.: Annual Meeting of the Development and Peace Foundation*, 8 June, www.sef-bonn.org/download/veranstaltungen/2006/2006_sd_dresden_martin_speaking_notes.pdf.

Maull, Hanns W. (1994), 'Germany at the Summit', in *The Future of the G-7 Summits*, 112-39 (*The International Spectator*, 29:2 Special Issue).

Merlini, Cesare (1994), 'The G-7 and the Need for Reform', in *The Future of the G-7 Summits*, 5-25 (*The International Spectator*, 29:2 Special Issue).

Putnam, Robert D. (1994), 'Western Summitry in the 1990s: American Perspectives', in *The Future of the G-7 Summits*, 81-93 (*The International Spectator*, 29:2 Special Issue).

Roach, Stephen (2004), 'How to Fix the World', *Global Economic Forum*, 9-10, December, www.morganstanley.com/GEFdata/digests/20041217-fri.html#anch or0.

Sachs, Jeffrey (1998), 'Global Capitalism: Making It Work', *The Economist*, 348:8085, 23-25, September 12.

Said Aly, Abdel Monem (2005), 'The L20 and the Restructuring of the International Economic Order: An Egyptian Perspective', in *Reforming from the Top: A Leaders' 20 Summit*, 260-80. English, et al. (eds), Centre for International Governance Innovation; United Nations University Press, New York; Tokyo.

Sennes, Ricardo U. and Alexandre de Freitas Barbosa (2005), 'Brazil's Multiple Forms of External Engagement: Foreign Policy Dilemmas', in *Reforming from the Top: A Leaders' 20 Summit*, 201-29. English, et al. (eds), Centre for International Governance Innovation; United Nations University Press, New York; Tokyo.

Shadow G-8 (2003a), 'Letter of Transmittal to the Leaders of the G-8 Member Countries', in *Restoring G-8 Leadership of the World Economy*, www.iie.com/publications/papers/g8-2003.pdf.

Shadow G-8 (2003b), *Restoring G-8 Leadership of the World Economy: Recommendations for the Evian Summit from the Shadow G-8*, [4th report] [Paris], www.ifri.org/files/policy_briefs/WP_SHADOW_G8.pdf, www.iie.com/publicat ions/papers/g8-2003.pdf

Shadow G-8 (2004), Interview, 1 December.

Shadow G-8 (2005), Interview, May.

Shadow G-8 (2006), Correspondence, April.

Slaughter, Anne-Marie (2005), 'Government Networks, World Order, and the L20', in *Reforming from the Top: A Leaders' 20 Summit*, 281-95. English, et al. (eds), Centre for International Governance Innovation; United Nations University Press, New York; Tokyo.

Smyser, W.R. (1993), 'Goodbye, G-7', *The Washington Quarterly*, 16:1. 16, 23, 26.

Stephens, Philip (1992), 'Major Calls for Overhaul of G7 Summits', *Financial Times*, 1, September 10, London.

Taylor, Ian (2005), 'South Africa: Beyond the Impasse of Global Governance', in *Reforming from the Top: A Leaders' 20 Summit*, 230-259. English, et al. (eds), Centre for International Governance Innovation; United Nations University Press, New York; Tokyo.

Truman, Edwin M. (2004), 'The Euro and Prospects for Policy Coordination', draft paper prepared for the conference on 'The Euro at Five: Ready for a Global Role', 26 February, www.iie.com/publications/papers/truman0204-3.pdf.

United Nations, High-level Panel on Threats, Challenges and Change (2004), *A More Secure World: Our Shared Responsibility: Report of the High-level Panel on Threats, Challenges and Change*, United Nations, New York. Also available as UN, General Assembly, Fifty-ninth Session (2004), *Follow-up to the Outcome of the Millennium Summit: A More Secure World: Our Shared Responsibility; Report of the [Secretary-General's] High-level Panel on Threats, Challenges and Change*, A/59/565; 2 December.

Whyman, William E. (1995), 'We Can't Go On Meeting Like This: Revitalizing the G-7 Process', *The Washington Quarterly*, 18:3, 149-63.

Yu, Yongding (2005), 'China's Evolving Global View', in *Reforming from the Top: A Leaders' 20 Summit*, 187-200. English, et al. (eds), Centre for International Governance Innovation; United Nations University Press, New York; Tokyo.

Chapter 13

Documentation of the Summits

Introduction

The G7 and G8 system has generated a great many varied and often significant documents in the course of its work. Because this public documentation is the principal primary source of information about the G7 and G8 and its activities, and because of the absence of a G8 secretariat to gather, disseminate and analyze the document output, there is a clear need for systematic assessment of this source material. This chapter surveys the types, characteristics, subject matter, production and dissemination of the documents of the G7 and G8 summits; and assesses the evolution and importance of the documentation. The documentation of ministerial meetings and other sub-summit entities of the G7 and G8 system is discussed in Chapter 14 and the documentation of the G20 in Chapter 11. Information on other sources of information, including a detailed discussion of archives, can be found in Chapter 15.

Underlying public documentation are the actual negotiations of the G7 and G8 leaders. These are private and confidential, but after 32 years of summitry records of such discussions at early summits are becoming available in government archives of G7 countries. There are, for example, two sets of papers in the Gerald R. Ford Library (hereafter referred to as Ford Library) that yield the detailed notes of verbatim discussions at the 1975 Rambouillet summit, taken by US presidential adviser (and National Security Council Senior Staff Member for International Economic Affairs) Robert Hormats in the meeting room. (Memorandum, Robert Hormats to [Assistant to the President for Economic Affairs] L. William Seidman, 2 December 1975; Box 312, L. William Seidman Files, 1974-77, International Economic Summit, November 15-17, 1975 – Memoranda of Conversations and Notes on Discussions; and Memorandum, Robert Hormats to [Assistant to the President for National Security Affairs] Brent Scowcroft, 2 December 1975; Box 16, National Security Adviser Memoranda of Conversations, November 15-17, 1975 – Rambouillet Economic Summit.)[1] Memoirs of certain prominent personalities who were present at the leaders' discussions also contain excerpts from what went on behind the scenes. Another indication of other G7 countries' versions of such notes can be found in the Library and Archives Canada. A 4 February 1976 letter to Basil Robinson, [Canadian] Under-Secretary of State for External Affairs to Ivan L. Head, Prime Minister Trudeau's sherpa, refers to a partial draft of the Japanese record of the Rambouillet summit given to Trudeau by the Japanese ambassador. The letter states that the leaders' interventions in that record are coded thus: A – Giscard, B

---

1   References to records in official archives follow the form suggested by those archives.

– Wilson, C – Ford, D-Schmidt, E – Miki, F – Moro, and G – Kissinger. (MG26019, Vol. 139, File 17: 1975-1977, P. E. Trudeau Fonds, Staff Series, Ivan Head – Subject Files – Economic Summit 1975-1976.)

Summit Documentation

Collective documents of G7 and G8 summits fall into the following categories:

- The communiqué;
- Declarations and statements on political and global or regional issues;
- Chair's statements and summaries, and leaders' statements of other types;
- Action plans;
- Reports of sub-summit G7 and G8 bodies submitted to the leaders;
- Documents released jointly by the G8 leaders and invited heads of non-G8 countries and international organizations; and
- Documents of selected bilateral meetings of G8 leaders when the host leader chooses to release them as summit documents.

In addition to primary collective documents, three other types of closely related public information should be noted:

- Transcripts of news conferences – particularly those at the end of the summits – of the host leader and his or her peers;
- Outside communications addressed to the G7 and G8; and
- Websites of the host and other G8 governments (for a description of these see Chapter 15).

As well, G7 and G8 officials give numerous briefings at summits; these often do not result in actual press releases but serve as background information to the media.[2]

The Communiqué

The principal summit document during the period 1975-2001 was the communiqué, a consensus document. It was 'a text agreed upon by all participants, which [did] not reflect the debate's progress nor the scale of priorities attached to the issues under discussion, but which [acted] as a position paper on a broad range of international issues' (Sherifis and Astraldi 2001: 195-95). The subjects of the communiqué

---

2   In addition to major collective and individual G8 country documents, before and during the summit the host country issues a number of minor documents for the information of the attending media. These include items such as notices of upcoming briefings and photo opportunities, and a detailed media handbook that gives information on the composition of official delegations, hotel assignments for the delegations, location of briefing rooms, and schedules of the leaders' meetings (this last is subject to change due to the progress of the leaders' negotiations and, as the case may be, unexpected events that interfere with the schedule).

ranged from exchange rates, interest rates, inflation, unemployment and economic growth to North-South and East-West relations, the environment and sustainable development, Third World debt, international organizations, and any other issue on the agenda. The communiqué was often entitled 'final communiqué', 'declaration' or 'economic declaration'. Philippe Moreau Defarges (1994: 184) wrote: '[f]inal declarations resemble Jacques Prévert's inventories or Jorge Luis Borges' lists: they can include the whole world'. William E. Whyman (1995: 153-54), too, noted: '[t]he communiqué has grown into a long, unwieldy "Christmas tree" with each country adding its cherished special interest "ornament"'.

At the inaugural summit at Rambouillet in 1975, it was not at all certain that a communiqué or declaration would be issued at all. Henry Kissinger recalls: 'The confidence of the leaders [in the ability of the G6 to handle the economic problems] was shown by the fact that they would talk about general principles and then turned over the drafting to either Ministers or experts and that the leaders only spent about an hour on the declaration. At first we didn't want any declaration because we were afraid that we would spend our whole time drafting it and it didn't turn out that way.' (White House Press Release, November 17, 1975: Press Conference of Henry A. Kissinger, Secretary of State, and William E. Simon, Secretary of the Treasury aboard Air Force One; Ford Library, Box 5, John W. 'Bill' Roberts Papers, 1973-1977, Presidential Subject File, Foreign Trips, November 14-17, 1975 – France – Press Releases.)

The communiqué then became the rule at subsequent summits, with infrequent exceptions. The last communiqué was produced by the 2001 Genoa summit; for the first time in summit history, the 2002 Kananaskis summit issued no formal communiqué – only a brief, more informal chair's summary. This was a result of long-standing aversion by some G8 leaders to lengthy, pre-scripted communiqués that, according to some, more people wrote than read. (There had been chair's summaries at earlier summits but those were issued in addition to formal communiqués.) Summits from then on continued this practice and issued chair's summaries only. At the 2005 Gleneagles summit, the two documents corresponding to the two central items of the agenda – one on Africa, the other on climate change, clean energy and sustainable development – that had first been released separately, also appeared together and were called 'communiqué' when signed by the leaders but they did not constitute a true communiqué. (The Africa document also included two annexes: the G8 and International Response; and Financing Commitments as submitted by individual G8 members.) Host Tony Blair's innovation of asking all G8 leaders to affix their signatures to the combined document (for the first time in summit history) was meant to underline their personal commitment to what they agreed to at the summit.

In earlier years of summitry, the text of the communiqué was often carried in full in *The New York Times* and other newspapers of record, but this practice was discontinued, partly because the communiqués had grown progressively longer, and partly because the media lost interest in publishing them *in extenso*.[3] On the

---

3   The University of Toronto G8 Information Centre website has a comprehensive set of G7/G8 summit documents at <www.g8.utoronto.ca/summit/index.htm>. Sets of documents related to particular summits – and in some cases archival sets of documents of several summits

other hand, with the rise of the internet, several websites have published full texts of communiqués and other G7 and G8 documents.

Andrea De Guttry (1994: 70-71), analyzing summit communiqués from an international law point of view, identified the following types of formulations the communiqués contained: 'international obligations for the participant states ..., [r]ecommendations to the G-7 member states ..., [s]imple invitations to international organizations ... [and] acts relative to international organizations'. Instruments available to the G7 to achieve implementation included direct formulation of recommendations, invitations to member states, delegation of various tasks to other organizations, and the establishment of new international bodies.

Preparing the Communiqué and Other Summit Documents

Rossella Franchini Sherifis and Valerio Astraldi (2001: 195) noted: 'the initial impetus behind the [c]ommuniqué traditionally lies with the G7/G8 [p]residency' when the host leader first reveals the agenda of the forthcoming summit. The preparation of the communiqué was a long, involved process unfolding during the lead-up to each summit. The sherpas played a crucial role in developing this document in the course of their series of meetings during the year, first to follow up on the previous summit and begin discussion of the priorities and political constraints of their leaders; then to shape the structure and preliminary agenda of the forthcoming summit, isolating specific issues for the leaders' discussion, beginning the draft of the summit documents (and, at their final pre-summit meeting, completing the 'thematic paper' closely resembling the final draft communiqué during the years when communiqués existed). In Michael R. Hodges's (1994: 150) words, the thematic paper 'simply serves as a quarry for the preparation of the final communiqués'. Between the 2004 Sea Island and 2005 Gleneagles summit the sherpas met six times: their first, 15 October 2004 meeting was the last under the US G8 presidency; in 2005 before the Gleneagles summit they met under UK presidency on 18-19 February, 23-24 March, 25-26 May, 14-16 June and 1-2 July. (The post-summit follow-up meeting took place on 9-10 November 2005.) Since the disappearance of the communiqué, the sherpas' drafting efforts formerly exerted on thematic papers are mostly given to action plans (see below).

In Naples (1994), Halifax (1995) and Lyon (1996), the communiqué was released on the second day rather than at the end of the summit, in order to allow the last day

---

– are available on the official websites of G8 host and other G8 member governments; for example, the UK website for the 2005 Gleneagles summit has documents of the 1998-2005 summits, at <www.g8.gov.uk/servlet/Front?pagename=OpenMarket/Xcelerate/ShowPage& c=Page&cid=1078995910202>; and the Russian website has documents of the 1997-2006 summits at <http://en.g8russia.ru/g8/history/shortinfo/> and <http://en.g8russia.ru/docs/>. For printed collections of summit documents see Hajnal (1989); Hajnal (1991); The Twenty... (1994). Other sources of the texts of the final communiqués include the now-defunct US Department of State *Bulletin* and its successors, the *US Department of State Dispatch* and *Foreign Policy Bulletin: The Documentary Record of United States Foreign Policy*; *La politique étrangère de la France* (issued by the Documentation française for the Ministère des relations extérieures of France), and other official publications of the summit countries.

to be devoted to P8 discussions with the Russians. This pattern changed with the 1997 Denver 'Summit of the Eight' when the communiqué was again released at the end of the summit, this time reflecting the consensus of the Eight. The communiqué (which, according to Defarges (1994: 179), reflected 'a soft consensus', contrasted with Whyman's (1995: 142) characterization of it as 'a fully negotiated, binding statement') was presented by the leader of the host country with considerable ceremony. In a departure from the practice at earlier summits where the host leader had read out the full text, at Houston in 1990 President Bush (the elder) simply summarized it with the evident approval of the guest leaders assembled on the stage while the full text was being distributed to the media. This simplified procedure took hold following Tokyo III (1993) where the leaders had signalled their intention to have more informal meetings and to produce shorter documents once again.

It is interesting to compare the economic components of the summit communiqué with the communiqué issued by the OECD ministerial meeting usually held a few weeks before the summit. As Hisashi Owada (1994: 111) put it: 'each year the communiqué of the OECD ministerial meeting offers a reference model for preparation of the summit's economic declaration'. For example, the communiqué of the OECD ministerial meeting held on 26-27 May 1997 raised many of the economic and political concerns that figure prominently in the Denver communiqué. The 27-28 April 1998 OECD ministerial communiqué, in its discussion of the effects of the Asian financial crisis, the multilateral trading system, harmful tax competition and other issues, again foreshadowed topics covered by the Birmingham G7 and G8 documents.[4]

The Draft Communiqué

Draft communiqués were not distributed (but were sometimes leaked) to the media before or at the summits. An interesting development occurred before the 1995 Halifax summit when, on 6 June, Canadian New Democratic Party Member of Parliament Nelson Riis released to the press a draft communiqué dated 27 May 1995 (BNA 1995: S12-S16). Comparing the missing sections and especially the square-bracketed passages in the leaked draft with the appropriate parts of the agreed communiqué throws additional light on the preparatory process and the role of the leaders in working out final agreement on the main document of the summit. There had been earlier as well as subsequent instances of leaked draft communiqués and other draft documents of summits; some of these attracted more attention than others.[5]

More than a month before the 2006 St. Petersburg summit, *The New York Times* revealed and described a draft of the energy action plan of the summit. This leaked

---

4   The texts of OECD ministerial communiqués are accessible at the organization's website (for example, the 2006 *Chair's Summary* is at <www.oecd.org/document/43/ 0,2340,en_2649_201185_36781483_1_1_1_1,00.html>) and can also be found in each issue of the *Annual Report of the OECD*.

5   See, for example, Summit... (1988). The texts of the 1997 Denver and 1998 Birmingham draft communiqués can be accessed, respectively, at <www.g8.utoronto.ca/ summit/1997denver/comden.htm>   and   <www.g8.utoronto.ca/summit/1998birmingham/ comdraft.htm>.

draft, still subject to negotiation before the summit, stipulated that Russian access to investment in natural gas facilities, pipelines, infrastructure and utilities in the US and Europe be matched by Western access to investment in Russian energy industry. This type of *quid pro quo* was indicative of what the Russian hosts of the summit had in mind for the central point of their St. Petersburg agenda: energy security (Weisman 2006: A1, A6).

Official archives of G7 countries are a good source of draft communiqués for earlier summits. They yield successive drafts as they were developed. See, for example, 'Rambouillet Declaration (Draft as of November 16, 1975)', Ford Library, Box 32, WHCF-Subject File, FO 6: International Conferences, Rambouillet Economic Summit.

Declarations on Political and Other Global and Regional Issues

The declaration is another major document type. These were traditionally used for foreign policy issues or other non-economic matters. The first such declaration was issued by the 1978 Bonn summit, on the subject of aircraft hijacking. Prior to that time, because of initial French opposition to wider political and security discussions and Japanese reluctance to engage in those areas, 'final declarations contained no political statements' (Garavoglia and Padoan 1994: 51). Tokyo I (1979) also deplored air hijackings, and issued a special statement on Indochinese refugees. Declarations, which have subsequently proliferated in number, have ranged in subject from refugees and terrorism through East-West security concerns to drug trafficking and human rights. 'In order to preserve the [essentially] economic nature of the [final] communiqué, these political statements have been issued as separate documents' (Kirton 1989: xxxiii). This changed with the 1997 Denver Summit of the Eight and with the 1998 Birmingham G8 summit, as discussed later.

The non-economic concerns of Venice 1980, expressed in special statements, were Afghanistan and the occupation of the US Embassy in Teheran. In Ottawa 1981 there was a separate statement on terrorism. The main political statement of the 1982 Versailles summit addressed the situation in Lebanon after the Israeli invasion. The 1983 'Williamsburg Declaration on Security', the first summit initiative on this issue, called for arms control and greater co-operation in that field between the Soviet Union and the G7; it also covered the stationing of US missiles in Europe. In London 1984 there were declarations on democratic values, terrorism, and East-West security relations, as well as a statement on the Iran-Iraq conflict.

The 1985 Bonn summit produced a political declaration commemorating the fortieth anniversary of the end of World War II. One of the political declarations at Tokyo in 1986 commented on the Chernobyl nuclear accident. 'Venice II' (1987) brought forward statements on East-West relations, terrorism, the Iran-Iraq war, AIDS, and narcotic drugs. The 1989 (Paris) Summit of the Arch also issued declarations on human rights (to commemorate the bicentennial of the Rights of Man and of the Citizen), on China (following the Tiananmen Square massacre of June 1989), on East-West relations (especially in connection with post-Cold War democratization in Eastern and Central Europe), and on terrorism. The 1991 London summit produced a 'Political Declaration' subtitled 'Strengthening the International Order', a separate 'Declaration on Conventional Arms Transfers and NBC [nuclear, biological and chemical] Non-proliferation' and a 'Chairman's Statement (As Prepared)' in which UK Foreign Secretary Douglas Hurd commented on the first two documents.

In 1992, in Munich, the political declaration, with the subtitle 'Shaping the New Partnership', dealt with specific economic, political and security areas of the new partnership with countries of Central and Eastern Europe and the new independent states of the former Soviet Union, nuclear non-proliferation, and the further strengthening of the UN. In addition, there was a separate declaration on the crisis in the former Yugoslavia, and a 'Chairman's Statement' (from German Foreign Minister Klaus Kinkel) on problems and developments in the Nagorno-Karabakh region, the Baltic States, the Middle East, Iraq, Korea, China, the Mediterranean, Africa and Latin America, as well as questions of drugs and terrorism. The 1993 Tokyo political declaration, issued on the second day of the summit, was subtitled 'Striving for a More Secure and Humane World'. The declaration condemns Serbia and Croatia for their aggression in Bosnia and affirms human rights and nuclear non-proliferation, among other points. Writing in early 1994, Robert D. Putnam (1994: 91) remarked that the formerly 'largely autonomous process of preparation of the summit "political declarations" has been taken over by the "G-7 political directors" in foreign offices outside the purview of the sherpas themselves'. A more recent example of a declaration is the *G8 Summit Declaration on Counter-Terrorism* issued by the 2006 St. Petersburg summit.

Chair's Statements and Chair's Summaries

In this type of document the host leader expresses 'his own point of view, for which he [takes] personal responsibility, on the common position … [of all the leaders], without committing the other participants to this specific wording' (Sherifis and Astraldi 2001: 196-97). Thus, the chair's statement, unlike the communiqué, does not represent a full consensus.

The chair's summary of earlier summits had, for a number of years, been used by the host leader to sum up his or her assessment of the achievements of the summit. It appeared as an oral statement, a prepared written document, or an agreed collective statement read by the host leader. An example is the 1981 Ottawa summit where the host leader, Prime Minister Pierre Trudeau, presented a summary of political issues. Toronto 1988 issued a chairman's summary on the Middle East, South Africa and Cambodia. The chair's summary was not issued at every summit.

At the 1994 Naples summit the chair's statement acquired a new meaning when it was issued by the host leader on behalf of the P8 ('Political 8' – the G7 + Russia before the latter became a full member of the G8 in 1998). There, as well as in Halifax in 1995 and Lyon in 1996, it reflected Russia's increased role in the summit's political discussions and was drafted with Russian participation, thus expressing the sense of the P8.

The Naples *Chairman's Statement [Political]* dealt with a number of issues ranging from Bosnia and the Israeli-Palestinian agreement, through North Korea and Rwanda, to the role of the UN and of the CSCE (Conference on Security and Cooperation in Europe). Following the pattern set at Naples, the 1995 Halifax summit, at its conclusion, issued a *Chairman's Statement*, reaffirming the commitment of the P8 to multilateral engagement, arms control and disarmament, new approaches in dealing with environmental and other global challenges, and fighting terrorism and other international crime. It also reviewed European achievements (the advance of democracy and market economy) and problems (especially Bosnia); the situation in the Middle East and Africa; the Asia-Pacific region; and the Americas. The main feature of the Halifax Chairman's Statement, though, was a thematic, generic approach to conflict prevention and resolution, rather than a regional focus.[6] The 1996 Lyon summit's *Chairman's Statement* covered a broad range of global and regional issues. It also included a long supplementary section reviewing UN reforms since Halifax, with a catalogue of achievements and a commitment by the Eight to 'continue and reinforce our efforts to improve the functioning of the UN in the economic and social fields and its impact on development ... [and to] continue to work in partnership with other members to complete processes underway ... and initiate further processes as required'.

The Denver Summit of the Eight (1997) associated Russia more closely with the G7, and the concept of the chair's statement changed again. With the advent of the G8 in Birmingham in 1998, accompanied nonetheless by the continuing survival of the G7, the chair's statement appeared as '*G7 Chairman's Statement*', reflecting the position of the G7 (G8 minus Russia) (Sherifis and Astraldi 2001: 197). In it, the G7 leaders and the President of the European Commission covered economic policies of the seven and the proposed 'New Financial Architecture'. From Cologne (1999) through Genoa (2001) each summit issued a *G7 Statement*. Starting with the 2002 Kananaskis summit, the G7 heads have not met separately from the G8 at summits.

G8 chair's summaries first appeared in 2002 at the Kananaskis summit. These summaries are not circulated in advance; they are intended to summarize the issues actually discussed by the leaders; it is the action plans, declarations, statements and reports which include commitments prepared in advance.

In 2005 at Gleneagles, the *Chair's Summary* was presented by host leader Tony Blair at his final press conference at the end of the summit. It gave a concise account of the highlights and achievements of Gleneagles. It noted the London terrorist bombings on the first day of the summit, and summarized the results of discussions on climate change; Africa and development; the global economy, oil and trade; and regional issues and proliferation of weapons of mass destruction. It noted as well the significant degree of participation by non-G8 countries and international organizations: the invited leaders of Brazil, China, India, Mexico and South Africa and heads of the International Energy Agency, International Monetary Fund, United Nations, World Bank, and the World Trade Organization in the summit's discussions on climate change and the global economy; and those invited for the discussions on Africa and development: the leaders of Algeria, Ethiopia, Ghana, Nigeria, Senegal, South Africa and Tanzania and

---

6   This and other summit documents cited in this chapter are accessible at the G8 Information Centre website, at <www.g8.utoronto.ca/summit/index.htm>. A few documents, not found on that website, are referenced separately.

the heads of the African Union Commission, International Monetary Fund, United Nations and the World Bank. In the 2006 St. Petersburg *Chair's Summary*, Vladimir Putin reviewed the summit's results – on the priority themes of energy security, education and infectious diseases, as well as other issues discussed by the G8 leaders: the world economy, trade, intellectual property piracy, corruption, Africa, weapons of mass destruction, terrorism, the Middle East and other regional issues.

The French term for the *Chair's Statement* is *communiqué de la Présidence* (communiqué of the presidency); an example was the one issued during the 1989 Paris summit by President Mitterrand, in his capacity as summit host leader, on the Arab-Israeli conflict, Southern Africa, Central America, Panama, Cambodia, and Lebanon. Other examples include host leader Italian Prime Minister Amintore Fanfani's statements on AIDS and narcotic drugs at the 1987 Venice summit. The 1995 Halifax summit saw Canadian host Prime Minister Jean Chrétien deliver a statement on Bosnia – unusually this was done in the first evening of the summit before Russian President Boris Yeltsin's arrival. This indicated that the Halifax summit was indeed a 'leaders' summit' of the seven, contrasted with many previous summits at which the initial working dinner of the heads had largely confined its agenda to previously prepared economic issues.

The 1998 G8 Birmingham summit produced another document in this category, entitled *Response by the Presidency on Behalf of the G8 to the Jubilee 2000 Petition*. At midday on the first day of the 2005 Gleneagles summit, host leader Tony Blair issued a statement reacting to, and condemning, the terrorist attacks that morning on the London transportation system: *Prime Minister's Statement on London Explosions*, 7 July (UK 2005c). (Blair appears to have made the statement as UK Prime Minister rather than as G8 president.) The leaders of the other G8 countries and the President of the European Commission also made individual statements condemning the terrorist attacks.

An interesting type of leaders' document is exemplified by the *G7 Leaders' Statement on the World Economy*, issued on 30 October 1998 without a formal summit meeting. In it, the leaders welcome the declaration of the same day of their finance ministers and central bank governors and announce their agreement on further reforms needed to create a stronger financial architecture (G7 1998). And following the 11 September 2001 terrorist attacks in the US, the G8 leaders issued a joint statement on 19 September, also without a meeting, deploring the attacks and pledging to prevent terrorism and take countermeasures (G8 2001).

Leaders' Action Plans, and Reports of Other G8 Bodies Submitted to the Leaders

Action plans related to main agenda items of each summit have become a regular feature of summitry. The 2002 Kananaskis summit's *G8 Africa Action Plan* and the 2005 *Gleneagles Plan of Action: Climate Change, Clean Energy and Sustainable Development* are two important examples of documents in this category. The 2006 summit released the *St. Petersburg Plan of Action on Global Energy Security*. It is an annex to the G8 statement, *Global Energy Security*. Such action plans (along with reports and declarations) have proliferated, particularly since the 2003 Evian summit.

Progress reports and other reports mandated by an earlier summit and prepared by sub-summit bodies are subsequently submitted to the leaders. Such reports have become more common in recent years. Examples follow:

- DOT Force (Digital Opportunities Task Force] *Report Card: Digital Opportunities for All*, submitted to the Kananaskis summit;
- *Progress Report by the G8 Africa Personal Representatives on Implementation of the Africa Action Plan* and the *Secure and Facilitated International Travel Initiative: Summit Progress Report*, both submitted to the Gleneagles summit.
- At St. Petersburg the leaders received the *Report of the Nuclear Safety and Security Group* and the *Report on the G8 Global Partnership* [against the proliferation of weapons and materials of mass destruction], the latter accompanied by a progress report on implementation of the partnership (which is considerably broader than the G8) in the following areas: the destruction of chemical weapons; dismantling nuclear submarines; disposition of fissile materials; employment of former weapons scientists; and other areas of co-operation. There is a lengthy annex reporting on related activities of members of the partnership: the G8 countries, the European Union, plus Australia, Belgium, Denmark, Finland, the Netherlands, New Zealand, Norway, South Korea, Sweden, Switzerland and Ukraine.

Joint Declarations by G8 Leaders and Other Invited Leaders

The Gleneagles summit gave birth to joint declarations issued by G8 leaders with other invited leaders participating in summits. These reflect the recent trend to involve other leaders more and more closely in the summit process. At Gleneagles, there were two such joint declarations: *Terrorist Attacks on London: Statement by the G8, the Leaders of Brazil, China, India, Mexico and South Africa and the Heads of the International Organisations Represented Here* [at Gleneagles] – this was a summit first in that the 2005 'G5' and the administrative heads of the UN, the IMF, the WTO and the World Bank formally associating themselves with a summit document – and *Statement by the G8 and AU* [African Union]: *Sudan*. Communications of individual invited participating leaders are, too, more closely related to the work of the G8 than outside communications to the summits (discussed below). An example at Gleneagles is a document by the Mexican President, *Mexico's General Position on Climate Change and Energy, Prepared for the Outreach Session of the G-8 Summit* (Mexico 2005).

The St. Petersburg summit's documentation includes the *Statement by the G8, the Leaders of Brazil, China, India, Mexico, South Africa, Chairman of the Council of the Heads of State of the CIS, Chairman of the African Union, and the Heads of the International Organizations*. In this statement, the leaders express their outrage at the 11 July 2006 terrorist acts in Mumbai and other parts of India.

Bilateral Declarations Issued as Summit Documents

Bilaterial meetings of leaders have always been a feature during the G7 and G8 summits. But at the St. Petersburg summit, host leader Putin released four of these statements as summit documents for the first time: two were based on Putin's meetings with Bush (one a joint statement announcing the Global Initiative to Combat Nuclear Terrorism, the other on co-operation in the peaceful uses of nuclear energy; there is also a related joint fact sheet); and two more on his meetings with Canadian Prime Minister Stephen Harper (on Canada-Russia relations and on Canada-Russia energy co-operation).

Transcripts of Press Conferences

At a level below the agreed public documents of the summits, transcripts of press conferences constitute another important category of document. Many press conferences and briefings are held throughout the summits. Each summit country, as well as the EU, goes to great lengths to present its own initiatives and positions on various issues to the world news media so as to reflect itself in the best possible light internationally as well as back home. Hodges (1994: 155) notes that 'the press does not know what really goes on in the summit meetings and relies heavily on briefings from the press secretaries of the various heads. Each of these briefings gives a different idea of who succeeded.' Because the press (and whatever else the summits are, they are also big media events, with thousands of print, radio and television journalists covering the scene) cannot attend the actual meetings of the leaders (or the ministers at their conferences), journalists must rely on briefings and press conferences. Even though they tend to be self-serving, news conferences nonetheless allow media representatives to ask probing questions of major officials and other spokesmen. The press conference given at the conclusion of each summit by the leader of the host country is particularly important because it allows the host to present not only his or her evaluation of the summit but also a summation in his or her capacity as president of the summit. Examples are President Clinton's news conference at the conclusion of the Denver Summit of the Eight, Prime Minister Blair's press conference marking the end of the Birmingham G8 summit; Blair's final press conference at Gleneagles, and Putin's end-of-summit press conference in St. Petersburg.

Press conferences of non-host leaders at the end of each summit are good sources of evaluation of the summit reflecting the position of each G8 country and the EU; for example, French President Jacques Chirac held a press conference at the end of the Gleneagles summit and his office issued a press release of his remarks and the question-and-answer period that followed (France 2005). Bilateral meetings of leaders during summits usually produce press releases as well. For example, on the first working day of the Gleneagles summit, on 7 July 2005, host leader UK Prime Minister Tony Blair met with US President Bush; a press release was then issued reproducing the remarks and answers to questions of both leaders (US 2005).

The host government sometimes produces fact sheets. At Gleneagles the UK Presidency of the G8 issued 21 of those, including fact sheets on the G8-Africa relationship, the Millennium Development Goals, peace and security, Dialogue on Climate Change, and sustainable development.

To indicate the full range of summit documentation (this, of course, varies greatly from summit to summit), a list of all 22 documents of the 2006 St. Petersburg summit follows, by date of release. (These are accessible on the Russian government's official G8 website at <http://en.g8russia.ru/docs/> as well as on the G8 Information Centre website, at <www.g8.utoronto.ca/summit/2006stpetersburg/index.html>.)

15 July:

- *Joint Statement by President George Bush and President V.V. Putin* [on co-operation in the peaceful uses of nuclear energy];
- *Joint Statement by U.S. President George Bush and Russian Federation President V.V. Putin announcing the Global Initiative to Combat Nuclear Terrorism;*
- *Global Initiative to Combat Nuclear Terrorism: Joint* [US-Russia] *Fact Sheet;*
- *Joint Policy Statement by Prime Minister Stephen Harper and President of the Russian Federation Vladimir Putin on Canada-Russia Relations;*
- *Joint Statement by Prime Minister of Canada Stephen Harper and President of the Russian Federation Vladimir Putin on Canada-Russia Energy Cooperation.*

16 July:

- *Global Energy Security;*
- *Education for Innovative Societies in the 21st Century;*
- *Fight against Infectious Diseases;*
- *Trade;*
- *Update on Africa;*
- *Fighting High Level Corruption;*
- *Combating IPR* [Intellectual Property Rights] *Piracy and Counterfeiting;*
- *G8 Summit Declaration on Counter-Terrorism;*
- *G8 Statement on Strengthening the UN's Counter-Terrorism Program;*
- *G-8 Declaration on Cooperation and Future Action in Stabilization and Reconstruction* [in post-conflict countries];
- *Statement on Non-Proliferation* [of weapons of mass destruction];
- *Middle East;*
- *Report on the G8 Global Partnership* [against the proliferation of weapons and materials of mass destruction], and Annex;
- *Report of the Nuclear Safety and Security Group.*

17 July:

- *Chair's Summary;*
- *Statement by the G-8, the leaders of Brazil, China, India, Mexico, South Africa, Chairman of the Council of the Heads of State of the CIS, Chairman of the African Union, and the Heads of the International Organizations* [on the 11 July 2006 terrorist acts in Mumbai and other parts of India].

Outside Communications to the Summit

Although not summit documents in the strict sense, outside communications to the summit are important related documents. Especially significant are President Gorbachev's 14 July 1989 letter to President Mitterrand expressing the Soviet Union's wish to be associated with the summits; and Gorbachev's letter to President Bush, received a few days before the 1990 Houston summit.[7] Gorbachev's letter was discussed and commented on by the leaders and reflected in summit documents, although the texts were not released to the public. Gorbachev's 23-page message (together with a 31-page annex) to the leaders at the 1991 London summit, delivered by Yevgeni Primakov on 12 July, caused a flurry of journalistic speculation and comment even though its text had not been officially released. The message – a synthesis of the Yavlinski reform plan and the Soviet government's plan for economic reform – was discussed intensively by the G7, although the personal dialogue, made possible by the Gorbachev visit to London, eclipsed the written communication.

Other examples of outside communications:

- A press release issued just before the 1989 Paris summit by four Third World leaders: President Hosni Mubarak of Egypt, Prime Minister Rajiv Gandhi of India, President Abdou Diouf of Senegal, and President Carlos Andrés Pérez of Venezuela. The four, in the name of the fifteen major developing countries, wished to initiate regular consultations with the developed world at the summit level. The fifteen later formed their own 'G-15', alluded to earlier.
- The co-ordinated but separate letters addressed to the 1991 London summit by the President of Poland, the Prime Minister of Hungary, and the President of Czechoslovakia. These letters (whose text was not released) expressed concern about the collapse of those countries' trade with the Soviet Union, and about their access to Western markets.[8]
- An address to the seven heads of summit delegations, dated 26 June 1992, from the Council of the Baltic States, dealing with the continued presence of Russian forces in Estonia, Latvia, and Lithuania.
- At the 2005 Gleneagles summit several religious leaders, led by the Dalai Lama, along with representatives of the Russian Orthodox Church, the World Council of Churches, the Central Conference of American Rabbis, the Latin American Council of Churches and the Interreligious Council of Mexico, signed a 'joint declaration on climate change and the defense of life'. The declaration called upon 'all the people of our world for a critical common

---

7   The text of President Gorbachev's letter to President Mitterrand is reproduced in Hajnal (1989: 429-36). Bayne and Putnam (1995: 7) note that the letter 'was identified by the British Foreign Secretary, Geoffrey Howe, as a cry for help'. Maull (1994: 128) reports that, in addition to Gorbachev's letter, there was another one from German Chancellor Kohl, on economic and political cooperation with Moscow.

8   Disclosed at a British press briefing, given by Gus O'Donnell (the Prime Minister's Chief Press Secretary), Francis Cornish (Press Secretary to the Secretary of State for Foreign and Commonwealth Affairs) and Dick Saunders (Press Secretary to the Chancellor of the Exchequer), 15 July 1991.

effort to preserve and promote life on this planet Earth', to respect and protect the environment, and to reduce emissions and other pollutants. It was given to a UK summit representative on 5 July (Dalai Lama 2005; Inter-religious… 2005).

- Recommendations of the Civil G8 forum of 3-4 July 2006 to the G8 leaders on 9 themes: social and economic policies for sustainable human development; genetically modified organisms; the interaction of business and society; infectious diseases; global security; energy security; education; biodiversity; and human rights (Civil G8 2006).

Assessing G7 and G8 Documentation

A number of observers have commented on the content of summit documents and the extent to which those documents reflect or fail to reflect actual deliberations. Cesare Merlini (1994: 19) remarks that 'distinction will have to be made in the final declarations at the end of the summits between qualifying and routine positions, between matters that have actually been discussed at the summit and matters that have been assigned to the structure … [Conversely, w]hile it is essential that the heads of state and government exchange views and concerns, these do not necessarily all have to be listed in communiqués and declarations.' G. John Ikenberry (1993: 132) laments the 'bland official communiqués that paper over dysfunctions in the global economic system, or vague joint commitments to growth and prosperity that substitute for actual accord'.

Guido Garavoglia and Pier Carlo Padoan (1994: 53-55) recall the early years of the summit when '[f]inal documents were rather short and reflected rather accurately the issues dealt with by the heads of state and government, although the tendency to increase the length and number of subjects was already evident'. Later, '[t]he increase in the number of subjects discussed has gradually led to a lengthening and a diversification of the final documents … These documents reflect a nominal agenda, which in many cases does not correspond to the matters actually discussed by the heads of state and government.'

An example of this lack of correspondence: almost one third of the communiqué of the 1989 Summit of the Arch was taken up by the topic of the environment contrasted with the relatively short time the leaders actually spent discussing that subject during their working dinner, as revealed in a background briefing by a senior official. Despite genuine efforts by the leaders to correct that kind of imbalance between released documents and actual discussions, and some real successes in this respect in more recent summits, a certain imbalance remains. For example – according to a background briefing by a senior official – Russian brutality in the war in Chechnya was brought up in Halifax in 1995, with several G7 leaders expressing unhappiness if not protest to Russian President Yeltsin. The Halifax *Chairman's Statement* of the P8, however, is silent on Chechnya, although remarks by the host leader prior to the release of the *Chairman's Statement* voiced 'concern at the continuing conflict and the resulting loss of life and civilian casualties … [and the participants'] strong belief that the situation in Chechnya should *not* be resolved by military means'. Dissatisfaction with the French decision to resume nuclear testing in the South Pacific was also voiced by several delegations in Halifax, but – keeping with the G7 tradition of not openly criticizing summit colleagues – this sentiment did not find its way into the public documentation of the summit.

C. Fred Bergsten (1996: 19), a frequent critic of the G7, decries this hesitancy, stating that '[t]he "nonaggression pact" now pervades the behavior of the G7. The members have decided not to criticize each other, especially in public, where it can sometimes be more effective, because they have lost confidence in their ability to influence events and because they fear being criticized themselves.' Later, in the lead-up to the 2006 St. Petersburg summit, this unspoken convention changed when officials of other G8 countries, particularly the US, openly, pointedly and repeatedly criticized the Russian government for backpedalling on democracy.

Several analysts have called for changes in summit documentation. Hisashi Owada (1994:110) advocates the necessity of 'a more structured approach to many vital issues through the summit process, while avoiding a bureaucratic straitjacket involving spending much time on preparing a document which basically lacks substance'. Hanns W. Maull (1994: 121, 136) criticizes the 'ever longer, broader and more non-committal communiqués, which tried to hide substantive policy disagreements by focusing on elements of consensus and mutual recognition of different national approaches'. He mentions the German desire to see shorter communiqués and separate chairman's summaries of political topics. Philippe Moreau Defarges (1994: 184) concurs: the French view is that 'declarations should be shorter, focusing on a few key points... . [If they] are shorter, they will be read more carefully and become more binding.' John J. Kirton (1994: 163), similarly, points to Canada's 'strong preference for a short, straightforward, comprehensible communiqué – one that reflect[s] what the leaders actually cared about, talked about and meant, and one that [is] easily understood not just by the officials ... but by the media and public at large'.

Garavoglia and Padoan (1994: 63), writing in early 1994, also suggest that:

> [o]nly one final document should be issued at the end of the summit and it should integrate economic and political aspects as much as possible. Furthermore, it should reflect the matters actually discussed by the leaders. This means that it would be much shorter than current communiqués, facilitating immediate public understanding of the matters discussed ... If the non-decisional nature of the summit is to be underlined, this could be done by a less demanding 'summary by the chairman' illustrating the main points on which the heads of state and government reached agreement.

It is worth noting how quickly events can overtake even the best-considered proposals from outside the G7. One of the major new developments at the Naples summit that took place only a few months after the above-cited proposal was written was Russia's formal participation in the political discussions. This resulted in an immediate change in the pattern of summit documentation, described previously: the communiqué of the 1994, 1995 and 1996 summits was issued at the end of the G7 part of the summit, on the second day, so that it was no longer the 'final' document. The 'chairman's statement' came to express the conclusions of the P8 which followed.

The new configuration of the 1997 Denver 'Summit of the Eight' changed the nature and scope of the communiqué. Now a document of the Eight, the *Communiqué* was released at the conclusion of the summit, on 22 June. In other documents released in Denver, financial and other economic issues – still in the purview of the G7 – were represented in a separate statement by the seven heads, entitled *Confronting Global Economic and Financial Challenges*, released on the second day of the summit. This statement dealt with promoting economic growth, strengthening the stability of the global financial system and building an integrated global economy. Significantly, the statement also discussed Ukraine at the level of the Seven, rather than the Eight. Also at the G7 level, the seven finance ministers submitted a *Final Report to the G-7 Heads of State and Government on Promoting Financial Stability* – a document with a separately issued two-page *Executive Summary*, a summit innovation. On the G8 level, in addition to the communiqué, the heads issued a *Statement on Bosnia and Herzegovina*, a *Statement on Cambodia* and a *Foreign Ministers' Progress Report*.

The innovations in summit format, agenda and participation introduced in 1998 in Birmingham were discussed earlier. These major changes were reflected in the pattern of documentation. The G8 produced a *Communiqué* at the conclusion of the summit, and political statements on regional issues (Indonesia, Kosovo, Bosnia/ Herzegovina; the Middle East peace process; and the Indian nuclear explosions of 11 and 13 May which the leaders condemned without agreeing on sanctions). A separate statement on Northern Ireland was issued, supporting the Good Friday agreement to end sectarian violence; another statement dealt with drugs and international crime.

At the G7 level, the leaders at Birmingham released a *G7 Chairman's Statement* on the world economy and on the strengthening of the global financial system, and supported the eight-page report submitted to them by the G7 finance ministers entitled *Strengthening the Architecture of the Global Financial System*. In it, the ministers identified five areas needing action: enhanced transparency; helping countries prepare for integration into the global economy and for free global capital flows; strengthening national financial systems; ensuring that the private sector takes responsibility for its lending decisions; and further enhancing the role of and cooperation among the IMF, the BIS (Bank for International Settlements), the World Bank, and other international financial institutions.

Although the Birmingham summit issued fewer documents than its recent predecessors, the reduction in volume was more than offset by the proliferating output of the joint pre-summit meeting of G7/G8 finance and foreign ministers in London on 8-9 May 1998. This shows a shifting of the workload and documentation from the leaders to their ministers, thereby allowing the leaders to concentrate on issues worthy of their time and attention. It is, moreover, a reflection of greater transparency in the work of the G7 and G8 – far from complete transparency, however: as discussed elsewhere in this chapter, the actual negotiations of the leaders behind the scenes have remained confidential.

Despite the uncertain equivalence between the leaders' time spent on a particular topic and summit documents, there is a relationship – albeit not a consistent one – between the length of the agenda and the summit documents. Sherifis and Astraldi (2001: 195) see the evolution of the communiqué thus: 'In the early G7 meetings, when the distinction between a "nominal agenda" and a "real agenda" was not evident, the Communiqué text was compact and quite brief … As the issues under discussion expanded … and as controversial themes were kept in successive Summits' agenda, the document ended up lengthening, diminishing its incisiveness and effectiveness as a communications tool.' The chair's summaries, which replaced the communiqués starting with the Kananaskis summit, have remedied the situation to the extent that these documents reflect more closely the actual deliberations of the leaders.

Nicholas Bayne (2005b: 6, 10, 37, 44, 56, 91, 150, 155, 166) observes that with the expansion of the summit agenda the corresponding documentation increases, and when the agenda is more concentrated, it is reduced. The Birmingham documents (but not the ministerial documents, as mentioned above) were fewer in number compared to earlier summits because the summit itself dealt with fewer topics. But by the following year, at Cologne, the agenda was less focused and the G7 statement (though not the communiqué) was longer than before. In Genoa it was shorter again; in Kananaskis, the summit was focused but there was voluminous documentation with action plans, reports and other material; Sea Island, with a more diffuse agenda, produced 'prolific and often confusing documentation'. At Gleneagles and St. Petersburg the agenda was generally concentrated but the documentation was voluminous.

Summit documents not infrequently contain ambiguities – likely by design rather than negligence – leading to different interpretations. A good example is the St. Petersburg summit's statement on the Middle East, released on the second day of the summit. French President Jacques Chirac 'characterized the statement … as a call for a cease-fire – a word the Bush administration has sidestepped at every turn over the last few days … R. Nicholas Burns, the [US] undersecretary of state for political affairs, said that the statement does not present any specific order for steps to solve the crisis but rather presumes that Israel will stand down only after Hezbollah and Hamas stop shelling Israeli towns and release captured soldiers' (Rutenberg 2006: A10).

Concluding Remarks

The documentation of the G7 and G8 system, in all its variety and dynamism, is an essential source of information not only about that G7 and G8 but also on a whole gamut of vital economic, political and other global issues. It is a potentially rich mine of political, economic and historical data, although it calls for a fair amount of interpretation to get beyond its jargon-laden language and somewhat repetitive nature. One must also look beyond the primary G7 and G8 documentation to complementary sources, notably archives, memoirs, and informed writings about the G7 and G8 and related issues.

References

Note on internet addresses (URLs): Websites tend to appear, change or disappear, often without warning. Addresses cited in this source list were accurate and active at the time of writing (August 2006) unless otherwise noted.

Bayne, Nicholas (2005b), *Staying Together: The G8 Summit Confronts the 21st Century*, Ashgate, Aldershot, UK.

Bayne, Nicholas and Robert D. Putnam (1995), 'Introduction: The G-7 Summit Comes of Age', in *The Halifax G-7 Summit: Issues on the Table*, 1-13, Sylvia Ostry and Gilbert R. Wynham (eds), Centre for Foreign Policy Studies, Dalhousie University, Halifax.

Bergsten, C. Fred (1996), 'Grade "F" for the G7', *The International Economy: The Magazine of International Economic Policy* 10:6, 18-21, 68, November/ December.

Bureau of National Affairs (1995), 'Draft Halifax Summit Communiqué, dated May 27, 1995, released June 6 by Canadian Member of Parliament Nelson Riis', *Daily Report for Executives: Preview of the G-7 Summit, Halifax, Canada, June 15-17*, 114, Special Issue, Washington, DC.

Civil G8 (2006), *Final Documents of the Forum*, 3-4 July, http://en.civilg8.ru/ forum0407_res.

Defarges, Philippe Moreau (1994), 'The French Viewpoint on the Future of the G-7', in *The Future of the G-7 Summits*, 177-85, (*The International Spectator* 29:2, April/June, Special Issue).

France, President (2005), *Conférence de presse de M. Jacques Chirac, Président de la République, à l'issue du sommet du G8 de Gleneagles*, www.elysee.fr.

G7 (1998), *G7 Leaders' Statement on the World Economy*, 30 October, www. g8.utoronto.ca/finance/g7_103098.html.

G8 (2001), *Terrorism: Statement by the leaders of the G8 over last week's terrorist attacks in New York and Washington*, 19 September, www.g8.utoronto.ca/ terrorism/sept192001.html.

Garavoglia, Guido and Pier Carlo Padoan (1994), 'The G-7 Agenda: Old and New Issues', in *The Future of the G-7 Summits*, 49-65, *The International Spectator* 29:2 April/June, Special Issue.

Guttry, Andrea de (1994), 'The Institutional Configuration of the G-7 in the New International Scenario', in *The Future of the G-7 Summits*, 67-80, (*The International Spectator* 29:2; April/June, Special Issue).

Hajnal, Peter I. (comp. and ed.) (1989), *The Seven-Power Summit: Documents from the Summits of Industrialized Countries, 1975-1989*, Kraus International Publications, Millwood, NY.

Hajnal, Peter I. (comp. and ed.) (1991), *The Seven-Power Summit: Documents from the Summits of Industrialized Countries; Supplement: Documents from the 1990 Summit*, Kraus International Publications, Millwood, NY.

Hodges, Michael R. (1994), 'More Efficiency, Less Dignity: British Perspectives on the Future Role and Working of the G-7', in *The Future of the G-7 Summits*, 141-159, (*The International Spectator* 29:2, April/June, Special Issue).

Ikenberry, G. John (1993), 'Salvaging the G-7', *Foreign Affairs*, 72:2, 132-39.

'Inter-religious Declaration Presented to the G8 Summit Leaders' (2005), [London,] 6 July.

Kirton, John J. (1989b), 'Introduction', in *The Seven-Power Summit: Documents from the Summits of Industrialized Countries, 1975-1989*, xxi-li, Peter I. Hajnal (ed.), Kraus International Publications, Millwood, NY.

Kirton, John J. (1994), 'Exercising Concerted Leadership: Canada's Approach to Summit Reform', in *The Future of the G-7 Summits*, 161-176, (*The International Spectator* 29:2, April/June, Special Issue).

Maull, Hanns W. (1994), 'Germany at the Summit', in *The Future of the G-7 Summits*, 112-39 (*The International Spectator*, 29:2 Special Issue).

Merlini, Cesare (1994), 'The G-7 and the Need for Reform', in *The Future of the G-7 Summits*, 5-25 (*The International Spectator*, 29:2 Special Issue).

Mexico, [President] (2005), *Mexico's General Position on Climate Change and Energy, Prepared for the Outreach Session of the G-8 Summit*, Gleneagles, Scotland, 7 July.

Office of the Dalai Lama (2005), 'Leaders Joint Declaration on Climate Change and the Defense of Life', [Dharamshala, India] July.

Owada, Hisashi (1994), 'A Japanese Perspective on the Role and Future of the G-7', in *The Future of the G-7 Summits*, 95-112, *The International Spectator*, 29:2, April/June, Special Issue.

Putnam, Robert D. (1994), 'Western Summitry in the 1990s: American Perspectives', in *The Future of the G-7 Summits*, 81-93 (*The International Spectator*, 29:2 Special Issue).

Rutenberg, Jim (2006), 'Despite Joint Statement on Mideast, Strains Emerge as U.S. Appears To Support Israel', *The New York Times*, 17 July, A10.

Sherifis, Rossella Franchini and Valerio Astraldi (2001), *Il G7/G8 da Rambouillet a Genova = The G7/G8 from Rambouillet to Genoa*, FrancoAngeli, Milano.

'Summit Part of Larger Process' (1988), *The Financial Post*, 22 June, www.g8.utoronto.ca/fp/ed880622.htm.

The Twenty G-7 Summits (1994), On the Occasion of the Twentieth Summit, Naples, July 8-10, Adnkronos Libri in Collaboration with Istituto Affari Internazionali, Rome.

United Kingdom, Prime Minister's Office (2005c), *Prime Minister's Statement on London Explosions*, 7 July, www.number-10.gov.uk/output/Page7853.asp.

United States, President, Office of the Press Secretary (2005), *Remarks by President Bush and Prime Minister Blair in a Photo Opportunity, Gleneagles Hotel*, Auchterarder, Scotland, 7 July.

Weisman, Steven R. (2006), 'Russia Bargains for Bigger Stake in West's Energy', *The New York Times*, 12 June, A1, A6.

Whyman, William E. (1995), 'We Can't Go On Meeting Like This: Revitalizing the G-7 Process', *The Washington Quarterly*, 18:3, 149-63.

Chapter 14

Documentation of Ministerial Fora, Task Forces, Working Groups and Expert Groups

This chapter discusses the documentation of parts of the G7 and G8 system apart from documentation of the leaders' summits (which is analyzed in Chapter 13). Chapter 6 provides a history of and information about the ministerial fora and other official bodies apart from the documentary aspects. For a discussion of the G20 and its documentation, see Chapter 11.

Ministerial Fora

Documentation of G7 and G8 ministerial meetings varies greatly. The G8 Information Centre website, <www.g8.utoronto.ca>, is a good source in which to find published statements of the G7 and G8 ministerial fora (see under 'ministerial meetings' <www.g8.utoronto.ca/meetings.html>) and documents of other official bodies related to the G7 and G8 (see under 'official-level meetings', <www.g8.utoronto. ca/meetings-official.html>). Websites of relevant ministries of G8 countries are additional sources, although these cover the meetings inconsistently and references tend to disappear later or migrate elsewhere within those websites.

The G7 and G8 employment ministers' meetings have issued public documents. For example, the G8 Conference on Growth, Employability and Inclusion, held in London on 21-22 February 1998, released 'Chairman's Conclusions'. The G8 Labour and Employment Ministers Conference ('Growth and Employment: The Future of the Working Society in a Changing World'), which met in Stuttgart, on 14-16 December 2003, issued 'Chair's Conclusions'. The G8 Labour Ministers, meeting in Turin, Italy on 10-11 November 2000, released not only 'Chair's Conclusions' but also the 'G8 Turin Charter: Towards Active Ageing'.

G7 and G8 environment ministers generally produce documents. For example, the 'Environment Leaders' Summit of the Eight' meeting in Miami, Florida, US, on 5-6 May 1997 issued a 'Chair's Summary' as well as a declaration on children's environmental health. Starting with the 3-5 April 1998 G8 environment ministers' meeting at Leeds Castle in Maidstone, Kent, UK, the annual meetings released communiqués until the Banff, Canada meeting of 12-14 April 2002 which produced instead the 'Banff Ministerial Statement on the World Summit on Sustainable Development'. There was a detailed press release of the 17-18 March 2005 joint meeting of environment and development ministers in Derbyshire, UK; and the

1 November 2005 joint meeting of environment and energy ministers in London issued 'Chairman's Conclusions'.

A recent example of G8 energy ministers' statements is the 'Chair's Statement' of the Moscow meeting of 15-16 March 2006. Earlier, the G8 energy ministers' meeting 'on the world energy future' of 31 March-1 April 1998, also held in Moscow, issued a 'Communiqué'.

The meetings of the finance ministers of the G5 were conducted in secret, with no official documentation. Nonetheless, as the records of archives of G7 countries covering the 1970s gradually become available, detailed notes of the proceedings of these meetings have begun to surface, along with references to information about the nature of the record of such meetings. For example, a letter from Sir Derek Mitchell (UK Treasury) to Sir Donald Maitland (Superintending Under Secretary, Economists Department, FCO), dated 11 September 1974, refers to the fact that another Treasury official was able to sit in at the 7-8 September 1974 meeting of the G5/G6 finance ministers (held in Champs-sur-Marne, France) and to produce a full record. The letter then states: 'I would not wish to arouse expectations that it would be physically possible to produce an equally full record of future meetings, ... [moreover] the record can only be regarded as background on a highly restrictive distribution given the importance of safe-guarding the ability of Ministers to speak freely to each other on these occasions.' ([UK] National Archives [hereafter referred to as TNA], FCO 59/1097, p. 27B, 2 pages.)[1]

In fact, the G5 took great pains to preserve secrecy. A 24 September 1974 telegram from the UK embassy in Washington cites official guidance to embassies from the US State Department:

> There will be no (repeat no) announcement of any kind about the [28 September 1974 G5 foreign and finance ministers'] meeting, ... there will be no (no) statement after the meeting, nor any official press briefing.... There [will] be no (no) agenda or formal papers tabled. To all legitimate enquiries United States departments here are saying merely that Dr Kissinger wanted to take advantage of ministers' presence in New York and Washington to hold informal (informal emphasised) discussions. (TNA, FCO 59/1098: 77)

Although G7 and G8 finance ministers operate with much more openness and publicity, texts of the actual deliberations of ministers in the G7 and G8 system have remained confidential, and it is not even clear that there always exists a completely detailed record. What emanates officially from the G7 and G8 bodies (not just the finance ministers' forum) are the communiqués, declarations and other documents intended for the media and the public.

The G7 and G8 finance ministers usually issue a chairman's summary or other statement at the end of their meetings, but there have also been meetings without public statements and, conversely, statements without formal meetings. Michael Hodges recalled that the G7 finance ministers issued no communiqué after their 1993 Washington meeting, 'and indicated to the heads at Tokyo that they too were striving to make their meetings more substantive and informal ...' (Hodges 1994:

---

1   References to records in official archives follow the form suggested by those archives.

142-43). In 2006, Russia's year of the G8 presidency, the Russian finance ministry created a special website covering the G8 finance ministers' forum <www.g8finance.ru/home.htm>.

Examples of statements issued at the conclusion of a meeting are: *Statement by G7 Finance Ministers and Central Bank Governors, April 16, 2005, Washington,* and *Pre-Summit Statement by G8 Finance Ministers, June 10-11, 2005, London.* Examples of statements issued by the finance ministers without a physical meeting: *Declaration of G7 Finance Ministers and Central Bank Governors*, 30 October 1998, and *Statement by G7 Finance Ministers on Assisting Countries Devastated by the Indian Ocean Tsunami*, January 7, 2005. Ministers agreed on these statements by verbal and written communication (G7 Finance Ministers 1998; G7 Finance Ministers 2005).[2]

In addition, the finance ministers have issued special statements and reports at their meetings. *Agenda for Growth: Progress Report*, Boca Raton, Florida, February 7, 2004; *G8 Finance Ministers' Conclusions on Development*, London, June 10-11, 2005; and *G8 Finance Ministers' Statement on Access to Energy Services for the Millennium Development Goals*, St. Petersburg, June 9-10, 2006, are examples of such special statements and reports.

The London joint meeting of G7 and G8 finance and foreign ministers on 8-9 May 1998 had a complex set of meetings and produced these documents: the two G7 sessions resulted in *Conclusions of G7 Finance Ministers*, which was the basis of the G7 finance ministers' report to the G7 leaders for their subsequent Birmingham meeting, entitled *Strengthening the Architecture of the Global Financial System.* Two other G7 finance-related documents were distributed at that meeting: *Financial Stability: Supervision of Global Financial Institutions; A Report by G7 Finance Ministers*, dated May 1998; and *Promoting Financial Stability: Recent Initiatives of the Basle Committee on Banking Supervision; Submission for the G-7 Heads of Government at the 1998 Birmingham Summit*, dated Basle, March 1998 (Financial Stability 1998; Promoting Financial Stability 1998). Following the release of the *Conclusions of G7 Finance Ministers*, there was a brief meeting of the G8 finance ministers on 9 May; there, the eight ministers decided to publish eight separate national employability action plans.

Parallel with the 8 May 1998 meetings of the G7 finance ministers, the G8 foreign ministers met for a working session in the afternoon, followed by a working dinner. On the morning of 9 May, the G8 foreign ministers had another working session at the end of which they issued a document, *Conclusions of G8 Foreign Ministers*. In it, the ministers deal with the following global issues: the environment, nuclear safety, UN matters, non-proliferation/arms control/disarmament, antipersonnel land mines, democracy and human rights, terrorism, infectious diseases, and intellectual property related crime. They also discussed many regional issues: Bosnia and Herzegovina, Croatia, Kosovo, Albania, Cyprus, the Middle East peace process, Iran, Iraq, Algeria, Afghanistan, Cambodia, Myanmar, the Korean peninsula, the African Great Lakes region, Nigeria, Angola, and Somalia.

---

2   A good source of G7 finance ministers' statements, in addition to the G8 Information Centre website at www.g8.utoronto.ca/finance/index.htm, is the periodical *IMF Survey*.

In late morning, 9 May, the G8 foreign ministers and G8 finance ministers met for a plenary meeting, followed by a working lunch of these ministers with the IMF Managing Director, the World Bank President and the Director-General of the WTO to discuss the Asian financial crisis and its implications. The ministers then released their *Conclusions of the Joint Meeting of G8 Foreign and Finance Ministers*. That document deals with two main issues: development, and electronic commerce.

Thus, the relatively meagre documentation of the Birmingham G8 summit was more than offset by the proliferating output of the joint meeting of G7 and G8 finance and foreign ministers in London on 8-9 May 1998. This is a downward shift of the workload and documentation from the leaders to their ministers, perhaps indicative of a welcome new trend. It is, moreover, a reflection of greater transparency in the work of the G7 and G8.

G7 and G8 foreign ministers do not issue public statements on their September annual meetings, but one can trace indirectly certain of their other reports; for example, their *Report on Aid to Africa* was submitted to the 1986 Tokyo summit which called for implementation of the recommended measures. Other documents, however, are available from meetings attended – sometimes with ministers holding other portfolios – by foreign ministers; for example, the G7 foreign and finance ministers meeting in Tokyo on 15 April 1993 in preparation for the 1993 Tokyo summit (with partial Russian participation), issued a *G-7 Chairman's Statement on Support for Russian Reform*; and the October 1994 Winnipeg G8 foreign ministers' Conference on Partnership for Economic Transformation in Ukraine released a Chairman's Summary, as noted earlier. The special meeting of the G8 foreign ministers held in London on 12 June 1998 issued a *G8 Foreign Ministers Communiqué on Indian and Pakistani Nuclear Tests*. Starting with 6 May 1999 when the G8 foreign ministers met in Bonn, this forum has issued 'statements', 'chairman's statements', 'conclusions' and other similar documents. For the documentation of the 1998 pre-summit joint meeting of the foreign and finance ministers, see above. In addition, special statements have become more frequent; for example, the 23 June 2005 London meeting's statement on Afghanistan. On 25 October 2002 the G8 foreign ministers, without having a formal meeting, issued a statement on the terrorist hostage-taking in Moscow.

The February 1995 Brussels Global Information Society ministerial meeting resulted in a fair amount of documentation, including 'chair's conclusions', a thematic paper, and other documents. Information on continuing activities related to SMEs in the G7 countries plus the European Union, as well as several other countries, can be found through the website of the Global Information Network for small and medium enterprises: <www.gin.sme.ne.jp/index.html>.

The G8 Justice Ministers' first meeting was hosted on 10 December 1997 in Washington by the US Attorney General who issued a statement at the end of the meeting. The virtual meeting of the G8 Justice Ministers on 15 December 1998 released a 'backgrounder' on organized crime and terrorist funding. The meeting of the G8 Ministers of Justice and Interior in Milan on 26-27 February 2001 issued a communiqué; the 13-14 May 2002 meeting in Mont-Tremblant, Canada, a 'Chairpersons' Summary'; the Paris meeting of G8 ministers of justice and home affairs, 5 May 2003, a 'Presidents' Summary'; and the 11 May 2004 Washington meeting, a communiqué. There is a set of documents of the 16-17 June 2005 meeting of G8 Justice and Interior Ministers in Sheffield, UK. The UK Home Office issued a background document for this meeting, reviewing the history and evolution of the G8's work on transnational organized crime. The meeting also released the following documents: 'Best Practices for Law Enforcement Interaction with Victim-Companies during a Cybercrime Investigation' (produced by the G8 Subgroup on High-Tech Crime); a communiqué entitled 'Critical Information Infrastructure Protection'; and a document also produced by the Subgroup on High-Tech Crime, 'Challenges Associated with Emerging Technologies for Law Enforcement: Wireless Local Area Networks (WLANS)'. The Russian host minister of the G8 justice and home affairs ministers' meeting in Moscow, 16 June 2006, published a release of the press conference on the results of the meeting.

The G7 and G8 science ministers do not, as a rule, issue public communiqués, but indications of when and where meetings were held can be found in various sources, for example on the official Russian government website for the G8 in 2006, at <http://en.g8russia.ru/page_work>. Background information on the G7 and G8 science ministers' forum can be found at <http://phe.rockefeller.edu/ccstg+10/bromley.html> and <www.ost.gov.uk/ostinternational/world/2_3.htm>.

The P8 ministerial meeting on terrorism resulted in the 'Ottawa Ministerial Declaration on Countering Terrorism' of 12 December 1995; the 30 July 1996 Paris Ministerial Meeting on Terrorism released its agreement on 25 measures to fight terrorism; and the French President's office issued a G7/P8 communiqué on 28 December 1996 on the Peruvian hostage incident.

The Trade Ministers Quadrilateral (The Quad) rarely released public communiqués at first. In the Quad's later years of activity it did issue statements; for example, a Chair's Statement was released after its 30 April-2 May 1997 meeting in Toronto.

An example of an *ad hoc* – as contrasted with regularly held – ministerial meeting was the October 1994 Winnipeg conference on assistance to Ukraine. It issued a chairman's summary, accessible at <www.g8.utoronto.ca/adhoc/94ukrai.htm>.

Task Forces, Working Groups and Expert Groups

Many task forces, working groups and expert groups issue public releases and reports, in addition to producing confidential documents; others do not. Examples follow.

The Global Fund to Fight AIDS, Tuberculosis and Malaria has created an excellent plurilingual website at <www.theglobalfund.org>. There, information can be found on the Fund's history and activities and programmes, governance and administrative structure, and funds pledged, raised and expended. The site also contains texts of press releases as well as meeting reports and other substantive publications.

The Lyon Group released the 40-point 'Recommendations' on 12 April 1996. The G8 justice and interior ministers' meeting on crime, held in Washington, DC on 10 December 1997, reviewed the work of the Senior Experts' Group; a summary of this review is included in a statement by US Attorney-General Janet Reno, host of the ministerial meeting. The 1996 Lyon summit's *Chairman's Statement* endorsed the 40 recommendations (Ministerial Meeting 1995; Ministerial Conference 1996; Senior Experts 1996; US 1997).

The Expert Group on Misuse of International Data Networks, at its meeting in Rome from 16 to 17 October 1997, submitted a report to the G8 science ministers. It is accessible at <www.g8.utoronto.ca/expert_group_g8/report_expert_group_rome_1997.html>.

The DOT force submitted a report to the Genoa summit in 2001. On the completion of its work it presented its final report, *Digital Opportunities for All: Report Card* to the 2002 Kananaskis summit.

The Financial Action Task Force (FATF) has a well-designed website, rich in content <www.fatf-gafi.org>. The task force publishes annual reports, periodic lists of non-cooperative countries and territories, standards, methodological works, 'best practices' papers, and special publications including the *Handbook for Countries and Assessors* (FATF 2006). The standards of FATF consist of the 40 recommendations on money laundering (which were originally developed by the Lyon Group, as indicated above); and nine special recommendations on terrorist financing.

The Financial Stability Forum has its website at <www.fsforum.org>. It publishes texts of press releases, the semiannual *Ongoing and Recent Work Relevant to Sound Financial Systems*, and a compendium of 12 key standards for sound financial systems; the standards themselves originate from the IMF, the OECD, FATF and various other international organizations.

The G8 Renewable Energy Task Force submitted its final report to the 2001 Genoa summit. The report, with annexes, is accessible at <www.worldenergy.org/wec-geis/focus/renew/g8.asp>.

The Working Group on Technology, Growth and Employment was established by the 1982 Versailles summit. One version of the report of the group appeared as a British government publication (UK 1983).

The GPWG under the Global Partnership against Weapons and Materials of Mass Destruction submitted its consolidated report on Global Partnership projects to the 2004 Sea Island summit. The report is accessible at <www.g8.utoronto.ca/summit/2004seaisland/consolidatedreport.pdf>. There is a report on the Partnership to the St. Petersburg summit and the Working Group, with a lengthy annex detailing the relevant activities of a number of G8 and other countries (G8 2006l).

Also at St. Petersburg, the Nuclear Safety and Security Group reported to the leaders who released the report as a summit document, accessible at <http://en.g8russia.ru/docs/24.html> and <www.g8.utoronto.ca/summit/2006stpetersburg/nuclear_report.html>. The report covers a wide range of issues, including recent international agreements to combat nuclear terrorism, consequences of the Chernobyl reactor accident, control of radioactive sources, and the decommissioning of the Armenian nuclear power plant.

The existence of otherwise publicly unavailable reports of task forces and working groups can often be verified through references in summit documents. For example, studies prepared by the International Nuclear Fuel Cycle Evaluation Group are acknowledged in the *Declaration* of the 1980 Venice summit. The *Declaration* also expresses support for the recommendations of the International Energy Technology Group. The Chemical Action Task Force submitted its report to the 1991 London summit which welcomed and endorsed it. The 1985 Bonn summit's communiqué, *The Bonn Economic Declaration*, refers to the establishment of the Expert Group on Aid to Sub-Saharan Africa, and to the group's to report to the G7 foreign ministers by September 1985; the following year, the Tokyo summit, in its economic declaration, acknowledges a 'Report on Aid to Africa adopted and forwarded to us by our Foreign Ministers.'

Conclusion

Public information and documentation generated by ministerial meetings, task forces and other expert groups constitute a complex system in itself. But the pattern over the years of the existence of this system clearly indicates increasing transparency and at times even eagerness to communicate with the media and the public. The exact details of actual deliberations nonetheless tend to remain confidential.

References

Note on internet addresses (URLs): Websites tend to appear, change or disappear, often without warning. Addresses cited in this source list were accurate and active at the time of writing (June 2006) unless otherwise noted.

Digital Opportunity Task Force (2002), *Digital Opportunities for All: Report Card*, DOT Force, New York.

Financial Action Task Force (2006), *AML/CFT Evaluations and Assessments: Handbook for Countries and Accessors*, Paris, www.fatf-gafi.org/dataoecd/3/26/36254892.pdf.

Financial Stability: Supervision of Global Financial Institutions; A Report by G7 Finance Ministers (1998), London, May (unpublished).

G7 Finance Ministers (1998), *Declaration of G7 Finance Ministers and Central Bank Governors*, www.g8.utoronto.ca/finance/fm103098.htm.

G7 Finance Ministers (2005), *Statement by G7 Finance Ministers on Assisting Countries Devastated by the Indian Ocean Tsunami*, www.g8.utoronto.ca/finance/fm050107.htm.

G7 Ministerial Meeting on Terrorism (1995), *Ottawa Ministerial [P8] Declaration on Countering Terrorism*, Ottawa, 12 December, www.g8.utoronto.ca/terrorism/terror96.htm.

G7 Ministerial Conference on Terrorism (1996), *Agreement on 25 Measures*, Paris, 30 July, www.g8.utoronto.ca/terrorism/terror25.htm.

G8 (2006l), *Report on the G8 Global Partnership*, http://en.g8russia.ru/docs/22.html and www.g8.utoronto.ca/summit/2006stpetersburg/gp_report.html.

Hodges, Michael R. (1994), 'More Efficiency, Less Dignity: British Perspectives on the Future Role and Working of the G-7', in *The Future of the G-7 Summits*, 141-159, (*The International Spectator* 29:2, April/June, Special Issue).

Promoting Financial Stability: Recent Initiatives of the Basle Committee on Banking Supervision; Submission for the G-7 Heads of Government at the 1998 Birmingham Summit (1998), Basle, March (unpublished).

Senior Experts on Transnational Organized Crime (1996), *P8 Senior Experts Group Recommendations*, Paris, 12 April, www.g8.utoronto.ca/crime/40pts.htm.

United Kingdom, Parliament, House of Commons, Session 1982/1983 (1983), *Technology, Growth and Employment: Report of the Working Group Set Up by the Economic Summit Meeting of 1982*, Science and Technology Secretariat, Cabinet Office (Cmnd. 8818; London: HMSO, 1983).

United States, Department of Justice (1997), *Statement by Attorney General Janet Reno on the Meeting of Justice and Interior Ministers of the Eight*, Washington, DC, 10 December, www.usdoj.gov/opa/pr/1997/December97/518cr.html.

Chapter 15

Other Sources of Information about the G7 and G8 System and the G20

In addition to public documents released by the G7 and G8 summits, ministerial and other bodies of the G7 and G8, and the G20 finance ministers' forum, various other important information sources exist about the G7 and G8 system and the G20. This chapter highlights several types of such sources, with illustrative examples: writings about the G7 and G8; research groups active in G8-related projects; archives; memoirs and other writings by former prominent summit participants; and websites. Chapter 12 discusses two policy groups that are concerned with G7 and G8 issues: the Shadow G-8 and the InterAction Council.

Writings about the G7 and G8

There is a large and growing corpus of writings – printed and electronic – about the G7 and G8 system and the G20, and about issues of concern to those institutions: scholarly analyses; compilations of texts of documents, often accompanied by additional material of reference value; government publications including parliamentary reviews in summit countries; memoirs and other writings by prominent former summit participants; reference works of various types; and media accounts including reportage and analysis in newspapers, journals, radio and television. On the subject of media accounts, quality of reportage is worthy of comment. It is clear that there are knowledgeable reporters, especially with prominent media such as the *Financial Times* of London, who follow economic and other summit-related issues the year round and are well able to interpret and analyze fast-breaking news at the summits. Others are often sent to the summit site by their news organizations simply because they are posted nearby and thus available at lower cost; their work can be quite uneven. Still others are interested in photo opportunities or in 'lifestyle' reporting (What dress did Cherie Booth Blair [UK Prime Minister Tony Blair's wife] wear? What were German Chancellor Helmut Kohl's food preferences? How did Russian President Boris Yeltsin handle his drinks? With whom was US President Bill Clinton photographed?). Finally, when summits are held in an isolated venue with limited communication to the public, media reporting naturally turns its focus more on demonstrations and other events or activities critical of, or different from, the summit.

The following examples illustrate the range of writings about the G7 and G8 and the G20:

- Robert D. Putnam and Nicholas Bayne, *Hanging Together: Cooperation and Conflict in the Seven-Power Summits*, rev. ed.; Nicholas Bayne, *Hanging in There: The G7 and G8 Summit in Maturity and Renewal*; and Nicholas Bayne, *Staying Together: The G8 Summit Confronts the 21st Century*. These three volumes together comprise a comprehensive, authoritative history and analysis of the G7 and G8.
- Andrew Baker's *The Group of Seven: Finance Ministries, Central Banks and Global Financial Governance* explores the role of the G7 finance ministers and central bank governors as a major actor in global financial governance.
- Andre Belelieu, 'The G8 and Terrorism: What Role Can the G8 Play in the 21st Century?' *G8 Governance*. Examines the historical and potential role of the G8 in the fight against terrorism.
- C. Fred Bergsten, and C. Randall Henning. *Global Economic Leadership and the Group of Seven*. Analyzes the economic role of the G7.
- Theodore H. Cohn, *Governing Global Trade: International Institutions in Conflict and Convergence*. With a strong focus on the trade role of the G7 and G8 including the Trade Ministers Quadrilateral.
- There is a relative paucity of book-length works analyzing a particular country's position vis-à-vis the G7 and G8. An example of such books is Hugo Dobson's *Japan and the G7/8, 1975-2002* – a study of a particular G8 country and its participation in the G7 and G8. Another example is Vadim Borisovich Lukov's, *Rossiia v Klube Liderov* [Russia in the Leaders' Club]. This Russian-language work examines Russia's role in the G8.
- John English, Ramesh Thakur, and Andrew F. Cooper, (eds). *Reforming from the Top: A Leaders' 20 Summit*. Analyzes the ramifications of the potential transformation of the G20 finance ministers' forum into a leaders' level L20.
- Gill Hubbard and David Miller (eds), *Arguments against G8*. A collection of essays highly critical of the G8, issued on the eve of the 2005 Gleneagles summit.
- Joseph Hanlon and John Garrett, *Crumbs of Comfort: The Cologne G8 Summit and the Chains of Debt*, Jubilee 2000 Coalition. Civil society critique of the G8's debt relief efforts.
- John J. Kirton, 'Contemporary Concert Diplomacy: The Seven-Power Summit and the Management of International Order'. Paper prepared for the annual meeting of the International Studies Association and the British International Studies Association. Presents a model of the G7 as a modern concert of powerful countries.
- Eleonore Kokotsis, *Keeping International Commitments: Compliance, Credibility, and the G7, 1988-1995*. Transnational Business and Corporate Culture series. Based on the author's PhD thesis, presents an elaborate system of measuring and evaluating compliance by the G7 of its commitments.
- David Mepham and James Lorge, *Putting our House in Order: Recasting G8 Policy towards Africa*. Study of a major concern of recent G8 summits: Africa.
- Sylvia Ostry, *'Globalization and the G8: Could Kananaskis Set a New Direction?'* (O.D. Skelton Memorial Lecture, Queen's University). Highlights the G8's role in globalization.

- Risto E. J. Penttilä, *The Role of the G8 in International Peace and Security.* Analyzes the security role of the G8.
- Rossella Franchini Sherifis and Valerio Astraldi, *Il G7/G8 da Rambouillet a Genova = The G7/G8 from Rambouillet to Genoa.* An example of a government publication, this history and analysis of the summits was issued before the 2001 Genoa summit by the Italian host government.
- Junichi Takase's *Samitto: Shuyô Shunô Kaigi.* [Summit: The Meeting of the Main Heads of State] is an example of works on the summit in languages other than English (Japanese in this case).

The rest of this chapter highlights four special types of source material, and the originators of those sources, on the G7 and G8 and the G20: research groups and other organizations active in related projects; archives; memoirs and other writings by prominent former summit participants; and websites.

Research Groups

G8 Research Group (University of Toronto)

The group's mission is '[t]o serve as the world's leading independent source of information, analysis, and research on the institutions, issues and members of the G8 Summit' (G8 Information Centre). The group was established at the University of Toronto in 1987 in the run-up to the Toronto summit of 1988. Over the years, the group has expanded its membership and activities, as well as the level and geographical location of participants. It has grown into a global network that includes academics, media professionals, personnel in business and government, and researchers, as well as students interested in the G7 and G8, the G20, and related issues.

The group's activities include research (resulting in a number of books and other publications as well as conference papers), teaching, information and public education. Notable among publications of group members and associates are two book series published by Ashgate in the United Kingdom: 'G8 and Global Governance' and 'Global Finance'. Group members have also produced a series of refereed working papers, *G8 Governance* (beyond members of the group, academics and other experts also submit manuscripts for these papers), and analytical studies of the summits and summit-related issues. Teaching activities comprise senior undergraduate/graduate level seminar courses, presentation of special seminars with invited speakers (including conferences in summit host countries just before the summits), and sponsorship of an annual scholarship for excellent and deserving students. Information and public education activities include the G8 research collection – located at the Graham Library of Trinity College, University of Toronto – of primary documents of the summits and other official G7 and G8, the G20, and related groups, commentary and writings about the G7 and G8 and the G20, as well as related issues; the websites G8 Information Centre and G8 Online; and media commentary before, at and after the summits. The G8 Information Centre website is widely used and continues to receive wide recognition for its comprehensiveness, up-to-date nature and as an excellent reference source.[1]

Moscow State Institute on International Relations G8 Research Centre

The Moscow State Institute on International Relations (MGIMO) announced on 29 June 2006 the establishment of a G8 research centre in partnership with the G8 Research Group. The new centre's mandate is to contribute to keeping alive the legacy of the St. Petersburg summit and to strengthen Russia's contribution to the G8 as an instrument of international co-operation. The centre will be linked with MGIMO's Department of International Relations and Foreign Policy of Russia. It will encourage students to engage in G8-related research. It plans to have a G8-related library and to establish a mutual web link with the G8 Information Centre. See <www.g8.utoronto.ca/mgimo/mgimo-launch.html> and <www.g8.utoronto.ca/mgimo/mgimo-g8.pdf> for more information.

The Higher School of Economics of the State University (Moscow)

The Higher School of Economics formed an Institute for International Organizations and International Relations in 2005 and established the G8 Research Team in the same year. The team's focus of research is on the G8 and its role in performing the functions of collective management and reconciling domestic and international pressures, as well as on the interaction of the G8 with IGOs in the context of global governance. In co-ordination with the University of Toronto's G8 Research Group, the team prepared a report on Russia's compliance with commitments at the 2005 Gleneagles summit. The report, released in 2006, is available at <www.g8.utoronto.ca/hse/hse-g8.pdf>. The continuing aims of co-operation between the two groups are: to provide informational, analytical and methodological support to effective Russian participation in the G8; to conduct internationally comparative research in the areas of G8 compliance with commitments; to assess G8 summits; and to assess the contribution of IGOs to compliance with G8 commitments.

Archives

Primary materials in presidential, prime ministerial, as well as foreign, finance and other ministry archives are a significant source of information on the G7. These archives can yield authoritative, first-hand information and a reliable record of the preparation, conduct and follow-up of meetings, and bilateral and summit-wide issues. Rules of access to archives and their contents vary greatly from country to country, and

---

1   The websites of the G8 Information Centre and G8 Online are, respectively, www. g8.utoronto.ca and www.g8online.org. For a detailed account of the concept, context, planning, establishment and early record of the www.g8.utoronto.ca website, see Meikle (1999).

from archive to archive within each country. As and when these archives are opened, their holdings can be explored profitably by researchers seeking access to first-hand accounts by participants of summits and G7 and later G8 ministerial meetings. The following section describes briefly the pertinent resources of the archives of G8 countries and the European Union, and then gives more detailed examples from four archives as authoritative primary sources of information. Subject-related information based on research in these archives is incorporated in several chapters of this book.

Canada has centralized archives, the Library and Archives Canada. Address: 395 Wellington Street, Ottawa ON Canada K1A 0N4; telephone: 613-996-5115 or 1-866-578-7777 (toll free in Canada and the US); website: <www.collectionscanada. ca>. There are no electronic finding aids; for information on online research tools see <www.collectionscanada.ca/archivianet/0201_e.html>. The 'closed' period is 30 years for public records; for private papers it is set individually. For illustrative examples of Canadian archival sources, see below.

The European Union, too, has centralized archives. Address: Historical Archives of the European Union, Villa il Poggiolo, Piazza T.A. Edison, 11, 50133 Firenze, Italy; telephone: ++ 39 055 4685620; fax: ++ 39 055 573728; website: <www.iue. it/ECArchives>. There is an online searchable database at <www.arc.iue.it/dcs/ SearchTools.html>. Records are closed for 30 years.

In France the name of the relevant archives is Centre des archives contemporaines; post-1958 records are preserved there, but Foreign Ministry archives are kept at the Quai d'Orsay in Paris. Address: Centre des archives contemporaines, 2 rue des archives, 77300 Fontainebleau, France; telephone: [33] (0)1.64.31.73.00; fax: [33] (0)1.64.31.73.03; website: <www.archivesnationales.culture.gouv.fr> (the English version of the website is less complete than the French). There is an online catalogue, Priam3, at <www.culture.fr/documentation/priam3/pres.htm>. The 'closed' period is as long as 60 years for certain types of records, but this is mitigated by new access-to-information legislation (Ordinance No. 2005-650 of 6 June 2005).

The German Bundesarchiv (Federal Archives) houses all post-1945 official government records except for those of the Foreign Office. Political party records and Foreign Office materials are held in Berlin. Address: Bundesarchiv, Potsdamer Str. 1, 56075 Koblenz, Germany; telephone: (0261) 505-0; fax: (0261) 505-226; website (primarily in German): <www.bundesarchiv.de>. The online finding aid is at <www.bundesarchiv.de/foxpublic/index.html>, see also <www.bundesarchiv.de/ bestaende_findmittel/bestaendeuebersicht/index_frameset.html?id_bestand=58>. The 'closed' period generally is 30 years.

In Italy, the archives, Archivio Centrale dello Stato (Central State Archives), are partially centralized. The archives of the Ministry of Foreign Affairs, Parliament and the President of the Republic are managed by professional archivists but preserved by the creators of the records. Address: Archivio Centrale dello Stato, Piazzale degli Archivi, 27 00144 Roma, Italy; telephone: +39 06 545481; fax: +39 06 5413620; e-mail: <acs@archivi.beniculturali.it>; websites: <http://archivi.beniculturali.it/ACS> and <www.esteri.it/ita/5_47_187.asp> (the latter for Foreign Affairs). Online finding aids may be accessed at <www.archivi.beniculturali.it/strumenti.html>. Records are generally closed for 30 years; researchers may ask for permission to see more recent records for purposes of study as long as data privacy is respected.

In Japan, the centralized National Archives of Japan hold all ministry and government agency documents. Address: National Archives of Japan, 3-2 Kitanomaru Koen, Chiyoda-ku, Tokyo 102-0091, Japan; telephone: +81-3-3214-062; fax: +81-3-3212-8806; website: <www.archives.go.jp/index_e.htm>. There is excellent English-language access although the documents themselves are in Japanese. Online catalogue, digital archives and finding aids are at <www.digital.archives.go.jp/index_e.html>. Many documents have been digitized. The Ministry of Foreign Affairs has G8-related information at <www.mofa.go.jp/policy/economy/summit/index.html>. The 'closed period' varies; it is 30 years for Ministry of Foreign Affairs records. The national policy stipulates public access to all documents except where privacy or security concerns exist.

Russia did not become a full member of the G8 until 1998, so that access to its G7- and G8-related records will be unlikely for some years. Russia has non-centralized archives, under the umbrella of the Federal Archive Agency of Russia (Rosarkhiv). Addresses: 119817 Moscow, ul. Bol'shaia Pirogovskaia, 17; and 121883 Moscow, Berezhkovskaia nab., 26, Russia; telephone and fax: (095) 245-12-87; websites: <www.rusarchives.ru> and <http://garf.ru>. A finding aid in Russian is available at <http://katyn.codis.ru/kdocs2.htm> and an English-language guide to Russian archives is at <www.iisg.nl/~abb/>. Presidential materials are classified Top Secret and not accessible. Under legislation enacted in October 2004 all other materials are to be transferred to a centralized archive after 15 years but are generally not available to researchers and the public for 30 years.

In the United Kingdom, public records are preserved centrally in The National Archives. Private papers (for example, Prime Ministers' personal papers) may be held at various academic libraries. Address: The National Archives, Kew, Richmond, Surrey, TW9 4DU United Kingdom; telephone: +44 (0) 20 8876 3444; website: <www.nationalarchives.gov.uk>. General catalogue and research guides are available at <www.catalogue.nationalarchives.gov.uk>; a research guide to Prime Ministers' papers is at <www.catalogue.nationalarchives.gov.uk/RdLeaflet.asp?sLeafletID=371>. Under the *Freedom of Information Act* of 2005 information is available on request from the date of creation of records, unless there are grounds to withhold it. Once a record is released to the requesting individual, it automatically becomes open to everyone. Otherwise, a 30-year closure applies. For illustrative examples of UK archival sources, see below.

The United States has perhaps been the most open. There, the central archival authority is the National Archives and Records Administration (NARA), an umbrella organization that administers – through its Office of Presidential Libraries – eleven presidential libraries plus the Nixon Presidential Materials Staff, College Park, Maryland <http://nixon.archives.gov/index.php>. Legislation passed by Congress in January 2004 provides for the establishment of the Nixon Presidential Library in Yorba Linda, California; this would turn the now-private Richard Nixon Library and Birthplace into a federally-operated institution. Bush's 2007 budget provides for $10.6 million for conversion of the privately funded Yorba Linda library into a full presidential library run by NARA. Should Congress approve the Bush budget proposal, $6.9 million would be used for a new wing for the Nixon library and $3.7 million would be earmarked for NARA staff for processing 46 million pages of documents from Nixon's presidency, seized by the US government upon Nixon's resignation in 1974 (Pasco 2006, B3). (The House approved the appropriations bill in June 2006 but the Senate had not passed the bill as of mid-February 2007.) These records, when processed and opened for public use, would be a good potential source of information on G7 pre-history (Bush Budget... 2006).

Increased US concern about national security in the aftermath of the 11 September 2001 terrorist attacks in New York and Washington has affected access to archival resources. One example of the implications of this is a March 2002 memorandum of understanding between NARA and the US Air Force which reveals that thousands of previously declassified documents have been gradually reclassified, and even the identity of personnel involved in the reclassification was being kept confidential. The belated release of the text of the memorandum of agreement prompted US Archivist Allen Weinstein to say that that was an 'important first step in finding the balance between continuing to protect national security and protecting the right to know by the American public' (NARA Cooperated ... 2006: 16).

The presidential libraries are:

- Herbert Hoover Presidential Library-Museum, West Branch, Iowa <http://hoover.archives.gov>;
- Franklin D. Roosevelt Presidential Library and Museum, Hyde Park, New York <www.fdrlibrary.marist.edu>;
- Harry Truman Presidential Museum and Library, Independence, Missouri <www.trumanlibrary.org>;
- Dwight D. Eisenhower Library and Museum, Abilene, Kansas <www.eisenhower.archives.gov>;
- John F. Kennedy Library and Museum, Boston, Massachusetts <www.jfklibrary.org>;
- Lyndon Baines Johnson Library and Museum, Austin, Texas <www.lbjlib.utexas.edu>;
- Gerald R. Ford Library (Ann Arbor, Michigan) and Museum (Grand Rapids, Michigan) <www.fordlibrarymuseum.gov>;
- Jimmy Carter Library and Museum, Atlanta, Georgia <www.jimmycarterlibrary.gov>;
- Ronald Reagan Presidential Library, Simi Valley, California <www.reagan.utexas.edu>; see also <www.reaganlibrary.com>;
- George Bush [Senior] Presidential Library and Museum, College Station, Texas <http://bushlibrary.tamu.edu>;
- William J. Clinton Presidential Library and Museum, Little Rock, Arkansas <www.clintonlibrary.gov>.

The address of the National Archives and Records Administration (NARA) is 8601 Adelphi Road, College Park, MD 20740-6001, USA; telephone: 1-866-272-6272 or 301-837-0482; website: <www.archives.gov>. There is an online catalogue at <http://arcweb.archives.gov/arc/basic_search.jsp>; other databases, catalogues and finding aids are identified at <www.archives.gov/research/tools>.

The following US presidential archives are relevant to early G7 history and pre-history: Nixon, Ford, Carter, Reagan, Bush senior and Clinton, and, eventually, a George W. Bush library if and when one is established. Scope and completeness of archival records are uneven among presidential libraries, some of which are more akin to museums, though this is likely to change over time as archival documents find their way into those libraries.

US archive rules allow the opening of records after 30 years but the Presidential Records Act of 1978 (44 U.S.C. Chapter 22) generally allows public access to presidential materials on request, starting with Reagan (because the Reagan Library was the first one to open after the enactment of the Presidential Records Act) and applying as well to his successors, beginning five years after the end of each President's term of office. In practice, it may take longer; at the end of each president's term (but not necessarily immediately), NARA takes possession of the records, and it needs a full five-year period for intellectual and technical processing before the records become subject to request under the Freedom of Information Act. As with the UK, under its Freedom of Information Act, in the US, too, once a record is released to the requesting individual, it automatically becomes open to all. Other rules that apply include, notably, Reagan's Executive Order 12667 of January 1989 that governs NARA procedures and the implementation of the Act; and Bush's Executive Order 13233 of 1 November 2003 which supersedes the previous Executive Order and seeks to restrict access to records of former and future presidents and vice presidents. Also of interest are Clinton's Executive Order 12958 of 17 April 1995 and its amending (Bush's) Executive Order 13292 of 25 March 2003, both dealing with classified national security information.

NARA's excellent website, <www.archives.gov>, is informative, relatively easy to use, and increasingly rich in content. It allows detailed and sophisticated searches of one, several or all presidential libraries. Archival material on summits spans confidential memoranda, analytical papers, pre-summit briefing books for the presidents, annotated travel schedules, correspondence and other exchanges of messages among summit principals and their supporting officials, candid assessments of other countries' positions and economic and political constraints, strategy documents, successive drafts of proposals including draft versions of summit communiqués, post-summit evaluations by various officials, press clippings and wire service dispatches (some with comment by administration officials), and much else. The archives of two presidents, Ford and Carter, were examined for this study, and illustrative examples are given below.

The Gerald R. Ford Library (hereafter referred to as Ford Library) is an excellent repository of primary sources for research into the first two summits: the 1975 G6 summit in Rambouillet, France, and the 1976 (the first G7) summit held in San Juan, Puerto Rico, as well as on the broader economic and political situation giving rise to, and prevailing during, these summits. The following very selective list shows the range and type of information available at Ford Library.[2]

- Memorandum, [Assistant to the President for Economic Affairs] L. William Seidman to President Ford, 22 October 1975; Ford Library, Box 32, WHCF-

---

2   References to records in official archives follow the form suggested by those archives.

Subject File, FO 6-1, International Economic Summit Preparation. Outlines the schedule of meetings and tasks for various US government officials (with the Economic Policy Board, the Council of Economic Advisers, the Special Trade Representative, departments of Treasury, Commerce, and State; National Security Council, and other offices) in preparing briefing papers and other material on the US position, objectives and strategy for the 1975 Rambouillet summit.

- Memorandum, [Secretary of State and Assistant to the President for National Security Affairs] Henry A. Kissinger, [Secretary of the Treasury] William E. Simon, [Deputy Assistant to the President for National Security Affairs] Brent Scowcroft, L. William Seidman to President Ford, 12 November 1975; Ford Library, Box 49, Presidential Handwriting File, Trips – Foreign, Economic Summit, 1975 (1), (2), (3). This and other documents in these three folders include briefing papers for the President, with background and analysis to support the US position at the Rambouillet summit, proposed talking points for Ford, assessments of the economic situation and policies in the other G7 countries, and other source material. This type of preparation has been typical before each summit.

- Memorandum, [National Security Council Senior Staff Member for International Economic Affairs] Robert Hormats to L. William Seidman, 2 December 1975; Ford Library, Box 312, L. William Seidman Files, 1974-77, International Economic Summit, November 15-17, 1975 – Memoranda of Conversations and Notes on Discussions; and Memorandum, Robert Hormats to Brent Scowcroft, 2 December 1975; Ford Library, Box 16, National Security Adviser Memoranda of Conversations, November 15-17, 1975 – Rambouillet Economic Summit. These two groups of records yield detailed notes of verbatim discussions at the summit. The National Security Adviser's papers contain the more complete text because those papers were declassified later than the Seidman papers by the archivists at the Ford Library; in the Seidman papers a great deal of text is blacked out. Thus, ironically, files that were originally more confidential actually yield more complete texts in this case. Yet, neither set is complete, missing some information on the opening session of the summit; fortunately, this can be reconstructed; for example, from Harold Wilson's memoirs (see the 'memoirs' section below and Chapter 3).

- Memorandum of Conversation: Excerpts from Conversations at the Quadripartite Luncheon in Helsinki (US, UK, France, FRG), 31 July 1975; Ford Library, Box 14, National Security Adviser, Memoranda of Conversations. It was during that luncheon that Giscard proposed the Rambouillet summit to his US, UK and German counterparts who all accepted. The Memorandum records that the relevant part of the conversation took place without note-takers, so the excerpts in the Ford Library do not yield the crucial information (it can, however, be found elsewhere; see Chapter 2).

- Joint Announcement of the International Summit, Puerto Rico, June 27-28, 1976, June 3, 1976 [White House Press Release], Folder 'Economic Summit – Puerto Rico'; Ford Library, Box 7, Vernon C. Loen and Charles Leffert Files (WH Congressional Relations Office). Includes Ford's invitation to Canada to participate, thus turning the G6 into the G7.

- Letter, Nicolás Nogueras Rivera [president of the Puerto Rico Free Federation of Labor], to President Ford, 23 June 1976; Ford Library, Box 33, WHCF-Subject File, FO 6-5, Economic Summit Conference, Puerto Rico, 6/27-28/76. Likely the very first civil society approach to a summit leader.

The Jimmy Carter Presidential Library in Atlanta, Georgia (hereafter referred to as Carter Library), has a wealth of source material related to G7 summits held during that President's administration (London 1977, Bonn 1978, Tokyo 1979 and Venice 1980). The following, again partial and selective, list, related to the 1978 Bonn summit, illustrates the kinds of sources housed in this repository:

- Memorandum, [Carter's sherpa] Henry Owen to President Carter, 11 July 1978; Carter Library, Box 6, JC-CEA, Charles L. Schultze's Subject File, on the Summit and energy.
- Memorandum, [Chairman of the Council of Economic Advisers] Charles L. Schultze to President Carter, 27 June 1978; Carter Library, Box 51, JC-CEA, Charles L. Schultze's Subject File, reporting on his conversation with German Economics Minister Count Lambsdorff on the *quid pro quo* of US action on energy for German economic growth stimulus.
- Telex, Hans Tietmayer of Germany to Charles L. Schultze, 24 April 1978; Carter Library, Box 7, JC-CEA, Charles L. Schultze's Subject File, on the international economic situation.
- Memorandum, Henry Owen to President Carter, 23 June 1978; Carter Library, Box 28, JC-SWO, Chronological File, revealing that '[t]he main purpose of US participation in the Summit is to strike a three-way deal…: a. the US pledging action to limit oil imports and control inflation; b. the Germans and Japanese pledging additional measures to stimulate domestic demand; c. all Summiteers agreeing to freer trade policies….'
- Transcript of President Carter's impromptu candid interview with journalists aboard Air Force One on the way back from Germany, transcribed by Don Campbell of Gannett and David Garcia of ABC, 18 July 1978; Carter Library, Box 104, JC-WHPO, Rex Granum's White House Office Files Relating to Trips. This transcript quotes Carter as saying: 'I think every political leader … [in Bonn] was pushing his own political options to the limit, and I think the leaders … on economic affairs recognize always the political [restraints] in one's own country…. I think that the other leaders understand clearly what we are trying to do in the energy field, they understand our special problems …, but there was a good recognition of a common purpose, and we don't pull any punches in our private meetings. We are very forceful, we are very evocative, very argumentative at times, but the sum total of it is that we understand each other well.'
- Memorandum, Henry Owen to President Carter, 9 May 1978; Carter Library, Box FO-44, WHCF-Subject File, on meetings with labour and business leaders about the Summit.
- Memorandum, [Secretary of Transportation] Brock Adams to President Carter, 21 July 1978, Box FO-44, WHCF-Subject File, on the Bonn Summit agreement on hijacking (the first non-economic G7 agreement and declaration).

- Memorandum, [National Security Adviser] Zbigniew Brzezinski to President Carter, [3?] July 1978; Carter Library, Box 13, JC-NSA, Zbigniew Brzezinski's Trip Files, on non-economic issues, notably German Chancellor Schmidt's proposal for a four-power (US, UK, France and Germany) breakfast meeting to discuss intra-German relations including Berlin, East-West relations including arms control, Africa, and the Middle East.
- Memorandum, Henry Owen to President Carter, 3 July 1978; Carter Library, Box 13, JC-NSA, Zbigniew Brzezinski's Trip Files, with briefing book for the President prepared by the departments of State, Treasury, Energy, the Council of Economic Advisers, the Special Trade Representative, the Central Intelligence Agency and others. The briefing book includes papers on the main agenda items of the summit, analysis of economic trends and constraints of the other G7 countries, proposed summit strategy with assessments of attitudes of other summit leaders, and a draft communiqué with some sections left blank pending decisions of the summit leaders.

It is interesting – and perhaps not unusual in government archives – that personal diaries are not included in the Carter Library. Also, because of classification rules and practices, certain other documents – such as Carter's 1980 letter to Schmidt – remain classified (unavailable for public consultation) in that library but are discussed in the respective leaders' memoirs. Such memoirs (discussed below) can thus be an invaluable source of 'inside' information, even though they tend to be subjective.

The National Archives (UK) (hereafter referred to by its official acronym, TNA) is a treasure trove of source material on the pre-history of the G7, particularly in the years 1972-1974. At the time of this writing, papers for 1975 were gradually being opened to researchers; material covering later dates can be requested through the UK Freedom of Information Act. Records from the Prime Minister's Office are nearing the point of access, but files from the Treasury, and the Foreign and Commonwealth Office (some originally classified 'secret' or 'confidential' and opened only in 2005), are already available to shed much light on the preparation, conduct and aftermath of meetings of the G4/G5/G6 finance ministers – many of the meetings themselves were held in secret – and the involvement of other branches of government, notably foreign ministers, in the process. Some examples:

- 'Note of a Meeting at the Chateau de Champs, France, over the Week-end of 7-8 September 1974.' Gives a fairly detailed record of the G5/G6 meeting of the finance ministers' and central bank governors' 7-8 September 1974 meeting (of first G5, then G6) in Champs-sur-Marne, France. (TNA, FCO 59/1097, p. 27A ff.)
- P. Wilson [Higher Executive Officer, Private Secretary, Treasury], 'Note of a meeting in Sir Derek Mitchell's office at the UK Department of Treasury on 12 September 1974.' Introduces the US proposal for a joint meeting of the G5 finance and foreign ministers on oil prices; the meeting took place in Washington on 28 September 2004. (TNA, FCO 59/1097, p. 29, 2 pages.)
- Telegram, Sir Peter Ramsbotham [UK Ambassador in Washington], 24 September 1974. Throws light on the length to which the US hosts of the 28

September 1974 G5 finance/foreign ministers' meeting went. There would be no announcement, no post-meeting statement, no press briefing, and no formal agenda. (TNA, FCO 59/1098, p. 77.)

- Letter, Peter H. R. Marshall [Under-Secretary, Financial Relations Department, Treasury] to J. G. Littler [Under-Secretary, General, Treasury], 13 December 1973. Reveals that the G5 finance ministers' deputies also met periodically, to prepare the finance ministers' meetings. (TNA, T354/52, pp. 43-45.)
- Memorandum, C. W. France [Assistant Secretary, Principal Private Secretary, Treasury], 10 July 1974) to Sir Derek Mitchell, on Schmidt's proposal of a meeting of the G4 finance ministers (US, UK, France and Germany) in London on 26 July 1974. (TNA, T354/167, p. 189/7, 2 pages).

The Library and Archives Canada (hereafter referred to as LAC), whose archives component was previously known as the National Archives of Canada, is an excellent source of primary information on all Canadian aspects of the G7. Here are some examples related to the first two summits:

- On 26 November 1975, shortly after the Rambouillet summit, French President Giscard wrote a long letter to Canadian Prime Minister Trudeau, giving a detailed narrative of the deliberations and participants of the summit, stating: 'the main objective of this meeting was to bring together top-level officials of the six industrialized democratic countries represented, in order to examine from a political viewpoint the problems posed by the world economic situation, and to determine the direction to be taken in acting to solve them.' [Translation by Canadian government sources.] (LAC, P. E. Trudeau Fonds, MG 26 O, Staff Series, O19, Volume 139, File 17: 1975-1977, Ivan Head – Subject Files – Economic Summit 1975-1976.)
- Memorandum, Secretary of State for External Affairs Allan J. MacEachen, to Prime Minister Trudeau, Puerto Rico Summit, 25 June, 1976, stating that as the leaders will have an informal discussion 'which may well be devoted to political issues', attaches, on a contingency basis, detailed notes on major foreign policy issues: nuclear relations with India and Pakistan; China after Mao; détente; build-up of Warsaw Pact forces; Lebanon; and the status of the Law of the Sea conference. (LAC, P. E. Trudeau Fonds, 1968-1978 PMO Priority Correspondence Series, MG26 O7, Vol. 536, File 1203: 1975-1977, 1976 Files.)
- Memorandum, Ivan L. Head [the Prime Minister's special representative] to Prime Minister Trudeau, 25 June 1976. This is a covering letter accompanied by a set of confidential biographical and political profiles of the other G7 leaders to attend the 1976 Puerto Rico summit. The aim of these profiles is to help in ascertaining 'the political wavelength on which the men are operating'. Giscard's profile, for example, includes this: 'Fresh evidence has appeared to make it quite clear that the French were obstinately opposed to the Puerto Rico meeting. They did not want the Rambouillet summit to become institutionalized, largely because of the difficulties in which this would place France with the "small five" of the European Community. This being so,

Giscard may be somewhat annoyed at the willingness with which all other invitees accepted President Ford's proposed meeting. It will explain as well why Giscard, in a somewhat petulant fashion, proposes to arrive in Puerto Rico literally minutes before the meeting begins Sunday afternoon and to depart instantly on its conclusion Monday afternoon.' (LAC, MG26 O7, Vol. 536, File 1203.) Similar confidential biographical and political sketches of the other leaders have also been found in the other countries' archives, so this may well be part of each G8 country's preparatory process.

- Letter, Prime Minister Trudeau to President Ford, 30 June 1976, thanking Ford for his hospitality at the 1976 Puerto Rico G7 summit and reiterating Canada's satisfaction to be able to participate. (LAC, MG26 O7, Vol. 536, File 1203.)

Memoirs and Other Writings by Former Prominent Summit Participants

Personal recollections and accounts of G7 and G8 heads of state or government, and of other prominent participants in earlier summits, are not only informative but often revealing, given the unique insight and perspective of these leaders. Examples of their 'inside stories' of summit meetings are discussed in Chapter 3 while illustrations of personal interaction between leaders follow here.

Harold Wilson, UK Prime Minister at the time of the 1975 Rambouillet summit, in his account of the discussions and the atmosphere at Rambouillet, relates that he agreed with Helmut Schmidt's economic analysis, and encouraged Gerald Ford's optimism vis-à-vis the state of the US economy. He comments on Takeo Miki's and Aldo Moro's stance against trade protectionism, and on Giscard's surprise at 'American bullishness' (Wilson 1979: 185-86).

The two former US presidents, Ford and Carter, expose very different personal perspectives on the dynamics between each of them and their German peer, Chancellor Schmidt. Carter writes about his uneasy and at times antagonistic relationship with Schmidt. Drawing on his personal diary, Carter recalls an acrimonious meeting with Schmidt during the 1979 Tokyo G7 summit: 'We ... had a luncheon that was very bitter and unpleasant. Schmidt got personally abusive toward me when I pushed the individual target position [on oil imports by G7 countries]. For instance, he alleged that American interference in the Middle East trying to work for a peace treaty was what had caused the problems with oil all over the world' [the Japanese and French leaders eventually mediated an acceptable compromise] (Carter 1982: 112-13).

Ford, on the contrary, highlights how well he and Schmidt saw eye to eye on economic and political questions (Ford 1979: 221). The very different nature of those two relationships is confirmed by Schmidt's own memoir. He relates that not only was there good understanding between him and Ford in the political and economic arenas, but that they had developed a close personal friendship that had endured well beyond their terms as leaders. By contrast, Schmidt had a stormy relationship with Carter not only at and around G7 summits but also elsewhere. This had to do with their personality differences but also with genuine policy disagreements that had become public knowledge. For example, US anger over Schmidt's perceived support for the Soviet Union on arms limitation negotiations led to critical statements in the

US press, originating from US government officials, about the loyalty of Schmidt and Giscard to western interests. Beyond media accounts, Schmidt 'received an astonishing letter from Carter' dated 12 June 1980, repeating the US position on opposing any moratorium on intermediate missile development, but 'the real source of Carter's anger was my [Schmidt's] impending meeting with Brezhnev. The release of the letter to the Washington press was pure spite.' In his terse reply, Schmidt suggested further talks with Carter during the upcoming Venice G7 summit. Schmidt transcribes part of that testy conversation (Schmidt 1989: 176-77, 209-19). Carter, in his own account of the same incident, comments on their confrontation at the 1980 Venice summit: 'Shortly after arriving I had an unbelievable meeting with Helmut Schmidt ... ranting and raving about a letter that I had written him, which was a well-advised message. He claimed that he was insulted' (Carter 1982: 536-37).

Former US President Clinton participated in several summits: Tokyo 1993, Naples 1994, Halifax 1995, Lyon 1996, Denver 1997 (under his chairmanship), Birmingham 1998, Cologne 1999 and Okinawa 2000. His memoir gives his personal accounts of these summits and of his interaction with various leaders, including Yeltsin whose presence (and Russia's membership in the club) was strengthened at the Denver 'Summit of the Eight' (Clinton 2005).

Jacques Attali was French President François Mitterrand's sherpa for all summits from 1982 to 1990. He was perhaps closer to the thinking of his leader than any other sherpa to his or her leader in summit history. His *Verbatim*, in three volumes, is a lively and candid account of his years working with Mitterrand; it includes fascinating insights into the inside story of those summits, notwithstanding the fact that some of his assertions have been disputed, for example by Pierre Favier and Michel Martin-Roland in their *La décennie Mitterrand.*

Websites

A few websites are dedicated to the G7 and G8 system and the G20 on a permanent basis but most arise in an *ad hoc* manner, only to disappear later. Some are developed and maintained by G8-G20 governments; others by outside entities such as research groups. Some are entirely dedicated to G7 and G8-related content, while others deal with selected developments in those institutions, and issues and programmes as and when needed by the concerned organization. The following selection introduces several representative sites, indicating their content and, when applicable, their demise. Unless otherwise stated, all websites were still active as of November 2006.

Governmental G8 Websites

Canada. Canada's G8 Website. <www.g8.gc.ca>   Maintained by the Department of Foreign Affairs of the government of Canada, this website includes – in English and French – background information on the forthcoming G8 summit and past summits, full text of collective documents of summits and ministerial meetings back to the 2001 Genoa summit, other documents and news releases emanating from the Canadian government, links to relevant websites, and other information.

France. Le Sommet 2003. [Evian Summit] <www.g8.fr/evian>   In addition to texts of collective G8 documents of Evian and transcripts of the French President's press conferences, the site contains background information about the G8, videos of the Evian summit, guidance for the media, information about the Evian region, and archives of previous summits back to Lyon 1996. It replaces the French government's summit site for their previously-hosted 1996 Lyon summit. In English and French.

Germany. [2007] G8 Presidency Homepage <www.g-8.de/Webs/G8/EN/Homepage/ home.html>   Gives background information on the G8 and Germany's place in it; information on summit agenda, 'outreach countries' and civil society relations; news releases; and information for media representatives. Will add summit documents and other material as the year 2007 progresses. In German and English.

Italy. Vertice di Genoa. <www.g8italia.it>   This was Italy's official website for the Genoa summit of 2001. It also has archives of earlier summits: Birmingham 1998, Cologne 1999, and Okinawa 2000; as well as the previous three Italian-hosted summits: Venice 1980, Venice 1987, and Naples 1994. In Italian and English.

Japan. The Ministry of Foreign Affairs of Japan. G7/G8. <www.mofa.go.jp/policy/ economy/summit/index.html>   Contains summit and ministerial documents, and press conference transcripts for the period 1996 to the present, with archives of earlier summit documents from Rambouillet 1975 to Halifax 1995. In Japanese and English.

Russia. G8/Saint Petersburg, Russia, 2006. <www.g8russia.ru>   Russia's official G8 website, in Russian and English, was launched on 8 July 2005, the last day of the 2005 Gleneagles summit. Provides information on the G8, on the summit agenda, working meetings including ministerial meetings scheduled for 2006, background information on Russia, news briefings, media information, and contact information. Also includes texts of major documents of the 1997-2005 summits.

Switzerland. Sommet d'Evian, côté suisse   The Swiss government's website for aspects of the 2003 Evian summit affecting Switzerland. No longer accessible.

United Kingdom. [Gleneagles] G8 Summit 2005. <www.g8.gov.uk>   Gives background information about preparations for and events leading up to the Gleneagles summit, media and public information (including information about Gleneagles and its environs), policy issues for the summit, links to other websites, photographs of past summits from Genoa 2001 to Sea Island 2004 and communiqués or chair's summaries of past summits going back to the 1998 Birmingham summit, the last previous summit hosted by the UK. It replaces the official UK summit website for Birmingham.

United States. Department of State. Economic Summits. <www.state.gov/e/eb/ ecosum>   Contains archives, including documents and background information, of previous summits starting with Halifax 1995. (The original official US website for Sea Island is no longer active.)

United States. Office of the President. [White House web page for the G8 2004 and 2005 Summits.] <*www.whitehouse.gov/g8*>   Has summit documents, background information, transcripts of news conferences, photographs and other material.

G8-Related Bodies and Programmes

Digital Opportunity Task Force (DOT Force)   Ironically – given the nature of the DOT Force – this entity's website is no longer accessible and has not been archived since the group completed its work. The summary of the DOT Force's first meeting is available at the G8 Information Centre website, at <www.g8.utoronto.ca/dot_force/summary-nov-00.html>.[3]

Financial Action Task Force on Money Laundering. Paris: FATF Secretariat. <*www.fatf-gafi.org*>   Originally a G7-established body, it has become autonomous, with a larger membership. For a number of years it functioned at OECD headquarters. The website gives background information, list of member states and of non-cooperative countries, text of publications and documents, information about meetings and other events, links, and additional information. In English and French.

Financial Stability Forum. <*www.fsforum.org*>   Provides background information, information on meetings, compendium of standards, text of documents and press releases, and other material.

G7 Support Implementation Group in Moscow   The group functioned from 1993 to 1997. Its website is no longer accessible.

G8 Renewable Energy Task Force   This group functioned in 2000-2001. Its website is no longer active, but its report and annexes are available on the website of the World Energy Council, at www.worldenergy.org/wec-geis/focus/renew/g8.asp.

Global Fund to Fight AIDS, Tuberculosis and Malaria <*www.theglobalfund.org*> Gives information on programmes, funds raised and spent, calendar of events, HIV/ AIDS-related stories, publications and press releases. In English, French, Russian, Arabic and Chinese.

The New Partnership for Africa's Development (NEPAD) <*http://nepad.org*>   Was initiated by five African heads of state (Abdelaziz Bouteflika of Algeria, Hosni Mubarak of Egypt, Olusegun Obasanjo of Nigeria, Abdoulaye Wade of Senegal and Thabo Mbeki of South Africa) under a mandate of the Organization of African Unity (OAU; now African Union, AU) in response to Africa's pressing economic and social needs. (It is not a G8-inspired project but one that enjoys the support of the G8.) The primary objectives of NEPAD are poverty eradication, sustainable growth and development, Africa's integration into the global economy, and the empowerment of

---

3   The final report of the DOT force, *Digital Opportunities for All* (2002) was presented to the Kananaskis summit.

African women. The website provides a brief history of NEPAD, text of documents and speeches, information about workshops and other events, a discussion list, links, and other information. In English and French.

Strengthening the Global Partnership Project: Protecting Against the Spread of Nuclear, Biological and Chemical Weapons (SGP) <www.sgpproject.org>   Contains documents and background material in English, French and Russian. The SGP Project is related to the G8's Global Partnership Program, but is a consortium of 22 research institutes in 17 countries of Europe, Asia and North America, with the mandate to build political and financial support for G8 initiatives to reduce the dangers from nuclear, biological and chemical weapons everywhere, beginning with the countries of the former Soviet Union. Has documents and background material in English, French and Russian. A related website (Canada, Department of Foreign Affairs, *Global Partnership Program*. <http://geo.international.gc.ca/cip-pic/library/globalpartnership-en.asp> is an example of a governmental website, in English and French, dedicated to a particular aspect of the G8, preventing terrorist groups from obtaining weapons and materials of mass destruction. The Global Partnership Program was mandated by the 2002 Kananaskis summit.

G20 Websites

Australia. [Website of the Australian chairmanship, 2006]. <www.g20.org> Contains background information about the G20 and its members, list of all previous meetings of finance ministers and central bank governors, texts of all communiqués, media information and other material. Includes intranet for members only.

Canada. Department of Finance. [Archival G20 Website]   Canada chaired the G20 from its inception in 1999 to 2001. This site is no longer accessible. The G8 Information Centre website (see below), at <www.g8.utoronto.ca/g20>, includes the texts of available G20 documents, background information, and links to G20 websites.

Germany. [Archival website of the German chairmanship, 2004]   The original website of the German Ministry of Finance is no longer active, but it is archived by the German Bundesbank: <www.bundesbank.de/g20/public>. Contents are similar to the website of the 2006 Australian chairmanship, including intranet for members, but also including texts of case studies and other publications.

Mexico. Secretaría de Hacienda y Crédito Público. [Website of the Mexican chairmanship, 2003]   No longer active. Similarly, there is no trace of the website of the Indian chairmanship, 2002.

Universities and Research Groups

University of Toronto and G8 Research Group. G8 Information Centre. <www.g8.utoronto.ca>   Designed as a permanent, authoritative and comprehensive electronic repository, in all G8 languages, of available collective documents of the G7 and G8 summits and ministerial and other related documents from the beginning of summitry, documents of the G20, and a great deal of other material: text of scholarly publications including the refereed series of working papers *G8 Governance*, analytical studies produced by members of the group, seminar and conference papers, news of the G8 and G20, information on research and publications, online finding aid to the University of Toronto's G8 Research Collection, and an extensive set of links to governmental, international organization and civil society websites relevant to the G7 and G8 system and the G20.

University of Toronto and G8 Research Group. G8 Online. <www.g7.utoronto.ca/ g8online/>   Educational website of the G8 Research Group, in English and French. Date of coverage begins with the 1999 Cologne summit. Contains lectures, pre-summit academic conferences and interviews. Also has student discussion forums and other material, including video and audio links. A third website, <www.g8live. ca>, was launched at the time of the St. Petersburg summit and is devoted to blogs and other short pieces by student members of the group.

Lyon-Sommet du G7 (Lyon-G7 Summit). Lyon: Institut d'Etudes Politiques, 1996. <http://sung7.univ-lyon2.fr/sommet-lyon.html>   Archival website of the Institut d'Etudes Politiques, Université de Lyon. Contains texts of official documents of the 1996 Lyon summit, and background information on the summit and related events of 1995-1996, in French. Its links have not been kept up and many no longer work.

NGO-Civil Society Websites

Civil G8. <www.civilg8.ru>   Dedicated to matters of civil society consultations with the Russian host government of the 2006 summit. Includes: background information on the G8, Russian government priorities for the summit, and civil society and official G8 activities during the year's Russian G8 presidency; information on the group's advisory council and technical support for consultations; news briefings and reports; invitation to participate; and links to other sites of interest. In Russian and English.

Dissent ('a network of resistance against the G8') <www.dissent.org.uk>   A British-based coalition, formed in 2003 by radical ecological and other anti-globalization groups, with a full programme to protest against the 2005 Gleneagles summit.

G6B People's Summit [Alternative event related to the Kananaskis Summit 2002]   Its website is no longer active.

G8 Activism. [Alternative events related to the Kananaskis Summit, 2002]. <http:// g8.activist.ca>   This website archives information about selected events that took place around the Kananaskis summit, from the point of view of anti-G8 NGOs. Many links from this site no longer work.

G8 NGO Platform. *<www.g8-germany.info>*   Launched in preparation of the 2006 Heiligendamm summit, this is a website of a German civil society group of social movements, with international NGO participation. In German and English.

J8 [youth forum]. *<www.j82006.com>*   The group's activities began at the 2005 Gleneagles summit. The website provides basic information about the J8, its annual pre-summit competition, news, and resources for teachers.

Make Poverty History, *<www.makepovertyhistory.org>*   A coalition of a large number of British and international NGOs and other civil society organizations and individual citizens. Its objectives are debt cancellation for the poorest countries, more and better aid including a timetable to reach 0.7% of GNP, and more justice in international trade. The website is activist, aiding civil society mobilization. Also includes documents, press releases and other information.

Sommet pour un autre monde [Alternative events related to the Evian Summit 2003]   The website is no longer active.

TOES (The Other Economic Summit) [Alternative summits]. *<www.ese.upenn.edu/~rabii/toes/>*   Background information about TOES, with some coverage of the alternative events around the 1997 Denver Summit of the Eight, and brief references to later countersummits.

TOES/USA: The Other Economic Summit. *<www.toes-usa.org>*   Archival website of the alternative summit held at the time of the 2004 Sea Island summit.

WOMBLES. *<www.wombles.org.uk>*   Anti-G8 NGO website begun around the time of the 2003 Evian summit. Still active as of June 2006, with coverage of opposition to the 2005 Gleneagles summit.

Conclusion

The more than three decades of the existence and functioning of the G7 and G8 system and the G20 have inspired a considerable body of scholarly and other analytical and critical writings. Several research groups have focused their attention on these institutions and related issues. Governmental archives of some G7 countries have opened their records to the public, revealing a great deal of valuable information and many authoritative details of the 'inside story' of the early years of the G7 and developments leading to its formation as a new forum. Memoirs and other writings by prominent former participants in G7 and G8 deliberations provide unique personal perspective. And proliferating – albeit sometimes ephemeral – websites created by governments, G7 and G8 bodies, universities and research groups, and nongovernmental/civil society organizations, add immediacy, critical comment and background material. All of these information sources contribute to greater understanding of the complexities of the G7 and G8 system, the G20 and their relevant processes.

References

Note on internet addresses (URLs): Websites tend to appear, change or disappear, often without warning. Addresses cited in this source list were accurate and active at the time of writing (June 2006) unless otherwise noted.

Baker, Andrew (2006), *The Group of Seven: Finance Ministries, Central Banks and Global Financial Governance*, Routledge/Warwick Studies in Globalisation, 10, Routledge, London; New York.

Bayne, Nicholas (2000), *Hanging in There: The G7 and G8 Summit in Maturity and Renewal*, Ashgate, Aldershot, UK, The G8 and Global Governance Series.

Bayne, Nicholas (2005b), *Staying Together: The G8 Summit Confronts the 21st Century*, Ashgate, Aldershot, UK, The G8 and Global Governance Series.

Belelieu, Andre (2002), 'The G8 and Terrorism: What Role Can the G8 Play in the 21st Century?', *G8 Governance*, 8, www.g8.utoronto.ca/governance/belelieu2002-gov8.pdf.

Bergsten, C. Fred and C. Randall Henning (1996), *Global Economic Leadership and the Group of Seven*, Institute for International Economics, Washington DC.

'Bush Budget Funds Archives Transfer to Nixon Library' (2006), *American Libraries Direct*, February 15, www.ala.org/ala/alonline/currentnews/newsarchive/2006abc/february2006a/nixonbudget.htm.

Carter, Jimmy (1982), *Keeping Faith: Memoirs of a President*, Bantam, New York.

Clinton, Bill (2005), *My Life*, Vintage, New York. (Originally published by Knopf in 2004.)

Cohn, Theodore H. (2002), *Governing Global Trade: International Institutions in Conflict and Convergence*, Ashgate, Aldershot, UK, The G8 and Global Governance Series.

Digital Opportunity Task Force, (2002), *Digital Opportunities for All: Report Card*, DOT Force, New York.

Dobson, Hugo (2004), *Japan and the G7/8: 1975-2002*, RoutledgeCurzon, London.

English, John, Ramesh Thakur and Andrew F. Cooper (eds) (2005), *Reforming from the Top: A Leaders 20 Summit*, Centre for International Governance Innovation; United Nations University Press, New York, Tokyo.

Favier, Pierre and Michel Martin-Roland (1990-91), *La décennie Mitterrand*, 3 vols, Seuil, Paris.

Ford, Gerald R. (1979), *A Time to Heal: The Autobiography of Gerald R. Ford*, Harper & Row, New York.

G8 Information Centre, www.g8.utoronto.ca.

G8 Live, www.g8live.ca.

G8 NGO Platform, www.g8-germany.info.

Hanlon, Joseph and John Garrett (1999), *Crumbs of Comfort: The Cologne G8 Summit and the Chains of Debt*, Jubilee 2000 Coalition, London.

Hubbard, Gill and David Miller (eds) (2005), *Arguments against G8*, Pluto Press, London, Ann Arbor.

InterAction Council, www.interactioncouncil.org.

Kirton, John J. (1989a), '*Contemporary Concert Diplomacy: The Seven-Power Summit and the Management of International Order*', Paper prepared for the annual meeting of the International Studies Association and the British International Studies Association, London, March 29-April 1. Unpublished in print. www.g7.utoronto.ca/scholar/kirton198901/index.html.

Kokotsis, Ella (1999), *Keeping International Commitments: Compliance, Credibility, and the G7, 1988-1995*, Garland, New York, Transnational Business and Corporate Culture series.

Lukov, Vadim Borisovich (2002), *Rossiia v Klube Liderov* [Russia in the Leaders' Club], Nauchnaia Kniga, Moscow. [In Russian.]

Meikle, Sian (1999), 'G7/G8 Information: Internet Resources', in *The G7/G8 System: Evolution, Role and Documentation*, 107-24, Peter I. Hajnal, Ashgate, Aldershot, UK, The G8 and Global Governance Series.

Mepham, David and James Lorge (2005), *Putting our House in Order: Recasting G8 Policy towards Africa*, IPPR, London.

'NARA Cooperated in Document Reclassification' (2006), *American Libraries*, 37:5, 16-17.

Ostry, Sylvia (2002), '*Globalization and the G8: Could Kananaskis Set a New Direction?-La Mondialisation et le G8: Kananaskis marquera-t-il le début d'une nouvelle orientation?*', O.D. Skelton Memorial Lecture, Queen's University, Department of Foreign Affairs and International Trade. www.utoronto.ca/cis/skeltonlecture_ostry2002.doc.

Pasco, Jean O. (2006), 'Nixon Library Could Get a Lift in 2007 Budget', *Los Angeles Times*, February 8, B3.

Penttilä, Risto E. J. (2003), *The Role of the G8 in International Peace and Security*, Adelphi Paper, 355. Oxford University Press for the International Institute of Strategic Studies, Oxford.

Putnam, Robert D. and Nicholas Bayne (1987), *Hanging Together: Cooperation and Conflict in the Seven-Power Summits*, rev. ed., Harvard University Press, Cambridge, Mass.

Schmidt, Helmut (1989), *Men and Powers: A Political Retrospective*, Random House, New York.

Takase, Junichi (2000), *Samitto: Shuyô Shunô Kaigi* [Summit: The Meeting of the Main Heads of State], Ashi Shobô, Tokyo. [In Japanese.]

Wilson, Harold (1979), *Final Term: The Labour Government, 1974-1976*, Weidenfeld and Nicolson, and Michael Joseph, London.

Chapter 16

Conclusion

The detailed examination of the Group of Seven/Group of Eight contained in this book leads to several conclusions. It surveys the G7's origins; the economic and political context of the G7 and G8; the summit meetings; the very slow and cautious growth in membership and the question of potential members; the progressively expanding agenda; the evolving relationship with non-member countries, international organizations, civil society and business; the nature of G7 and G8 information and documentation and the growing corpus of writings about the G7 and G8; the broader G7 and G8 system beyond the leaders' forum itself; the G20 finance ministers' forum; and the long and continuing story of initiatives to reform the G7 and G8.

First, the rationale for the emergence of this forum or institution: the economic and political context of the oil crisis, the breakdown of the exchange rate system and other major disruptions in the 1970s caused the leaders of the five major democracies – France, West Germany, the UK, the US and Japan (they were later joined by Italy) to recognize their common vulnerability to economic shocks and other major international developments. The six were joined by Canada in 1976, by the then European Community (now European Union) in 1977 and, in a difficult multi-year incremental process, by Russia which finally became a full member in 1998 and hosted a G8 summit for the first time in 2006. The leaders saw the need to find solutions to problems and challenges in a co-ordinated fashion. Because existing international institutions could not cope adequately with these changes, a new forum arose in the 1970s, first in the form of periodic meetings of the finance ministers of the original five countries, and eventually as summit meetings of the countries' leaders. These heads of state and government saw that through their political leadership, they would be able 'to launch new ideas and resolve disputes that had persisted at lower levels'; that they could pool 'their capacity to reconcile domestic and international pressures [italics removed] on policy-making'; and that 'they could introduce a system of collective management [italics removed], where Europe, North America and Japan would share responsibilities hitherto exercised by the United States alone' (Bayne 2005b: 4).

The 32-year evolution of the membership of the institution reveals the difficult and contentious incremental increase from the original G6 of 1975 to the G8 of 2006. Several potential trajectories for further development can be envisioned. But the question remains: What is the likeliest scenario of the G8's evolution: Into a larger group? A smaller core group? A looser grouping based on the agenda of each summit? An expanded-membership institution?

Over the 32-year history of the G7/G8, the leaders' summits have evolved from the first meeting in 1975 (as G6 that year, without Canadian membership) in Rambouillet, near Paris – seen then as a one-time event – to an elaborate annual occasion, central to the foreign policy endeavours, priorities and prestige of the host country, providing many opportunities ranging from substantive joint, bilateral and other meetings to photo sessions and entertainment for delegates, their spouses and the attending media. The informality and flexibility of the summits have allowed the relatively like-minded leaders of these major democratic, market-economy countries to exchange views freely and in confidence, as G7 from 1975 to 1997 and as G8, with Russia, since 1998. Such candid and private interaction would be unlikely in larger, more cumbersome, and economically and politically more diverse formal organizations with large bureaucracies.

The role of the G7 and G8 embraces deliberation, direction-giving and decision-making as well as global governance and domestic political management functions (Kirton 2006b: 6, App A). The summit allows the attending heads of state and government to exercise political leadership, reconcile domestic and international concerns, develop collective management, and integrate economics and politics in their negotiations and decisions. Present and former leaders and other high officials of the G7 and G8 appreciate the value of this forum and invest considerable political, financial and personal resources in preparing, conducting and following up the summits.

The early summit meetings were conducted with a limited agenda, a restricted number of participants and a high degree of secrecy, but they laid the foundation on which later summits were built and from which an expanded system of ministerial and other meetings evolved. These later meetings proceeded in a generally more transparent manner, with a steadily broadening agenda, and much greater participation by other countries, international organizations, civil society and the private sector.

It is the prerogative of the leader hosting a particular summit to set the agenda, but the agenda develops in the context of global economic and political realities and the force of continuity in case of persistent and particularly important issues; these factors are all reflected in the topics discussed at the summits. In view of those changing realities – and with input from other G7 and G8 countries – the agenda undergoes numerous changes, additions or deletions by the time the summit is reached. The host leader, his fellow leaders and their personal representatives (sherpas) all have a crucial role in honing and completing the agenda, through an intensive process of year-round negotiations with their counterparts and with other G7 and G8 officials. From the original focus of the summits on economic and financial issues, the summit agenda has evolved over 32 years to embrace more and more topics: political concerns, and later a great number of diverse transnational, global issues from the environment to terrorism and infectious diseases. As well, major unexpected events occurring just before or during summits inevitably make an impact on the actual agenda.

The leaders' G7 and G8 forum has been accompanied by an expanding G7 and G8 system, with ministerial fora ranging from finance, foreign, trade, environment and other ministers' regular and special meetings to diverse task forces and expert groups established by the leaders or their ministers. These fora and groups have performed a wide variety of specialist functions, freeing the leaders to concentrate on issues that they alone have the authority to handle and providing valuable technical and practical channels for deliberation and action.

In a special category of its own is the G20 finance ministers' and central bank governors' forum. It was created to address the need to deal adequately with key issues of the international monetary and financial system, to strengthen the international financial architecture, and to serve as a platform for discussing other pressing international economic questions. The G20 – a creation of the G7 – has developed as an autonomous informal group. It is composed of systemically important developing and emerging-market countries; thus, it reflects a much broader global constituency, and therefore greater legitimacy, than its parent, the G7. Although the G20 brings together countries that, together, account for two-thirds of the world's population and some 90 per cent of global gross domestic product, the group still excludes representation of the poorest developing countries. Its agenda has expanded considerably over its now seven-year lifespan, but its mandate and therefore its capacity are limited so that it cannot deal with many of the global issues linked to economic and financial matters.

The G7 and G8 have always recognized the crucial role of international governmental organizations (IGOs), and have continually widened and deepened links with them. There has been increasing IGO participation in and around the summits themselves, although the same organizations are not consistently involved in each summit. Issues dealt with by the G7 and G8 are routinely remitted to IGOs for action within the competence of those bodies.

The private sector, too, has long been recognized as an essential interlocutor of the G7 and G8. This recognition is mutual, as reflected by G7 and G8 statements and other documents, by papers and analysis originating from business organizations, and by G8 initiatives affecting business (and, in particular, corporate responsibility). Both state and non-state actors have come to value multi-stakeholder approaches and have, on occasion, followed this by establishing working partnerships. This has certainly been true also for civil society, and its growing role in influencing G8 processes and – to a smaller extent – outcomes. Four dimensions of civil society action – dialogue, demonstrations, parallel summits and partnerships – have played an important role in the evolving relations with the G8. The usefulness of productive dialogue, forceful but peaceful demonstrations and creative parallel summits has been clearly shown. As well, multi-stakeholder partnerships can produce public good in ways that a single type of actor (governments, civil society or the private sector) cannot do alone.

For almost as long as summitry itself, there has been interest in evaluating G7 and G8 achievements. In addition to media reports and civil society and other stakeholder evaluations, a body of scholarly work has emerged over the years. These works differ in their objectives and approaches. Three important projects have been the Putnam and Bayne (later Bayne) examination and analysis of the leaders' co-operative achievements; the Kirton/Kokotsis series of studies of compliance with summit commitments, and the more recently developed 'scorecard' method of assessing the performance of each year's summit host country. The fact that each of these methods starts from different premises and each one measures or evaluates different aspects of the subject makes them difficult to compare. Nonetheless, the studies, covering the period from the inception of the summits in 1975 to 2006, yield evaluations over a period of thirty-two years. They reveal relatively high success rates on certain issues and by some summit countries, and lower rates (in some cases, negative values) for other issues and countries. They do, however, make a good case that, over all, there has been a fairly significant degree of compliance with summit undertakings.

The documentation of the G7 and G8 system, in all its variety and dynamism, is an essential source of information not only about that G7 and G8 but also on a whole gamut of vital economic, political and other global issues. It is a potentially rich mine of political, economic and historical data, although it calls for a fair amount of interpretation to get beyond its jargon-laden language and somewhat repetitive nature.

One must also look beyond the primary G7 and G8 documentation to complementary sources. The more than three decades of the existence and functioning of the G7/G8 system (and the shorter history of the G20) have inspired a considerable body of scholarly and other analytical and critical writings. Several think tanks and research groups have focused all or part of their attention on the G7 and system and the G20, as well as related issues. Governmental archives of some G7 countries have opened their records to the public, revealing a wealth of valuable information and many authoritative details of the 'inside story' of the early years of the G7 and developments leading to its formation as a new forum. Memoirs and other writings by prominent former participants in G7 and G8 deliberations provide unique personal perspectives. And proliferating websites – created by governments, G8 bodies, universities and research groups, and civil society organizations – lend immediacy, critical comment and background material. All of these information sources contribute to greater understanding of the complexities and processes of the G7 and G8 system and the G20.

There is a wide perception of the structural, procedural, democratic and other shortcomings of the G8 as it is now constituted, and of the need to reform or replace it. This perception is not restricted to the news media, academia and civil society but has also been expressed by some former and even present officials of various G8 governments associated with summit preparation, conduct and follow-up. There have been many reform proposals ranging from abolishing the G8 to expanding or reducing its membership, rationalizing its agenda and processes, increasing its legitimacy and representativeness, replacing it with a new body, or supplementing it with additional bodies. Many of these proposals have merit, and some have had high-level advocates. The ultimate outcome may be promoted by various constituencies, but will have to be endorsed and agreed by the leaders of the present G8 (and perhaps the present G20).

The G8 could follow several trajectories. It could continue with fixed membership but a flexible agenda and dynamic processes that would allow involving other important countries without absorbing them as members. It could function in parallel with a revived G7. It could expand and become more representative, more responsive to global issues, and bring together greater capacity to deal with those issues, by inviting key countries (particularly China, India, Brazil and South Africa). It could be turned into a more representative (but perhaps less efficient) Leaders' 20 (L20), or continue as G8 but work alongside with an L20. It could disappear. Or it could evolve in ways unforeseen by anyone today. To remain relevant, the G8 must become more flexible and more representative, and it must transform itself significantly if it is to rise to the challenges of our age.

References

Note on internet addresses (URLs): Websites tend to appear, change or disappear, often without warning. Addresses cited in this source list were accurate and active at the time of writing (August 2006) unless otherwise noted.

Bayne, Nicholas (2005b), *Staying Together: The G8 Summit Confronts the 21st Century*, Ashgate, Aldershot, UK.

Kirton, John J. (2006b), *A Summit of Significant Success: The G8 at St. Petersburg*, G8 Research Group, Toronto, 19 July, www.g8.utoronto.ca/evaluations/2006stpetersburg/kirton_perf_060719.pdf.

Bibliography

For a more comprehensive bibliography on the G7, G8, G20 and related issues, compiled by Peter I. Hajnal, see the G8 Information Centre website, at <www. g8.utoronto.ca/bibliography/index.htm>.

Web addresses and links (URLs): websites tend to appear, change or disappear, often without warning. URLs cited in this bibliography were accurate and active at the time of final compilation (2006) unless otherwise noted.

'Activists Keep up Pressure on G-8 Leaders to Alleviate Poverty' (2006), Associated Press, 15 July.

'Aid to Africa: The $25 Billion Question' (2005), *The Economist*, 376:8433, 24-26, July 2.

Alagh, Yoginder K. (2005), 'On Sherpas and Coolies: The L20 and Non-Brahmanical Futures', in *Reforming from the Top: A Leaders' 20 Summit*, 169-86. English, et al. (eds), Centre for International Governance Innovation; United Nations University Press, New York; Tokyo.

Amnesty International (2002), Telephone Interview, 30 August.

Amnesty International (2003a), *A Catalogue of Failures: G8 Arms Exports and Human Rights Violations*, 19 May, IOR 30/003/2003, http://web.amnesty.org/library/Index/ENGIOR300032003?open&of=ENG-366.

Amnesty International (2003b), *G8: No Trade Off for Human Rights*, Press release, 2 June, POL 30/002/2003, http://web.amnesty.org/library/Index/ENGPOL300022003.

Amnesty International (2006), *UN: Security Council Must Adopt Urgent Measures to Protect Civilians in Israel-Lebanon Conflict*, Press release, 18 July, http://news.amnesty.org/index/ENGIOR410122006

Annan, Kofi (2005), 'Here is What the G8 Leaders Should Do', *The Globe and Mail*, 6 July, A15.

Appel du Forum des Peuples, (2003), 'Consensus des peuples face au consensus du g8', Siby. www.attac.info/g8evian/index.php?NAVI=1016-114297-14fr.

Ardouin, Estelle (1996), *Sherpas et sommets des 7* [Sherpas and Summits of the 7], Institut d'Etudes Politiques, Lyon.

Åslund, Anders (2006), *Russia's Challenges as Chair of the G-8*, Policy Briefs in International Economics, PB06-3, Institute for International Economics, Washington, DC, www.iie.com/publications/pb/pb06-3.pdf.

Atlantic Council of the United States (1980), *Summit Meetings and Collective Leadership in the 1980's*, Charles Robinson and William C. Turner, co-chairmen; Harald B. Malmgren, rapporteur, Atlantic Council of the United States Policy Papers, Working Group on Political Affairs, Washington, DC.

Attali, Jacques (1993-95), *Verbatim*, Fayard, Paris. [Tome 1: Chronique des années 1981-1986; Tome 2: Chronique des années 1986-1988; Tome 3: Chronique des années 1988-1991].

Bailin, Alison (2001), 'From Traditional to Institutionalized Hegemony', *G8 Governance*, 6, www.g8.utoronto.ca/scholar/bailin/bailin2000.pdf.

Bailin, Alison (2005), *From Traditional to Group Hegemony: The G7, the Liberal Economic Order and the Core-Periphery Gap*, Ashgate, Aldershot, UK.

Baker, Andrew (2000), 'The G-7 as a Global 'Ginger Group': Plurilateralism and Four-Dimensional Diplomacy', *Global Governance: A Review of Multilateralism and International Organizations*, 6:2, 165-89.

Baker, Andrew (2006), *The Group of Seven: Finance Ministries, Central Banks and Global Financial Governance*, Routledge/Warwick Studies in Globalisation, 10, Routledge, London; New York.

Baker, Gerald (1998), 'G7 Attempts to Restore Calm to World Finance', *Financial Times*, 31 October/1 November, 2.

Barnes, Hugh and James Owen, comp[ilers] (2006), *Russia in the Spotlight: G8 Scorecard*, Foreign Policy Centre, London, http://fpc.org.uk/fsblob/686.pdf and http://fpc.org.uk/events/past/224.

Baxter, Joan (2003), 'Poor People's Summit Held in Mali', BBC News, 1 June, http://news.bbc.co.uk/1/hi/world/africa/2957372.stm.

Bayne, Nicholas (1995), 'The G7 Summit and the Reform of Global Institutions', *Government and Opposition*, 30:4, 492-509.

Bayne, Nicholas (1997), 'Changing Patterns at the G7 Summit', *G7 Governance*, 1, May, www.g8.utoronto.ca/governance/gov1/.

Bayne, Nicholas (2000), *Hanging in There: The G7 and G8 Summit in Maturity and Renewal*, Ashgate, Aldershot, UK, The G8 and Global Governance Series.

Bayne, Nicholas (2004), *Impressions of the 2004 Sea Island Summit*, 29 June, www.g7.utoronto.ca/evaluations/2004seaisland/bayne2004.html.

Bayne, Nicholas (2005a), *Overcoming Evil with Good: Impressions of the Gleneagles Summit, 6-8 July 2005*, Gleneagles and London: G8 Research Group, 18 July, www.g8.utoronto.ca/evaluations/2005gleneagles/bayne2005-0718.html.

Bayne, Nicholas (2005b), *Staying Together: The G8 Summit Confronts the 21st Century*, Ashgate, Aldershot, UK.

Bayne, Nicholas and Robert D. Putnam (1995), 'Introduction: The G-7 Summit Comes of Age', in *The Halifax G-7 Summit: Issues on the Table*, 1-13, Sylvia Ostry and Gilbert R. Wynham, (eds), Centre for Foreign Policy Studies, Dalhousie University, Halifax.

Beattie, Alan (2001a), 'Aid Groups Could Miss G8 Talks', *Financial Times*, 2 July.

Beattie, Alan (2001b), 'Protests Aim to Breach G8 Cordon', *Financial Times*, 5 July.

Beattie, Alan (2005a), 'Campaigners Divided on Aid Promises for Africa', *Financial Times*, 9/10 July, 8.

Beattie, Alan (2005b), 'G8 Mood and Doha Talks "Show Disconnect"', *Financial Times*, 9/10 July, 8.

Beattie, Alan (2006), 'G8 Legitimacy Queried as Russia Plays Host', *Financial Times*, 13 July.

Belelieu, Andre (2002), 'The G8 and Terrorism: What Role Can the G8 Play in the 21st Century?', *G8 Governance*, 8, www.g8.utoronto.ca/governance/belelieu2002-gov8.pdf.

Benoit, Bertrand (2006), 'Hedge Fund Transparency Put on G8 Agenda', *Financial Times*, 18 October.

Benoit, Bertrand and Mark Schieritz (2006), 'Germany Plans to Shake Up G8 Agenda', *Financial Times*, 27 July.

Bergsten, C. Fred (1996), 'Grade "F" for the G7', *The International Economy: The Magazine of International Economic Policy* 10:6, 18-21, 68, November/December.

Bergsten, C. Fred (1998), 'The New Agenda with China', *International Economics Policy Briefs*, 98-2, May.

Bergsten, C. Fred (2004a), 'The Euro and the Dollar: Toward a "Finance G-2"?', paper prepared for the conference on 'The Euro at Five: Ready for a Global Role', 26 February, www.iie.com/publications/papers/bergsten0204.pdf.

Bergsten, C. Fred (2004b), 'Foreign Economic Policy for the Next President', *Foreign Affairs*, 83:2, 88-101, March/April.

Bergsten, C. Fred and C. Randall Henning (1996), *Global Economic Leadership and the Group of Seven*, Institute for International Economics, Washington DC.

Bergsten, C. Fred and Caio Koch-Weser (2004), 'The G-2, a New Conceptual Basis and Operating Modality for Transatlantic Economic Relations', in *From Alliance To Coalitions: The Future of Transatlantic Relations*, 237-49, Werner Weidenfeld et al. (eds), Bertelsmann Foundation Publishers, Gütersloh, Germany.

Berridge, G. R. (1995), *Diplomacy: Theory and Practice*, Prentice Hall/Harvester Wheatsheaf, London; New York.

Blair, Tony (2006), 'Our Values Are Our Guide', *The Globe and Mail*, 27 May, A19.

Blitz, James (2005), 'Blair Contrasts G8 with "Politics of Terror"', *Financial Times*, 9/10 July, 4.

Blomfield, Adrian (2006), 'Far-Right Racists Join the Protests', *The Daily Telegraph*, 14 July.

'Bono, Geldof Win Ear of Bush' (2005), *Toronto Star*, 7 July, A7.

Bonvicini, Gianni and Wolfgang Wessels (1984), 'The European Community and the Seven', in *Economic Summits and Western Decision-Making* 167-91, Cesare Merlini (ed.), Croom Helm; St. Martin's Press in association with the European Institute of Public Administration, London; New York.

Bradford, Colin I. (2005a), 'Anticipating the Future: A Political Agenda for Global Economic Governance', in *Reforming from the Top: A Leaders' 20 Summit*, 46-62. English, et al. (eds), Centre for International Governance Innovation; United Nations University Press, New York; Tokyo.

Bradford, Colin I. (2005b), 'Global Governance for the 21st Century', prepared for the Brookings Institution/Centre for International Governance Innovation Governance Project, Spring, Washington, DC, www.brookings.edu/views/papers/20051024bradford.pdf.

Bradford, Colin I. and Johannes F. Linn (2004), 'Global Economic Governance at a Crossroads: Replacing the G-7 with the G-20', *Brookings Institution Policy Brief* No. 131.

Brundtland, Gro Harlem and Michel Camdessus (2005), 'The World Expects Bold Action', *Toronto Star*, 23 June, A25.

Brzezinski, Zbigniew (1983), *Power and Principle: Memoirs of the National Security Adviser, 1977-1981*, Farrar Straus Giroux, New York.

Brzezinski, Zbigniew (1996), 'Let's Add to the G-7', *The New York Times*, 25 June, A11.

Brzezinski, Zbigniew (2004), *The Choice: Global Domination or Global Leadership*, Basic Books, New York.

Bureau of National Affairs (1995), 'Draft Halifax Summit Communiqué, dated May 27, 1995, released June 6 by Canadian Member of Parliament Nelson Riis', *Daily Report for Executives: Preview of the G-7 Summit, Halifax, Canada, June 15-17*, 114, Special Issue, Washington, DC.

'Bush Budget Funds Archives Transfer to Nixon Library' (2006), *American Libraries Direct*, February 15, www.ala.org/ala/alonline/currentnews/newsarchive/2006abc/february2006a/nixonbudget.htm.

Business Action for Africa (2005), *Conference Statement*, 5-6 July, London.

Callaghan, James (1987), *Time and Chance*, Collins, London.

Camé, François (1989), 'Comment les sherpas avaient ficelé le sommet [How the Sherpas Had Wrapped Up the Summit]', *Libération*, 8-15, 17 juillet.

'Campaigners Say G8 AIDS Pledge Not Enough' (2006), Reuters Health E-Line, 17 July.

Carin, Barry and Gordon Smith (2005), 'Making Change Happen at the Global Level', in *Reforming from the Top: A Leaders' 20 Summit*, 25-45. English, et al. (eds), Centre for International Governance Innovation; United Nations University Press, New York; Tokyo.

Carter, Jimmy (1982), *Keeping Faith: Memoirs of a President*, Bantam, New York.

Centre for Global Studies, *L20: The G20 at the Leaders' Level*, www.l20.org.

Centre for International Governance Innovation, *L20 Project*, www.cigionline.org/research/l20_events.php.

Centre for International Governance Innovation (2003a), *The G-20 at Leaders' Level?: Record of the Discussion at Bellagio, 9-11 December*, www.cigionline.ca/publications/docs/Bellagio.pdf.

Centre for International Governance Innovation (2003b), *The G-20 at Leaders' Level?: Report of a Meeting Hosted by the Centre for International Governance Innovation and the Centre for Global Studies, Waterloo, Ontario, 26-27 October*, www.cigionline.ca/publications/docs/G-20 Conference Report November 2003. pdf.

Centre for International Governance Innovation (2004), *CFGS/CIGI Report: 'The G-20 at Leaders' Level?'*, www.cigionline.ca/publications/docs/G20 Feb 2004 Report.pdf.

Centre for International Governance Innovation (2005), *Report on L-20 Stocktaking Conference*, Ottawa, 19-20 February.

Chase, Steven (2005), 'Alarm Bells Raised over WTO Talks', *The Globe and Mail*, 6 September, B1-2, Toronto.

Chirac, Jacques (2006), 'The G8's Raison d'être', *The Globe and Mail*, 13 July, A17.

Chivers, C.J. (2006), 'Rights Activists Gather to Call for Russian Evolution', *The New York Times*, A3, 12 July.

Clark, Joe (1995), 'The PM [Prime Minister] and the SSEA [Secretary of State for External Affairs]: Comment 2', *International Journal*, 50:1, 213-15, Winter.

Clinton, Bill (2005), *My Life*, Vintage, New York. (Originally published by Knopf in 2004.)

Cohn, Theodore H. (2002), *Governing Global Trade: International Institutions in Conflict and Convergence*, The G8 and Global Governance Series, Ashgate, Aldershot, UK.

Commission for Africa (2005), *Our Common Interest: Report of the Commission for Africa*, London, www.commissionforafrica.org/english/report/thereport/english/11-03-05_cr_report.pdf.

Cooper, Andrew F. and Thomas Fues (2000), 'L20 and ECOSOC Reform: Complementary Building Blocks for Inclusive Global Governance and a More Effective UN', *Briefing Paper* 6/2005, Deutsches Institut für Entwicklungspolitik, Bonn.

Council on Foreign Relations (2006), *Russia's Wrong Direction: What the United States Can and Should Do*, Task Force Report, 57, CFR, New York, March.

'Counter G8 Summit Disappointed at Little Attention Paid to Africa' (2006), Agence France Presse, 17 July.

Culpeper, Roy (2003), 'Systemic Reform at a Standstill: A Flock of "Gs" in Search of Global Financial Stability', in *Critical Issues in International Financial Reform*, 203-36, Albert Berry and Gustavo Indart (eds), Transaction Publishers, New Brunswick, NJ; London.

Daniels, Joseph P. (1993), *The Meaning and Reliability of Economic Undertakings, 1975-1989*, Garland Publishing, New York.

DATA (2004a), *Disappointment, but Door Left Open to Progress on Debt Relief*, 10 June, www.data.org/archives/000527.php.

DATA (2004b), *G8 and African Leadership in the War on AIDS and Extreme Poverty*. June, www.data.org/archives/G82004report.pdf.

DATA (2006), *DATA Calls on G8 and EU Political Leaders to Make Good on Their Promise to Make Trade Work for Africa*, Media release, 24 July, www.data.org/archives/000798.php.

'Day of Hope Turns to Day of Violence' (2005), *The Scotsman*, 7 July, 1-5.

Defarges, Philippe Moreau (1994), 'The French Viewpoint on the Future of the G-7', in *The Future of the G-7 Summits*, 177-85, (*The International Spectator* 29:2, April/June, Special Issue).

Dent, Martin and Bill Peters (1999), *The Crisis of Poverty and Debt in the Third World*, Ashgate, Aldershot, UK.

Digital Opportunity Task Force, (2002), *Digital Opportunities for All: Report Card*, DOT Force, New York.

Dobson, Hugo (2004), *Japan and the G7/8: 1975-2002*, RoutledgeCurzon, London.

Dobson, Wendy (1995), 'Summitry and the International Monetary System: The Past as Prologue', *Canadian Foreign Policy*, 3:1, 5-15, Spring.

Dobson, Wendy (2001), 'Broadening Participation in G-7 Summits', in *Toward Shared Responsibility and Global Leadership: Recommendations for the G-8 Genoa Summit from the G-8 Preparatory Conference, 23-29.* [Turin, Italy: G-8 Preparatory Conference].

Drache, Daniel (2005), 'The Political Economy of Dissent: Global Publics after Cancún', in *Reforming from the Top: A Leaders' 20 Summit*, 121-40. English, et al. (eds), Centre for International Governance Innovation; United Nations University Press, New York; Tokyo.

Drop the Debt (2001a), *Bono, Bob Geldof and Lorenzo Jovanotti Meet G8 Leaders in Genoa*, Press Release, 20 July, www.dropthedebt.org. No longer accessible.

Drop the Debt (2001b), *Drop the Debt Response to the G7 Communiqué*, Genoa, 20 July, www.dropthedebt.org. No longer accessible.

Drop the Debt (2001c), *Verdict on Genoa Summit*, Press Release, 22 July, www.dropthedebt.org. No longer accessible.

Ekins, Paul (ed.) (1986), *The Living Economy: A New Economics in the Making*, Routledge & Kegan Paul, London & New York.

English, John, Ramesh Thakur and Andrew F. Cooper (eds) (2005), *Reforming from the Top: A Leaders 20 Summit*, Centre for International Governance Innovation; United Nations University Press, New York; Tokyo.

Evans, David (1981a), '"Popular Summit" Calls for World Disarmament', *Ottawa Citizen*, 20 July, 3.

Evans, David (1981b), 'Summit Security Noose Tightens around Ottawa Core', *Ottawa Citizen*, 21 July.

Evans, Gareth (2005), 'UN Missed the Chance of a Lifetime', *The Globe and Mail*, 11 October, A19.

50 Years is Enough (2002), 'Activists Disappointed, But Not Surprised, As G7 Africa Decisions Affirm Economic Status Quo', www.50years.org/cms/updates/story/9.

Favier, Pierre and Michel Martin-Roland (1990-91), *La décennie Mitterrand*, 3 vols, Seuil, Paris.

Fedorov, Yury E. (2006), *'Boffins' and 'Buffoons': Different Strains of Thought in Russia's Strategic Thinking*, REP BP 06/01, Chatham House, London, March, www.chathamhouse.org.uk/pdf/research/rep/BP0306russia.pdf.

Financial Action Task Force (2006), *AML/CFT Evaluations and Assessments: Handbook for Countries and Accessors*, Paris, www.fatf-gafi.org/dataoecd/3/26/36254892.pdf.

Financial Stability: Supervision of Global Financial Institutions; A Report by G7 Finance Ministers (1998), London, May (unpublished).

Finn, Peter and Peter Baker (2006), 'At Carefully Staged G-8, Dissenters Kept in Wings', *The Washington Post*, A13, 16 July.

'For Slimmer and Sporadic Summits' (2001), *Financial Times*, 10, 23 July.

Ford, Gerald R. (1979), *A Time To Heal: The Autobiography of Gerald R. Ford*, Harper & Row, New York.

Fowler, Robert (2003), 'Canadian Leadership and the Kananaskis G-8 Summit: Towards a Less Self-centred Foreign Policy', in *Coping with the American*

Colossus: Canada among Nations 2003, 219-41, David Carment et al. (eds), Oxford University Press, Don Mills, Ontario.

France, Assemblée Nationale, Douzième Legislature (2003), *Second Meeting of the Parliamentary Presidents of the G8 Countries*, 9 September, www. assembleenationale.fr/12/rap-dian/dian018-2004-english.asp#P58_1649.

France, President (2005), *Conférence de presse de M. Jacques Chirac, Président de la République, à l'issue du sommet du G8 de Gleneagles*, www.elysee.fr.

Fratianni, Michele, Paolo Savona and John J. Kirton (forthcoming 2007). 'Governance amid Globalisation: Corporations, Governments, and the G8', in *Corporate, Public, and Global Governance: The G8 Contribution*, Michele Fratianni, Paolo Savona, and John J. Kirton (eds), Global Finance Series, Ashgate, Aldershot, UK.

Freeland, Chrystia and Matthew Kaminski (1997), 'Helsinki Talks Reach Nuclear Breakthrough', *Financial Times*, 22-23 March.

Friedmann, Harriet (2001), 'Forum: Considering the Quebec Summit, the World Social Forum at Porto Alegre and the People's Summit at Quebec City: A View from the Ground', *Studies in Political Economy: A Socialist Review* 66, 85-105.

Friends of the Earth International (2005), *G8 Summit Agrees More Talk, No Action*, Final G8 Media advisory, 8 July, www.foei.org/media/2005/0708.html.

Friends of the Earth International (2006), *G8 to Feed Oil Addiction, Fuelling Climate Change*, Media advisory, 14 July, www.foei.org/media/2006/0714.html.

Funabashi, Yoichi (1989), *Managing the Dollar: From the Plaza to the Louvre*. 2nd, rev. ed., Institute for International Economics, Washington, DC.

Furstenberg, George M. von and Joseph P. Daniels (1991), 'Policy Undertakings by the Seven "Summit" Countries: Ascertaining the Degree of Compliance', *Carnegie-Rochester Conference Series on Public Policy* 35, 267-308.

Furstenberg, George M. Von and Joseph P. Daniels (1992), *Economic Summit Declarations, 1975-1989: Examining the Written Record of International Cooperation*, Princeton Studies in International Finance, 72, International Finance Section, Dept. of Economics, Princeton University, Princeton, NJ.

G05 (2005), *Global Democracy: Civil Society Visions and Strategies Conference*, Montreal, 31 May, www.g05.org.

G7 (1978), *Declaration*, Bonn, 17 July, www.g8.utoronto.ca/summit/1978bonn/communique/index.html.

G7 (1979), *Declaration*, Tokyo, 29 June, www.g8.utoronto.ca/summit/1979tokyo/communique.html.

G7 (1995), *Halifax Summit Communiqué*, Halifax, June 16, in United States, Department of State, Bureau of Public Affairs, *US Department of State Dispatch* 6:4, 6, July, www.g8.utoronto.ca/summit/1995halifax/communique/growth.html and www.g8.utoronto.ca/summit/1995halifax/communique/challenge.html.

G7 (1996a), *Chairman's Statement*, Lyon, 29 June, www.g8.utoronto.ca/summit/1996lyon/chair.html.

G7 (1996b), *Economic Communiqué*, Lyon, 28 June, www.g8.utoronto.ca/summit/1996lyon/communique.html.

G7 (1997a), *Communiqué*, Denver, 22 June, www.g8.utoronto.ca/summit/1997denver/g8final.htm.

G7 (1997b), *Confronting Global Economic and Financial Challenges: Denver Summit Statement by Seven*, Denver, 21 June, www.g8.utoronto.ca/summit/1997denver/confront.htm.

G7 (1998a), *G7 Chairman's Statement*, Birmingham, www.g8.utoronto.ca/summit/1998birmingham/chair.htm.

G7 (1998b), *G7 Leaders' Statement on the World Economy*, 30 October, www.g8.utoronto.ca/finance/g7_103098.html.

G7 Environment Ministers (1996), *Chairman's Summary*, Cabourg, 9-10 May, www.g8.utoronto.ca/environment/1996cabourg/summary_index.html.

G7 Finance Ministers (1998), *Declaration of G7 Finance Ministers and Central Bank Governors*, www.g8.utoronto.ca/finance/fm103098.htm.

G7 Finance Ministers (2005), *Statement by G7 Finance Ministers on Assisting Countries Devastated by the Indian Ocean Tsunami*, www.g8.utoronto.ca/finance/fm050107.htm.

'The G7 Lays Its Plans' (1998), *Financial Times*, 31 October/1 November, 6.

G7 Ministerial Conference on Terrorism (1996), *Agreement on 25 Measures*, Paris, 30 July, www.g8.utoronto.ca/terrorism/terror25.htm.

G7 Ministerial Meeting on Terrorism (1995), *Ottawa Ministerial [P8] Declaration on Countering Terrorism*, Ottawa, 12 December, www.g8.utoronto.ca/terrorism/terror96.htm.

G8 (1998a), *G8 Birmingham Summit Communiqué*, Birmingham, 17 May, www.g8.utoronto.ca/summit/1998birmingham/finalcom.htm.

G8 (1998b), *Response By the Presidency on Behalf of the G8 to the Jubilee 2000 Petition*, Birmingham, 16 May, www.g8.utoronto.ca/summit/1998birmingham/2000.htm.

G8 (2000a), *G8 Communiqué Okinawa 2000*, Okinawa, 23 July, www.g8.utoronto.ca/summit/2000okinawa/finalcom.htm.

G8 (2000b) *Okinawa Charter on Global Information Society,* Okinawa, 22 July, www.g8.utoronto.ca/summit/2000okinawa/gis.htm.

G8 (2001a), *Communiqué*, Genoa, 22 July, Genoa, www.g8.utoronto.ca/summit/2001genoa/finalcommunique.html.

G8 (2001b), *G7 Statement*, Genoa, 20 July, www.g8.utoronto.ca/summit/2001genoa/g7statement.html.

G8 (2001c), *Genoa, City of Dialogue*, Genoa, www.genoa-g8.it/eng/attualita/primo_piano/primo_piano_2.html. No longer accessible.

G8 (2001d), *Terrorism: Statement by the leaders of the G8 over last week's terrorist attacks in New York and Washington*, 19 September, www.g8.utoronto.ca/terrorism/sept192001.html.

G8 (2002a), *G8's Africa Action Plan*, Kananaskis, 27 June, www.g8.utoronto.ca/summit/2002kananaskis/africaplan.html.

G8 (2002b), *The Kananaskis Summit Chair's Summary*, Kananaskis, 27 June, www.g8.utoronto.ca/summit/2002kananaskis/summary.html.

G8 (2005), *Joint Declaration of the Heads of State and/or Government of Brazil, China, India, Mexico and South Africa Participating in the G8 Gleneagles Summit*, Gleneagles, www.g8.utoronto.ca/summit/2005gleneagles/plusfive.pdf.

G8 (2006a), *Chair's Summary*, http://en.g8russia.ru/docs/25.html and www.g8.utoronto.ca/summit/2006stpetersburg/summary.html.

G8 (2006b), *Education for Innovative Societies in the 21ˢᵗ Century*, St. Petersburg, 16 July, www.g8.utoronto.ca/summit/2006stpetersburg/education.html.

G8 (2006c), *Final Press Briefing with President Putin*, St. Petersburg, 17 July, www.g8.utoronto.ca/summit/2006stpetersburg/putin060717.html.

G8 (2006d), *G8 Declaration on Cooperation and Future Action in Stabilization and Reconstruction*, http://en.g8russia.ru/docs/19.html and www.g8.utoronto.ca/summit/2006stpetersburg/stabilization.html.

G8 (2006e), *G8 Statement on Strengthening the UN's Counter-Terrorism Program*, http://en.g8russia.ru/docs/18.html and www.g8.utoronto.ca/summit/2006stpetersburg/counterterrorism-un.html.

G8 (2006f), *G8 Summit Declaration on Counter-Terrorism*, St. Petersburg, 16 July, www.g8.utoronto.ca/summit/2006stpetersburg/counterterrorism.html.

G8 (2006g), *Global Energy Security*, St. Petersburg, 16 July, www.g8.utoronto.ca/summit/2006stpetersburg/energy.html and http://en.g8russia.ru/docs/11.html.

G8 (2006h), *NGO Leaders Pleased with Meeting with Putin, Hope Their Dialogue with G8 Leaders Will Become Regular*, St. Petersburg, http://en.g8russia.ru/news/20060704/1167339.html.

G8 (2006i), *Press Statement Following the G8 Summit*, St. Petersburg, 18 July, http://en.g8russia.ru/podcast/001/246/115/putin4_en.mp3. http://en.g8russia.ru/news/20060717/1246115.html (transcription).

G8 (2006j), *Putin Does Not Rule Out Permanent Dialogue Between the G8 and the NGOs*, St. Petersburg, http://en.g8russia.ru/news/20060704/1166906.html.

G8 (2006k), *Report of the Nuclear Safety and Security Group*, St. Petersburg, 17 July, www.g8.utoronto.ca/summit/2006stpetersburg/nuclear_report.html.

G8 (2006l), *Report on the G8 Global Partnership*, http://en.g8russia.ru/docs/22.html and www.g8.utoronto.ca/summit/2006stpetersburg/gp_report.html.

G8 (2006m), *Trade Union Statement to the G8 Saint-Petersburg Summit*, St. Petersburg, 6 July, http://en.g8russia.ru/news/20060706/1169801.html.

G8 (2006n), *World Summit of Religious Leaders. Message*, http://en.g8russia.ru/news/20060712/1174296.html.

'G8 Auditing Agencies to Monitor Implementation of Programs' (2006), http://en.g8russia.ru/news/20060707/1169602.html and www.ach.gov.ru/psp/in/12.php.

G8 Business and University Leaders Symposium on Innovation (2006), *Working Meetings Summit 2006*, Moscow, 11 July, http://en.g8russia.ru/page_work/27.html.

G8 Development Ministers (2002), *Chair's Summary*, Windsor, 27 September, www.g8.utoronto.ca/development/09-2002-chair.html.

G8 Information Centre, www.g8.utoronto.ca.

G8 Information Centre (2005), www.g8.utoronto.ca/evaluations/csed/CIVIL/events.html.

G8 Live, www.g8live.ca.

G8 NGO Platform, www.g8-germany.info.

G-8 Preparatory Conference (2000), Strategies for the New Century: A Report to the Leaders of the G-8 Member Countries: Recommendations for the G-8 Okinawa Summit from the G-8 Preparatory Conference, [1ˢᵗ report] [Tokyo]. www.iie.com/publications/papers/g8-2000.pdf.

G-8 Preparatory Conference (2001), Toward Shared Responsibility and Global Leadership: Recommendations for the G-8 Genoa Summit from the G-8 Preparatory Conference, [2nd report] [Turin]. www.iie.com/publications/papers/g8-2001.pdf.

G-8 Preparatory Conference (2002), Global Responses to the New Global Challenges: Recommendations for the G-8 Kananaskis Summit from the G-8 Preparatory Conference, [3rd report] [Washington, DC]. www.iie.com/publications/papers/g8-2002.pdf.

'G8 to Step Up Pressure on India and Pakistan' (1998), *Financial Times*, 3, June 13-14.

G20 (1999), *Communiqué* (Berlin).

G20 [Australian Chair] (2006), www.g20.org/Public/index.jsp.

G22 (1998), *Summary of Reports on the International Financial Architecture* (Washington, D.C.), www.imf.org/external/np/g22/summry.pdf.

Garavoglia, Guido (1984), 'From Rambouillet to Williamsburg: A Historical Assessment', in *Economic Summits and Western Decision-Making*, 1-42, Cesare Merlini (ed.) Croom Helm; St. Martin's Press in association with the European Institute of Public Administration, London; New York.

Garavoglia, Guido and Pier Carlo Padoan (1994), 'The G-7 Agenda: Old and New Issues', in *The Future of the G-7 Summits*, 49-65, *The International Spectator* 29:2 April/June, Special Issue.

Garten, Jeffrey (2005), 'Russia's Leadership of the Group of Eight Will Be Farcical', *Financial Times*, 28 June, 23.

George, Susan (2001), 'L'ordre libéral et ses basses oeuvres', *Le Monde diplomatique* 48:569, 6.

'German Ambassador for Russia's Full Membership of G8 Financial Forum' (2006), 5 July http://en.g8russia.ru/news/20060705/1167611.html.

'German G8 Presidency to Focus on Hedge Funds, Product Piracy, Africa' (2006), *BBC Monitoring European*, 18 October.

'G-Force: The G7 No Longer Governs the World Economy: Does Anyone?' (2004), *The Economist*, 373:8396, 72, October 9.

Gill, Stephen (1999), 'Structural Changes in Multilateralism: The G7 Nexus and the Global Crisis', in *Innovation in Multilateralism*, 113-65, M. Schechter (ed.), St. Martin's Press, New York.

Gilmore, William C. (ed.) (1992), *International Efforts to Combat Money Laundering*, Cambridge International Documents Series, 4, Grotius Publications in association with the Commonwealth Secretariat, Cambridge.

Giscard d'Estaing, Valéry (1988), *Le pouvoir et la vie* [*Power and Life*], Compagnie 12, Paris.

Global Call to Action against Poverty (2005a), *Reflections on the G8 Summit*, by Kumi Naidoo, CIVICUS Secretary General and Chair of the Global Call to Action against Poverty, 13 July, www.civicus.org/new

Global Call to Action against Poverty (2005b), *Statement by the Global Call to Action against Poverty Marking the End of the G8 Summit*, 8 July.

Graham, Bill (2006), 'Civil Society and Institutions of Global Governance', in *Sustainability, Civil Society, and International Governance: Local, North*

American, and Global Contributions, 367-74, John J. Kirton and Peter I. Hajnal (eds), Ashgate, Aldershot, UK.

Graham, Robert (2003), '"Enlarged Dialogue" May Fall on Deaf Ears', *Financial Times*, 29 May.

Greenhill, Romilly et al. (2003), *Did the G8 Drop the Debt? Five Years after the Birmingham Human Chain, What Has Been Achieved, and What More Needs to Be Done?*, Jubilee Research, Jubilee Debt Campaign and CAFOD, www. jubileeresearch.org.

Greenpeace International (2006), *G-8 Fails to Develop Strategy for Energy Security*, 17 July, www.greenpeace.org/international/press/releases/g-8-fails-to-develop-strategy.

'Greens Glum as World Environment Day Heads for 30th Anniversary' (2003), Agence France-Presse, 4 June, Paris.

'Gryzlov to Meet Parliamentarians in Chicago' (2004), *RIA Novosti* [wire service report], 10 September.

Gurria, Angel (2005), 'A Leaders' 20 Summit?', in *Reforming from the Top: A Leaders' 20 Summit*, 63-71. English, et al. (eds), Centre for International Governance Innovation; United Nations University Press, New York; Tokyo.

Guttry, Andrea de (1994), 'The Institutional Configuration of the G-7 in the New International Scenario', in *The Future of the G-7 Summits*, 67-80, (*The International Spectator* 29:2; April/June, Special Issue).

Haas, Richard (2005), 'Leaders Have a Flawed Gleneagles Agenda', *Financial Times*, 1 July, 19.

Hainsworth, Susan (1990), *Coming of Age: The European Community and the Economic Summit*, Country Study No. 7, University of Toronto, Centre for International Studies, www.g8.utoronto.ca/scholar/hainsworth1990/index.html.

Hajnal, Peter I. (comp. and ed.) (1989), *The Seven-Power Summit: Documents from the Summits of Industrialized Countries, 1975-1989*, Kraus International Publications, Millwood, NY.

Hajnal, Peter I. (comp. and ed.) (1991), *The Seven-Power Summit: Documents from the Summits of Industrialized Countries; Supplement: Documents from the 1990 Summit*, Kraus International Publications, Millwood, NY.

Hajnal, Peter I. (2001), 'Civil Society at the 2001 Genoa G8 Summit', *Behind the Headlines* 58:1.

Hajnal, Peter I. (2002), 'Civil Society Encounters the G7/G8', in *Civil Society in the Information Age*, 215-42, Peter I. Hajnal (ed.), Ashgate, Aldershot, UK.

Hajnal, Peter I. (2006a), *Civil Society and the Gleneagles Summit*, paper presented at the Civil G8 International Forum, Moscow, 9 March, www.g8.utoronto.ca/scholar/hajnal_060309.html.

Hajnal, Peter I. (2006b), 'Civil Society, the United Nations, and G7/G8 Summitry', in *Sustainability, Civil Society, and International Governance: Local, North American, and Global Contributions*, 279-318, John J. Kirton and Peter I. Hajnal (eds), Ashgate, Aldershot, UK.

Hajnal, Peter I. and John J. Kirton (2000), 'The Evolving Role and Agenda of the G7/G8: A North American Perspective', *NIRA Review* 7:2, 5-10.

Handelman, Stephen (2006), 'They're Back!', *The Globe and Mail*, 3 June, F1, F6.

Hanlon, Joseph and John Garrett (1999), *Crumbs of Comfort: The Cologne G8 Summit and the Chains of Debt*, Jubilee 2000 Coalition, London.

Haynal, George (2005), 'Summitry and Governance: The Case for a G-XX', in *Setting Priorities Straight: Canada among Nations 2004*, 261-74, David Carment, Fen Osler Hampson and Norman Hillmer, (eds), McGill-Queens University Press, Montreal.

Healey, Denis (1989), *The Time of My Life*, Michael Joseph, London.

Helleiner, Gerald K. (2001), 'Markets, Politics and Globalization: Can the Global Economy Be Civilized?', *Global Governance* 7:3, 243-63.

Higgott, Richard (2005), 'Multilateralism and the Limits of Global Governance', in *Reforming from the Top: A Leaders' 20 Summit*, 72-96. English et al. (eds), Centre for International Governance Innovation; United Nations University Press, New York; Tokyo.

Hodges, Michael R. (1994), 'More Efficiency, Less Dignity: British Perspectives on the Future Role and Working of the G-7', in *The Future of the G-7 Summits*, 141-59, (*The International Spectator* 29:2, April/June, Special Issue).

Hodges, Michael R. (1999), 'The G8 and the New Political Economy', in *The G8's Role in the New Millennium*, 69-73, Michael R. Hodges, John J. Kirton and Joseph P. Daniels (eds), Ashgate, Aldershot, UK.

Hubbard, Gill and David Miller (eds) (2005), *Arguments against G8*, Pluto Press, London, Ann Arbor.

Ikenberry, G. John (1993), 'Salvaging the G-7', *Foreign Affairs*, 72:2, 132-39.

Illarionov, Andrei (2006), 'Moscow and the G8: Membership Has Its Privileges', *The Globe and Mail*, 18 April, A17.

Indymedia UK (2005), *GW8 Audio: Global Warming 8 Counter Conference Recordings*, www3.indymedia.org.uk/en/2005/07/317152.html.

Inoguchi, Kuniko (1994), 'The Changing Significance of the G-7 Summits', *Japan Review of International Affairs*, 8:1, 21-38.

InterAction Council, www.interactioncouncil.org.

Inter-European Parliamentary Forum on Population and Development (2005), *Outcome of the G-8 International Parliamentarians' Conference on Development in Africa*. www.iepfpd.org.

International Chamber of Commerce (1999), *Business and the Global Economy: ICC Statement on Behalf of World Business to the Heads of State and Government Attending the Cologne Summit*, www.iccwbo.org/home/statements_rules/statements/1999/g7_statement.asp.

International Chamber of Commerce (2000), *Business and the Global Economy: ICC Statement on Behalf of World Business to the Heads of State and Government Attending the Okinawa Summit*, www.iccwbo.org/home/statements_rules/statements/2000/g8_statement.asp.

International Chamber of Commerce (2001), *Business and the Global Economy: ICC Statement on Behalf of World Business to the Heads of State and Government Attending the Genoa Summit*, www.iccwbo.org/home/statements_rules/statements/2001/genoa_summit_trade.asp.

International Chamber of Commerce (2002), *Business and the Global Economy: ICC Statement on Behalf of World Business to the Heads of State and Government*

Attending the Kananaskis Summit, www.iccwbo.org/home/statements_rules/statements/2002/G8kananskis.asp.

International Chamber of Commerce (2003), *Business and the Global Economy: ICC Statement on Behalf of World Business to the Heads of State and Government Attending the Evian Summit*, www.iccwbo.org/home/statements_rules/statements/2003/G8.asp.

International Chamber of Commerce (2004), *Business and the Global Economy: ICC Statement on Behalf of World Business to the Heads of State and Government Attending the Sea Island Summit*, www.iccwbo.org/home/statements_rules/statements/2004/G8_statement.asp.

International Chamber of Commerce (2005), *Business and the Global Economy: ICC Statement on Behalf of World Business to the Heads of State and Government Attending the Gleneagles Summit*, www.iccwbo.org/uploadedFiles/ICC/policy/economic/Statements/G82005.pdf.

International Chamber of Commerce (2006a), *Business and the Global Economy: ICC Statement on Behalf of World Business to the Heads of State and Government Attending the St. Petersburg Summit*, www.iccwbo.org/uploadedFiles/ICC_G8_St_Petersburg_statement.pdf.

International Chamber of Commerce (2006b), *ICC Urges Strong Follow Up to G8 Statement on Intellectual Property*, 26 July, www.iccwbo.org/iccicij/index.html.

International Confederation of Free Trade Unions (2004), *Outcome of the Sea Island G8 Summit, 8-10 June 2004: Evaluation by the TUAC Secretariat*, www.icftu.org/displaydocument.asp?Index=991220130.

International Monetary Fund (1998), 'Work Program on Strengthening the Architecture of the International Monetary System', (Office Memorandum), 30 October, IMF, www.imf.org/external/np/g7/103098ed.htm.

International Monetary Fund (2005), *Annual Report of the Executive Board for the Financial Year Ended April 30, 2005*, IMF, www.imf.org/external/pubs/ft/ar/2005/eng/index.htm.

International Monetary Fund (2006a), *A Guide to Committees, Groups, and Clubs: Factsheet*, IMF, www.imf.org/external/np/exr/facts/groups.htm.

International Monetary Fund (2006b), *IMF Board of Governors Approves Quota and Related Governance Reforms*, Press Release 06/205, 18 September.

'Inter-religious Declaration Presented to the G8 Summit Leaders' (2005), [London,] 6 July.

Jha, Alok (2005), 'How Many People Does it Take to be Right?', *The Guardian*, 7 July, G2:2,4.

'Joint Press Conference Given by the Prime Minister, Mr John Major and the Soviet President, Mr Mikhail Gorbachev' (1991), London, 17 July, www.g8.utoronto.ca/summit/1991london/joint.html.

Jubilee Plus (2001), *Jubilee Movement International for Economic and Social Justice Statement on G7 Final Communiqué*, Press Release, 21 July, Genoa, www.jubileeresearch.org.

Junior 8 (2006), *J8 Delegation Meets the G8 Leaders*, St. Petersburg, 15 July, http://juniorg8.com/press/main/?page=28, http://en.g8russia.ru/news/20060718/1254740.html.

Kasparov, Garry (2006), 'What's Bad for Putin is Best for Russians', *The New York Times*, A21, 10 July.

Katada, Saori N. (2005), 'Balancing Act: Japan's Strategy in Global and Regional Financial Governance', in *Reforming from the Top: A Leaders' 20 Summit*, 97-120. English, et al. (eds), Centre for International Governance Innovation; United Nations University Press, New York; Tokyo.

Kenen, Peter B., et al. (2004), *International Economic and Financial Cooperation: New Issues, New Actors, New Responses*, Centre for Economic Policy Research, London.

Kerevan, George (2005), 'How UN Failure Cleared the Way for G8 Power', *The Scotsman*, 26, 7 July.

Kirton, John J. (1989a), '*Contemporary Concert Diplomacy: The Seven-Power Summit and the Management of International Order*', paper prepared for the annual meeting of the International Studies Association and the British International Studies Association, London, March 29-April 1. Unpublished in print. www.g7.utoronto.ca/scholar/kirton198901/index.html.

Kirton, John J. (1989b), 'Introduction', in *The Seven-Power Summit: Documents from the Summits of Industrialized Countries, 1975-1989*, xxi-li, Peter I. Hajnal (ed.), Kraus International Publications, Millwood, NY.

Kirton, John J. (1994), 'Exercising Concerted Leadership: Canada's Approach to Summit Reform', in *The Future of the G-7 Summits*, 161-76, (*The International Spectator* 29:2, April/June, Special Issue).

Kirton, John J. (1995), 'The Diplomacy of Concert: Canada, the G7 and the Halifax Summit', *Canadian Foreign Policy* 3:1, 63-80.

Kirton, John J. (1997), 'Economic Cooperation: Summitry, Institutions, and Structural Change', Paper prepared for a conference on 'Structural Change and Co-operation in the Global Economy', Center for International Business Education and Center for Global Change and Governance, Rutgers University, New Brunswick, NJ, 19-20 May, www.g7.utoronto.ca/scholar/kirton199702/index.html Also in *Structural Change and Co-operation in the Global Economy* (1999), John Dunning and Gavin Boyd (eds), Edward Elgar , London.

Kirton, John J. (1999), *The G7 and China in the Management of the International Financial System*, paper prepared for the Forum 'China in the 21st Century and the World', Shenzen, China, 11-12 November, www.g8.utoronto.ca/scholar/kirton199903/index.html.

Kirton, John J. (2000), 'Broadening Participation in Twenty-First Century Governance: The Prospective and Potential Contribution of the Okinawa Summit', paper presented at the conference 'The Kyushu-Okinawa Summit: The Challenges and Opportunities for the Developing World in the 21st Century', co-sponsored by the United Nations University, the Foundation for Advanced Studies in Development, and the G8 Research Group, Tokyo, July 17, www. g8.utoronto.ca/scholar/kirton20000717/.

Kirton, John J. (2004a), *Getting the L20 Going: Reaching out from the G8*, paper prepared for a workshop on 'G20 to Replace the G8: Why Not Now?', sponsored by the Brookings Institution, Institute for International Economics and the Centre for Global Governance, Washington, DC, September 22. www.g7.utoronto.ca/scholar/kirton2004/kirton_040922.html.

Kirton, John J. (2004b), *What the G8's Sea Island Summit Means for the World Ahead*, Paper prepared for a seminar at the Canadian Embassy, Tokyo, Japan, July 27, www.g8.utoronto.ca/scholar/kirton2004/kirton_040727.html.

Kirton, John J. (2005a), 'From Collective Security to Concert: The UN, G8 and Global Security Governance', paper prepared for the conference 'Security Overspill: Between Economic Integration and Social Exclusion', Centre Études Internationales et Mondialisation, Université de Québec à Montréal, Montreal, Appendix A, 27-28 October.

Kirton, John J. (2005b), 'From G7 to G20: Capacity, Leadership and Normative Diffusion in Global Financial Governance', paper presented for the annual convention of the International Studies Association, Honolulu, March 1-5, www.g8.utoronto.ca/scholar/kirton2005/kirton_isa2005.pdf.

Kirton, John J. (2005c), 'New Perspectives on the G8', in *New Perspectives on Global Governance: Why America Needs the* G8, 231-57, Michele Fratianni et al. (eds), Ashgate, Aldershot, UK.

Kirton, John J. (2005d), 'A Promising Push: Complying with the Gleneagles G8 Africa Commitments and Parliamentarians' Role', Paper prepared for the conference 'Partnership Beyond 2005: The Role of Parliamentarians in Implementing NEPAD Commitments', 19-22 October, London. www.g8.utoronto.ca/scholar/kirton2005/kirton_london2005.pdf.

Kirton, John J. (2005e), 'Toward Multilateral Reform: The G20's Contribution', in *Reforming from the Top: A Leaders' 20 Summit*, 141-68. English, et al. (eds), Centre for International Governance Innovation; United Nations University Press, New York; Tokyo.

Kirton, John J. (2006a), 'Building Democratic Partnerships: The G8-Civil Society Link', in *Sustainability, Civil Society, and International Governance: Local, North American, and Global Contributions*, 319-35, John J. Kirton and Peter I. Hajnal (eds), Ashgate, Aldershot, UK.

Kirton, John J. (2006b), *A Summit of Significant Success: The G8 at St. Petersburg*, G8 Research Group, Toronto, 19 July, www.g8.utoronto.ca/evaluations/2006stpetersburg/kirton_perf_060719.pdf.

Klein, Naomi (2002), *Fences and Windows: Dispatches from the Front Lines of the Globalization Debate*. Debra Ann Levy (ed.), Vintage Canada, Toronto.

Kokotsis, Ella (1999), *Keeping International Commitments: Compliance, Credibility, and the G7, 1988-1995*, Garland, New York, Transnational Business and Corporate Culture series.

Kokotsis, Ella (2004), *Background on Compliance Assessments: Methodology*, www.g8.utoronto.ca/evaluations/methodology/g7c2.htm.

Kokotsis, Ella (2006), *G8 Compliance Coding and Reference Manual*, G8 Research Group, Toronto, www.g8.utoronto.ca/evaluations/compliance_manual_2006.pdf.

Krickus, Richard J. (2006), *Iron Troikas: The New Threat from the East*, Strategic Studies Institute, US Army War College, Carlisle, PA, www.strategicstudiesinstitute.army.mil/pubs/display.cfm?pubID=643.

'Leaders Boost African Aid by $25b' (2005), *Toronto Star*, 9 July, A10.

Lewis, Flora (1992), 'The 'G-7½' Directorate', *Foreign Policy*, 85, 25-40.

Lewis, Stephen (2005), *Race against Time*, House of Anansi Press, Toronto.

'Live 8 Launched' (2005), www.makepovertyhistory.org/2005/index.shtml.

'The Lost U.N. Summit Meeting' (2005), *The New York Times*, editorial, 14 September.

Lugo, Chris (2004), *From the G8 to Africa to You – The Other Economic Summit*, Tennessee Independent Media Center, 10 June, www.tnimc.org/newswire/display/2189/index.php.

Lukov, Vadim Borisovich (2002), *Rossiia v Klube Liderov* [Russia in the Leaders' Club], Nauchnaia Kniga, Moscow. [In Russian.]

'La Lutte contre la récession passe par une solution monétaire' (1975), *Le Monde*, 9 July, 24.

Make Poverty History (2005), *Response to G8 Summit Communiqué*, Press release, [8 July], www.makepovertyhistory.org/response.shtml.

Mander, Jerry and Edward Goldsmith (eds) (1996), *The Case against the Global Economy and for a Turn Toward the Local*, Sierra Club Books, San Francisco.

Martin, Lawrence (2006), 'Miles to Go before Martin Sleeps', *The Globe and Mail*, A1, A7, 1 June.

Martin, Nigel (2005), 'Not Representative, but Still Legitimate', *Alliance*, 10:2, June, 16-17.

Martin, Paul (2005), 'A Global Answer to Global Problems: The Case for a New Leaders' Forum', *Foreign Affairs*, 84, 2-6, May/June.

Martin, Paul (2006), *Speaking Notes for the Right Honourable Paul Martin P.C., M.P.: Annual Meeting of the Development and Peace Foundation*, 8 June, www.sef-bonn.org/download/veranstaltungen/2006/2006_sd_dresden_martin_speaking_notes.pdf.

Maull, Hanns W. (1994), 'Germany at the Summit', in *The Future of the G-7 Summits*, 112-39 (*The International Spectator*, 29:2 Special Issue).

McHugh, David (2006), 'Germany Sets Agenda for Next Year's G-8', *The Associated Press*, 18 October, Berlin.

Médecins Sans Frontières (2001), 'Violence Grants No Perspectives', Press Release, 20 July, Genoa.

Meikle, Sian (1999), 'G7/G8 Information: Internet Resources', in *The G7/G8 System: Evolution, Role and Documentation*, 107-24, Peter I. Hajnal, Ashgate, Aldershot, UK, The G8 and Global Governance Series.

Mepham, David and James Lorge (2005), *Putting our House in Order: Recasting G8 Policy towards Africa*, IPPR, London.

Mercu, Francesca (2006), 'Opposition is Split after "Other Russia"', *The Moscow Times*, 4, 14 July.

Merlini, Cesare (1994), 'The G-7 and the Need for Reform', in *The Future of the G-7 Summits. The International Spectator*, 29:2, 5-25, April/June, Special Issue, www.library.utoronto.ca/g7/italiano/merlini_i1.html (Italian).

Mexico, [President] (2005), *Mexico's General Position on Climate Change and Energy, Prepared for the Outreach Session of the G-8 Summit*, Gleneagles, Scotland, 7 July.

Montreal International Forum (2002), *Civil Society and the G8*, 21-23 May, consultations in Montreal and Ottawa, www.fimcivilsociety.org/english/CivilSocietyG8.html.

Myers, Steven Lee (2005), 'Bill to Increase Russia's Control over Charities Moves Ahead', *The New York Times*, 22 December, A3.

Myers, Steven Lee (2006), 'Strong Rebuke for the Kremlin from Cheney', *The New York Times*, 5 May, A1, A10.

'NARA Cooperated in Document Reclassification' (2006), *American Libraries*, 37:5, 16-17.

Nelson, Fraser (2005), 'After the Revelry Comes the Cold Political Reality', *The Scotsman*, 4 July, 2-3.

Neslen, Arthur (2001), 'Mean Streets: On Location, Genoa Summit', *Now* (Toronto), No.1019, 26 July-1 August, 18-20.

Nichol, Jim, Steven Woehrel and Bernard A. Gelb (2006), *Russia's Cutoff of Natural Gas to Ukraine: Context and Implications*, CRS Report for Congress, RS22378, Washington, DC, 15 February.

Nybo, Thomas and Maya Dollarhide (2005), 'Young People at C8 Children's Summit Insist World Leaders Listen', www.unicef.org/policyanalysis/index_27604.html.

Office of the Dalai Lama (2005a), 'Inter-religious Declaration Presented to the G8 Summit Leaders', [London,] 6 July.

Office of the Dalai Lama (2005b), 'Leaders Joint Declaration on Climate Change and the Defense of Life', [Dharamshala, India] July.

Organisation for Economic Co-operation and Development (2000a), *Report of the Task Force for the Safety of Novel Foods and Feeds*, OECD Council document C(2000)86/ADD1, 17 May.

Organisation for Economic Co-operation and Development (2000b), *Report of the Working Group on Harmonization of Regulatory Oversight in Biotechnology*, OECD Council document C(2000)86/ADD2, 25 May.

Ostry, Sylvia (2002), '*Globalization and the G8: Could Kananaskis Set a New Direction?-La Mondialisation et le G8: Kananaskis marquera-t-il le début d'une nouvelle orientation?*', O.D. Skelton Memorial Lecture, Queen's University, Department of Foreign Affairs and International Trade. www.utoronto.ca/cis/skeltonlecture_ostry2002.doc.

The Other Russia (2006), *Closing Statement of the Participants of the Other Russia Conference*, www.theotherrussia.ru/eng/.

'Outspoken Putin Aide Quits, Scolding Kremlin' (2005), *The New York Times*, A1, 28 December.

'The Outspoken Silenced' (2005), *The Economist*, 374:8408, 47, 8 January.

Owada, Hisashi (1994), 'A Japanese Perspective on the Role and Future of the G-7', in *The Future of the G-7 Summits*, 95-112, *The International Spectator*, 29:2, April/June, Special Issue.

Owen, Henry (1978), Memorandum to President Jimmy Carter. Jimmy Carter Library, WHCF-Subject File, Box FO-44, Memorandum, Henry Owen to President Carter, May 9, 1978.

Oxfam (2004), *The 2004 Summit of the G8: Trick or Retreat? Joint Statement from African NGOs and Trade Unions at the Conclusion of the 2004 Summit*, www.oxfam.org.uk/what_we_do/issues/panafrica/rich_countries.htm.

Oxfam International (2001), *Genoa Fails: Big Promise for Next Year*. Press release, 22 July, Genoa, www.oxfam.org/eng/pr010722_G8_Reaction_to_Genoa.htm. No longer accessible.

Oxfam International (2004), *Oxfam on G8 2004: More Said than Done, and Not Enough Said*, Press release, 10 June, www.oxfam.org/en/news/pressreleases2004/pr040610_G8_final.htm.

Oxfam International (2005a), *Oxfam International Reaction to the G8 Outcome*, Press release, 8 July, www.oxfam.org/en/news/pressreleases2005/pr050708_g8.htm.

Oxfam International (2005b), *What Does $50 Billion by 2010 Actually Mean?* Press release, 8 July.

Oxfam International (2006), *Oxfam Verdict on St. Petersburg G8 Summit*, 17 July, www.oxfam.org/en/news/pressreleases2006/pr060717_g8verdict.

Page, Jeremy (2006), 'Fear Silences the Voices of Russian Revolution', *The Times*, 17 July.

Pamfilova, Ella (2006), 'The Civil G8 2006', in *G8 Summit 2006: Issues and Instruments*, 23, Maurice Fraser (ed.), Newsdesk Communications, London.

Pasco, Jean O. (2006), 'Nixon Library Could Get a Lift in 2007 Budget', *Los Angeles Times*, February 8, B3.

Pauly, Louis W. (1997), *Who Elected the Bankers? Surveillance and Control in the World Economy*, Cornell University Press, Ithaca, NY; London.

Penttilä, Risto E. J. (2003), *The Role of the G8 in International Peace and Security*, Adelphi Paper, 355. Oxford University Press for the International Institute of Strategic Studies, Oxford.

People's Summit (1995), *Communiqué from the People's Summit*, 16 June, Halifax.

Peston, Robert (1998), 'Blair To Urge Full Overhaul of IMF and WB', *Financial Times*, 21 September, 1.

'Picking Up the Pieces: After the Genoa Summit' (2001), *The Economist* 360:8232, 28 July, 49-50.

'"Poor People's Summit" Slams G8 Policies' (2006), *All Africa*, 18 July, http://allafrica.com/stories/200607180812.html.

'Pope Takes up Live 8 Message' (2005), *Toronto Star*, 4 July, A7.

Porter, Tony (2000), 'The G-7, the Financial Stability Forum, the G-20, and the Politics of International Financial Regulation', paper prepared for the International Studies Association Annual Convention, Los Angeles, March 15, www.g8.utoronto.ca/g20/g20porter/index.html.

'La Presse Internationale Conteste l'Utilité du Sommet' (2001), *Le Monde*, 24 July.

Promoting Financial Stability: Recent Initiatives of the Basle Committee on Banking Supervision; Submission for the G-7 Heads of Government at the 1998 Birmingham Summit (1998), Basle, March (unpublished).

Putnam, Robert D. (1994), 'Western Summitry in the 1990s: American Perspectives', in *The Future of the G-7 Summits*, 81-93 (*The International Spectator*, 29:2 Special Issue).

Putnam, Robert D. and Nicholas Bayne (1984), *Hanging Together: Cooperation and Conflict in the Seven-Power Summits*, Harvard University Press, Cambridge, MA.

Putnam, Robert D. and Nicholas Bayne (1987), *Hanging Together: Cooperation and Conflict in the Seven-Power Summits*, rev. ed., Harvard University Press, Cambridge, MA.

'Report on Russian Crisis Prepared for G7' (1998), *Financial Times*, 15 September, 2.

Risbud, Sheila (2006), 'Civil Society Engagement: A Case Study of the 2002 G8 Environment Ministers Meeting', in S*ustainability, Civil Society and International Governance: Local, North American and Global Contributions*, 337-42, John J. Kirton and Peter I. Hajnal (eds), Ashgate, Aldershot, UK.

Rivera, Nicolás Nogueras (1976), Letter to President Gerald Ford. Gerald R. Ford Library, WHCF-Subject File, FO 6-5, Box 33, Economic Summit Conference, Puerto Rico, 6/27-28/76.

Roach, Stephen (2004), 'How to Fix the World', *Global Economic Forum*, 9-10, December, www.morganstanley.com/GEFdata/digests/20041217-fri.html#anchor0.

Rudich, Denisse V. (2005), 'Performing the Twelve Labors: The G8's Role in the Fight against Money Laundering', *G8 Governance*, 12, www.g8.utoronto.ca/governance/rudich_g8g.pdf.

'Russia's Anti-West Offensive' (2005), *The New York Times*, 27 December, A22.

Rutenberg, Jim (2006), 'Despite Joint Statement on Mideast, Strains Emerge as U.S. Appears To Support Israel', *The New York Times*, 17 July, A10.

Sachs, Jeffrey (1998), 'Global Capitalism: Making It Work', *The Economist* 348:8085, 23-25, 12 September.

Said Aly, Abdel Monem (2005), 'The L20 and the Restructuring of the International Economic Order: An Egyptian Perspective', in *Reforming from the Top: A Leaders' 20 Summit*, 260-80. English, et al. (eds), Centre for International Governance Innovation; United Nations University Press, New York; Tokyo.

Sanger, David E. (1998), 'Clinton Presents Strategy To Quell Economic Threat', *The New York Times*, 15 September, A1, A16.

Sanger, David E. (2001), 'Two Leaders Tell of Plot to Kill Bush in Genoa', *New York Times*, 26 September, B1.

Sauzey, François (ed.) (1978), *The London Summit Revisited*, T16, Trilateral Commission, Washington, DC.

'Scares Ahead: Can the World Economy Sustain its Stunning Pace of Growth?' (2004), *The Economist*, 373:8395, 11, 2 October.

Scherrer, Amandine (2005), 'Le G8 face au crime organisé' [G8 and organized crime], *G8 Governance*, 11, www.g8.utoronto.ca/governance/scherrer_g8g.pdf.

Schmidt, Helmut (1989), *Men and Powers: A Political Retrospective*, Random House, New York.

Schroyer, Trent (ed.) (1997), *A World That Works: Building Blocks for a Just and Sustainable Society*, A TOES Book. Bootstrap Press, New York.

Schroyer, Trent and Susan Hunt (2004), *TOES 2004 Experience in Georgia*, www.toes-usa.org/TOESBrunswick.html.

Senior Experts on Transnational Organized Crime (1996), *P8 Senior Experts Group Recommendations*, Paris, 12 April, www.g8.utoronto.ca/crime/40pts.htm.

Sennes, Ricardo U. and Alexandre de Freitas Barbosa (2005), 'Brazil's Multiple Forms of External Engagement: Foreign Policy Dilemmas', in *Reforming from the Top: A Leaders' 20 Summit*, 201-29. English, et al. (eds), Centre for International Governance Innovation; United Nations University Press, New York; Tokyo.

Shadow G-8 (2003a), 'Letter of Transmittal to the Leaders of the G-8 Member Countries', in *Restoring G-8 Leadership of the World Economy*, www.iie.com/publications/papers/g8-2003.pdf.

Shadow G-8 (2003b), *Restoring G-8 Leadership of the World Economy: Recommendations for the Evian Summit from the Shadow G-8*, [4th report] [Paris]. www.ifri.org/files/policy_briefs/WP_SHADOW_G8.pdf, www.iie.com/publications/papers/g8-2003.pdf.

Shadow G-8 (2004), Interview, 1 December.

Shadow G-8 (2005), Interview, May.

Shadow G-8 (2006), Correspondence, April.

Sherifis, Rossella Franchini and Valerio Astraldi (2001), *Il G7/G8 da Rambouillet a Genova = The G7/G8 from Rambouillet to Genoa*, FrancoAngeli, Milano.

Silvestri, Stefano (1994), 'Between Globalism and Regionalism: The Role and Composition of the G-7', in 'The Future of the G-7 Summits', 27-48, *The International Spectator*, 29:2, April/June, Special Issue.

Slaughter, Anne-Marie (2004), *A New World Order*, Princeton University Press, Princeton; Oxford.

Slaughter, Anne-Marie (2005), 'Government Networks, World Order, and the L20', in *Reforming from the Top: A Leaders' 20 Summit*, 281-95. English, et al. (eds), Centre for International Governance Innovation; United Nations University Press, New York; Tokyo.

Smith, Janel and Montana Burnett (2004). *Report on Civil Society Presence at 2004 G8 Summit*, G8 Research Group, 10 June, Savannah, www.g8.utoronto.ca/g8online/2004/english/featured-content5.html.

Smyser, W.R. (1993), 'Goodbye, G-7', *The Washington Quarterly*, 16:1, 15-28.

Stephens, Philip (1992), 'Major Calls for Overhaul of G7 Summits', *Financial Times*, 1, 10 September, London.

'Summit Part of Larger Process' (1988), *The Financial Post*, 22 June, www.g8.utoronto.ca/fp/ed880622.htm.

Sunderland, Laura (2006), *The Prospective Agenda for the 2007 G8 Heiligendamm Summit*, G8 Research Group, www.g8.utoronto.ca/evaluations/2007heiligendamm/2007agenda.html.

Tagliabue, John (2003), 'Chirac To Call for a Shift from Battling Terrorism to Helping Poorer Nations', *The New York Times*, 1 June, YT13.

Takase, Junichi (2000), *Samitto: Shuyō Shunō Kaigi* [Summit: The Meeting of the Main Heads of State], Ashi Shobō, Tokyo. [In Japanese.]

Taylor, Ian (2005), 'South Africa: Beyond the Impasse of Global Governance', in *Reforming from the Top: A Leaders' 20 Summit*, 230-59. English et al. (eds), Centre for International Governance Innovation; United Nations University Press, New York; Tokyo.

Teslenko, Peter (2005), 'Press Conference on Co-operation between Civil Society and the Group of Eight during Russia's Presidency', Moscow, 20 December, [Canadian embassy official in Moscow], www.g8.utoronto.ca/whatsnew/cs051220.html.

Thatcher, Margaret (1993), *The Downing Street Years*, Harper-Collins, London.

Transparency International (2006), *The G8 Communiqué: Strong Words on Global Fight against Corruption, Treading Water on Africa and Oil*, 17 July, http://transparency.org/news_room/latest_news/press_releases/2006/2006_07_17_g8_communique.

Traub, James (2005), 'The Statesman[: Why, and How, Bono Matters]', *The New York Times Magazine*, 18 September, 80-89, 96, 98, 113, 120, 180, 187.

Truman, Edwin M. (2004), 'The Euro and Prospects for Policy Coordination', draft paper prepared for the conference on 'The Euro at Five: Ready for a Global Role', 26 February, www.iie.com/publications/papers/truman0204-3.pdf.

The Twenty G-7 Summits (1994), On the Occasion of the Twentieth Summit, Naples, July 8-10, Adnkronos Libri in Collaboration with Istituto Affari Internazionali, Rome.

Ullrich, Heidi and Alan Donnelly (1998), 'The Group of Eight and the European Union: The Evolving Partnership', *G8 Governance*, 5, www.g7.utoronto.ca/governance/gov5/intro.html.

UNICEF UK (2005), 'C8 Children in Urgent Plea to G8 Leaders on Murrayfields Stage To Make a World Fit for Children', Press release, [8?] July.

United Kingdom, Parliament, House of Commons, Session 1982/1983 (1983), *Technology, Growth and Employment: Report of the Working Group Set Up by the Economic Summit Meeting of 1982*, Science and Technology Secretariat, Cabinet Office (Cmnd. 8818; London: HMSO, 1983).

United Kingdom, Prime Minister's Office (1998), *Press Conference Given by the Prime Minister*, Birmingham, 17 May, www.g8.utoronto.ca/summit/1998birmingham/blaira.html and www.g8.utoronto.ca/summit/1998birmingham/blairb.html.

United Kingdom, Prime Minister's Office (2005a), *British Prime Minister Tony Blair Reflects On 'Significant Progress' Of G8 Summit*, Press Conference at the Conclusion of the Gleneagles Summit, 8 July, www.g8.gov.uk/servlet/Front?pagename=OpenMarket/Xcelerate/ShowPage&c=Page&cid=1078995903270&a=KArticle&aid=1119520262754.

United Kingdom, Prime Minister's Office (2005b). *A Comparison between the Recommendations of the Commission for Africa Report and the G8 Commitments* (2005). www.number-10.gov.uk/output/Page7894.asp. No longer accessible.

United Kingdom, Prime Minister's Office (2005c), *Prime Minister's Statement on London Explosions*, 7 July, www.number-10.gov.uk/output/Page7853.asp.

United Kingdom, Prime Minister's Office (2005d), *Special Address by Tony Blair, Prime Minister of the United Kingdom at the World Economic Forum in Davos*, 27 January, www.g8.gov.uk/servlet/Front?pagename=OpenMarket/Xcelerate/ShowPage&c=Page&cid=1078995903270&a=KArticle&aid=1106749656900.

United Nations, High-level Panel on Threats, Challenges and Change (2004), *A More Secure World: Our Shared Responsibility: Report of the High-level Panel on Threats, Challenges and Change*, United Nations, New York. Also available as UN, General Assembly, Fifty-ninth Session (2004), *Follow-up to the Outcome of the Millennium Summit: A More Secure World: Our Shared Responsibility; Report of the [Secretary-General's] High-level Panel on Threats, Challenges and Change*, A/59/565; 2 December.

United States, Department of Justice (1997), *Statement by Attorney General Janet Reno on the Meeting of Justice and Interior Ministers of the Eight*, Washington, DC, 10 December, www.usdoj.gov/opa/pr/1997/December97/518cr.html.

United States, Department of State, Bureau of Public Affairs (1995), *US Department of State Dispatch* 6, Supplement No. 4, July.

United States, President, Office of the Press Secretary (2005), *Remarks by President Bush and Prime Minister Blair in a Photo Opportunity, Gleneagles Hotel*, Auchterarder, Scotland, 7 July.

United States, White House, Office of the Press Secretary (1997), *Press Conference of the President*, 22 June, Denver, www.g8.utoronto.ca/summit/1997denver/clint22.htm.

Wallace, William (1984), 'Political Issues at the Summits: A New Concert of Powers?', in *Economic Summits and Western Decision-Making*, 137-52, Cesare Merlini (ed.), Croom Helm; St. Martin's Press in association with the European Institute of Public Administration, London; New York.

Wanyeki, L. Muthoni (2005), Remarks as Executive Director of the African Women's Development and Communications Network (FEMNET) at the conference 'Global Democracy: Civil Society Visions and Strategies', Montreal, 29 May-1 June.

Weisman, Steven R. (2006), 'Russia Bargains for Bigger Stake in West's Energy', *The New York Times*, 12 June, A1, A6.

'Welcome to China, Mr Clinton' (1998), *The Economist*, 347:8074, 17, June 27.

Whyman, William E. (1995), 'We Can't Go On Meeting Like This: Revitalizing the G-7 Process', *The Washington Quarterly*, 18:3, 149-63.

Wickstead, Myles (2005), Presentation as Head of the Secretariat to the Commission for Africa, Munk Centre for International Studies, University of Toronto, 25 April.

Wilkinson, Rorden (2006), 'Ghost of a Chance: ACUNS in Hong Kong', *ACUNS* [Academic Council on the United Nations System] *Informational Memorandum*, 65.

Wilson, Harold (1979), *Final Term: The Labour Government, 1974-1976*, Weidenfeld and Nicolson, and Michael Joseph, London.

World Bank (2005), *The World Bank Annual Report*, World Bank, Washington, DC.

World Economic Forum (2006a), 'Developing the Future Framework for Climate Change and Energy Policy with the G-20', *The World Economic Forum on East Asia: Initiative Activity*, www.weforum.org/en/events/eastasia/InitiativeActivity/InitiativeActivityAsia.

World Economic Forum (2006b), 'Obasanjo, Brown and Gates Call on Leaders to Fund New TB Plan', *Annual Meeting 2006*, www.weforum.org/en/events/annualmeeting/AnnualMeetingContent.

'World Leaders Back Joint Action in Face of Financial Turmoil' (1998), *Financial Times*, 15 September, 1.

Yeltsin, Boris (2000), *Midnight Diaries*, Weidenfeld & Nicolson, London.

Yu, Yongding (2005), 'China's Evolving Global View', in *Reforming from the Top: A Leaders' 20 Summit*, 187-200. English, et al. (eds), Centre for International Governance Innovation; United Nations University Press, New York; Tokyo.

Zupi, Marco (2001), 'The Genoa G-8 Summit: Great Expectations, Disappointing Results', *The International Spectator* 36:3, 59.

Index